THE CAMBRIDGE COMPANION TO
MARTIN LUTHER

Martin Luther (1483–1546) stands as one of the giant figures in history.
His activities, writings, and legacy have had a huge effect on the Western
world. This *Cambridge Companion* provides an accessible introduction to
Martin Luther for students of theology and history and for others interested
in the life, work, and thought of the first great Protestant reformer. The
book contains eighteen chapters by an international array of major Luther
scholars. Historians and theologians join here to present a full picture of
Luther's contexts, the major themes in his writings, and the ways in which
his ideas spread and have continuing importance today. Each chapter serves
as a guide to its topic and provides further reading for additional study. The
*Companion* will assist those with little or no background in Luther studies,
while teachers and Luther specialists will find this accessible volume an
invaluable aid to their work.

DONALD K. MCKIM has served as Academic Dean and Professor of Theology at Memphis Theological Seminary and Professor of Theology at the
University of Dubuque Theological Seminary, in addition to being a pastor
in Presbyterian Church (USA) churches. He is the author and editor of over
twenty-five books and currently works as Academic and Reference editor
for Westminster John Knox Press.

D1427132

CAMBRIDGE COMPANIONS TO RELIGION

A series of companions to major topics and key figures in theology and religious studies. Each volume contains specially commissioned chapters by international scholars which provide an accessible and stimulating introduction to the subject for new readers and non-specialists.

*Other titles in the series*

THE CAMBRIDGE COMPANION TO CHRISTIAN DOCTRINE
edited by Colin Gunton (1997)
ISBN 0 521 47118 4 hardback      ISBN 0 521 47695 8 paperback

THE CAMBRIDGE COMPANION TO BIBLICAL INTERPRETATION
edited by John Barton (1998)
ISBN 0 521 48144 9 hardback      ISBN 0 521 48593 2 paperback

THE CAMBRIDGE COMPANION TO DIETRICH BONHOEFFER
edited by John de Gruchy (1999)
ISBN 0 521 58258 x hardback      ISBN 0 521 58751 6 paperback

THE CAMBRIDGE COMPANION TO LIBERATION THEOLOGY
edited by Chris Rowland (1999)
ISBN 0 521 46144 8 hardback      ISBN 0 521 46707 1 paperback

THE CAMBRIDGE COMPANION TO KARL BARTH
edited by John Webster (2000)
ISBN 0 521 58476 0 hardback      ISBN 0 521 58560 0 paperback

THE CAMBRIDGE COMPANION TO CHRISTIAN ETHICS
edited by Robin Gill (2001)
ISBN 0 521 77070 x hardback      ISBN 0 521 77918 9 paperback

THE CAMBRIDGE COMPANION TO JESUS
edited by Markus Bockmuehl (2001)
ISBN 0 521 79261 4 hardback      ISBN 0 521 79678 4 paperback

THE CAMBRIDGE COMPANION TO FEMINIST THEOLOGY
edited by Susan Frank Parsons (2002)
ISBN 0 521 66327 x hardback      ISBN 0 521 66380 6 paperback

THE CAMBRIDGE COMPANION TO MARTIN LUTHER
edited by Donald K. McKim (2003)
ISBN 0 521 81648 3 hardback      ISBN 0 521 01673 8 paperback

*Forthcoming*

THE CAMBRIDGE COMPANION TO THE GOSPEL
edited by Stephen C. Barton

THE CAMBRIDGE COMPANION TO ST PAUL
edited by James D. G. Dunn

THE CAMBRIDGE COMPANION TO MEDIEVAL JEWISH THOUGHT
edited by Daniel H. Frank and Oliver Leaman

THE CAMBRIDGE COMPANION TO ISLAMIC THEOLOGY
edited by Tim Winter

THE CAMBRIDGE COMPANION TO

# MARTIN LUTHER

Edited by Donald K. McKim

CAMBRIDGE
UNIVERSITY PRESS

PUBLISHED BY THE PRESS SYNDICATE OF THE UNIVERSITY OF CAMBRIDGE
The Pitt Building, Trumpington Street, Cambridge CB2 1RP, United Kingdom

CAMBRIDGE UNIVERSITY PRESS
The Edinburgh Building, Cambridge, CB2 2RU, UK
40 West 20th Street, New York, NY 10011–4211, USA
477 Williamstown Road, Port Melbourne, VIC 3207, Australia
Ruiz de Alarcón 13, 28014 Madrid, Spain
Dock House, The Waterfront, Cape Town 8001, South Africa

http://www.cambridge.org

First published 2003

Printed in the United Kingdom at the University Press, Cambridge

*Typeface* Severin 10/13 pt.      *System* LATEX 2$_\varepsilon$   [TB]

ISBN 0 521 81648 3 hardback
ISBN 0 521 01673 8 paperback

Dedicated to

Richard E. Brown
Respected friend and valued colleague
With gratitude

# Contents

# Notes on contributors

**Oswald Bayer** is Professor of Systematic Theology in the Evangelical Theological Faculty of Eberhard-Karls-Universität, Tübingen. Among his numerous books is *Promissio: Geschichte der reformatorischen Wende in Luthers Theologie.*

**Albrecht Beutel** is University Professor of Church History in the Evangelisch-Theologische Fakultät, Westfälische Wilhelms Universität, Münster, Germany. Professor Beutel has written *Martin Luther* and *In dem Anfang war das Wort: Studien zu Luthers Sprachverständnis.*

**Mark U. Edwards, Jr.** is formerly President of St. Olaf College, Northfield, Minnesota and has also taught at Harvard University. He has written *Luther's Last Battles: Politics and Polemic, 1531–46, Printing, Propaganda, and Martin Luther,* and *Luther and the False Brethren.*

**Günther Gassmann** is formerly Director of the Commission on Faith and Order, World Council of Churches and Distinguished Visiting Professor, Lutheran Theological Seminary at Gettysburg, Gettysburg, Pennsylvania. He has written, in cooperation with Duane H. Larson and Mark W. Oldenburg, the *Historical Dictionary of Lutheranism* and written with Scott H. Hendrix, the *Fortress Introduction to the Lutheran Confessions.*

**Eric W. Gritsch** is Professor of Church History Emeritus, Lutheran Theological Seminary at Gettysburg, Gettysburg, Pennsylvania. Among his books are *A History of Lutheranism: What Happened to the Movement Begun by Luther,* the *Fortress Introduction to Lutheranism, Martin, God's Court Jester: Luther in Retrospect,* and, with Robert W. Jenson, *Lutheranism: The Theological Movement and Its Confessional Writings.*

**Hans J. Hillerbrand** is Professor of History and Religion, Duke University, Durham, North Carolina. He has edited *The Oxford Encyclopedia of the Reformation,* the *Historical Dictionary of the Reformation and the Counter-Reformation* and the *Encyclopedia of Protestantism.* His numerous contributions to Reformation studies include *The World of the Reformation,* and his editing of *The Protestant Reformation* and *The Reformation.*

**Robert W. Jenson** is Senior Scholar for Research, Center of Theological Inquiry, Princeton, New Jersey. He previously taught at St. Olaf College. Among his books are *Systematic Theology* (2 vols.) and *The True Identity: God According to the Gospel*. He has edited, with Carl W. Braaten, *Christian Dogmatics, Union with Christ: The New Finnish Interpretation of Luther*, and *The Catholicity of the Reformation*.

**Helmar Junghans** is University Professor of Church History in the Theological Faculty of the University of Leipzig, Germany. He is the author of *Wittenberg als Lutherstadt, Martin Luther und Wittenberg* and the CD ROM *Martin Luther: Exploring His Life and Times (1483–1546)*.

**James M. Kittelson** is Professor of Church History, Luther Seminary, St. Paul, Minnesota. He formerly taught at Ohio State University. He is the author of *Luther the Reformer* and editor with Pamela J. Transue of *Rebirth, Reform, and Resilience: Universities in Transition 1300–1700*.

**Robert Kolb** is Missions Professor of Systematic Theology and Director of the Institute for Mission Studies, Concordia Theological Seminary, St. Louis, Missouri. He has edited, with Timothy Wengert, *The Book of Concord: The Confessions of the Evangelical Lutheran Church* and written *Martin Luther as Prophet, Teacher, Hero: Images of the Reformer, 1520–1620, Confessing the Faith: Reformers Define the Church, 1530–1580*, and *Nikolaus von Amsdorf (1483–1565): Popular Polemics in the Preservation of Luther's Legacy*.

**Carter Lindberg** is Professor of Church History, Boston University School of Theology, Boston, Massachusetts. Among his writings are *The European Reformations* and *Beyond Charity: Reformation Initiatives for the Poor*. He has edited *The European Reformations Sourcebook* and *Reformation Theologians: An Introduction to Theology in the Early Modern Period*.

**Timothy F. Lull** is President and Professor of Systematic Theology, Pacific Lutheran Theological Seminary, Berkeley, California. He has edited *Martin Luther's Basic Theological Writings* and written *My Conversations with Martin Luther*.

**Fred W. Meuser** is President Emeritus, Trinity Lutheran Seminary, Columbus, Ohio where he served as President from 1971 to 1988. He is the author of *Luther the Preacher* among other works on Luther and American Lutheran history.

**James Arne Nestingen** is Professor of Systematic Theology, Luther Seminary, St. Paul, Minnesota. He has written *Martin Luther: His Life and Teachings* and *The Faith We Hold: The Living Witness of Luther and the Augsburg Confession* and has edited, with Robert Kolb, *Sources and Contexts of the Book of Concord*.

**Jane E. Strohl** is Associate Professor of Reformation History and Theology, Pacific Lutheran Theological Seminary, Berkeley, California where she has taught since 1996. She has written "Martin Luther in Daily Readings" in *Spiritual Classics*, ed. Paul Ofstedhl and "Ministry in the Middle Ages and the Reformation" in *Called* *and Ordained: Lutheran Perspectives on the Office of the Ministry*, ed. Marc Kolden and Todd Nichol.

**Bernd Wannenwetsch** is University Lecturer in Ethics, Harris Manchester College, University of Oxford, Oxford, England. He is the author of *Die Freiheit der Ehe: das Zusammenleben von Frau und Mann in der Wahrnehmung evangelischer Ethik* and *Gottesdienst als Lebenform: Ethik für Christenbürger*.

**David M. Whitford** is Assistant Professor of Religion and Philosophy, Claflin University, Orangeburg, South Carolina where he has taught since 1999. He is the author of *Tyranny and Resistance: The Magdeburg Confession and the Lutheran Tradition*, "Learning a Lesson from Luther," *Journal of the Historical Society* and "Martin Luther" in the *Internet Encyclopedia of Philosophy*.

**Markus Wriedt** is Research Professor in the Institut für Europäische Geschichte in the University of Mainz as well as Visiting Professor of Historical Theology at Marquette University, Milwaukee, Wisconsin. He is the author, among other works, of *Gnade und Erwählung: eine Untersuchung zu Johann von Staupitz und Martin Luther*.

# Preface

The name Martin Luther evokes many reactions. Known primarily as the initiator of the Protestant Reformation in Europe in the sixteenth century, Luther through the centuries has had his advocates and detractors. But his influence has been immense. The essays that follow display the far-reaching importance of his words and deeds as well as the significance of Luther's life and thought – an impact that continues today.

This *Companion* is written to introduce the life and work of Martin Luther (1483–1546). All the writers are experts on the aspects of Luther on which they write. Scholars will mine much from this treasury but beginning students even more.

The two opening essays in the collection set Luther's life and context in terms of the main events he experienced and the city where he spent most of his time. These elements are important for becoming acquainted with Luther's struggles, triumphs, joys, and sorrows.

Luther's wide-ranging work is considered in Part II of this book. Here we encounter the vastness of his writings and work in translating and interpreting Holy Scripture. We consider the main themes in his developing theology, a theology that took shape in light of the issues with which Luther dealt. Luther's views on theological topics had their counterparts in his moral theology or ethics. He spent his life as a professor and preacher who proclaimed the Word of God, undergirded by the spiritual resources of his understandings of Scripture and his own religious experience. Luther's struggle with social-ethical issues emerged as he encountered the concerns of his culture and the church. His responses took shape in the political contexts of his setting in Germany. In establishing the reform movement that became associated with Luther's name, he found himself engaged in numerous polemical controversies in which he sought to set forth his understanding of the Word and will of God in light of opponents who were equally vehement.

Those who followed Luther and built on his views appropriated his work in various ways. The essays in Part III describe ways in which Luther's image and insights were developed by his followers and the legacy that his person, theology, and ecclesiastical influence have engendered. Luther has been variously interpreted and approaches to the magisterial reformer have changed and developed in the centuries since his death.

The final part of this *Companion* presents assessments of Martin Luther's relation to modern church history, his contemporary theological significance, and his importance in the worldwide church today. These topics point to Luther's enduring legacy and his towering importance for Christian life and thought.

Among the countless comments made about Luther during his life and in the centuries since, one of the most affecting was made by John Calvin (1509–1564). Calvin, along with Luther, was one of the most eminent of the Protestant reformers. Though they never met, Calvin summed up his understanding of Luther in a single sentence: "We regard him as a remarkable apostle of Christ, through whose work and ministry, most of all, the purity of the Gospel has been restored in our time."[1]

Thanks are due to those who provided key help in bringing this volume to completion. Kevin Taylor of Cambridge University Press has aided this venture from the very start with excellent suggestions and continuing support and advice. I value our friendship. Kevin has been ably assisted by Gillian Dadd who has splendidly contributed her competence and geniality to this project as well. In addition, I would like to thank all the contributors who here provide their expertise to introduce us to the multi-faceted Luther. Katharina Gustavs and Mark Mattes have rendered superb English translations, both stepping into the breach to provide their skills for this work. As always, I thank my wonderful family, LindaJo, Stephen, and Karl McKim, for constant care and support. Their love means more to me than I can express.

This volume is dedicated with gratitude to Richard E. Brown, my esteemed former colleague and firm friend. Richard has always supported my scholarship and has been unfailingly kind in numerous ways. I deeply respect who he is and truly appreciate all he has done for me.

### Note

1. Cited in B. A. Gerrish, "The Pathfinder: Calvin's Image of Martin Luther," in *The Old Protestantism and the New: Essays on the Reformation Heritage* (Chicago: University of Chicago Press, 1982), p. 38. Calvin made this comment in a treatise against Albertus Pighius, *Defensio sanae et orthodoxae doctrinae de servitute et liberatione humani arbitrii adversus calumnies Alberti Pighii Campensis* in *Ioannis Calvini opera quae supersunt omnia*. Ed. Wilhelm Baum, Edward Cunitz, and Edward Reuss. 59 vols. *Corpus Reformatorum*, vols. XXIX–LXXXVII. Brunswick: C. A. Schwetschke and Son (M. Bruhn), 1863–1900, VI:250.

# Chronology of Martin Luther

# Abbreviations

| | |
|---|---|
| BoC | *The Book of Concord: The Confessions of the Evangelical Lutheran Church.* Ed. Robert Kolb and Timothy J. Wengert, trans. Charles Arand et al. Minneapolis: Fortress Press, 2000. |
| BR | Martin Luther, *D. Martin Luthers Werke: Kritische Gesamtausgabe, Briefwechsel.* 18 vols. Weimar: Hermann Böhlaus Nachfolger, 1930–85. |
| DB | Martin Luther, *D. Martin Luthers Werke: Kritische Gesamtausgabe, Deutsche Bibel.* 12 vols. Weimar: Hermann Böhlaus Nachfolger, 1906–61. |
| Dillenberger | John Dillenberger, ed., *Martin Luther: Selections from His Writings.* Garden City: Doubleday, 1961. |
| LCC | Library of Christian Classics |
| Lull | Timothy F. Lull, ed., *Martin Luther's Basic Theological Writings.* Philadelphia: Fortress Press, 1989. |
| LW | Martin Luther, *Luther's Works.* American Edition. 55 vols. St. Louis and Philadelphia: Concordia and Fortress Press, 1958–86. |
| RGG | Friedrich Michael Schliel and Leopold Zscharnack, eds., *Die Religion in Geschichte und Gegenwart.* 5 vols. Tübingen: J. C. B. Mohr (Paul Siebeck), 1909–13. Later editions followed. |
| TR | Martin Luther, *D. Martin Luthers Werke: Kritische Gesamtausgabe, Tischreden.* 6 vols. Weimar: Hermann Böhlaus Nachfolger, 1912–21. |
| WA | Martin Luther, *D. Martin Luthers Werke: Kritische Gesamtausgaber [Schriften].* 65 vols. in 127. H. Böhlau, 1883–1993. |
| ZThK | *Zeitschrift für Theologie und Kirche* |

**Part I**

*Luther's life and context*

# 1  Luther's life

ALBRECHT BEUTEL
Translated by Katharina Gustavs

## YEARS AS A STUDENT

From the outside, Luther's life passed by simply and steadily.[1] With few exceptions, his whole life took place within the territories of Thuringia and Saxony, mostly in Wittenberg, the electoral capital at the Elbe river, and its surroundings. Only a few journeys led Luther beyond this small sphere of life: on behalf of his order to Rome (1510/11), to Cologne (1512) and Heidelberg (1518); later on behalf of a Reformation consensus to Marburg (1529), and also on his own behalf to Augsburg (1518) and Worms (1521). Equally, with regard to his profession, Luther's was a remarkable and steady character. From entering the monastery through to his last moment, Luther always remained a man of the word: as a preacher, professor and writer.

During Luther's life the horizon of world history and humanities was in the process of becoming radically changed. The following names must stand for many others representing this era: the two emperors Maximilian I and Charles V, the popes Leo X, Clemens VII and Paul III (Council of Trent), as well as the names of such artists and scientists as Raphael, Michelangelo, Dürer, Copernicus and Paracelsus. However, as far as Luther is concerned these changes could be deceptive because his childhood and youth had not been touched by the spirit of humanism or of the Renaissance. Limited to the provincial surroundings of his hometown, Luther grew up as a typical child of the late Middle Ages – just like thousands of other boys around him.

On November 10, 1483 Luther was born as the eldest of probably nine sisters and brothers at Eisleben in what was then the county of Mansfeld. The next morning he was baptized and named Martin after the saint of that day. Coming from a Thuringian family of farmers, his father Hans Luder, not being entitled to inherit, sought his luck in one of the most advanced business opportunities: the copper mines of Mansfeld. During the course of his life he was able to gain a well-respected economic and social position through enormous hard work and thrift. We know only a very little about his wife Margarethe, Luther's mother. She came from a family named

*1483*

Lindemann, resident in Eisenach. As the wife of a venturesome entrepreneur and as mother of her large family, she had to work hard throughout her whole lifetime. Martin Luther was well aware of the fact that, as he put it, the bitter sweat of his parents had made it possible for him to go to the university.

CHILDH.

Their parenting principles were strict, but not unusual for that time. Luther does not seem to have come to any harm. In fact, he honored the memory of his parents with love and respect. The devotional life at home also followed common church practices. Luther lived most of his life away from his parents' home after he turned fourteen.

Between about 1490 and 1497 Luther attended the town school in Mansfeld. Thereafter his father sent him to Magdeburg, probably because one of his friends also changed to the cathedral school there. Luther found accommodation with the "Brethren of the Common Life," a modern religious movement emanating from the Netherlands. Only a year later he moved to the parish school of St. George in Eisenach. Closeness to his mother's relatives may have played a role in this decision. Later Luther criticized the rigidity in late medieval schools. At any rate he owed them his proficiency in the Latin language, his familiarity with ancient Christian culture and his love for poetry and music.

In spring 1501 Luther enrolled at the University of Erfurt. He stayed at a hostel, whose life followed strict monastic rules. To the prerequisite studies of liberal arts, which were mandatory for any prospective theologian, lawyer, or medical doctor, Luther devoted himself passionately. And after four years, in the shortest time possible, he graduated with excellence. When he was awarded his master's degree in spring 1505, he took second place out of seventeen candidates.

Then Luther turned toward the study of law, as was his father's desire. After having visited his parents, Luther got caught in a summer thunderstorm nearby Stotternheim on his way back home on July 2, 1505. A lightning bolt, which struck right beside him, scared him to death and caused

MONAST.

him to vow: "Help me, Saint Anna, I will become a monk!" That Luther entered the monastery, but not before another fifteen days had passed, shows that he did not act under the effect of mere emotions, but that he became a monk only after careful self-examination. We will have to see his decision against the background of a deep existential fear, whose resolution he tried to force but whose dramatic expression it only became, since even in the Erfurt convent of the Augustinian Hermits, he was barred from the religious peace for which he had longed.

Luther's father was outraged by his son's unexpected turn: All plans he had made for his eldest son's life and career seemed to be thwarted. This conflict would cast a shadow over the relationship between father and son for many years to come and only in 1525 when Luther got married was it finally resolved.

*CONSC.*

During his first year as a novice, Luther subjected himself to an intense study of the Bible. He also familiarized himself with the rules and regulations of the monastic life. The strict way of living, which was predominant there, did not pose any problems to him. But soon it became apparent that even the most painstaking obedience to the three monastic vows Luther had taken at his profession (obedience, poverty, chastity) did not lead to the inner peace for which he had longed. An excessively pursued practice of confessing did not help either. It only increased his religious distress. Thus it was no coincidence that Luther got stuck in the high prayer during the first mass he had to read as a newly ordained priest. The young man who all of a sudden found himself facing God so closely was left speechless in his fear. Filled with awe of the sacred he tried to run away from the liturgy but his teacher admonished him to stay and finish mass.

*AWE DURING MASS*

In the figure of the *pantocrator* – the ruling and judging Christ – Luther's fear of God became symbolically intensified. The anxieties and melancholies that haunted Luther throughout his entire life were fed from this image of the Judge of the World, so real for him during his early years. Yet Luther never lost himself to his religious anxieties. He rather felt spurred on to study the Bible more intensely. Unlike the approach of the scholastic tradition, Luther would not read the Scriptures for intellectual purposes but for existential meditation. Even later the professors at Wittenberg were always quite impressed by their young colleague's outstanding knowledge of the Bible. The fact that Luther felt at home in this book more than in any other became the characteristic trademark of his theology: No matter what he read from the fathers and teachers of the church, he would always relate it to the Bible and compare it with its original message.

In 1507, the same year he was ordained as a priest, Luther was selected by his superior to study theology. In Erfurt the Augustinian Hermits had established a general course of studies for their members. As a doctor of theology the respective chair had to fill the professorship of theology at the university as well. Through the works of Gabriel Biel, also von Ockham, Duns Scotus, Petrus of Ailly and Thomas Aquinas, Luther was introduced to Christian dogmatics. However, Augustine was the figure who became of utmost importance to Luther. Having studied his works most diligently, Luther preferred him over all other scholastics, turning him King's evidence for his reformational renewal. In addition to these scholastics, he also came in contact with the Aeropagitic (Dionysios, Gerson), the Roman (Bernhard von Clairvaux) and the German mysticism (Tauler) as well as the German

*1507*

humanism (Reuchlin, Wimpfeling), though in a more limited, philology-oriented manner.

STAUPITZ

At that time Johannes von Staupitz served as vicar general of the German monasteries of the Augustinian Hermits. Today there is still very little known about his theology, which was highly influenced by Augustine. He attached great importance to the study of the Bible in his monasteries. To Luther he became an important supporter and father confessor, seeking to alleviate Luther's fear of punishment and eternal damnation by pointing out that God only intends to punish the sinful nature in humans but seeks to win the person of the sinner for himself. In a somewhat modified manner this distinction can also be found later in Luther's writings. At one point Luther tormented himself with an almost maniacal urge to confess, when von Staupitz, a pastor of high standing, objected that he could not even produce any real sins, but just hobbling stuff and puppet's sins.

From fall 1508 to fall 1509 Luther was sent to the newly established university in Wittenberg where the Augustinian Hermits from Erfurt were in charge of one of the teaching positions. Due to a temporary vacancy Luther had to fill in as a Master of Arts, reading about the *Nicomachean Ethics* of Aristotle. After this interim in Wittenberg, Luther returned to the monastery in Erfurt. From there he accompanied an older fellow friar on a trip to Rome in winter 1510/11, where the latter was engaged by his order to settle business with the curia. Only in the late summer of 1511 did Luther move for good into the city which would make history through him and in which he himself would make history.

As his very own creation Elector Frederick the Wise had established a new university in Wittenberg in 1502, for which the imperial privilege had been granted whereas papal confirmation of the university was not given until 1507. Georg Spalatin, electoral court chaplain and tutor of the princes, became the crucial intermediary between court and university. Though Spalatin also cherished other theological ideas at first, Luther did not have much trouble in winning him for his own opinions. The bond of friendship that grew immediately between them turned out to be an essential cornerstone of the Reformation, lasting through the storms of decades.

In Wittenberg the two convents of the mendicant orders were each engaged with a professorship in theology. For the Augustinian hermits von Staupitz was the one giving the lectures. However, he wished to free himself from this responsibility and it was obvious he built Luther up into being his successor right from the start. Under his spiritual guidance Luther graduated through all levels of theology studies up to and including his doctorate – and all that within the shortest time frame possible, as five years of study were the minimum requirement.

On October 18 and 19, 1512 Luther was solemnly awarded his doctor of theology. The required fee of fifty guilders was paid by the elector himself. With the doctorate came the right of independent academic work. Anyone with a doctoral degree was entitled to voice his own opinion, which could then be heard in theological disputes – of course this was only as long as it resonated within the accepted teachings of the church. Even though at first Luther was most reluctant to pursue the academic career intended for him, it did not take him long to adjust and he would refer to his doctoral degree without any reservation whenever his authority as a teacher was questioned, be it toward the papal legate Cajetan, the elector Albert of Mainz, or the pope himself.

With his promotion Luther entered into a stage of his life which was characterized by extremely intense academic and spiritual work. Beside his academic responsibilities, he already faced an enormous workload as sub-prior and chairman of the general course of studies in Wittenberg, adding even more duties when he became district vicar of his order in 1515.

## A TIME OF NEW DEPARTURES (1512–21)

Luther's series of early lectures – first on Psalms (1513/14), then on the Letters to the Romans (1515/16), Galatians (1516/17) and Hebrews (1517/18) – is an invaluable source of information for understanding Reformation theology. Those lectures document an exciting and far-reaching process during whose course of discoveries Luther got out of the rut of conventional theology more rigorously with each new insight: He interpreted the passages not with a scholastic's eye any more, but from the Bible's perspective, not on the background of traditional interpretations by church authorities, but within the framework of the whole biblical tradition. The debate as to whether Luther experienced his Reformation breakthrough in 1514/15 or somewhat later, in 1518, which has not been settled as yet, loses more and more of its importance when Luther's Reformation theology is not looked at as a sudden event, which might even have occurred overnight, but rather as a complex developmental process spreading out over several years, furthering sudden insights on a continuous basis. Without a doubt the most famous discovery of all is about God's righteousness (Rom. 1:17) – which is not based on demanding but on giving, not on the law but on the gospel.

Luther's early lectures seemed to make a fundamental reform of the theological course of studies absolutely necessary. His criticism of Aristotelian prerequisites for thinking grew steadily into a criticism of the entire scholastic theology. The call for a new reform of the theological study course was the inevitable consequence: away from Aristotelianism and the interpretation of the Lombard's *Sentences* toward a study of the Bible and, with a proper distance, the church fathers as well. Luther's criticism found its preliminary peak in his – partly harshly termed – disputation theses "Against Scholastic Theology,"[2] which were published in September 1517, only two months before his famous Ninety-five Theses "On the Power of Indulgences" were announced, triggering a snowball effect. Strangely enough, at this time everything appeared to remain largely calm on the outside.

Beside his academic work Luther had also assumed responsibility for the parish of Wittenberg as a preacher. In their inseparable connectedness these two, lectern and pulpit, formed together the decisive continuum of Luther's theological existence. No later than 1514 he must have already filled in the preaching position at the town church of Wittenberg. Some of his sermons Luther sent immediately to press. However, the majority of his sermons – in the end somewhat over 2,000 – were handed down to us in form of shorthand transcripts. As a preacher Luther preferred a homiletic approach, which would closely follow the Bible passage. His interpretations were crafted in a down-to-earth manner without rhetorical pathos, but full of experiences from real life and faith. Beside the interpretation of individual passages from the Bible, Luther also liked to teach about central texts such as the Ten Commandments or the Lord's Prayer. Those catechistic series of sermons formed the basis from which, later, the two catechisms grew.

The turning point in society, which Luther brought about not as an act of daring but unintentionally, was kicked off by his criticism of the widespread but not canonized practice of selling indulgences. By means of indulgences the church offered an opportunity to compensate for one's unatoned sin and punishments through money. Pope Leo X had reissued a plenary indulgence in 1515 for, among other territories, the church province of Magdeburg, near to Wittenberg. Many members of Luther's parish made eager use of this opportunity, lulling them into a false sense of religious certainty. First of all, Luther voiced his pastoral concerns from the pulpit. On October 31, 1517 he presented his critique of the indulgences in a concerned letter to Margrave Albert of Brandenburg, who was at the same time Archbishop of Mainz as well as of Magdeburg. His Ninety-five Theses "On the Power of Indulgences"[3] were also enclosed in this letter. In his writing he called repentance a lifelong attitude expected of Christians. He expressed his particular disapproval of the fact that humans were more frightened of punishments set by the church than of sin whose forgiveness lies in God's power alone. Thus Luther's criticism of the indulgences aimed at the church's instrumentalization of Christian repentance.

Whether Luther actually posted his Ninety-five Theses on the castle church of Wittenberg remains uncertain – Melanchthon at least talks about

that only decades later. However, it is beyond any doubt that his theses
spread throughout all Germany in no time and launched a meteoric development after they had been released at the end of 1517 and explained in
German by Luther in March 1518.[4] This marks the beginning of Luther's
unprecedented writing activities. At the end of April 1518, when he visited
his order's chapter in Heidelberg, he was already a famous man. With his
theses of the "Heidelberg Disputation," in which he gave the theology of
the cross as promoted by him a distinct image, he won some of his most
important connections in southern Germany, among them Johannes Brenz,
Martin Bucer, and Erhard Schnepf.

In summer 1518 Rome opened a trial for heresy against Luther. The situation appeared to be hopeless: The ban of the church would most certainly
be followed by the ban of the empire. Luther asked his territorial ruler,
Elector Frederick the Wise, to lend him his support with the emperor's
consent so that the whole cause could come to negotiations in Germany.
Frederick complied with his request, and because Rome had political reasons to reach an agreement with Frederick, Luther was indeed examined
by a papal legate on German soil in October 1518, following the Diet of
Augsburg. The interrogations were led by the papal legate Cajetan, a highly
educated Dominican, who had the authority to readmit Luther to the community of the church if he would recant, but also to excommunicate him
if need be. Through it all Luther remained steadfast. Therefore Cajetan demanded that Luther be extradited to Rome. That of course was flatly declined
by Frederick the Wise, who demanded instead that Luther be heard before
an unbiased court of scholars. Since Rome did not intend to bargain away
Frederick's favor in view of the upcoming imperial election, no particular
measures were enforced in the *causa Lutheri* for the moment.

Yet the debate continued. In summer 1519 the theology professor
Johann Eck from Ingolstadt sought a confrontation with Luther. In the
"Leipzig Disputation" they first debated about indulgences, but soon moved
on to the question of papal authority. Provoked by Eck, Luther disputed
that the pope's primacy was grounded in divine right and at the same time
he also disputed the infallibility of the church councils: Those *might* not
only err, but had certainly already erred, as with the Council of Constance
(1414–18), for example, in the case of the Bohemian Jan Hus. The Leipzig
Disputation helped clarify positions: From now on Duke George of Saxony
saw his enemy in Luther. On the other hand many humanists, such as
Erasmus of Rotterdam, sided with Luther or at least showed solidarity while
keeping their distance.

The breathing space which the year 1520 seemed to grant was used by
Luther to give his theology a more clearly defined image in writing. With the

*1520*
*WRITINGS*

four main reformational works of this year he showed that he did not only aim at the criticism of a specific, ill-developed, practice of piety, but that he was on his way to renew the whole church and theology based on the gospel. He started out with the treatise *Von den guten Werken (Of Good Works)*.[5] This fundamental writing of Reformation ethics Luther clothed in the form of an interpretation of the Ten Commandments. Faith alone, he stated at the beginning, is able to fulfill the first commandment. However, when a person in faith knows herself accepted by God without any contributing works of her own, she will not need to speculate about attaining God's salvation through her own activities, but fueled by her confidence in God will feel free to do good works as the most natural thing in the world. Following this line to practice a life lived out of faith, Luther also interpreted all the remaining nine commandments.

In his writing *An den christlichen Adel deutscher Nation von des christlichen Standes Besserung (To the Christian Nobility of the German Nation Regarding the Improvement of the Christian Estate)*,[6] Luther encouraged the target group to make active use of their right as secular authorities to lend their active support to a reform of Christianity. And all the more, Rome would take cover behind a threefold wall against all legitimate reform efforts: First, through the unbiblical division of Christianity between priests and lay people; second, through the claim that the pope holds the supreme power of teaching; third, through the presumptuous pretension that the pope alone was allowed to convene a council.

The "Nobility Treatise," written in German, was selling like hot cakes. Only a few days after its publication the 4,000 copies of the first printing were sold out. The Latin writing *Von der babylonischen Gefangenschaft der Kirche (On the Babylonian Captivity of the Church)*,[7] however, was geared toward a theologically educated audience. In it Luther unfolded the baseline for a biblical understanding of the sacraments, which on the one hand sorted out confirmation, marriage, ordination and extreme unction, and with some reservation also repentance, as unbiblical, and on the other hand announced his fundamental opposition to the Roman Catholic understanding of the Lord's Supper. The explosive potential of Luther's new teaching on the sacraments can hardly be overestimated, not to mention its practical implications which, for example, would render private masses pointless. This in turn would also put many priests out of work and in general would make the separation between clergy and lay people irrelevant. Luther certainly did not have an impious destruction of the church in mind, but rather its basic Christian renewal. Yet Luther hit the vital nerve of current church practices. Erasmus commented on this writing with the laconic remark that the break with Rome could hardly be healed any more.

The best-known writing of them all explored *Von der Freiheit eines Christenmenschen (On the Freedom of a Christian)*.[8] Luther portrayed Christians in their relationship to God as free, in their relationship to the world, however, as obliged to the service and compassion of their neighbor: Faith would set humans free from the compulsion for self-justification and therefore would render them free to serve their neighbors. In short, humans would be free out of faith in love.

The programmatic writings of the Reformation were hereby established. In the same year the proceedings against Luther were taken up again. As early as 1519 the two universities of Cologne as well as Löwen had already condemned Luther. On June 15, 1520 the bull threatening Luther with excommunication was finally issued, and in October 1520 it was publicly announced to have the force of law. Somehow Frederick the Wise was able to negotiate that Luther was not to be arrested at once but would first be interrogated at the Diet of Worms. On March 6, 1521 Luther was summoned before the emperor with the promise of safe-conduct.

*1520*
*BULL*

*1521*
*WORMS*

The journey to Worms turned into a triumphal procession. Wherever Luther went, he was eagerly greeted with public interest and good will. In Leipzig the magistrate welcomed him with an honorary cup of wine, in Erfurt the rector of the university received him at the city wall with great splendor as if a prince was to be honored. Here in Erfurt Luther also preached in his order's church, which was overfilled to the point of mortal danger. When the creaking of the wooden gallery caused panic to spread, with great presence of mind he was able to avert the danger: Please stand still, he called into the crowd, nothing evil will happen, the devil just tried to frighten us.

Finally, on April 18, 1521, his crucial appearance in Worms became reality. In front of the emperor and the imperial estates Luther refused to follow their demand of renunciation. He did not feel the slightest obligation to the authority of the pope, he stated. Instead his conscience was bound to Holy Scripture. Therefore he could not and would not recant as long as his teachings could not be refuted through Scripture or clear reasoning. With reference to his conscience as solely obliged to the word of God, Luther had denied access to human faith to the two world powers, represented by the emperor and the pope.

Though the effort was made to continue negotiations in Worms, they did not produce successful results. On April 26, 1521 Luther set out on his return trip. Shortly before, Frederick the Wise had informed Luther that he would have him kidnapped on his way home so he could be brought to safety. This is exactly what happened on May 4: To all appearances an attack was launched and Luther was taken to his new refuge at the Wartburg castle. Since Worms, Luther's life was in danger: The Edict of Worms had placed him under the imperial ban. Furthermore, all his books were to be destroyed and a censorship of religious writings was to be introduced in all territories of the empire.

Soon it became obvious that the orders of the Edict of Worms defied enforcement in this form. Yet it should not be underestimated that as a legal instrument they served their purpose in the imperial religious politics until the Peace of Augsburg in 1555.

## A TIME OF CREATIVE PROWESS (1521–25)

Often enough Luther found his isolation difficult to bear while locked up at the Wartburg castle. An immense work schedule was his way of going about coping with it. He studied the Bible and beside numerous letters he also wrote some of his most important works, such as the *Wartburgspostille* (*Church Postil*)[9] – a collection of exemplary sermons – and also an interpretation of the Magnificat (Luke 1:46–56),[10] a broadsheet against the theologian Latomus von Löwen,[11] and a fundamental treatise on monastic vows,[12] whose rejection of the binding force of the vows soon triggered far-reaching practical consequences. The exodus from the monasteries began.

But above all Luther translated the New Testament from the Greek original, a first since Wulfila, at the Wartburg castle within just eleven weeks. Luther's German translations of the Bible outshone all those before him by far: in their linguistic beauty and power, but also in their spiritual authority and theological precision. Luther's New Testament was released in September 1522 (*Septembertestament*) with 3,000 copies and a rather high retail price, notwithstanding which it was out of print within a few days. By December a revised edition (*Dezembertestament*) was published. Between 1522 and 1533 Luther's New Testament saw a total of eighty-five editions. Soon after 1522 Luther set out to translate the Old Testament. This endeavour, which engaged several collaborators, came to its fruition with the first edition of a complete Luther Bible in 1534. It is said that the print shop of Hans Lufft in Wittenberg sold about 100,000 copies of the *Biblia, das ist die gantze Heilige Schrift Deudsch* (*Biblia, That Is the Entire Holy Scripture in German*) over fifty years. The number of non-local reprints or illegal copies, however, is beyond our knowledge. From 1531 Luther presided over a revision commission, whose goal it was to improve the texts of the German Bible on a continuous basis and whose work can still come alive for us through some extant commission protocols.

During the creative break Luther had been forced to take at the Wartburg castle, the call for restructuring the church system became more and more urgent. Now it all depended on shaping this critical potential, fed from all those forces across Germany that aligned themselves with Luther's protest, into a positive and creative power that would be able to give this new faith, which claimed to be the truly old and evangelical one, a visible and credible expression of life. That Luther met this challenge without hesitating and dedicated his entire life to it without sparing himself is what really shows his greatness and at the same time has given the cause he represented its lasting historic meaning.

In 1522 turmoil broke out in Wittenberg. Blind enthusiasm for reform got out of hand. First Luther responded in written form only, with his *Treue[n] Vermahnung zu allen Christen, sich zu hüten vor Aufruhr und Emporung (Earnest Exhortation to All Christians Against Insurrection and Rebellion).*[13] When he realized that written encouragement would not help, he came in person. At the beginning of March 1522 Luther preached for a whole week every single day. Thus he was able to stop the radical iconoclasm, cooling down the very heated feelings. *Non vi sed verbo* – not through violence, but through the word alone. This was the message of the "Invocavit Sermons"[14] he preached very eloquently. This was also the start for the reorganization of the budding church of the Reformation.

Luther reformed the current form of worship service cautiously but also with consequences. So that the congregation could play its active role as set forth by the new evangelical approach, Luther initiated congregational singing in the native language. As early as 1524 the first three evangelical hymnbooks could be released, with a large portion of the new hymns contributed by Luther himself.

Furthermore, the church assets had also to be reorganized. In Wittenberg a satisfying solution was quickly found. After a temporary trial of the so-called "begging ordinance," the *Gemeine Kasten* ("common chest") was established in 1522. This new institution was responsible for the finances of church and school and also for the social services to be granted in support of poor local residents. The begging of foreigners was hereby prohibited.

The school system Luther regarded as an excellent object for reform work. Over and over again he complained about the lack of interest in schooling among citizens and the magistrates. In 1524 he therefore appealed *An die Ratsherren aller Städte deutschen Lands, daß sie christliche Schulen aufrichten und halten sollen (To the Councillors of all Cities in Germany that they Establish and Maintain Christian Schools).*[15] A solid knowledge of the original languages of the Bible seemed to be indispensable for a preacher in Luther's opinion, and likewise the professional skills to access the whole of the education currently available. This was the only way that an evangelical preacher could fulfill his task satisfactorily, just as the opposite opinion, that of a fanciful and low regard for school and academic education, would inevitably lead to a bargaining away of the cause of the church. The gospel, Luther was certain, could not be deliberately trivialized. The educational responsibility of the Lutheran Church as put forth by Luther became an essential factor in the modern history of humanities.

Not only for the history of the Reformation, but also for Martin Luther himself the year 1525 meant a deep caesura. It was marked by the Peasants' War as well as the suspect role Luther played in it. As early as 1523 Luther noticed that Thomas Müntzer, one of his followers during the first years, began to drift further off from him: The rigoristic mysticism that Müntzer began to spread, Luther regarded as much against the gospel as was its objective, to execute the punishment of the godless through violent-revolutionary means. At the beginning of 1525 Müntzer became one of the protagonists of the peasants' movement in Thuringia.

The Peasants' War turned into a trial of strength for Luther's political ethics. Luther regarded most of the peasants' demands as legitimate. However, he disliked the fact that the peasants did not voice their concerns in a political and pragmatic manner, but rather justified their cause from the Bible, thereby revoking the secular system of laws in the name of the gospel. Luther asked for a clear distinction between law and religion. When open rebellion broke loose in Thuringia, Luther became outraged about the peasants: They had violated their obligation of allegiance and were guilty of violation of the peace as well as blasphemy. At the same time Luther admonished the princes to take up their duties as rulers, that is, to protect the system of laws and to go into action against the rebellious peasants.

Of course, Luther could not hinder the rebellion. After all, we should not overestimate the influence he exerted over the course of events. However, the consequences followed really hard upon him: The Roman Catholic party sought to make him legally responsible for the uproar as its spiritual father. Among Luther's friends there was irritation due to his hard line. The peasants were disappointed by him, and most of them remained embittered. From now on Luther kept reminding the secular authorities of their duties to be the chosen patrons of the Reformation. The *Landesherrliche Kirchenregiment* (territorial church government), which grew out of this development, would define the Protestant church governance in Germany until 1918.

Beside the Peasants' War the year 1525 also brought another caesura: the break with Erasmus. Humanism and Reformation, Erasmus and Luther: They were a pair of brothers, sometimes arguing but certainly cast in the same mold. Not only in their criticism of ecclesiastical incrustations and the traditional scholastic education system were they connected, but also in their philological dedication toward the original documents of the Western world and in their deep respect for the ancient languages of the civilized world.

At first Erasmus had been kindly disposed towards Luther's appearance. No later than 1521 he considered the break between Rome and Luther as irreparable. At best he had preferred to keep silent. Yet because he was increasingly suspected of being one of Luther's secret followers and also because he had felt hurt by some of Luther's adverse remarks, he could hardly avoid making a public statement. In September 1524 he began to take a stand against Luther with his treatise *On Free Will*.[16] The topic was chosen cleverly: It hit the core of the argument over which Luther had become involved with the church.

Erasmus opted for the path of the golden mean: On the way to salvation, many things would have to be ascribed to divine grace and others to human will. Luther replied with his counter-writing *On the Bondage of the Will*[17] in fall 1525. To the question whether the human will can be thought of as being free, he also answered: half and half. Unlike Erasmus he drew a line of categorical distinction: With respect to its relationship to God, the human will is totally bound. On the other hand, with respect to its dealing with worldly things, freedom of choice belongs to humans. If humans were to ascribe freedom to themselves, then, stated Luther, God's gift of faith becomes a human effort. According to Luther, this was exactly the position toward which Erasmus was leaning. For Erasmus, human faith in God would become a moral postulate.

Erasmus responded once more with a detailed defense statement.[18] Luther did not react to it any more. The break between the two scholars was complete by then. The relationship between the two movements they represented did not suffer the same fate, fortunately for both.

## A TIME OF TRIALS (1525–1546)

With respect to his personal life the year 1525 also meant an essential caesura to Luther. He left monkhood and entered into marriage. From the union with Katharina von Bora, a former nun, six children were born: Hans (1526), Elizabeth (1527), Magdalena (1529), Martin (1531), Paul (1533) and Margarethe (1534). Two of the girls died young: Elizabeth after eight months, Magdalena – Luther's beloved *Lenchen* – in her thirteenth year.

The burden of Luther's household was immense. In addition to his own children, he also took in children of both his deceased sister, and an aunt of his wife. Some students found also accommodation in Luther's house as well as varying numbers of foreign guests; these alone could amount to twenty-five people. This large operation posed a continuous domestic challenge. And that Luther on the one hand was a man of warm generosity and on the other hand lacked a sense of finances did not make things easier. That Luther's wife not only managed the domestic matters but also secured their economic survival through husbandry and agriculture, Luther always appreciated with deep gratification. The relationship between the two spouses was conducted in mutual respect and happy love. In contrast to the law of his time, Luther appointed his wife as sole heir in his last will.

Luther's professional duties took up most of his time. As a preacher, often also as a father confessor or pastor, he served the parish of Wittenberg, unflustered in his faithful and reliable devotion despite many a dispute. From 1535 Luther was appointed again permanent dean of the theology faculty. Highlights of his academic work included the second lecture series on Galatians (1531) and the great interpretation of the Book of Genesis (1535–45), which took about ten years and was worked on with many an interruption. The practice of disputations, which had come to a standstill during the disturbances of the early 1520s, was revived in 1535. Luther had been involved in a total of fourteen circular as well as thirteen doctoral disputations. For the promotion of this literary style, by which the Reformation had been sparked off so to speak, Luther spared neither trouble nor care. Therefore nowhere else can greater examples of his outstanding writing and editing skills be found than in the series of disputation theses he drew up. As for the subject matter, he would always aim at the heart of the Reformation theology: The doctrine of justification, later also Christology, the doctrine of Trinity, as well as anthropology, were his favorite topics.

Again and again Luther emphasized the importance of disputation exercises for theological teaching and church life. In his opinion they offered prospective pastors and teachers an ideal opportunity to train their rhetorical-dialectical skills and to prepare them for all those arguments they would inevitably be confronted with owing to their profession. To Luther theology was a science of conflict par excellence: Its subject was the dispute about the truth of faith into which everybody had been baptized and into which each and every studying Christian would certainly and constantly become involved. In Luther's opinion, theological reality would not find its expression in unconditional neutrality but in a constantly raging debate: Only in the defense of life-threatening evil would the truth of faith manifest itself in concrete terms.

After the disaster of the Peasants' War Luther made an appeal to the elector to have visitations in the parishes carried out and to urge his villages to regard the support of schools and churches as at least as important as the maintenance of bridges and roads. Thus in 1527 the first visitation was conducted in Electoral Saxony. Luther contributed mainly in written form: the "German Mass,"[19] a new liturgy for baptism and marriage, a prayer book for children, new editions of hymnals, a series of sermons and of course the two Catechisms.[20]

Both Catechisms, the Large as well as the Small, were Luther's way of dealing with the depressing visitation results. In view of the alarming lack of biblical and theological knowledge encountered in the pastors – not to mention the congregations – Luther set out to tackle the challenge, whose effort can hardly be overrated, of putting the essence of the Christian faith in basic sentences without trivializing or reducing it excessively. Fortunately he could draw on some groundwork he had done earlier, in particular on three series of sermons from 1528, in which he had worked through the "Principal Themes of Faith" one after the other: Decalogue, Confession, Lord's Prayer, Baptism, and Lord's Supper. From that source the *Large Catechism* was born: a handbook for pastors designed to provide them with the necessary tools of the theological trade.

The *Large Catechism* was published in 1529 and the *Small Catechism* in the same year. The *Small Catechism* is first of all nothing more than its superbly phrased short form for domestic use. The one-page format made it possible for the individual pages of the entire Catechism to be put up on the wall as an educational aid for memorizing. With unsurpassed proficiency Luther knew how to summarize the heart of the Christian faith in concrete terms, always keeping his readership in mind so that its translation into the lives of those who would read and memorize the Catechism came alive with each sentence. "Your book says it all," commented his wife Käthe. And this is exactly how it was meant to be.

Beside the Luther Bible the *Small Catechism* in particular unfolded an incredible sphere of activity throughout the history of Protestant piety, extending to the dawn of our present time. The scheme of having the question "What is it?" constantly repeated was meant as an encouragement to render account to each other for the mystery of faith on a daily basis.

At the Diet of Speyer in 1529 the evangelical imperial estates submitted a formal protestation. An alliance of all "Protestants" came into sight then, for which Luther assumed as inevitable an agreement on all questions of teaching. The "Schwabach Articles"[21] which he had co-authored with Melanchthon were supposed to form the foundation. The teaching on the Lord's Supper led to an argument with the reformers from Zurich: Do we celebrate only the memory of Christ – as Zwingli said; or even his bodily presence – as Luther stated? In October 1529 the "Colloquy of Marburg" was set up to bring about the indispensable theological as well as political unity. Yet no agreement could be reached. From now on each party would go their own way. The consequences caused by the separation between the reformers of Wittenberg and Switzerland have reached right into the twenty-first century.

The separation from the Roman Catholic Church also remained tormenting. For the Diet of Augsburg in 1530 the emperor had promised a peaceful settlement of the religious issue. The "Augsburg Confession," written by Melanchthon since Luther was not allowed to leave his territory of Electoral Saxony, offered a careful and cautious summary of the Lutheran teachings. Unlike Melanchthon, Luther regarded the attempt to reconcile with Rome in theological and ecclesiastical matters as utopian. Therefore he aimed at a political settlement. The "Peace of Nuremberg" (1532) seemed to offer that. However, appearances were deceptive: The political reality only took root with the "Peace of Augsburg" in 1555. Though Luther did not trust the pope's plans for a church council, in his "Schmalkald Articles"[22] he did summarize the theological priorities of the Protestants, which ought not to be given up in the discussion with Rome. They became his theological will.

Luther's workload, which rested on his shoulders over decades on end, was enormous. Just a glance at his written legacy, collected in over one hundred thick volumes of the complete critical Weimar Edition – equivalent to one thousand and eight hundred pages per year –, makes one stand in wonder at so much creative power. Luther always worked on the verge of exhaustion.

His life became overshadowed by more and more illness. An angina pectoris ailed him over decades; a severe attack in 1527 had his family fearing the worst. Among other chronic disorders were headaches as well as a stubborn kidney disorder, which almost cost his life in 1537 while on a trip to Schmalkald.

Luther devoted his last energy to the mediation of a fight over an inheritance which had divided the counts of Mansfeld. In the end they asked Luther to help negotiate between the parties. At the end of 1545 Luther had become involved with several letters and visits, but in vain.

Thus he set out for another trip to Eisleben in January 1546. This time his arbitration efforts attained their goal. On February 16, 1546 a first arbitration contract could be signed. The next day Luther was unable to participate in the signing of the second contract due to acute bodily weakness. In the night of February 18 he died. Both of the friends who were with him asked the dying Luther if he would remain steadfast and intended to die in Christ and the teaching he himself had preached. Luther replied with a clear and audible: *Ja* ("Yes"). This was his last word.

During the two following days Luther's body remained laid out in Eisleben. Thereafter he was transferred to Wittenberg where he was taken to the castle and university church with a solemn escort. At the funeral service Bugenhagen as the town pastor preached in German and Melanchthon representing the university spoke in Latin. Then Luther was interred next to the pulpit. When the imperial troops entered Wittenberg a year later, Charles V ordered his soldiers to leave the grave of his adversary untouched. Luther had shaped his time in an extraordinary way. Now he had become history himself.

*Notes*

1. In addition to all the standard published "lives of Luther," see also Helmar Junghans, *Martin Luther: Exploring His Life and Times, 1483–1546* (Minneapolis: Fortress Press, 1998).
2. WA 1, 224–28 (*Disputatio contra scholasticam theologiam*; 1517). Luther's writings are quoted according to the Weimarer Ausgabe (Weimar Edition), the only complete critical edition of his works, letters, table talks and Bible interpretations: D. Martin Luther, *Werke: Kritische Gesamtausgabe*, Weimar: H. Böhlau, 1883–1993 (abbr. WA).
3. WA 1, 233–38 (*Disputatio pro declaratione virtutis indulgentiarum*; 1517).
4. WA 1, 243–46 (*Ein Sermon von Ablaß und Gnade [A Sermon on Indulgences and Grace]*; 1518).
5. WA 6, 202–76 (1520).
6. WA 6, 404–69 (1520).
7. WA 6, 497–573 (*De captivitate babylonica ecclesiae Praeludium*; 1520).
8. WA 7, 20–38 (1520).
9. WA 10, 1, 1 (1522).
10. WA 7, 544–604 (*Das Magnificat verdeutscht und ausgelegt*; 1521).
11. WA 8, 43–128 (*Rationis Latomianae pro incendiariis Lovaniensis scholae sophistis redditae, Lutheriana confutatio*; 1521).
12. WA 8, 573–669 (*De votis monasticis M. Lutheri iudicium*; 1521).
13. WA 8, 676–87 (1522).
14. WA 10, 3; 1–64 (1522).
15. WA 15, 27–53 (1524).
16. Erasmus von Rotterdam, *De libero Arbitrio diatribe sive collatio* (1524).
17. WA 18, 600–787 (*De servo arbitrio*; 1525; ET *The Bondage of the Will*, trans. J. I. Packer and O. R. Johnston. Westwood, NJ: Fleming H. Revell Company, 1957).
18. Erasmus von Rotterdam, *Hyperaspistes diatribae adversus servum arbitrium Martini Lutheri*, 2 vols. (1526/27).
19. WA 19, 72–113 (*Deutsche Messe und Ordnung Gottesdiensts*; 1526).
20. WA 30, 1; 125–425 (1529).
21. WA 30, 3; 178–82 (*Ein Bekenntnis christlicher Lehre und christlichen Glaubens durch D. M. Luther in 17 Artikeln verfaßt*; 1529).
22. WA 50, 192–254 (1536).

## 2 Luther's Wittenberg

HELMAR JUNGHANS

Translated by Katharina Gustavs

Wittenberg is Luther's Wittenberg in three distinct ways: The Wittenberg of the late Middle Ages provides the conditions for Luther's work, the Wittenberg of the Reformation era is shaped by Luther himself, and the Wittenberg of the post-Reformation period is formed by Luther's followers.

### WITTENBERG IN THE LATE MIDDLE AGES

A fortress of Wittenberg is mentioned for the first time in 1180. It belongs to the Ascanians, who call people from the Rhineland and the Netherlands to settle there around 1159/60. Situated next to the fortress, this settlement grows into a town, receiving its charter in 1293. The charter also includes permission for fortifications. Soon a town wall is erected.

The townspeople continue to gain in strength and about 1280 they begin the construction of a town church, the so-called St. Mary's Church. Well before 1300 the Gothic choir with its two aisles is completed. A keystone in the nave shows Christ giving a blessing. In the middle of the fourteenth century a mighty construction is begun on the west side, including two towers. In 1439 the finished hall church with its nave and two aisles running between the choir and the west end is consecrated. Thus the town church takes on the shape it has maintained to the present day.

At the end of the fourteenth century a big sandstone relief depicting Christ as judge of the world is erected in the cemetery next to the church. It instills into the people of Wittenberg the typical late-medieval demand: Prepare yourself for the final judgment through "good works" so that you may lessen your punishment. Masses read in memoriam of the deceased are also regarded as highly effective. For this reason the town church is equipped with side altars. About 1368 a chapel of Corpus Christi is founded, to be located on the south side of the church. Due to the increasing number of masses to be read by the hired priests, sermons are on the decline. In order to correct this situation, the town council creates the office of a municipal preacher (*Prädikant*), filled and paid for by the town council itself.

When in 1260 Duke Albert I (?1212–1261) divides his rule between his two sons, the duchy of Saxony-Wittenberg is formed. As a result Wittenberg becomes an electoral capital and in 1355 Duke Rudolf I (?1298–1356) becomes its elector. From that time on until 1806 the Saxon electorate stays connected with Wittenberg. After the death of Elector Albert III (?1419–1422) in 1422, this branch of the Ascanians dies out and Emperor Sigismund (b. 1368, ruled 1410–37) rewards the Wettin Frederick the Valiant (b. 1370, ruled 1381–1428), Margrave of Meissen, with the Saxon electorship. Therefore the entire territory of Wettin rule, covering Thuringia and Saxony of today, is given the designation "Saxony" and Wittenberg remains closely related to the fate of the Wettins until 1815.

Wittenberg owes three of its ecclesiastical institutions to the Ascanians. Duchess Helen (d. 1273) brings the first monks into town. In 1261 she establishes a Franciscan monastery, at which the Ascanians of Wittenberg are buried from 1273 to 1435. Duke Rudolf I builds a chapel on the grounds of the fortress and at the same time establishes the All Saints' chapter. Six chaplains under the leadership of a provost provide the masses, in particular memorial masses for the deceased members of the ruling dynasty. In 1346 the All Saints' chapter is placed directly under papal jurisdiction, thereby removing it from the jurisdiction of the Bishop of Brandenburg and putting it basically upon the dependence of the duke. In 1400 the town church is incorporated into the chapter of All Saints. Thus the core of a territorial church government (*landesherrliche Kirchenregiment*) is formed, as is common practice during the late Middle Ages. Rudolf I is also determined to make Wittenberg a centre of devotion. From France he brings an alleged thorn from Christ's crown, which is kept as a valuable relic in the castle chapel. As early as 1342 indulgences can be acquired from here. In 1398 the All Saints' chapter even acquires the portiuncula indulgence, which allows the granting of complete remission to confessing believers in the castle chapel on the eve and day of the festival of All Saints (November 1).

In 1485 the rule of the Wettins is divided between the two brothers Ernst (b. 1441, ruled 1464–86) and Albert of Leipzig (b. 1443, ruled 1464–1500). The older brother, Ernst, receives the electoral title and Wittenberg, including its surrounding district, whereas Albert receives the castles of Meissen, and Leipzig including its university. When Frederick III, also called the Wise, succeeds his father in his office in 1486, he decides to make Wittenberg his electoral capital. It had been rather neglected since 1423. First of all he has the Ascanian castle torn down and a magnificent Renaissance castle constructed. The construction of the castle church begins with its north wing in 1496/97. On January 17, 1503 it is consecrated by the cardinal-legate Raimund Peraudi (1435–1505). Thereby independence from the Bishop of

Brandenburg is once more emphasized. The vault continues to be worked on until 1505. Up to 1509 the castle church is generously furbished. In addition to the main altar by Lucas Cranach the Elder (1472–1553), nineteen side altars are built, many of which feature very valuable paintings. Four of them are by Albrecht Dürer (1471–1528). Liturgical books, vestments, and vessels are also lavishly decorated: The "Wittenberger Heiltumsbuch" of 1509 describes, and illustrates with woodcuts, more than 116 vessels containing 5,005 relics. This collection of relics is dear to Frederick the Wise, who keeps collecting until 1520 – a total of 19,013 holy objects. However, he also wishes to fill this precious church with church life. Therefore, in 1506 he establishes a cult of St. Mary and a cult of St. Anna. In 1519 the last such foundation is announced. At that time 1,138 masses are sung and 7,856 masses are read, year in, year out. In addition the hourly prayers are also celebrated every day. In one year alone 40,932 candles are put up and 6,600 weights of wax are burnt. In 1520 the records of the All Saints' chapter show that from the provost, the canons, vicars, and chaplains down to the choirboys eighty-one people receive an income from this foundation. Frederick the Wise is successful in establishing an outstanding center of late medieval devotion in Wittenberg at the beginning of the sixteenth century.

Elector Frederick also has a great interest in education and in having his own university. Since Leipzig is not part of his territory he decides to establish a new university, for which he chooses Wittenberg. For the preparation of its foundation he engages two men who are open-minded toward the humanist movement: the Leipzig Medical Professor Martin Pollich from Mellerstadt (d. 1513) and Johann von Staupitz (c. 1465–1524). On October 18, 1502 the Leucorea opens its doors. The university hires humanists who also start to teach, but never stay for too long. The humanist Nikolaus Marschalk (c. 1470–1525), for example, is among them. He had reprinted writings of mostly Italian humanists at his own print shop in Erfurt. Among his prints is an introduction to the study of the Hebrew language based on the teaching principle: If you wish to understand Holy Scripture, you have to know Hebrew. Nikolaus Marschalk brings his print shop along with him to Wittenberg. It will stay there when he leaves. The humanists' teachings appeal to quite a few, but are not indispensable to a professional career in the late Middle Ages.

By 1502 Augustinian Hermits have also come to Wittenberg, founding a monastery in the grounds of the hospital of the Holy Spirit whose chapel they use as their church. The establishment of a course in monastic studies leads to a close connection between the monastic order and the Leucorea. In 1504 the construction of the monastic complex starts off with the south wing next to the town gate in the east. In 1507/08 it is already transformed into an assembly house with lecture halls. In order to secure the financing of the Leucorea, the elector reminds all those of their duties who have benefited from his foundations: From 1507 not seven but twelve members of the All Saints' chapter have to follow teaching responsibilities at the university. The Franciscans are obligated to provide for a professor in theology, who lectures on the teachings of John Duns Scotus (*c.* 1265–1308), a member of their order. The Augustinian Hermits are responsible for providing for a professorship in moral philosophy and biblical exegesis (*in biblia*). Von Staupitz fills the latter position.

In 1505 the court painter Lucas Cranach, following his appointment by Frederick the Wise, moves to Wittenberg. The establishment of his extensive and productive workshop ensures that Wittenberg also becomes a center of the fine arts.

In 1512 Frederick the Wise founds a castle and university library. Georg Spalatin (1484–1545), a follower of Marschalk, is entrusted with its care. Spalatin acquires printed works mainly written by humanist authors and editions of church fathers, clearly pursuing the interests of a biblical humanist.

## WITTENBERG DURING LUTHER'S WORK

In October 1508 the monk Magister Martin Luther comes to Wittenberg for the first time in order to fill in the position of moral philosophy at the Leucorea, which had been assigned to the Augustinian Hermits. He enters a town with about two thousand inhabitants. Even though this town calls two impressive structures – the town church and the newly built castle – its own, it must have appeared to be rather unassuming to someone coming from Erfurt, a town that will number 16,117 inhabitants in 1511. Later in life Luther will sometimes disparage Wittenberg as a place located on the periphery of city culture. At the same time, he also tries to emphasize the miraculous side of it, that God brought the gospel to light again in such an insignificant place. To form an objective opinion on the size of Wittenberg, we should consider that more than 90 percent of all German towns have less than 2,000 inhabitants at that time and that Wittenberg is an up-and-coming town. In 1509 Luther is called back to Erfurt where he has to teach lectures on Peter Lombard's (1095/1100–1160) *Sentences*.

When Luther is finally transferred back to Wittenberg in 1511, his education is drawing close to its completion. He is familiar with scholastic philosophy in the Ockhamistic tradition and scholastic theology in the tradition of the late scholastic Gabriel Biel (1410–1495). Among the many books he brings along to Wittenberg, there is also one that has initiated a new school of thought: the handbook "De rudimentis hebraicis" by Johannes Reuchlin (1455–1522). It shows Luther's connection to the biblical humanist movement, which was also active in Erfurt. This movement focuses on language studies in philology and rhetoric. It demands a turning away from scholasticism and instead a turning toward the Bible and the church fathers as its authentic interpreters as well as toward philological exegesis that goes back to the original languages of the Bible.

Johann von Staupitz has been vicar general of the German observant Augustinian Hermits since 1503 and also dean of the Theology faculty of the Wittenberg university. As a consequence he is unable to fill in his Bible professorship properly. Therefore he persuades a most reluctant Luther, under a pear tree in the monastic court of Wittenberg, to become his successor. On October 19, 1512 Luther is awarded the doctorate in theology (*Doctor theologiae*) in the castle church, which also serves as university church, and is received into the academic staff of the theology faculty. By the winter semester 1513/14 Luther begins with his interpretation of biblical books, a practice he continues until November 17, 1545. For a study, Luther is given a room with a fireplace in a tower at the southwest corner of the monastery. Between 1515 and 1523 he interprets the Book of Psalms. As expected, he begins with late medieval exegesis. But he also consults books by biblical humanists and applies their philological principles. Sometimes he refers back to Hebrew words in the Psalms and offers – often with a polemic undertone – the difference between the scholastic and biblical meanings of the words. He finally comes to the conclusion that Holy Scripture can only be understood if scholastic terminology is cast off.

The interpretation of the Psalms is not only an academic assignment for Luther. At the same time he also searches for answers to his own personal experiences with faith. Luther's status as a monk, as well as his theology, motivates him to use strict asceticism, repentance, and prayers to fulfill the righteousness demanded by God to such an extent that he can be certain of God's merciful judgment. However, he suffers from the fact that he cannot feel such certainty.

So Luther researches the original meaning of "God's righteousness" as he has done with many other biblical terms before. In light of Romans 1:16–17, Luther is overwhelmed by the knowledge that God does not demand such justice from him, but that God himself justifies believers through faith alone. Luther experiences this insight as a liberation from his anxieties, which in turn opens up a whole new world of the gospel, Holy Scripture, even all theology and devotion. Named after the place of the event, this discovery of the gospel message is referred to as the "tower experience." While Luther left no clear notes about when this happened, there is every reason to believe that this event occurred during his first lecture series on Psalms.

Luther meets with little resistance at this young university, which is open toward humanist thinking and which does not have more experienced theologians, who might have already made their mark. His fellow friar Johannes Lang (c. 1487–1548), who had been transferred with him to Wittenberg, reads moral philosophy. Since he is also an expert in Greek, he sets off the church fathers against the scholastics in his publications. On September 25, 1516 Bartholomeus Bernhardi (d. 1551) defends his theses, whose fundamental arguments he gained from Luther's lecture series on the Book of Romans during 1515/16. Like Luther, he contradicts Biel's assumption that humans could fulfill God's commandments out of their own natural powers, drawing most of his arguments from the anti-Pelagian writings of Augustine (354–430). The professor of theology, Nikolaus von Amsdorf (1483–1565), who supports the teachings of John Duns Scotus, is won over to Luther's side as a result of this disputation. Andreas Bodenstein von Karlstadt (1486–1541), known as a supporter of the theology of Thomas Aquinas (1224–1274) and Scotus, opposes those theses. He, however, agrees to study Augustine and on April 26, 1517 presents his own version of 152 theses, which lead him to side with Luther. Under Luther's influence a new awareness is developing in the theology faculty at the Leucorea, which favors a biblical theology in accordance with the church fathers over scholasticism. This is in line with the biblical humanist school of thought. The monastic course of study offered through the Augustinian hermits in Wittenberg ensures that those monks returning to their home monasteries begin to spread word of this new theology at an early date.

By 1514, Luther becomes municipal preacher (*Prädikant*) of the town of Wittenberg. It is his obligation to preach at the town church on Sundays and holidays. Later he will also fill in on weekdays in the absence of the pastor, thereby interpreting entire biblical books consecutively. As a result of his preaching activity, the parishioners of Wittenberg and also those students who do not hear his lectures are updated on the latest insights in Reformation thinking.

Luther's theology reaches a dimension of church policy as he invites the academic world for a disputation on the power of indulgences with his Ninety-five Theses. When faith in God's promises as revealed in the gospel justifies, hope in purchased letters of indulgence must necessarily lead people astray and consequently cause the loss of salvation. Luther the pastoral care professional and theologian cannot keep silent about this. Johann Tetzel's (c. 1465–1519) most blatant way of selling plenary indulgence prompts Luther to take a closer look at the subject. The Saxon princes do not allow Tetzel to enter their territories, to prevent money from flowing to Rome. But because some people from Wittenberg buy letters of indulgence in Jüterbog (thirty-five kilometers away), belonging to the archdiocese of Magdeburg, this topic remains relevant in Wittenberg.

On October 31, 1517 Luther sends his Ninety-five Theses to Albert of Brandenburg, Archbishop of Magdeburg and Mainz (b. 1490, elected 1513, served 1514–45), who is responsible for this particular sale of indulgences. At the Reformation anniversary of 1967 the question was raised as to whether these theses had ever been made public in Wittenberg. Since it was common practice at the university of Wittenberg to post disputation theses on the door of the north side of the castle church, we have reason to assume that Luther's theses were also posted there – coincidentally on the same day on which the collection of relics was opened to benefit the acquisition of the portiuncula indulgence. With theses 42 and 44, propounding that it is more important to do works of mercy than buy letters of indulgence, Luther hits the nerve of an avaricious papacy, which launches a trial against him. Because of this, Wittenberg attracts the public's attention.

At the fringe of the Diet of Augsburg in October 1518, Cardinal Cajetan (1469–1534) tries in vain to persuade Luther to recant. In response to Cajetan's demand, Luther appeals to the pope for a general, all-Christian council in the presence of competent witnesses at the chapel of Corpus Christi on November 28, 1518. Thus he tries to take his trial out of the pope's hands and have it handed over to a church council. This Wittenberg appeal for a church council keeps being made during the whole Reformation period. Finally, between 1545 and 1563 the Council of Trent is summoned. However, it is not a general and all-Christian council at all but an exclusively Roman Catholic one.

In September 1516 Georg Spalatin becomes secretary to Frederick the Wise, who in September 1517 also entrusts him with the responsibilities for church and university affairs. Through Spalatin's new position Luther gains an ideal connection to the elector. And when the elector appoints Spalatin in fall 1517 to implement a university reform, Spalatin and Luther collaborate to carry it out. Though scholastic subjects are not removed immediately, as was Luther's desire, a whole series of new teaching positions concerning humanist subjects is established. The professorships include Hebrew, Greek, and Latin as well as rhetoric based on the "Institutio oratoria" by Marcus Fabianus Quintillianus (c. 30–c. 96).

The new chair for Greek is taken by Philip Melanchthon (1497–1560), who outlines a reform program in his inaugural speech on August 28, 1518, which finds Luther's full support. He becomes not only a follower of Luther, but his co-reformer and friend. As far as professors of Hebrew are concerned, the University of Wittenberg has bad luck until Mathias Auro-gallus (1490–1543) can be won. He is an outstanding specialist in Hebrew, possesses exceptional teaching skills, puts his knowledge into the service of the interpretation of Holy Scripture, and makes useful contributions to Luther's translation of the Bible. All these new professors dedicate their careers to the distribution of the Reformation message. The university reform of 1518 is only the beginning of many more reforms, which are later carried out by Melanchthon in co-operation with Luther. Through the university reform of 1518, however, a whole new movement is initiated, which serves other educational institutions as an example. The University of Wittenberg owes its success mainly to Luther's theology based on biblical humanist methods. While prior to his time humanist studies were irrele-vant for examinations, they now become a necessary prerequisite for the study of theology. In Wittenberg the professors from the two faculties of theology as well as that of the arts collaborate in such a way that a very fruitful educational reform can be instituted.

Students flock to Wittenberg, and Wittenberg is soon the most attended university in all Germany. Since there is not enough accommodation avail-able, a building boom sets in. Between 1519 and 1535 a new town hall is built at the market square. There is an ever-increasing demand for food; tai-lors and shoemakers have plenty of work. Since 1519 the frenzied demand for Luther's writings attracts more and more printers to Wittenberg so that at one point some thirty print shops are in operation at the same time, mak-ing Wittenberg the most important place of printing in Germany. Lucas Cranach sees to it that many printings are decorated with elaborate title-borders or illustrated with remarkable woodcuts. Precious book covers are created. Through Luther's work Wittenberg enjoys an export trade. Those printings – especially the printings of the Luther Bible – spread Luther's usage of the German language, thereby exerting a great influence on the development of a German literary language.

During the late Middle Ages begging becomes a plague. Town govern-ments try to contain the number of people allowed to beg through by-laws. However, they cannot prohibit begging entirely because almsgiving belongs to the good works by whose means a Christian believer is supposedly able to shorten his stay in purgatory. This motivation is cancelled through the Reformation message, which teaches that Christians are justified out of grace alone. The care of the poor needs to be put on different grounds. The "common chest" is established, in which all income from parish and church fiefs as well as foundations and collections flows together and from which the church, the school and a doctor for the poor are financed and people in need supported.

On June 15, 1520 Pope Leo X (b. 1475, reigned 1513–21) issues the bull "Exurge Domine" threatening excommunication against Luther. When the nuncio Johann Eck (1486–1543) demands the University of Wittenberg enforce this bull, the responsible authorities stand so steadfastly by Luther that they refuse to do so. As a consequence Eck adds Karlstadt, Melanchthon, and the electoral marshal Hans von Dolzig (d. 1551) to the list of those to whom the bull shall also be applied. Luther does not think of recanting. The morning of December 10, 1520 he prefers to burn a copy of the canon law and the bull threatening his excommunication to great applause by the members of the university in front of the Elstergate next to the Holy Cross hospital – the hospital reserved for infectious diseases. In the afternoon students get pleasure from deriding the bull and burning scholastic books. Thus Luther has publicly broken with the papacy.

After Luther refuses to renounce his writings at the Diet of Worms in April 1521, he is kept in hiding at the Wartburg castle from May 5. On May 26 the imperial ban follows, which calls upon all estates of the empire to take Luther captive after his safe-conduct expires and to do the same with all his followers. Any form of dissemination of Luther's writings is listed in great detail and put under punishment. Thus Frederick the Wise is obliged to silence the teaching of the Reformation in Wittenberg and to stop the printing of Luther's writings. But nothing of this nature happens. Luther's friends at Wittenberg show no inclination toward silence themselves.

On the occasion of disputations on June 20 and July 19, 1521 Karlstadt attacks the marital ban for priests and monks, the refusal to give the cup to the laity, and the reading of private masses, which were usually read as memorial masses for the alleged benefit of the deceased without any participation of a congregation. On August 1 Luther sends Melanchthon an encouraging letter, in which he gives his friends his general approval to put his teachings into practice.

At a Lord's Supper on September 29, 1521 Melanchthon, along with some of his students, not only receives the bread, but – in contrast to the current canon law – is also given the cup. Luther's fellow friar Gabriel Zwilling (1487–1558) abandons the mass at the monastic chapel, celebrating the Lord's Supper in both kinds. On November 12 thirteen Augustinian hermits leave the monastery for good. At the beginning of December Luther turns up in the disguise of Knight George to see for himself how things are going and to promote the printing of his writings. He then writes to Spalatin: "I am very pleased with everything I see and hear." Karlstadt celebrates a different style of worship service in the castle church as well as in the town church at Christmas 1521. He makes no use of liturgical robes, leaves some parts of the mass out – especially those that interpret the Lord's Supper as sacrifice – reads the words of institution, so far only silently uttered, out loud in German, and offers the cup also to the lay people.

On January 6, 1522 the assembled chapter of the German observant Augustinian Hermits makes a decision based on Luther's recommendation that it is up to each member of the order whether they wish to leave the monastery or stay. This decision in Wittenberg sets a signal for other monks and nuns in many other orders. On January 10 Zwilling cleans out the Chapel of the Holy Spirit by burning the altars, crucifixes, saints' pictures and statues in the monastic court.

Beside these spontaneous actions, which also included some tumultuous events when, for example, armed townspeople and students stopped a priest reading a private mass in the town church, on December 3, Karlstadt pursues the goal of giving the church a new order. He is successful in having members of the university ask Frederick the Wise on October 20, 1521 to prohibit the abuse of the mass. The elector refuses. On January 24, 1522 the town council of Wittenberg decides with no consideration for Frederick the Wise on a new parish order, which among other things stipulates a Protestant worship service and the removal of paintings and side altars so that only three altars without paintings remain. Since the council hesitates to have the paintings removed, iconoclasts storm the town church, destroying part of the furnishings. The new movement seems to get out of hand in Wittenberg.

Luther returns from the Wartburg castle and begins to preach for a whole week on March 9, the Sunday of Invocavit, 1522. In these "Eight Sermons at Wittenberg" he approves of the changes having taken place, but at the same time he criticizes their being performed with no consideration for the weak in faith but through the power of by-laws. Luther has great confidence in the impact of the preached Word, through which the Holy Spirit changes its listeners so that they will voluntarily and gladly do God's will and lead an evangelical lifestyle. As a consequence the receiving of the cup is possible then but not mandatory. Pictures of saints are not to be destroyed, but rather the unfounded confidence in them – this through the sermon. Luther hereby initiates a movement that leads eventually to the abandonment of the veneration of saints without destroying medieval works of art. The elaborate furnishings of the castle church remain untouched. Luther likes to use the altar as the table for the Lord's Supper. However, as soon as he realizes that there is still a strong desire to decorate the altar with a retable, he suggests a depiction of the Lord's Supper. When Lucas Cranach the Elder and his son – probably in 1539 – begin to decorate the main altar of the town church with depictions of the Lord's Supper, baptism, confession, and preaching, they do so in accordance with Luther's wishes.

The same holds true for depictions of stories from the Bible illustrating the epitaphs put up in the town church during the sixteenth century.

Luther not only attracts students. Justus Jonas (1493–1555) is awarded his juridical licentiate in Erfurt in 1518 and studies Greek with Johannes Lang, developing in the biblical humanist tradition. In 1512 he ostentatiously accompanies Luther on his way to the Diet in Worms. Thereafter he becomes provost of the All Saints' chapter in Wittenberg and is received into the theology faculty as a member in October 1521. He enjoys a close relationship with Luther and promotes the distribution of Luther's Latin writings through translating them effectively according to sense rather than literal meaning. In 1541 Jonas goes to Halle near the Saale river to introduce the Reformation there.

Johannes Bugenhagen (1485–1558) forms connections with biblical humanists. In 1517 he is awarded the newly established lectorate in biblical exegesis at the Premonstratensian Abbey at Belbuck, near Treptow in Pomerania. Luther's writings prompt him to go to study at Wittenberg in spring 1521, where he quickly makes friends with Melanchthon. During the summer semester Luther has continued his second series of lectures on the Psalms. When Luther does not return from Worms, Bugenhagen interprets the Psalms, first privately and then publicly. In 1523 the position of the town pastor becomes available. The majority of the canons of the responsible All Saints' chapter is not Reformation-minded and hesitates to fill the position.

Luther grants the congregation the right to choose their own pastor. Together with the town council, Luther is successful in having Bugenhagen appointed. In co-operation with Luther, Bugenhagen implements a new educational system in Wittenberg in fall 1523. He continues to give lectures in exegesis, finally being received as a member into the theology faculty in 1533. He becomes Luther's father confessor and turns out to be an invaluable advocate of the Reformation in the territories and towns of Northern Germany as well as in Denmark and Norway.

Luther, Jonas, Bugenhagen, and Melanchthon are the reformers of the core group in Wittenberg, who develop Protestant theology through their fruitful collaborations and shape the Protestant church order through their participation in church and school visitations.

Although in 1522 Luther demands emphatically that consideration should be shown for the weak, it is not his intention to tolerate something he is convinced is not in accord with the gospel. In 1522 he preaches against the celebration of All Saints' Day, which accordingly is not observed in 1524. In the process of teaching the essence of an evangelical worship service, he also introduces new changes. From January 1523 onward, all lay people are offered the cup. The reading of the daily mass ceases and new church services, in which the interpretation of biblical books is the main focus, take their place, starting on March 23, 1523. At the end of 1523 Luther displays his continuing reworking of the still Latin liturgy in his writing, the "Formula missae et communionis pro ecclesia Wittenbergensi." In 1525 he writes on a German mass. In a team effort, Luther and Johann Walter (1496–1570), the later cantor of Torgau, match the German words very carefully with the accompanying melodies of the liturgy. After its first test run in the parish of Wittenberg, "The German Mass and Order of Service," in which Luther outlines general considerations concerning the style of worship services, is published at the beginning of 1526. Within the next three years, a liturgy evolves in Wittenberg whose influence can still be seen in Protestant church services today. Even some of those who introduced a liturgy reform at the Vatican Council II took note of it.

While the parishioners of Wittenberg follow Luther readily, sometimes even urging him into action, the members of the All Saints' chapter fail to get involved. Due to Luther's insistence, the collection of relics is downsized and displayed for the last time in 1523. At the beginning of Advent 1524 Luther mobilizes princes, the mayor, the council, and the judges against the reading of private masses in the castle church. Finally the university and the town council urge the canons to abandon those masses, which they do at Christmas 1524. After the death of Frederick the Wise on May 5, 1525 his brother John the Constant (b. 1468, ruled 1525–32) dissolves the All Saints' chapter in October 1525. The collection of relics, gems, and liturgical vestments is secretly taken to Torgau. While the court tailor makes use of the precious fabrics, the goldsmith takes the vessels apart to extract the gold, silver, gems, and pearls. By 1530 the valuable collection of relics is dissolved. Luther is given a drinking glass from it, which was said to be part of the treasures of the landgravess Elisabeth of Thuringia (1207–1231) and which opened the collection of relics in 1509.

Wittenberg becomes a refuge for persecuted Protestant preachers and all those who leave their monasteries. On April 10, 1523 nine nuns arrive who escaped from the Cistercian cloister of Nimbschen near Grimma, among them Katharina von Bora (1499–1552). Families in Wittenberg take in the nuns. Since the Augustinian hermits left their Wittenberg monastery, Luther and the prior Eberhard Brisger (d. 1535) are the only ones left in fall 1523. Escaped preachers and monks find refuge here until they can take over a new task.

Luther marries Katharina von Bora on June 13, 1525 and this fills the monastery with new life. The birthdays of their children are: Johannes on June 7, 1526 (d. 1575); Elizabeth on December 10, 1527 (d. 1528); Magdalena on May 4, 1529 (d. 1542); Martin on November 9, 1531 (d. 1563);

Paul on January 28, 1533 (d. 1593); and Margarethe on December 17, 1534 (d. 1570). In 1529 six children of Luther's deceased sister join the family circle and some more from another sister. Students, who are supervised by masters of arts, find accommodation here. Refugees are always taken in. Furthermore, there are also guests who seek Luther's advice. Katharina is a competent hostess, capable of managing such a huge household. Luther acquires properties suitable for agricultural use so that they can become self-sufficient for the main part. From 1525 Luther receives a professor's salary from the Leucorea. In addition he is also given donations in the form of clothing, food, cups, and money. The donors honor Luther's hospitality in serving the cause of the Reformation. On February 4, 1532 Elector John transfers the title of the former monastery of the Augustinian Hermits to Luther. Thereafter, mainly between 1535 and 1540, he arranges for building activities. The late Gothic Katharine portal is installed and the so-called Luther study is built.

Not far from the university, Melanchthon acquires a piece of property with a modest "cabin" in 1520. With the support of Elector John Frederick (b. 1503, ruled 1532–47, d. 1554) and the city of Wittenberg, the co-reformer can tear down this cabin, expand the property and build a beautiful Renaissance house in 1536. Bugenhagen lives in a spacious parish house, which is named after him.

After the city of Wittenberg prohibits begging on January 24, 1522, the Franciscans leave their monastery. In 1524 Melchior Lotter the Younger (d. *c.* 1528) establishes his printing office there. In 1527 the former monastery is turned into a poorhouse. In 1537 the monastic church is rebuilt to serve for grain storage.

When Luther is interred in the castle church on February 22, 1546, all the medieval institutions have changed their function as a result of his theology. The town church with its private masses has been turned into a church where the Lord's Supper is offered in both kinds and a Protestant sermon is delivered. The Franciscan monastery has become a poorhouse and grain storage, the monastery of the Augustinian Hermits has become Luther's home. The scholastic Leucorea is transformed into a centre of Protestant theology and humanist education. The castle church is no longer a famous place of pilgrimage, the numerous private masses and hourly prayers are silenced. It is a Protestant university church now, which enjoys a high reputation because Luther's Ninety-five Theses were posted on its door and because the Reformation prince Frederick the Wise found his last resting place here in 1525, as did John the Constant in 1532. Luther's own burial here in 1546 will be followed by that of Melanchthon in 1560.

## WITTENBERG AFTER LUTHER'S DEATH

On May 19, 1547 Wittenberg has to surrender to Emperor Charles V (b. 1500, ruled 1519–56, d. 1558), who defeated the army of the Smalkald League. Wittenberg, including its electoral district and title, is given to Duke Moritz of Saxony (b. 1521, ruled 1541–53). Since 1539 the Duke had owned a Protestant university in Leipzig, which is why he could close the Leucorea. However, since the Protestants regard him as a traitor because of his support for the emperor, he must try to win their recognition. Therefore he assures Melanchthon that he will leave the University of Wittenberg untouched so that he can return. Melanchthon's reputation is held in such great esteem that professors and students flock to Wittenberg, quickly turning the Leucorea into the most attended German university again. Though the University of Wittenberg becomes entangled in the crypto-Calvinist controversies in 1574 and receives professors with inclinations towards the Reformed community through Elector Christian I (b. 1560, ruled 1586–91), it remains mainly a stronghold of Luther's theology. Between 1650 and 1686 Abraham Calov (1612–1686), an outstanding proponent of Lutheran ultra-orthodoxy, also known as the "Lutheran Pope," teaches here. Yet Wittenberg is not only Luther's town because of its university but increasingly also because of a Lutheran memorial culture finding its center here.

In 1565 Elector August of Saxony (b. 1526, ruled 1553–86) acquires the former Augustinian monastery from the Luther family and rebuilds it so that the university gains new lecture halls and the students find accommodation there. Between 1580 and 1582 he adds a wing on the west side of the property followed by another one on the north side. He intends to accommodate 150 scholarship holders. It is through those buildings that a "monastic court," as we know it today, is created.

In 1617 the University of Wittenberg proposes to celebrate the centennial anniversary of the Reformation. Elector John George I (b. 1585, ruled 1611–56) has the anniversary observed throughout his entire electoral territory and also invites other Protestant princes to do the same. In Wittenberg many guests join in the festivities between October 31 and November 2, 1617. In 1630 the centennial anniversary of the "Augsburg Confession" is celebrated, in 1646 Luther's day of death, and in 1655 the "Peace of Augsburg."

During the Seven Years' War the firing of the imperial troops forces the Prussian occupying army to surrender on October 13, 1760. During the course of the battle the northern half of the town is burnt to the ground. The former Franciscan monastery is destroyed, the castle is devastated, and the castle church including its theses door also burns down. Wittenberg becomes unsightly. In view of Enlightenment and pietism, the Leucorea is unable to present the Lutheran tradition in a convincing manner. None of the many Bible associations, which begin to flourish after 1710, makes its home in Wittenberg, so that the printing offices lose their importance. On January 13, 1814 the troops of emperor Napoleon's (b. 1769, ruled 1804–15, d. 1821) army take Wittenberg by storm, destroying the city and its castle church once more. After Wittenberg becomes Prussian in 1815, its university merges with the one in Halle, which in 1933 is given the name "Martin Luther University Halle-Wittenberg" in honour of Luther's 450th anniversary. In 1817 a new Protestant theological seminary is founded in Wittenberg. It owns the theological and philological part of the Wittenberg university library up to the present day.

Wittenberg gains new importance as the memorial of the Reformation during the nineteenth century, especially after it can be reached via railway in 1841. In 1821 a statue of Luther is erected in the marketplace, designed by Johann Gottfried Schadow (1764–1850) according to Cranach's altar painting in Weimar. Melanchthon's statue follows in 1865 and Bugenhagen's statue is put up on the north side of the town church in 1885. Since 1858 the depiction of Luther's Ninety-five Theses on a bronze door of the castle church has commemorated their posting there. In 1844 the dilapidated Luther house is renovated, a Gothic ornamental gable and terraced gablets on the roof providing this Luther monument with a very beautiful and appropriate decor. In 1883 the Luther hall opens its doors. Since then it has continued to expand its exhibition area with the aim of covering the entire Luther house by 2002. In 1897 Melanchthon's study and death room are turned into a memorial. Gradually the exhibition dedicated to Melanchthon expands into more and more rooms. After the Melanchthon house is completely renovated, the museum spreads throughout the entire house and the garden is newly arranged. It is reopened in 1997. In 1830 an oak tree is planted at the spot where Luther burnt the bull threatening him with excommunication on December 10, 1520. In 1925/26 it is surrounded by an additional green space and a fountain is also added.

Between 1885 and 1892 the castle church, which was burned out in 1760 and damaged again in 1814, is converted into an honorary monument of the German Reformation. Its architecture is updated in a neo-Gothic style. Nine statues, twenty-two medallions, coat of arms on the gallery and 198 coats of arms in the windows are exhibited to commemorate reformers and political supporters of the Reformation from the princes and electoral advisors down to the town governments. Luther's and Melanchthon's graves are highlighted through new decorations. In 1983 this national concept is further emphasized through twelve additional glass portraits of European reformers in three windows below the galleries.

In the nineteenth century anniversaries with a nationwide participation are on the increase, initiated by the commemoration of Bugenhagen in 1858, Melanchthon in 1860 and Cranach in 1872. After World War I more anniversaries are added, commemorating events of the Reformation such as the burning of the bull threatening excommunication in 1920, the Diet of Worms in 1921, Luther's return from the Wartburg castle in 1922, Luther's marriage in 1925 and the publication of Luther's German Mass in 1926. Since not only centennial anniversaries are celebrated, Wittenberg enjoyed a wealth of commemorative events during the twentieth century, events which have been promoted by the tourist industry over these last years.

Because Wittenberg is conceived as a central place of German Protestantism, Protestant societies prefer to hold founding events and meetings here. In 1848 the first German Protestant church congress (*Evangelischer Kirchentag*) assembled at the castle church. The Luther Society was founded in Wittenberg in 1918. In 1922 the founding certificate of the German Federation of Protestant Churches (*Deutsche Evangelische Kirchenbund*) was signed at Luther's table next to his grave. In 1933 the first German national synod gathered for its opening in the castle church, voting later in the town church for the old Prussian bishop Ludwig Müller (1883–1945) to become the Reichsbischof. In 1971 the Federation of the Reformed Churches (*Evangelische Kirche der Union*) brought international Luther researchers together to a Theologischer Arbeitskreis für Reformationsgeschichtliche Forschung (Theological Research Group on Reformation History) in Wittenberg. This group still meets regularly. As a result, international attention is drawn to the Luther hall so that it escapes being transformed into a purely Marxist museum of the early bourgeois revolution. The planned isolation of Luther researchers from East Germany and other Eastern bloc countries has been eased. In 1995 the Leucorea Foundation was established. Since 1996 it has run a congress center and various research institutions, such as the Centre for Reformation History and Lutheran Orthodoxy, located in the newly renovated buildings in the former university grounds.

The growing interest in Luther and the place of his work gained such great importance for the development of Wittenberg that the magistrate of the city introduced the official designation "Lutherstadt Wittenberg" in 1922. This was immediately adopted by the Protestant church assembly in Berlin, but the responsible ministry of internal affairs approved it only in 1938. The addition to its name is well justified because with ever-growing worldwide attention this town near the Elbe river was and is Luther's town.

# Part II

*Luther's work*

# 3 Luther's writings

TIMOTHY F. LULL

## FACING INTIMIDATION

The great pleasure of reading Luther is complicated by several problems. The greatest of these is the sheer mass of material. The critical edition in German and Latin, the Weimar Ausgabe, includes sixty-eight volumes of his published writings, seventeen of his letters, twelve of documents relating to the translation of the Bible, and six volumes of *Table Talk*. The American Edition of *Luther's Works* in English contains fifty-five volumes. Even this fraction of the whole can overwhelm the strongest student.

The mention of German and Latin reminds English-speaking readers of the difficulty of reading Luther in his original languages. Any knowledge of these languages will help, but Luther's German is difficult (think of English a century before Shakespeare!) and his Latin also is quite complex. While the most important documents are available in translation, a few significant ones are not. Some translations are not especially accurate, or not based on more recent critical texts.

Some Luther writings are hard to read. One current anthology begins with Luther's 1517 theses: *Disputation Against Scholastic Theology*.[1] The argumentation in a later and very central work, *The Bondage of the Will*, is quite complex and difficult to follow. Many other writings are much clearer, and some are simple and delightful. Luther had a great capacity to communicate with ordinary readers. But Heiko Oberman maintained that a false confidence can emerge when one is carried along by lucid passages and reaches a premature understanding by ignoring more obscure parts – which may in fact contain the very key to what Luther is arguing.[2]

There is also no agreed "canon" of Luther's writings nor a single central work like Philip Melanchthon's *Loci Communes* or John Calvin's *Institutes of the Christian Religion*. Luther's most important insights are scattered among several dozen writings. He was more a contextual theologian than a systematician – usually responding to specific opponents and immediate pastoral challenges. He did engage in an orderly exposition of major sections of the Bible, but there are many books on which we have no Luther commentary.

From time to time Luther spoke dismissively of his own writings. He was aware that he had written very many books, and sometimes at too great length.

> I'd rather that all my books would disappear and the Holy Scriptures alone would be read. Otherwise we'll rely on such writings and let the Bible go. Brenz wrote such a big commentary on twelve chapters of Luke that it disgusts the reader to look into it. The same is true of my commentary on Galatians. I wonder who encourages this mania for writing! Who wants to buy such stout tomes? And if they're bought, who'll read them? And if they're read, who'll be edified by them?[3]

Bernhard Lohse has pointed out "the absence of any pride of authorship" in Luther, partly from his wanting to point beyond his works to the Bible, and partly from his own ironic understanding of his unlikely mission as a reformer.[4] Luther's recommendations from his own writings can surprise modern readers, as in his placing his *Lectures on Deuteronomy* at the top of the list, next to his *Galatians*.[5]

### RESOURCES

This summary of Luther's writings will concentrate on works available in translation. Most of these will be found in the already mentioned American Edition of *Luther's Works* (hereafter LW). This is a fifty-five-volume translation of Luther produced jointly by Concordia Publishing House and Fortress Press under the editorship of Jaroslav Pelikan and Helmut T. Lehmann.[6] The first thirty volumes contain Luther's biblical writings – lectures, commentaries, and expository sermons. The next twenty-four contain the Reformation documents. This organization can be helpful for finding topics of interest, but materials from the same year are often in widely scattered volumes. Volume 55 is the index to the whole work. A companion volume by Pelikan, *Luther the Expositor*, introduces Luther's biblical interpretation.[7]

Four volumes of the Library of Christian Classics (hereafter LCC) published by Westminster Press contain extensive material from Luther, sometimes in editions that offer a good alternative to the American Edition. That series also includes Philip Melanchthon's *Loci Communes* in the original edition of 1521. Luther considered this one of the finest books of the Reformation and an excellent summary of their common teaching.[8]

Two anthologies have a large number of documents. John Dillenberger, ed., *Martin Luther: Selections from His Writings*[9] (hereafter Dillenberger) includes sixteen central writings of Luther. Timothy Lull, ed., *Martin Luther's Basic Theological Writings*[10] (hereafter Lull) contains thirty-seven of Luther's works.

The American Edition did not include three of Luther's most influential writings that were included in 1580 among the official confessions of the Lutheran Church: *Small Catechism* (1529), *Large Catechism* (1529) and *Smalcald Articles* (1537). Readers must seek these in one of the several editions of *The Book of Concord*,[11] (hereafter BoC). The *Small Catechism* and the *Smalcald Articles* are also included in the Lull anthology.

## CATEGORIES OF ORGANIZATION

In describing Luther's works, there are difficult decisions about what categories to use.[12] Luther operates in a way that challenges boundaries. One of his most famous writings, *The Freedom of a Christian* (1520) is partly a sermon, partly a treatise, and partly a work of polemic against the "bondage" of the church in his time – a sequel to the *Babylonian Captivity* of earlier that same year. Attached to it is a final appeal for understanding from Luther to Pope Leo X. A later work, *Against Hanswurst* (1541), is partly a polemic against a fierce Catholic prince, partly an autobiographical account of some of the key incidents in the Reformation, and partly a key to Luther's ecclesiology.

### 1. Luther's life – letters, autobiographical writings, table talk

Luther's theology cannot be understood without knowledge of the period and the course of his own life. Because Luther changed his mind on many topics, it is important to understand what the circumstances were when Luther made a particular statement. Many biographies and introductions provide such background,[13] but an exciting way to understand Luther is to study his life in his own words – particularly through his letters.

One of the glories of the American Edition is Gottfried Krodel's edition of three volumes of Luther's *Letters* (*LW* 48, 49, 50). They include 325 letters that Luther wrote from the time he was a young monk until days before his death. These provide an unparalleled resource for following Luther's story, and the critical notes, while now dated, are excellent. Especially notable are Luther's letters to his parents, wife, and children, and letters to his friends. Also important are letters to public figures, including Erasmus and the three Electors of Saxony in his lifetime. Particularly interesting are the 41 letters written from Luther's ten months in the Wartburg, and another 30 letters from 1530 when Luther waited for events at the Diet of Augsburg at Castle Coburg.

An earlier edition, extending only through 1530, is still very valuable because it also includes letters to and about Luther. This is *Luther's Correspondence and Other Contemporary Letters* (two volumes) edited by Preserved Smith and Charles M. Jacobs (Philadelphia: Lutheran Publication Society, 1918). Here one can read Melanchthon's deep disappointment in Luther's marriage as he writes to his friend Camerarius, or the very sharp exchange between Luther and his long-term enemy Duke George of Saxony at the end of 1525.

Theodore Tappert edited a volume in the Library of Christian Classics called *Luther: Letters of Spiritual Counsel* (Philadelphia: Westminster: 1955). This is not one of the volumes in this series currently in print from that publisher, but a reprint of this exceptional material is available from Regent College, Bellingham, Washington. This shows a side of Luther as counselor and spiritual director that is often missed in focusing on his public career.

Among Luther's own accounts of his life one of the most important is his *Preface to the Complete Edition of the Latin Writings* (1545 – LW 34, Dillenberger). Luther reviews the early events of the struggle – the controversy on indulgences, the hearing before Cardinal Cajetan in Augsburg, the debate with John Eck in Leipzig, the attempts at mediation of Karl von Miltitz, and especially his own theological struggle to understand the "righteousness of God." It is a compelling writing, but must be checked against other accounts.

Other autobiographical reflections can be found in *Letter to the Princes of Saxony* (1524 – LW 40), *Exhortation to All Clergy Assembled at Augsburg* (1530 – LW 34), and *Against Hanswurst* (1541 – LW 41). A delightful account of Luther's understanding of being a theologian is his *Preface to the Wittenberg Edition of Luther's German Writings* (1539 – LW 34, Lull). A chronological survey of Luther's career can be found in the forty-three sermons in *Sermons I* (LW 51).

Luther's *Table Talk* shows Luther at ease among his friends, making candid comments on events and people. Students should use the American Edition volume (LW 54) rather than several popular editions that have not been sorted critically. Since all of *Table Talk* represents notes taken by others, it is best used to confirm impressions given in the writings that come directly from Luther.[14]

## 2. The course of the Reformation

Many of Luther's most important writings were themselves events that shaped his career. An account of the first years is in the documents in volume 31 of the American Edition: *Career of the Reformer I*. This includes *Ninety-five Theses* or *Disputation on the Power and Efficacy of Indulgences* (LW 31, Dillenberger, Lull) and the much more elaborate *Explanations of the Ninety-five Theses* from the next year (LW 31). Luther's mind was changing on some key issues as the controversy grew. There is still no readily available translation of the *Sermon on Indulgences and Grace* (WA 1) – which was far more widely read than the *Ninety-five Theses*.

Within a year Luther was in danger as he faced the Pope's representative Cardinal Cajetan in a hearing at Augsburg. Luther's own account of *Proceedings at Augsburg* (1518 – LW 31), did much to persuade the public that he was being treated unfairly by the Roman party. Luther also wrote an account of his 1519 debate with John Eck in which he was forced to concede his doubts about papal authority – *The Leipzig Debate* (1519 – LW 31). This should be read with Luther's *Sermon Preached at the Castle at Leipzig for the Day of St. Peter and St. Paul* (LW 51) to see how he preached on such issues.

All Luther's great writings of 1520 were public events, but the most important in creating support for him was *To the Christian Nobility of the German Nation Concerning the Reform of the Christian Estate* (LW 44, Dillenberger). Here Luther presents a program for religious reform and social renewal for the whole nation, inviting the princes to take the lead in reforming the church (since the bishops were not willing to do so). This treatise shows Luther's great power as a rhetorician and his ability to envisage new social and religious orders.

By the end of 1520 a papal bull threatening excommunication had been issued, and Luther's writings were being burned in many of the Catholic strongholds of Germany and the Netherlands. In December of that year, Luther and his friends burned not only the bull, but volumes defending the papacy. Luther defended his action in *Why the Books of the Pope and His Disciples were Burned by Dr. Martin Luther* (1520 – LW 31). Despite his defiance, Luther was allowed to appear before Charles V at the Diet of Worms. This pivotal event is summarized in *Luther at the Diet of Worms* (1521 – LW 32).

The years 1521–29 were a time of Luther's working on concrete problems – worship in Wittenberg, social problems, biblical translation, and debates about the sacraments, discussed in several sections below. Crucial documents for Luther's later career include *The Marburg Colloquy* (1529 – LW 38), *To the Clergy Assembled at Augsburg* (1530 – LW 34), *Commentary on the Alleged Imperial Edict* (1531 – LW 34), and *Sermon in Pleissenberg Castle* (on the introduction of the Reformation in Leipzig: 1539 – LW 51, Dillenberger). Documents relating to Luther's last years include *Luther's Will*

(1542 – LW 34), the fascinating *Italianite Lie Concerning Dr. Martin Luther's Death* (1545 – LW 34), and Luther's *Last Sermon in Eisleben* (1546 – LW 51).

### 3. Luther's approach to theology

Many readers will explore Luther's life to get the background they need for studying his theology. Here the rewards are great, but again the challenges are considerable. No single writing spells out Luther's understanding of justification by faith, his theology of the cross, or the priesthood of all believers. Even where there is a logical starting point (the *Romans Lectures* of 1515/16 for justification, or the *Heidelberg Disputation* for the theology of the cross), one must see how these ideas develop, and how Luther spreads them in popular writings.

Early in 1517 Luther composed an attack on the way that he had been taught to do theology: *Disputation Against Scholastic Theology* (1517 – LW 31, Lull, LCC – *Luther: Early Theological Writings*).[15] This concern gave way for a time to the Indulgences crisis, but was resumed when Luther presented theses at a meeting of the Augustinian Order the next spring. These concepts are found in *The Heidelberg Disputation* (1518 – LW 31, Lull, Dillenberger, LCC – *Early Theological Works*).[16] Here Luther first presented his concept of the theology of the cross – the hidden and surprising ways of the God revealed in the cross of Jesus. An early popular version of these insights is found in the sermon, *Two Kinds of Righteousness* (1519 – LW 31, Dillenberger, Lull).[17] Luther worked out his views on justification in detail in the polemical treatise *Against Latomus* (1521 – LW 32, LCC – *Early Theological Works*) – whom he considered his most impressive opponent.

Luther's theology was developed in treatises, biblical lectures, and sermons in the 1520s. His view of how God acts in the world is found in his *Commentary on the Magnificat* (1521 – LW 21). Another milestone is his *Bondage of the Will* (late 1525 – LW 33, LCC – *Luther and Erasmus on Free Will*, selections in Dillenberger and Lull). It was written in response to Erasmus' attack from the previous year on one of Luther's long-held convictions about the depth and seriousness of human sin. This 300-page treatise gave Luther opportunity to develop his Pauline (and Augustinian) theology in great detail. He sometimes considered this difficult book his finest work.[18]

Luther's developed theology is summarized in Part III of *Confession Concerning Christ's Supper* (1528 – LW 37, Lull). Because Luther feared that he would die soon, he appended to a major work defending Christ's sacramental presence, this overview of his theological commitments. It should be read with *Luther's Small Catechism* (BoC, Lull), *Large Catechism* (BoC), and *Smalcald Articles* (BoC, Lull) as testaments concerning the issues he thought most worth defending. His continuing affirmation of the faith of the church catholic is found in *Three Symbols or Creeds* (1539 – LW 34).

Luther's late views can be found in *Theses Concerning Faith and Law* (1535 – LW 34), *Disputation Concerning Man* (1536 – LW 34) and *Disputation Concerning Justification* (1536 – LW 34). His views on the Antinomian Controversy with Agricola can be found in *Against the Antinomians* (1539 – LW 47).

### 4. Luther's work in piety, spiritual and pastoral care

The American Edition devotes two volumes to Luther's so-called *Devotional Writings* (LW 42, 43). These scarcely begin to indicate the centrality of the reform of faith and piety in Luther's vocation. When he returned from the dangerous encounter with Cardinal Cajetan at Augsburg in 1518, he tackled first the area of devotional life. He had already edited a partial and complete edition of *A German Theology* – a set of medieval mystical sermons that he found personally helpful.

Highly significant is his *Meditation Concerning Christ's Passion* (1519 – LW 42, Lull), which provides a new approach to Lent and Holy Week. Cautioning against excessive self-blame, he invites Christians to acknowledge their sin and then be lifted up to the kind parental heart of God revealed in Jesus. This should be read with *A Sermon on Preparing to Die* (1519 – LW 42, Lull) that gives counsel on true comfort in the face of death. Basic catechetical materials grew out of preaching at the town church in Wittenberg, such as *An Explanation of the Lord's Prayer for Simple Laymen* (1519 – LW 42). When his prince, Frederick the Wise, was very ill in the summer of 1519 he wrote the masterful *Fourteen Consolations* (1520 – LW 42), replacing the late medieval fourteen holy helper saints with an analysis of the seven evils that beset humanity, and the seven even greater promises of God in Christ.

In later years Luther's work in this area often took the form of commentaries on the Psalms. Significant are *Seven Penitential Psalms* (1525 – LW 14, a revision of an early publication from 1517) and *Four Psalms of Comfort* (1526, LW 14), dedicated to the sister of Charles V, the recently widowed Queen of Hungary. In his own considerable distress while waiting for the outcome of the Augsburg Diet in Coburg Castle, he wrote a commentary on his favorite psalm, *Psalm 118 – The Beautiful Confitemini* (1530 – LW 14). Also interesting is *Psalm 23 Expounded at Table* (1535 – LW 12).

Luther returned to the question of prayer in a famous treatise written for his barber, *A Simple Way to Pray* (1535 – LW 43), and came to a new understanding of the sorrows families could experience in *Comfort for Women Who Have Had a Miscarriage* (1542 – LW 43). Luther's gifts in spiritual direction are best seen in the amazing variety of letters found in Tappert, ed., *Letters of Spiritual Counsel* (LCC). The harsh polemicist can also be the tender comforter of parents whose child has died of illness at the university, or the guide to others who experienced depression and *Anfechtung* (Luther's word for the intense spiritual struggles that came with faith).

### 5. Luther's catechetical writings

The most influential of Luther's works over the past five centuries has been his *Small Catechism* (1529 – BoC, Lull). The occasion for the *Small Catechism*, and its companion the *Large Catechism* (also 1529 – BoC, written to provide more material for pastors), was the systematic visitation of all the churches in Elector Saxony in the late 1520s. Luther was appalled by the reports that he heard concerning ignorance of the Creed, the Ten Commandments, the Lord's Prayer, and the sacraments, especially in rural communities. He wrote in a clear and accessible way, without polemic (at least in the *Small Catechism*), using language simple enough for generations to memorize.

Helpful for the context for these works is *Instructions for the Visitors of Parish Pastors in Electoral Saxony* (1528 – LW 40). The Instructions were written by Melanchthon but reviewed by Luther who also supplied a preface. They give a fascinating checklist of Reformation concerns at this time. Earlier versions of Luther's catechetical material can be found in his *Personal Prayer Book* (1522, but several times revised and expanded – LW 43). Key ideas for the catechisms were worked out in *Sermons on the Catechism* (late 1528 – LW 51, Dillenberger).

### 6. Luther on the Bible: introduction and translation

Luther was ordered by Staupitz, his superior in his order, to study for his doctorate in theology specializing in the Bible. He initially fought this assignment, but in the end it shaped his identity. He not only lectured on the Bible in Wittenberg from 1513 to 1545, but also published versions of many of his lectures, and preached hundreds of sermons on biblical texts.

Luther finished his German New Testament during his stay at the Wartburg (1521/22), and the first edition was published the next September in Wittenberg after a thorough revision with the help of Melanchthon and others. He then published the Old Testament in several sections. This work was not completed until 1534. On the Old Testament Luther worked as part of a team and cherished the expert help of others.

Luther's views on interpretation were deeply influenced by Augustine, especially his development of the Pauline distinction between spirit and letter. An early polemical writing – *Against the Hyperchristian, Hyperspiritual, Hyperlearned Book by Goat Esmer in Leipzig* (1521 – LW 39, Lull) – contains a good discussion of Luther's views. Very important is a small essay he attached to his model sermons for the Christmas season – the *Christmas Postil* (1521 – LW 52) – called *A Brief Instruction on What to Look for and Expect in the Gospels* (LW 35, Lull). Along with his *Prefaces to the New Testament* (1522 – LW 35, Lull, Dillenberger) this writing explains Luther's understanding of the difference between gospel and Gospels, the difference between law and gospel, and his evaluation of the most important New Testament books – his so-called "canon within the canon."

Luther's view of the Old Testament is distinctive. He differed sharply with many of the other reformers in his limiting the validity of Old Testament law for Christians (unless it agreed with the natural law). Yet he found the Hebrew Bible authoritative and valuable for Christians in diverse ways, and spent a large proportion of the rest of his life interpreting Old Testament books. His views are summarized in *Prefaces to the Old Testament* (1523 – LW 35, Lull) and *How Christians Should Regard Moses* (1525 – LW 35, Lull).

To accompany his German Bible Luther wrote introductions to most of the individual books (all the books of the Old Testament beginning with Job, all the books of the New Testament beginning with Acts – LW 35). Especially important are his *Preface to Romans* (also in Dillenberger) and his several Prefaces to the Book of Revelation. Luther's introductions to the books of the Apocrypha (included in his German Bible, but as an appendix) are included in *Word and Sacrament I* (LW 35). His approach to translations is found in *On Translating* (1530 – LW 35) and *Defense of the Translation of the Psalms* (1531 – LW 35).

### 7. Luther's interpretations of the Old Testament

Twenty volumes of the American Edition are devoted to Luther as an expounder of the Old Testament. His first lectures were on the Psalms (1513–15). A version of these is available (LW 10, 11) but includes only the *scholia* (longer comments), and not the glosses (marginal notes). This is very challenging material, and probably not the place to begin. He returned to the Old Testament in 1523 with important lectures on Deuteronomy (LW 9).

Lectures on the Minor Prophets lasted from 1524 to early 1526. These coincide with the great events of 1525 including the death of Frederick the Wise, the Peasants' War, Luther's marriage, and his writing against Erasmus. Nine of the prophets are available from student notes (LW 18), but Luther reworked three others for subsequent German publication – Habakkuk and Jonah (LW 19), and Zechariah, on which Luther published an extensive commentary in 1527 (LW 20). The narrative material in Jonah was a great stimulus to Luther's imagination. The Habakkuk commentary is a key source for his understanding of faith.

In 1526 Luther turned to *Ecclesiastes* (LW 15). He found this a difficult assignment, as there were few commentaries to help him. Isaiah was more congenial material for him and a large commentary was produced in 1526/27 (LW 16, 17). Luther returned to the Old Testament with *Song of Solomon* (LW 15) in 1530/31. Luther saw this book as neither a love poem nor an allegory, but as a treatise on politics.

His *Commentary on Psalm 90* (1535 – LW 13) contains his understanding of death. The most massive interpretative task of his lifetime was the ten-year course of *Lectures on Genesis* (1535–45 – LW 1–8), a rich work that shows Luther's theological and interpretive power in his last years. Especially memorable are his treatment of creation and fall, his reflections on Abraham, and his interpretation of the Joseph story.

### 8. Luther's interpretations of the New Testament

In early years Luther turned to Paul in Romans, Galatians, and Hebrews (which he considered a Pauline epistle). These lectures were decisive for Luther's theological development, especially for his understanding of justification, Christian freedom, and Christology. They are more accessible than the earlier Psalms lectures, but still challenging to a beginner.

The Lectures on Romans (LW 25, LCC – *Lectures on Romans*) were delivered at 6 a.m. on Mondays and Fridays, 1515/16. Luther proceeded next to *Galatians*, lecturing in 1517/18 (LW 27). In these we have Luther's early thinking about these themes of faith, freedom, and the law. He returned to this epistle in 1531. His later *Commentary on Galatians* (published 1535 – LW 26–27, selections in Dillenberger) is considered one of his finest mature works. Luther's *Lectures on Hebrews* (1517/18, LW 29, LCC – *Early Theological Writings*) come from the very time in which Luther was emerging as a public and controversial theologian. The Library of Christian Classics version has both the glosses and the *scholia*, while the American Edition contains the *scholia* only.

Early in 1521 Luther was preparing a *Commentary on the Magnificat* (1521 – LW 21), Mary's Song from Luke 1:46–55, which he completed while a prisoner in the Wartburg. Luther was critical of some current theology and practices surrounding Mary, but he had a high view of her role as the model of faith. He considered the Magnificat to be one of the great texts of the theology of the cross – showing God's surprising and unexpected ways of working in the world.

On his return from the Wartburg Luther began a series of *Sermons on I Peter* (1522 – LW 30), which he considered among the most important biblical books. These sermons – somewhat ignored – are a crucial source for Luther's developing ecclesiology. He continued with *Sermons on II Peter and Jude* (1523 – LW 30), which are also interesting for his view of the antichrist. In 1523 he also wrote a *Commentary on I Corinthians 7* (LW 28) at a time when he was defending marriage against celibacy.

When the plague was raging in Wittenberg and most of the university had moved to Jena, Luther offered those who stayed a series of *Lectures on I John* (1527 – LW 30), another of his most valued biblical books. He then took up the Pastoral Epistles, beginning with *Lectures on Titus and Philemon* (late 1527 – LW 29), followed by *Lectures on I Timothy* (LW 29) in early 1528. These works provide continuing clues about his understanding of the order and structure of the church. The short *Lecture on Philemon* is a gem – a splendid example of Luther's insistence that right action stem from right motivation, freely offered.

From 1530 onward Luther's close colleague John Bugenhagen, town pastor and professor in the university, was often absent from Wittenberg as he helped with the introduction of the Reformation in Northern Germany and Denmark. Many of Luther's final New Testament works come from his preaching as a substitute for Bugenhagen. Luther's 1530–32 sermons from Matthew 5–7 have been collected as *Sermon on the Mount* (LW 21), a very important text for Luther's thinking on ethics and discipleship. In the same period on Saturdays he preached on the Gospel of John, forming the basis for *Sermons on John 6–8* (LW 23), with rich discussions of the Lord's Supper.[19]

In 1532/33 Luther delivered a long series of *Sermons on I Corinthians 15* (LW 28) – Paul's interpretation of the resurrection of Christ. The series was interrupted by the death of Luther's prince, John the Steadfast, and his burial in the castle church in Wittenberg. Luther preached *Two Funeral Sermons* on I Thessalonians 4 (August 1532 – LW 51).

The *Sermons on John 14–16* (LW 24) were given in 1537, just after Luther's return from Smalcald and his near-death from kidney stones. They are excellent sources for his developed understanding of the Trinity, Christology, and the Spirit. A final series of expository *Sermons on John 1–4* (LW 22) followed in 1537/38, important for Luther's understanding of the incarnation.

### 9. Luther's preaching and guides to preaching

Luther became a preacher when Staupitz assigned him this responsibility in the Augustinian monastery in Wittenberg. He also soon became preacher in the town church. Later in his life he came to identify himself even more as preacher than as Doctor of Theology. *Sermons I* (LW 51) provides an excellent overview of Luther's preaching, with forty-three sermons of various types and occasions. Most of Luther's sermons remain untranslated.

To support the improvement of preaching Luther produced a series of postils – model sermons or sermon helps for the entire cycle of the church year. He began a Latin series for Advent in 1521, but at the Wartburg he realized that this resource needed to be in German. He later completed the cycle for the whole church year. A reprint of an old translation of the 1544 *House Postil* by John Nicholas Lenker is available in eight inexpensive volumes; these are mostly Luther's sermons from 1531–35.[20]

Luther considered the postils among his most important works. They were influential for Lutheran preaching in the centuries after Luther. The American Edition contains only selections from the *Christmas Postil* (1521 – LW 52), with seven of Luther's eight Gospel texts for Christmas, but none of the epistles. A wonderful recent addition to Luther's church-year preaching is *The 1529 Holy Week and Easter Sermons*.[21] In these eighteen sermons we see how Luther spoke both about the death and resurrection of Christ, and how he discussed the Lord's Supper in the months before the Marburg Colloquy.

### 10. The sacraments

Luther's writings on the sacraments are vast. They constitute one of his finest contributions to Christian theology. He was not only a reformer of church practice, but reflected deeply both about the Lord's Supper and the sacrament of baptism. His views underwent considerable development. Most of the crucial documents are in the four volumes of the American Edition (*Word and Sacrament I, II, III, IV*) with good introductions and helpful notes.

While Luther's critique of the Roman Catholic sacramental system in *The Babylonian Captivity of the Church* (1520 – LW 36, Dillenberger, Part I in Lull) is justly famous, the reader needs to start with Luther's important earlier treatises on these subjects to chart his development. Critical are the three "sermons" from 1519 – *The Sacrament of Penance, The Holy and Blessed Sacrament of Baptism*, and *The Blessed Sacrament of the* Holy and True *Body of Christ and the Brotherhoods* (all LW 35, the last in Lull). The last document, which has been somewhat neglected, contains some of Luther's finest reflection on the communal nature of the sacrament. In *Treatise on the New Testament, that is, the Holy Mass* (1520 – LW 35) he begins to criticize the notion of the mass as sacrifice.

The development of Luther's views is charted in the documents in *Word and Sacrament II* (LW 36), especially *Misuse of the Mass* (1521) and *Receiving Both Kinds in the Sacrament* (1522). The differences with his more radical opponents, Karlstadt and Müntzer, can be found in the long but interesting *Against the Heavenly Prophets* (1525 – LW 40). His mounting disagreement with Zwingli and "the fanatics" is chronicled in several documents in volumes 36 and 37 and comes to sharp focus in the very important *Confession Concerning Christ's Supper* (1528 – LW 37). Luther's account of what actually happened when the contesting parties met at Marburg in October 1529 can be found in *The Marburg Colloquy* and the *Marburg Articles* (LW 38).[22]

Luther defended infant baptism and interpreted the sacrament in a broad and positive way in *Concerning Rebaptism* (1528 – LW 40, Lull) and in his *Large Catechism* (1529 – BoC). Treating baptism, the Lord's Supper, and confession (which he continued to value highly whether or not it was a sacrament) in his Catechisms gave him a chance to show how popular teaching could be done. He wrote persuasively about the meaning of the Lord's Supper in *Admonition Concerning the Sacrament of the Body and Blood of Christ* (1530 – LW 38) and explored the biblical basis for worship in his *Commentary on Psalm 111* (1530 – LW 13). Important late works are the *Disputation: "That the Word was Made Flesh"* (1539 – LW 38) and his critique of the sacramental theology of Schwenckfeld in *Short Confession on the Holy Sacrament* (1544 – LW 38).

### 11. Worship and hymns

Most of the important documents in this area are available in a single volume with good notes – *Liturgy and Hymns* (LW 53). Luther took personal charge of the reform of worship in Wittenberg on his return in Lent 1522. He restored order partly by his presence and partly through a series of famous sermons, *Eight Sermons in Wittenberg* (LW 51, Lull) that set out a cautious plan for sustainable reform.

He then developed a series of principles for worship, an order for the Sunday service of Communion, and finally an order for that service in German. These changes can be traced in *Concerning the Order for Public Worship* and *An Order for Mass and Communion* (both 1523, LW 53, Lull). Luther believed that local variation is allowable and even desirable. His finished project is found in *The German Mass* (1526 – LW 53).

Luther also revised the order for baptism, the service for marriage, and eventually the rite for the ordination of pastors. All these materials can be found in *Liturgy and Hymns*, along with Luther's appeal for the writing of hymns and introductions to various hymnals. Especially interesting is Luther's poem in praise of music in *Preface to All Good Hymnals* (1538) and a motet from the end of his life on Psalm 118:17, a crucial verse for his personal history: "I Shall Not Die, But Live" (1545). Luther's hymns are themselves worth study, both for their content and as a reminder of his creativity in finding ways to extend and reinforce his message. Some of them have been "cleaned up" considerably in modern hymnals; this makes the more literal translations and notes in *Liturgy and Hymns* very useful.

Beyond volume 53 of the American Edition, readers should note Luther's qualified praise of images or art for Christian use in *Against the Heavenly Prophets* (1525 – LW 40). Luther's developed ideas on worship are summarized in the important *Sermon at the Dedication of the Castle Church, Torgau* (1544 – LW 51).

### 12. Ecclesiology

Conflicting understandings of the church were at the heart of the Reformation struggle. *The Leipzig Debate* (LW 31) with John Eck first clarified the radical nature of Luther's approach. Neither the decrees of popes nor the vote of councils could be considered completely reliable, for each had erred and suppressed the gospel. Each must be judged against the standard of the Word of God. Luther criticized the papacy forcefully in *On the Papacy in Rome* (1520 – LW 39) and in *To the Christian Nobility of the German Nation* (1520 – LW 44), with its suggestions of a limited role for the papacy in the future.

*The Babylonian Captivity of the Church* (1520 – LW 36) claimed that the church had intentionally held Christians in bondage to its sacramental system. *The Freedom of a Christian* (1520 – LW 31, Dillenberger, Lull) was written in intentional juxtaposition to the *Babylonian Captivity* to explore what Christian freedom might mean. If such freedom were formed in the image of Christ, it could not mean doing whatever one pleased, but rather a fresh impulse to serve others, knowing that one had already been set free in Christ. While Luther tried to set sharp limits to the political and social implications of this freedom, he was committed to a church that respected freedom. These ideas were further developed in the *Sermons on I Peter* (LW 30), preached in 1522 soon after his return to Wittenberg.

In the post-Wartburg years Luther wrote often on specific issues of ministry. He defended the congregational choice of pastors (in consultation with the authorities) in *That a Christian Assembly or Congregation Has the Right and Power to Judge All Teaching, and to Call, Appoint and Dismiss Teachers, Established and Proven by Scripture* (1523 – LW 39). He advised the Bohemian Christians (heirs of Jan Hus) in *Concerning the Ministry* (1523 – LW 40). *Private Mass and the Ordination of Priests* (1533 – LW 38) addressed a persistent problem as the Reformation came to new territories.

Luther's positive exposition of church as community rather than hierarchy is well summarized in his most systematic statement about the nature of the church, *On the Councils and the Church* Part III (1539 – LW 41, Lull) with its important discussion of the seven marks of the church (including suffering – always a surprise to contemporary readers). Another list of ten signs of the true church and twelve symptoms of the false church is found in *Against Hanswurst* (1541 – LW 41). Issues of ordination and possible compromise with episcopacy were important in the last dozen years of Luther's life, but most key documents are not available in English. His rite for *The Ordination of Ministers of the Word* (1539 – LW 53) gives some clues.

### 13. The Christian life: foundations in freedom

As in Paul's letters, so in Luther's writings – questions of theology and ethics, of faith and life, come mixed together. Luther presented a fresh interpretation of how Christians ought to live in the world – both in their motivation (from justification), in their worldly vocation (as opposed to life in religious community), and in the content of their action (free service of their neighbor rather than religious good works). The basic pattern was worked out in *Two Kinds of Righteousness* (1519 or 1518 – LW 31, Dillenberger, Lull) and developed more systematically in *Treatise on Good Works* (1520 – LW 44), a notable and extended commentary on the Ten Commandments. This new thrust is further explored in *The Freedom of a Christian* (1520 – LW 31, Dillenberger, Lull). Unjustly neglected is his *Sermon on the Three Kinds of the Good Life* (1521 – LW 44).

Luther early began a positive reevaluation of marriage in his landmark *Sermon on the Estate of Marriage* (1519 – LW 44, Lull). This freedom to marry is further underscored in the very significant treatise *The Judgment of Martin Luther on Monastic Vows* (1521 – LW 44). Luther dedicated this treatise to his father, and it should be read with the accompanying letter of November 21, 1521 (LW 48). *Avoiding the Doctrines of Men* (1522 – LW 35) assembles biblical texts that support an ethic of freedom.

A series of writings further explores marriage issues in the 1520s: *The Estate of Marriage* (1522 – LW 45), *To the Knights of the Teutonic Order* (1523 – LW 45), *That Parents Should Neither Compel Nor Hinder their Children* (1524 – LW 45), and *On Marriage Matters* (1530 – LW 46). The biblical basis for discipleship and ethics is powerfully explored in *The Sermon on the Mount* (1530 – LW 21).

An ethic of freedom can generate problems of license or self-indulgence, and Luther often struggled with this misunderstanding. Helpful are both *Sermon on Soberness and Moderation Against Gluttony and Drunkenness*

(1539 – LW 51) and *Against the Antinomians* (1539 – LW 47). Occasionally his disappointment was overpowering, as one can read in his letter to his wife Käthe of July 28, 1545 (LW 50).[23]

### 14. Political writings

Luther seems always to have been critical of social disorder. A December 1521 visit to Wittenberg in disguise from the Wartburg led to the important pamphlet, *A Sincere Admonition by Martin Luther to All Christians to Guard Against Insurrection and Rebellion* (1522 – LW 45). Luther denied that God-pleasing changes could come except through rulers and other established authorities, but he challenged Christians to use their speech to demand such reforms and to refuse to participate in discredited Roman practices.

Luther's most systematic statement of his understanding of political order is *Temporal Authority: To What Extent It Should Be Obeyed* (1523 – LW 45, Dillenberger, Lull). Luther defends the divine authority of government (against the claim of the Roman Church that it derives from ecclesial sources), the limits of temporal authority (it cannot control faith or conscience), and the character of the wise Christian ruler. That the state should maintain order but not try to force people to believe nor interfere with the preaching is developed in Luther's critique of Müntzer, *To the Princes of Saxony Concerning the Rebellious Spirit* (1524 – LW 40).

For Luther's role in the Peasants' War see section 17 below. A defense of the calling of Christians to military service is *Whether Soldiers Too Can Be Saved* (1526 – LW 46). Luther's views about whether Christians could defend themselves against an attack from the emperor or the Turk can be explored in *Warning to His Dear German People* (1531, after the Diet of Augsburg – LW 47), *On War Against the Turk* (1529 – LW 46), and *Appeal for Prayer Against the Turks* (1541 – LW 43). His developed notions of the Christian prince can be found in *Commentary on Psalm 101* (1534 – LW 13), reflecting his early tensions with the court of John Frederick, Elector of Saxony.

### 15. Social challenges

Luther's stress on obedience to temporal authority and his deep hostility to rebellion suggest that he was a social conservative. This actual case is more complicated. The changes that came with the Reformation led to unforeseen problems in education, in social welfare, and even in care of the sick. There were longstanding economic grievances for peasants and town dwellers, and even Luther's extended family appealed for his help with economic hardships. Luther was simultaneously a theoretical conservative and a pragmatic reformer and innovator.

Beginning with *To the Christian Nobility of the German Nation* (1520 – LW 44, Dillenberger) Luther stressed the importance of financial support for schools at every level, especially universities. The professor advocated full funding from his princes. Equally significant is his support for starting local schools. He called for this in the influential *To the Councilmen of All Cities of Germany That They Establish and Maintain Christian Schools* (1524 – LW 45, Lull). He followed up this appeal with praise for territories that took such steps. He knew that parental attitudes were critical and addressed them in *On Keeping Children in School* (1530 – LW 46).

Luther had creative ideas for the reform of welfare that he developed in a series of writings to the town of Leisnig: *Preface to the Ordinance of a Common Chest* (1523 – LW 45) and *Fraternal Agreement on the Common Chest of the Entire Assembly at Leisnig* (1523 – LW 45).[24] Luther's views on economic matters are surprising and even offensive to many modern readers. He consistently opposed the earning of interest on borrowed money – which was the foundation of the Fugger Bank of Augsburg in his day. A good place to start is with his *Trade and Usury* (1524 – LW 45).

One of Luther's most visionary and persuasive writings about social issues came from his remaining in Wittenberg during the outbreak of plague in 1527. With Bugenhagen, the town pastor, he taught the students who remained and took an active role in the care of the sick and dying. From this experience he wrote the moving *Whether One May Flee from a Deadly Plague* (1527 – LW 43, Lull).

### 16. Apologetics and polemics

Modern readers of Luther are often appalled by what they consider his harsh language and personal attacks on his opponents. Luther does have a sharp tongue, but he was not unusual in using all available rhetorical devices to pursue his arguments. Peter Matheson's *The Rhetoric of the Reformation* helps set Luther and many of his contemporaries (Erasmus, Karlstadt, Müntzer, and Eck) in this context.[25]

In 1521 Luther wrote four times against a Catholic opponent, Jerome Emser – whom he called the "goat of Leipzig." These writings can be found in LW 39, *Church and Ministry I*. From the Wartburg Luther completed a significant treatise against the Louvain theologian Jacques Masson, also known as Latomus. *Against Latomus* (LW 32, LCC – *Early Theological Writings*) is a major statement of his understanding of justification by faith.

His continuing frustration with Albrecht of Mainz was expressed in *Against the Spiritual Estate of the Pope and the Bishops, Falsely So Called* (1522 – LW 39). His significant reply to the English King Henry VIII's attacks (*Contra Henricum Regem Angliae* – WA 10) has not been translated. Luther's later *Bondage of the Will* (1525 – LW 33, LCC, selections in Dillenberger and Lull) is partly a work of polemic in response to Erasmus, but even more deeply a personal testament to Luther's understanding of the nature of sin and grace.

Luther wrote *Against the Heavenly Prophets in Matters of Images and Sacraments* (1525 – LW 40) to clarify and publicize his differences with Karlstadt and Müntzer on the eve of the Peasants' War. *The Burning of Brother Henry* (1525 – LW 32) reads like an account of early Christian martyrdom. It is a very successful piece of Lutheran propaganda that tells the story of the death at the stake of a fellow Augustinian, his good friend Henry of Zutphen.

Luther continued to debate fellow Protestants, but his strongest polemics in later years were directed against the Roman Church. He mocked the report of a committee of cardinals appointed by Paul III to plan for the forthcoming council in *Counsel of a Committee of Several Cardinals with Luther's Preface* (1538 – LW 34). He used a book against the fierce Catholic prince Henry of Brunswick (*Against Hanswurst*, 1541 – LW 41) as occasion to review the corrupt practices of the Catholic Church. He was still taking aim at old opponents in *Against the Thirty-Two Articles of the Louvain Theologians* (1545 – LW 34).

### 17. The harsh books

Certain polemical writings were objectionable even to Luther's friends in Luther's lifetime. In 1519, a sympathetic observer said that Luther's fault was that he was "somewhat too violent and cutting in his reprimands, in fact more than is proper for one seeking to find new trails in theology, and certainly also for a divine..."[26] These writings include his three 1525 pamphlets on the Peasants' War, his writings from 1523 until his death about the Jews, and his final treatise on the papacy from 1545.

At a late point in the development of the peasant uprising, Luther attempted to mediate with his *Admonition to Peace: A Reply to the Twelve Articles of the Peasants in Swabia* (spring 1525 – LW 46). He rails against the princes in a way that should put to rest simplistic notions of Luther as their tool, but also confronts the peasants for hiding their demands behind a mask of Christianity. He urges both sides to submit their grievances to "certain counts and lords from among the nobility and certain councilmen from the cities, and ask them to arbitrate and settle this dispute amicably."[27]

As the situation became more violent Luther wrote *Against the Robbing and Murdering Hordes of Peasants* (May 1525 – LW 46), prepared as an addendum to a later printing of *Admonition to Peace*. In it Luther castigated the peasants sharply and called on them to repent of the sin of rebellion, and admonished the rulers to carry out their divine mandate to keep and restore order. Where peasant bands were threatening other peasants with violence unless they joined the rebellion, Luther called on the rulers to take the strongest measures possible to stop them: "Let whoever can stab, smile, slay." Luther considered the situation apocalyptic and ended the work by saying that "the destruction of the world is to be expected every hour."[28]

This later writing appeared when the princes were already engaged in wholesale slaughter. It gave the impression of Luther as one-sided and ill-tempered in his advice. By midsummer friends persuaded Luther to compose a third writing, *An Open Letter Against the Harsh Book of the Peasants* (July 1525 – LW 46). Luther continued to be defiant about the rightness of his course and clearly lost some of his popular following from this point.[29]

Luther's first major writing about the Jews was a hopeful breakthrough in Christian reflections: *That Jesus Christ Was Born a Jew* (1523 – LW 45). In the first part Luther affirmed his faith that Jesus was born of the line of Abraham, but by a miracle to a virgin mother. But in the second half of the treatise Luther criticized the shameful Christian treatment of Jews through the centuries and urged a new beginning, guided by love: "We must receive them cordially, and permit them to trade and work with us, hear our Christian teaching, and witness our Christian life. If some of them should prove stiff-necked, what of it? After all we ourselves are not all good Christians either."[30]

Much later Luther's attitude toward the Jews became more hostile. In *Against the Sabbatarians* (1538 – LW 47) he accused the Jews of stirring up Christians in Bohemia to give up their Sunday observance for the biblical Sabbath. The full course of Luther's rage against the Jews in the last period of his life is found in *On the Jews and Their Lies* (1543 – LW 47). Here Luther defended his christological interpretation of the Old Testament, but also made terrifying proposals for what rulers should do about the Jews – burn their synagogues, tear down their houses, destroy their prayer books, and eventually expel them from the country.

The treatise was not popular in Luther's time, and none of his more radical proposals was then adopted, though some princes did take certain steps to cancel earlier Jewish rights and privileges. But the outburst was not isolated, as can be seen from other late writings including *Last Words of David* (1543 – LW 15) and several of Luther's last letters from Eisleben to his wife in the weeks before his death (LW 50). Several contemporaries matched Luther in their strong anti-Judaism, including Erasmus and Zwingli, but no one could match the power of his rhetoric.[31] Such writings were given full publicity by the National Socialists in 1933–45.

Also extreme is Luther's final treatment of the claims of the popes in *Against the Roman Papacy: An Institution of the Devil* (early 1545, LW 41). This extremely bitter book makes an important theological critique of three papal claims, namely: to be the supreme Lord over Christendom, to be beyond judgment and deposition, and to be the only one who can crown a German emperor. The context was the attempt of the papacy to rescind measures of toleration toward Protestants granted by Charles V at the Diet of Speyer in 1544. Luther's abusive language was underscored in a set of woodcuts by his Wittenberg neighbor Lucas Cranach, which showed the pope being swallowed by the jaws of hell.[32]

### 18. Miscellaneous writings

Luther wrote many prefaces to books, generally for friends and for books that he admired. An example is his *Preface to Galeatius Capella's History* (1538 – LW 34). Luther wrote some interesting poetry, including a ballad in memory of the first Lutheran martyrs: *A New Song Here Shall Be Begun* (1523 – LW 53). While he was at the Coburg Castle in 1530, he worked at editing *Aesop's Fables*, a book that he had loved ever since his student days.


THE PLEASURE OF READING LUTHER

Despite having so many choices, readers should be able to discover possible starting points. It takes a few years of study to gain a comprehensive overview, but in a few months one may come to know some of Luther's most important writings and explore his ideas. One wise teacher used to insist that students read any three or four volumes of the American Edition – as Luther returns to his major themes repeatedly.[33]

Each of the anthologies is a proposal for how to read Luther and what to read. Bernhard Lohse provides a list of what he considers basic in *Martin Luther*: Some of the early lectures on the Bible, *Ninety-five Theses*, some of the sermons from 1519, the great treatises of 1520 – *To the German Nobility*, *The Babylonian Captivity of the Church*, and *The Freedom of a Christian*, *The Magnificat*, one of Luther's writings on political authority, *The Bondage of the Will*, and the *Smalcald Articles*.[34] Simply beginning with volume 31 (*Career of the Reformer I*) or volume 48 (*Letters I*) of the American Edition will get one started.

The best advice of all may be to read fewer items and to get to know those writings well. Luther suggested such a plan to his students:

A student who doesn't want his work to go for nothing ought to read and reread some good author until the author becomes part, as it were, of his flesh and blood. Scattered reading confuses more than it teaches. Many books, even good ones, have the same effect on the student. So he is like the man who dwells everywhere and therefore dwells nowhere. Just as in human society we don't enjoy the fellowship of every friend every day, but only of a few chosen ones, so we ought to do in our studies.[35]

Repeated reading of Luther provides delights, disappointments, and deeper understanding.

### Notes

1. See Timothy F. Lull, ed., *Martin Luther's Basic Theological Writings* (Philadelphia: Fortress Press, 1989), 20.
2. Heiko Oberman, *Luther: Man Between God and the Devil* (New York: Image Books, 1992).
3. Table Talk No. 4075 (September 29, 1538), in *Luther's Works* (Philadelphia: Fortress Press, 1967), 54:311.
4. Bernhard Lohse, *Martin Luther: An Introduction to His Life and Work* (Philadelphia: Fortress Press, 1986), 97.
5. Martin Luther, "Table Talk for Winter of 1542–3," in LW 54, 439–40.
6. See the highly useful resource *Luther's Works on CD-ROM* (Minneapolis and St. Louis: Fortress Press and Concordia Publishing House, 2002) which makes the 55-volume American Edition available in this format.
7. Jaroslav Pelikan, *Luther the Expositor* (St. Louis: Concordia, 1959).
8. Philip Melanchthon, "Loci Communes" (1521), in *Melanchthon and Bucer*, Library of Christian Classics (Philadelphia: Westminster, 1969).
9. John Dillenberger, ed., *Martin Luther: Selections from His Writings* (Garden City: Doubleday, 1961).
10. See note 1 above.
11. Theodore Tappert, ed., *Book of Concord* (Philadelphia: Fortress Press, 1959) or now preferably Robert Kolb and Timothy Wengert, eds., *Book of Concord* (Minneapolis: Fortress Press, 2000). Cf. the useful resource, *The Book of Concord on CD-ROM*, ed. Robert Kolb and Timothy J. Wengert (Minneapolis: Fortress Press, 2000).
12. See Lohse, *Martin Luther*, ch. 4.
13. Among the lives of Luther, the best current resource in English is the three-volume set by Martin Brecht: *Martin Luther: His Road to Reformation* (Philadelphia: Fortress Press, 1985), *Martin Luther: Shaping and Defining the Reformation* (Philadelphia: Fortress Press, 1990), and *Martin Luther: The Preservation of the Church* (Minneapolis: Fortress Press, 1993). Among the studies especially significant are Oberman, *Luther*, and Bernhard Lohse, *Martin Luther's Theology* (Minneapolis: Fortress Press, 1999). For background see Hans Hillerbrand, ed., *Oxford Encyclopedia of the Reformation*. 4 vols. (New York: Oxford, 1996) and Thomas Brady, Heiko Oberman, and James Tracy, eds., *Handbook of European History 1400–1600*. 2 vols. (Grand Rapids: Eerdmans, 1995).

14. An entry for November 1532 tells a charming story of the boy Luther's first encounter with the Bible. See LW 54, 13–14. Martin Brecht gives good reasons to doubt that this story is accurate in his *Martin Luther: His Road to Reformation*, 85. See Theodore Tappert's introduction to volume 54 for his principles of selection. Much more material is available in the six volumes of the Weimar Ausgabe.

15. James Atkinson, ed., *Luther: Early Theological Works*. Library of Christian Classics (Philadelphia: Westminster, 1962).

16. The translation of the *Heidelberg Disputation* in the American Edition has been criticized. An alternative is James Atkinson's translation in the Library of Christian Classics.

17. Martin Brecht has argued that the real date of this sermon is Palm Sunday, 1518 – rather than 1519 – which would put it just before Luther's trip to Heidelberg. See *Martin Luther: His Road to Reformation*, 230–1.

18. The reader has two good resources in the American Edition and in the Library of Christian Classics, both from the hand of English Luther scholar Philip Watson. The American Edition is a later volume, and Watson has improved his translation at various points, but the Library of Christian Classics version also includes the text of Erasmus' *On the Freedom of the Will* (1524), which makes much more sense of the debate.

19. It would be very helpful to have more Gospel material in English. Good possibilities could include the 1528/29 Sermons on Matthew 11–15 and John 16–20 (WA 28). The Sermon on Matthew 18–24 (1537–40) would contribute to our ability to study Luther's later interpretation of the Gospels (WA 47).

20. J. N. Lenker, ed., *Sermons of Martin Luther*. 8 vols. (Minneapolis: Lutherans of All Lands, 1904), rpt. Grand Rapids: Baker, 1992.

21. Martin Luther, *The 1529 Holy Week and Easter Sermons*, trans. and ed. Irving L. Sandberg and Timothy J. Wengert (St. Louis: Concordia, 1999).

22. Luther's letter to his wife on this occasion is also an important document and one of the signs that she was becoming an important theological confidante – a role that she surely played but which has been ignored until recently. Luther, "Letter to Katharina Luther" (October 4, 1529) in LW 49, 234–9.

23. The neglected story of this crisis at the end of Luther's life is found in Brecht, *Martin Luther: The Preservation of the Church*, 262–5.

24. There are also important letters about this project to Leisnig and to Frederick the Wise in LW 49.

25. Peter Matheson, *The Rhetoric of Reformation* (Edinburgh: T&T Clark, 1998).

26. Petrus Mosellanus, a Leipzig Greek scholar and humanist, gave this evaluation of Luther at the Leipzig Debate. He also praised his learning, his courteous and friendly behavior, and his "large store of words and ideas." The report is found in Brecht, *Martin Luther: His Road to Reformation*, 313.

27. *Admonition to Peace* (1525) in LW 46, 42.

28. *Against the Robbing and Murdering Hordes of Peasants* (1525) in LW 46, 54–5.

29. Brecht, *Martin Luther: Shaping and Defining the Reformation*, 172–94.

30. Luther, *That Jesus Christ Was Born a Jew* (1523) in LW 45, 229.

31. Helpful background for understanding the views of Luther and other Reformers toward the Jews is found in Heiko Oberman, *The Roots of Anti-Semitism* (Philadelphia: Fortress Press, 1984).

32. For examples of the woodcuts see Brecht, *Martin Luther: The Preservation of the Church*, 363, 365. Luther found at least one of them "too raw" and asked that it be suppressed.
33. The teacher was Ian D. K. Siggins, author of important books on Luther's Christology and Luther's family.
34. Lohse, *Martin Luther*, 123–4.
35. Luther, Table Talk No. 2894a (January, 1533), in LW 54, 179.

# 4 Luther as Bible translator

ERIC W. GRITSCH

Luther was not the first German translator of the Bible. Translations into old German dialects had already appeared at the time of Charlemagne (Charles the Great, 742–814), based on the first Latin Bible, the Vulgate (from the Latin *vulgare*, "to make common") offered by Jerome (348–420). He had used a Greek translation of the Old Testament by Christian scholars in Alexandria, Egypt, from the third century, known as the Septuagint (from the Greek for "seventy", an alleged legendary number of the scholars involved in the translation). The emperor had ordered a translation of portions of the Psalter and the Gospels from the Vulgate as part of his program to convert his subjects to Christianity. Rare whole German Bibles began to appear in the fourteenth century. When the Mainz German printer John Gutenberg refined the ancient Oriental art of printing by using movable type, one of his co-workers used an unknown German Bible from Nuremberg to produce the "Gutenberg Bible" of 1466. It became popular in a version of 1475, edited by Günther Zainer in Augsburg, with corrections based on the Vulgate and some linguistic updating. The Nuremberg printer Anton Koberger added stylistic refinements and published a revised version in 1483, the year of Luther's birth.

Church authorities tried to discourage the printing of German Bibles. The head of the German dioceses, Archbishop Berthold of Mainz, prohibited the publication of German Bibles because the poverty of the German language did not mediate the real meaning of the holy biblical texts of the Vulgate. Although such a powerful intervention slowed the speed of publication of German Bibles, eighteen German translations had been published by 1518, one year after Luther called for a biblically grounded church reform in his famous *Ninety-five Theses*. Luther was initially supported by influential "humanists", such as Erasmus of Rotterdam (1469–1536), who published the first text-critical Greek edition of the New Testament in 1516. In the preface he disagreed with those who wanted to prohibit the reading of the Bible by simple folk. On the contrary, he argued, the Bible should be read by everyone in every language. This Greek text of the New Testament paved the way for new biblical studies and translations.

Luther was educated to be a biblical scholar. Fluent in Latin as a monk and priest in the monastery of the Augustinian Hermits in Erfurt, he began studying Hebrew in 1506, based on the Hebrew grammar and dictionary of the German humanist John Reuchlin (1455–1522). He tried his linguistic skills in his lectures on his two favorite parts of the Old Testament, the Psalter and the Pentateuch. In 1518 Philip Melanchthon, one of the best young Greek scholars, joined the Wittenberg faculty and assisted Luther in the study of the Greek New Testament. Melanchthon loved ancient Greek so much that he even adopted a Greek translation of his German family name Schwarzerd ("black earth," *melan chtonos* in Greek). Another colleague and expert in ancient Hebrew, Matthew Aurogallus, joined the Wittenberg faculty in 1521 and assisted Luther in the translation of Old Testament texts. Luther's first translation of Old Testament texts in conjunction with the Vulgate was his edition of "seven penitential Psalms" in 1517 (Psalms 6, 32, 38, 51, 102, 130, 143).

Luther thought of a translation of the Bible into German during his voluntary exile at the Wartburg (May 4, 1521 – March 6, 1522), a castle in Saxony owned by his benefactor Elector Frederick the Wise. The protective custody had been arranged by the Saxon court after the anticipated condemnation of Luther at the imperial Diet of Worms on May 26, 1521. Luther was urged by colleagues and friends during a secret visit to Wittenberg in December 1521 to begin a translation of the New Testament from the Greek text provided by Erasmus. Melanchthon feared that translations of various parts of the New Testament might dismember the whole and thus undermine its significance. Luther threw himself into the project and translated the entire New Testament in eleven weeks, beginning in the middle of December 1521, working with the second edition of the Erasmus text of 1519. Accordingly, he translated about eleven pages every day, using the Greek and Latin texts. Though removed from the resources of Wittenberg University, he managed to have materials brought to him and to consult Melanchthon. He also did additional work of various sorts.

*The New Testament in German (Das neue Tyestament Deutsch)* was published shortly before September 25, 1522 in time for sale at the famous Leipzig Fair (September 29 to October 6). It became known as the "September Bible," printed by Melchior Lotther the Younger in Wittenberg, but without identifying the translator, printer or date of publication; perhaps because the "heretic" Luther was not allowed to publish anything. But since the location, Wittenberg, was revealed Luther became quickly known as the translator. The first edition of three thousand copies of the "September

Bible" was sold for about half a guilder per copy, the weekly earnings of a young traveling carpenter. Another edition was printed in Wittenberg and Basel in December 1522, known as the "December Testament." Luther followed the example of Jerome and added prefaces to the individual New Testament books as well as marginal notes (glosses). These additions offered reasons why Luther rearranged the sequence of the New Testament books. They were to be judged by the fact whether or not they "inculcate" (*treiben*) Christ,[1] that is, whether they expressed the core of the "gospel" as the good news about salvation from evil by Christ alone. Paul's Letter to the Romans clearly did so, summarizing the gospel in the phrase "justification by faith in Christ without the works prescribed by the law" (Rom. 3:28). This is why Luther assigned Romans to the beginning of the New Testament whereas the Letters of James, Jude, and Hebrews, as well as the Revelation of John, belonged to the end. Like the "inauthentic" (apocryphal) books of the Bible, they were insignificant parts of "Holy Scripture," the canon; they were generally good and useful to read but not edifying.

Luther moved quickly to the translation of the Old Testament, planning an edition in three parts: (1) Pentateuch (five books of Moses), (2) Historical books (Joshua to Esther) and (3) Prophetic and poetic books (Job to Malachi). The first part was done and published by Lotther in Wittenberg in 1523. Melanchthon and Aurogallus had worked with Luther. The second part appeared in January 1524, with the cost of printing provided by the Wittenberg artist Lucas Cranach the Elder and the goldsmith Christian Döring. Luther and his team had severe difficulties with this part. Job's peculiar style, simultaneously somber and dazzling, made the work stop and go. Luther remarked that Job would be as unhappy with the translation as he was with his friends! Luther, Melanchthon, and Aurogallus admitted that they had once been able to translate only three lines in four days.

Such delays, also caused by Luther's illness (kidney and gall stones), made him decide to publish the third part without the prophetic books in October 1524, preceded by the publication of the Psalter in September. During his lectures on the "minor prophets" (Jonah, Habakkuk, and Zechariah) from 1524 to 1526 he translated the texts with interpretations and published them in a special edition in January 1528. Two humanists linked to the "radical reformation" with their pacifist stance and mystical tendencies, Ludwig Hätzer and Hans Denck, had published a German translation of the Hebrew prophets in Worms in 1527. Luther grudgingly used their work to enhance his own. He and his team were sweating over the translation of Isaiah, comparing the work to childbirth and to the impossible attempt of the nightingale to teach the cuckoo a song. Since work was dragging, the Book of Isaiah was published separately in 1528.

Negotiations for toleration of the growing reform movement, resulting in the submission of *The Augsburg Confession* to the Diet of Augsburg in 1530, separated Luther from Melanchthon and other friends. He had to stay at the Coburg, another Saxon castle, while his friends defended his cause. So he translated on his own the apocryphal book of the Wisdom of Solomon which had been written in Greek. In the preface he compared the time of Solomon with his own, reminding readers to be aware of tyrants. In 1530 he published the translation of the Book of Daniel since he thought that some of its portions were linked to prophecies about the final ungodly reign of the Turks (Daniel 7:24–26) and to the pope as the antichrist (Daniel 8 and 11). Luther was certain that the fulfillment of these prophecies would bring the end of the world before the translation of the Bible was finished. But he did not interrupt his work. He just added a map of the world to the translation and presented it as a gift to Crown Prince John Frederick of Saxony, who gave Luther the now famous ring depicting Luther's theology in a coat of arms in the form of a rose.[2] The translation of prophetic books appeared in the summer of 1532. Left for translation were only the apocryphal (extra-canonical) books. Luther had great difficulties rendering the proverbial Wisdom of Sirach (Ecclesiasticus) into German in 1532. His colleagues Melanchthon and Caspar Cruciger did much of the work. The bulk of the translation of the apocrypha was mainly done by Luther's colleagues Melanchthon and Justus Jonas. Luther was less interested in this literature, which he labeled in the table of contents of the German Bible as books "unequal to Holy Scripture but good and useful to read." But he did compose the prefaces and marginal notes.

The first complete original High German Luther Bible left the Wittenberg printing shop of Hans Lufft in September 1534. Twelve years had been spent on the translation of the Old Testament. But the German Luther Bible was preceded by a Low German translation in April, edited by Luther's pastor John Bugenhagen and printed by Ludwig Dietz in Lübeck. Another German Bible, combining the work of Luther as well as the "Worms prophets" Hätzer and Denck, was edited by the Swiss humanist Leo Jud and was printed as "the whole Bible" (*Ganze Bibel*) by the enterprising book dealer Christoph Froschauer in Zurich in 1530. The Luther Bible was illustrated by 117 woodcuts from the workshop of Lucas Cranach. Luther supervised the selection. The Bible was unmistakably a *Luther Bible*. Prefaces and glosses read like an evolving catechism of Luther's theology. Its center is the doctrine of "justification by faith alone." The polemic is directed to the papal church. There is concrete advice about obedience to government, marriage, and family, with some critique of moral laxity. German readers quickly adopted this Bible as an indispensable, indeed fascinating, guide for life. That is why it became the cornerstone for an enduring Lutheran culture in Germany.

Luther discussed his work as a Bible translator in two publications. The first appeared in 1530 under the title *On Translating: An Open Letter*, responding to the question of a friend about Luther's translation of Romans 3:28: "We hold that a person is justified without the works of the law, by faith alone" (Lat. *solum*). The friend wanted to know why Luther added the word "alone" to the text. The second writing was composed a year later but was published in 1532 as an introduction to the German Psalter which appeared in 1533. Luther entitled it *Defense of the Translation of the Psalms*.

The first publication identifies the "friend" as someone who had heard of an ardent critique of Luther's "September Bible" of 1522 by the theologian Jerome Emser (1478–1527) who had taught in Erfurt while Luther studied law there. He was engaged by Duke George of Saxony, a zealous opponent of Luther and his cause, to investigate Luther's work of translation and reveal him as an incompetent and prejudicial translator who confused rather than edified simple folk with his German New Testament. The duke prohibited the selling of the "September Bible" in his territory and ordered the confiscation of the copies already sold. But the mandate only increased the sale of the translation. So it was up to Emser to stop the sales. One year after the publication of Luther's translation of the New Testament he published an extensive treatise entitled *Reasons why Luther's translation of the New Testament was rightfully prohibited to be read by common people. With a clear demonstration how, where and in which places Luther turned texts upside down or dealt with them unfaithfully or led them with false marginal notes and prefaces from the ancient Christian track to his own advantage and illusion.* Emser listed 1,400 "errors," but satirically conceded that Luther had translated more charmingly and with sweeter tones than some of his predecessors had done. But this only made his work more dangerous. Luther's prefaces and marginal notes became the chief targets of Emser's attack because they showed how Luther interpreted texts without considering the unquestionable authority of ecclesiastical doctrines based on the Latin Vulgate. Duke George also requested that Emser offer his own translation of the New Testament to show how wrong Luther was. Emser went to work and published his own translation in 1527. But in reality it was only a corrected version of Luther's work, looking like his and containing the same illustrations. Duke George offered a preface justifying the confiscation of Luther's translation with the accusation that Luther had destroyed ancient, dignified tradition, especially in regard to worship and piety. That is why Emser's work was to be a welcome substitute grounded in the tradition of the old "orthodox" faith. Luther's Dominican opponents, led by John

Dietenberger and John Eck, edited and advertised Emser's "Catholic" Luther Bible in thirty-eight editions from 1534. But this Bible never became a real competitor.

Luther began his treatise on translating with the advice to the reader that his papal critics opposed everything he did, having declared him a heretic. They had no idea what faith really meant, he contended, nor did they know good German. Luther called Emser a "scribbler" and "slanderer," unworthy of a response because he and his circle could not even come close to understanding any ancient Greek text, be it the Bible or Aristotle. Then he defended the addition of the word "alone" because it conveys the sense of the text in German. When Germans speak of two things, one of which is affirmed and the other denied, they use the word "alone" (*allein*) along with the word "no" (*kein*). Example: "The farmer brings grain *alone* (*allein*) and no (*kein*) money" (in idiomatic English "alone" becomes "only" and "no" becomes "not"; thus, "The farmer brings *only* grain and *not* money"). A totally literal translation would not convey the way people speak at home and in the marketplace. Luther confessed that he and his Wittenberg co-workers had to sweat and toil like a road-gang trying to remove boulders and clods to clear the way. But they found the best translation by listening to the way people spoke ("looking at their mouth," *auf das Maul sehen*). Example: If Christ's saying in the official Latin Bible, the Vulgate, were translated in its strictly literal sense it would read, "Out of the abundance of the heart the mouth speaks" (*Ex abundatia cordis os loquitur*, Matt. 12:34; Luke 6:45). But Germans would render it in a proverbial manner, "What fills the heart overflows the mouth" (*Wem das Herz voll ist, dem geht der Mund über*).

Luther's favorite example of how to translate best into German is the beginning of the popular "Magnificat" from the first words of the angelic salutation of Mary (Luke 1:28), "Hail Mary, full of grace" (Lat. *Ave Maria gratia plena*). Luther again refused to offer a literal translation since he thought that Germans would not use the word "full" in connection with grace because it was usually linked to being "full" with beer or money. Instead he translated, "Thou gracious one" (Ger. *Du holdselige*). The common people would have the angel say, "Hello there, Mary," meaning "God greet you, you dear Mary" (from the popular German greeting on arrival, *Gott grüsse dich, liebe Maria*, comparable to the English "God be with you"). Using such common language, Luther mused, would have made his hypocritical pious opponents hang themselves because he would have destroyed the salutation for them. But he did settle on the translation "dear (*liebe*) Mary" because the German word "love" (*Liebe*) expresses a sentiment that rings through the heart as it is reflected in the Greek *kecharitomene* (Luke 1:28), which means something or someone very lovely and attractive. Luther insisted on being right since no one had tried harder than he did to communicate with Germans in daily life.

Luther also created a linguistic think-tank, known as *collegium biblicum.* It consisted of Melanchthon, Aurogallus, Cruciger and the secretary George Rörer who also recorded many of Luther's lectures and sermons. Sometimes the group was joined by three other colleagues, Justus Jonas, Veit Dietrich and Bernhard Ziegler, all former students and/or strong supporters of Luther. Occasionally, literal meaning prevailed even though it was not easily understood in German. Example: John 6:27 has Christ say, "It is on him that the Father has set his seal" (*versiegelt* in German based on the Greek). It might have been better to substitute "signified" as the Vulgate had it (*gezeichnet,* or "marked" in English). But "sealed" means endowed with the Holy Spirit and thus conveys better the relationship between Christ and God, as John had intended. With such examples Luther wanted to defend his addition of the word "alone" to the German version of Romans 3:28. His final defense is the fact that the word highlights the passage as the fundamental text for the chief article of the Christian faith, "justification by faith alone." Luther's opponents claimed that the word "alone" was offensive because it tempted common people to exclude good deeds from faith. But Paul, Luther retorted, never meant to exclude "the works of the law" from Christian life. On the contrary, he insisted that "good works" are necessary, but not to earn salvation; that was done by Christ alone. The works need to be done as a witness to Christ in the world. If they were done to appease the wrath of God, for merit, they would dishonor Christ's ministry. Luther even regretted not having added another word in the translation, namely, the word "any" (*aller,* or *alle*), so that the saying would read "without the works of any laws."

The second treatise on translation, *Defense of the Translation of the Psalms,* deals largely with Luther's use of ancient Hebrew. He had intended to publish his explanation of the principles and procedures of translating the Hebrew Psalms together with the German publication of the whole Psalter. But the pressures of work prevented him from doing so. Now he was ready to defend his translation against the criticism that it was not literal enough, or did not agree with Jewish interpretations. Luther told readers that Hebrew is a language filled with rich images or pictures of the mind. Moreover, its translation depends heavily on the use of the rabbinical punctuation substituting for vowels.[3] Consequently, words and phrases often may have quite different meanings, and a strictly literal translation may miss what the text has in mind. Luther's major illustration of the problem is the translation of Psalm 68, which he liked because of its picturesque description of God's power over unjust nations. Verse 30 disclosed the difficulties of translation because the meaning of the Hebrew is uncertain. But Luther agreed with the rabbinical understanding: The psalm is a prayer to God to ward off the wild animals, bulls among calves, who have a large following. They signify greedy tyrants, politicians, and priests, who lust after money (or tribute); and they dislike the word of God that demands the sharing of riches with the needy. The phrase "who lust after money" can also be translated more literally with "who run with the tramplers for the sake of money."

Luther's translation team, the *collegium biblicum*, discussed the matter in great detail and decided to modify the phrase to read "who do everything for the sake of money" (*die da* treiben *um des Geldes willen*) in the edition of 1531 even though it appeared in the more literal translation in the first edition of the Psalter in 1524. Luther defended such shifts in translation by insisting on the best idiomatic German expression of the Hebrew sense. He insisted that one must always ask, "What would a German say in this situation?" Once the best meaning is found, Luther declared, one should let go of the literal meaning of a Hebrew word. Example: Psalm 68:13 speaks of "sheepfolds," "wings of the dove covered with silver" and "pinions with green gold." Verse 12 is much clearer by singing of kings who make war and turn over the spoils to the housewives. Luther suggested that the sense of verse 13 should be derived from verse 12: the kings have an army with shining armor, looking like a dove reflecting the colors of white and red in the sun as if they were silver and gold; the kings signify the apostles reflecting the glow of the Holy Spirit, taking the field against the devil and, after being victorious, turning people over as booty to the mistress of the house, the church, to govern and to lead. Luther recommended that such a "Christian" translation of Psalm 68 should be continued in verse 15 ("O mighty mountain of Bashan...a many-peaked mountain"). Here, he translated "great mountain" as "a fruitful region," called "fat land" or "lard-pit" (*Schmalzgruben*). For Germans like to think of food when they read the text. Another example is Psalm 91:5–6 ("You will not fear the terror of the night, or the arrow that flies by day, or the pestilence that stalks in the darkness, or the destruction that wastes at noonday"). Luther translated literally, but pointed readers to what he thought was implied by the "obscure and veiled words." "Fear of the night" points to threats, hatred, envy and harm, symbolizing hostility to the word of God; "arrows" are slander, contradiction, reviling, backbiting, symbolizing papal bulls, imperial edicts, factious spirits and other enemies Luther himself encountered. "Pestilence" points to intrigues, tricks, and pacts of the adversaries to the Word of God; "destruction" points to open persecution of devout Christians guided by the Word of God. Luther also compared his interpretation to that of the revered monk

Bernard of Clairvaux (1090–1153) who, however, was too "monkish" in his listing of vices (pride, cupidity, etc.).

Luther told readers that these and other examples of translating the Psalter reveal his "principle," namely, at times retaining the words quite literally, and at times rendering only the meaning. If someone criticized this principle, Luther declared, the critics should try to offer a good translation of the Hebrew word *chen*. It could mean "grace," "favor," "dear," all pointing to "grace" (*Gnade*), Luther's favorite translation. He would offer a hefty sum of money, Luther contended, if someone were to offer a totally acceptable translation of *chen* throughout the Old Testament.

Luther clearly translated the Bible from the viewpoint of what he, and others in the Christian tradition, viewed as its center: the Christ event, foreshadowed in the Old Testament and attested in the New Testament as an actual happening. Accordingly, his German Bible was *one* comprehensive "Holy Scripture" rather than a collection of writings with equal value in their own right. But Luther was different from other translators like Jerome in that he wanted to render the central meaning as well as the literary detail into a language used at home and in the marketplace. As a consequence, Luther expanded the use of consonants, and created new ways of pronunciation and composite words like *Sündenbock* (scapegoat), *Lockvogel* (decoy-bird), *Lückenbüsser* (stand-in) and similar words. In addition, he created new sentence structures with a tendency to put the verb at the end of the sentence. Luther always had a conversation with the Bible to let it speak to him with verve and rhythm. Readers could quickly make biblical sayings their own and recall them later. Composers of motets found it easy to use such texts in their compositions. Specific sayings exhibited alliterations, as does Matthew 5:16, "*Also lasset euer Licht leuchten vor den Menschen*" ("Thus let your light shine before all the people"). The words of institution in the celebration of Holy Communion were tuned to a solemn "a" sound (Matt. 26:25), "*Da sie aber assen, nahm Jesus das Brot, dankte und brachs und gab es seinen Jüngern und sprach…*". The Pauline description of love in 1 Corinthians 13 sounds like a poem in German. The Revelation of John was illustrated with twenty-one woodcuts from the workshop of the popular Wittenberg artist Lucas Cranach. Some disclose Luther's polemical allusions: a picture of Rome serves as illustration for the fall of Babel; the monster from the deep is crowned with a papal tiara; chapter 21 offered illustrations showing jewels from the Saxon treasury, supplied by Luther's good friend, Court Chaplain Georg Spalatin.

Philologists agree that Luther did not create the German language for subsequent generations. Three literary variants were used in Germany when Luther began his Bible translation: a "low" German, an "east-middle" German and a "south-east" German. The east-middle German became dominant during Luther's reformation because of its use in the rapidly increasing flow of Reformation tracts. Luther was already bilingual when he began his work as a Bible translator; he grew up learning Latin and "Saxon German." It was his intention to provide a German Bible for everyone in Germany, just as Jerome had supplied a Latin one for all of Western Christendom. Like Jerome, he first listened to the language of the noble and powerful. Accordingly, Luther used as his linguistic base the bureaucratic language of the Saxon court in Meissen, known as "Meissen officialese" (*Meissner Kanzleisprache*), which was used by all nobles in Germany and was preferred by printers. From this base Luther tried to reach all Germans, especially the common people. His extraordinary linguistic creativity is revealed in the way in which he combined noble, bureaucratic, and common idiomatic expressions. Thus Luther created an idiomatic linguistic consensus by rendering the ancient texts of the Bible into a language people used at home and in the marketplace. Using German mythology, proverbial wisdom, and even musical compositions, he mixed with great flair existing diverse dialect expressions in such a way that his readers became attracted by what he told them. He used existing German proverbs to encourage Germans to criticize a secularized pope ("if you have eyes, don't stick them in a bag," that is, clearly discern what the pope does); and he employed folk songs to announce the fall of Rome ("the cuckoo's fallen to his death, from off a hollow tree"). In this way, the creative, idiomatic language of the most popular German mind, the "Wittenberg nightingale" (as some admirers dubbed Luther), found its way into the world of common communication. If the German Bible had not become the most popular book in German households, a common German language would not have been born. When Luther's Bible appeared it was greeted like a new-born baby. Theologians, pastors and ordinary people expressed their delight that finally the Bible had come to be part of their lives. Even Luther's opponents talked with faint praise about his Bible, conceding that some had begun to learn portions by heart. It is, therefore, no surprise that Luther's "Bible German" became the ruling literary language within a century of its debut at the Wartburg castle, by the middle of the seventeenth century.

Besides, printers did everything possible to sell Luther's German Bible. The Wittenberg printer Hans Lufft joined two other businessmen to form a consortium dedicated to profit from the sale of Bibles. They, and others, quickly became rich without sharing any royalties with Luther who never requested any. When he died in 1546 half a million Bibles had been sold. The sales were accompanied by continual revisions of the translation, reflecting the evolution of a common German language rooted in Luther's translation.

Special luxury editions were sold from 1541 with an imprint by Luther, usually a Bible verse with a brief exposition. Such a Bible was very expensive and was bought only by nobles and other rich people. Typical is Luther's imprint of Joshua 1:8, "This book of law shall not depart out of your mouth." Luther's comment: "This is a splendid promise for him who likes to read, studies the Bible and does so with diligence. For he will be happy and will live wisely." To Luther the Bible was not just a book but a word addressing and changing life: "The Scriptures are a vast forest, but there is no tree in it that I have not shaken with my hand...This German Bible (this is not praise for myself but the work praises itself) is so good and precious that it is better than all other versions, Greek and Latin, and one can find more in it than in all the commentaries."[4]

### Notes

1. Luther used the verb *treiben* (literally "to drive," badly translated "inculcate") to indicate that biblical texts are "Holy Scripture" and/or "Word of God" when they are "driven by Christ" (*was Christum treibet*), "the true test by which to judge all [biblical] books." See his *Prefaces to the New Testament*, 1546 (1522), LW 35, 396.
2. A golden signet ring depicts a blue ground on which is a white rose within a *masoretgh*, golden circle; a red, glowing heart in the rose, with a black cross embedded in it. The cross signifies faith which makes the heart glow; the rose signifies peace and joy; the blue ground signifies hope; and the golden ring depicts eternity. All are consequences of the Christ event which, to Luther, was the focus of his life and work. Cf. Eric W. Gritsch, *Martin – God's Court Jester. Luther in Retrospect*, new edn. (Ramsey, NJ: Sigler Press, 1990; rpt. of 1983 edn.), 89.
3. The Hebrew text of the Old Testament supplied vowels by a system of punctuation. It was called the "masoretic" text (from the Hebrew *masoreth*, meaning "tradition"). Jewish scholars provided this text during AD 600–800. But translators and interpreters of the Hebrew Bible also used the unpointed texts in order to increase their meaning. Luther may have used the four volumes of the rabbinical Bible printed in 1516/17 in Venice by the Flemish Catholic printer Daniel Bomberg. The edition was prepared by a Jewish scholar, Felice da Pratio, who converted to Christianity and became a Friar of the Augustinians, Luther's order in Erfurt. See Guy Bedouelle, "Editions of the Bible," in Hans J. Hillerbrand, ed., *The Oxford Encyclopedia of the Reformation*, 4 vols. (New York and Oxford: Oxford University Press, 1996), 1:158. Luther's work with the Old Testament is summarized and analyzed by Heinrich Bornkamm, *Luther and the Old Testament*, new edn., trans. Eric W. Gritsch and Ruth C. Gritsch (Ramsey, NJ: Sigler Press, 2000. Rpt. 1969 edn.).
4. Table Talk No. 674 (early 1530s). LW, 54, 121. Table Talk No. 5324 (1540), LW, 54, 408.

# 5 Luther as an interpreter of Holy Scripture

OSWALD BAYER

Translated by Mark Mattes

## THE BIBLE AS A MIRROR OF THE WORLD

The philologist Friedrich Nietzsche maintained that Luther's translation of the Bible was "the best German book."[1] In connection to Luther's work, Goethe designated the Bible a "mirror of the world"[2] and thereby saw the world of this one book and the "book of the world" enfolded within each other.

Researchers of the German language are to a great extent agreed that Luther, not only with his translation of the Bible but also with his prefaces to the Bible, sermons, *Small Catechism*, and his songs, pamphlets, and tracts, is an event in the history of German literature to which no other can be compared. The event is of speech that comes out of hearing. Luther is linguistically creative by means of hearing and translating.

To recognize Luther's significance for the German language, one must not, as has indeed happened, make Luther into the creator of the modern High German literary language. Nevertheless, Klopstock wrote that among no nation has a single person so shaped the language of a whole people as Luther has done.[3] In fact, Luther's language – above all the language of his translation of the Bible – became the presupposition of understanding and communication throughout the whole of the German language.

Even Luther's sharpest opponents recognized the influence of his translation of the Bible. Johannes Cochlaeus had to admit:

> Luther's New Testament, through its printing, was disseminated to such an amazing extent that even cobblers and women and other simple people, if they had ever learned German at all and in so far as they were Lutherans, read it with greatest desire as the well of all truth. They carried the translation with themselves on their bosoms in order to impress it on their memory by means of frequent reading.[4]

Yet Luther's translation of the Bible had an effect not only in Protestantism but also, from the very beginning, in Roman Catholicism. It was even used by his opponents. Thus it grew into a common element in the communication and understanding of an entire people.

The common language was learned and used not only by means of the interpretation of Scripture, preaching, and the hymns of the worship service, but beyond that by means of reading the Bible at home and in school. On this basis, words and phrases from the translation of the Bible became indispensable in everyday life and even proverbial.

Until the period of the Enlightenment, the standard for German grammar was constructed from the Bible and Luther's other books. Luther's language also emphatically influenced the language of German literature. It was of decisive significance that until well into the nineteenth century Luther's translation of the Bible, in addition to the hymnbook and the catechism, was by far the most important means of instruction. This was not only for instruction in religion and for confirmation, but before that in the German language itself. The catechism and the Bible were the primers.

With Luther's translation of the Bible and its language, its figures and stories, whether of Abraham or Job, Sarah or Ruth, but above all the story of the life, suffering, and death of Jesus, an entire world was appropriated – the linguistic and picture world of specific archetypes, prototypes, models of orientation, and possibilities for identification. This linguistically shaped world interpreted its hearers and readers by allowing them to grow into it – permitting them to interpret themselves by means of this language and its images and enabling them to understand themselves by it. There are books that contain a great deal of the world – Homer or Shakespeare or the work of Goethe. But no book contains as much world as the Bible – as much world as Luther's Bible.

Still, the world, and the language of German history within the history of the world, are certainly not a purely biblical culture. If the history of the church is the history not only of the understanding of the Bible but also of its misunderstanding and misuse, how much more does this apply to universal history in which, in the choir and cacophony of many voices of most varied attractions and threats, demands and promises, the language and world of the Bible are intertwined with universal history but in no way removed from rivalry with it? Thus we quickly reach the boundary of what can be said in a literary and historical way where Luther is concerned. On the basis of the ambiguous effects that always remain – of receptions, overlappings, and distortions – we do not come to a true understanding of Luther's language and world. Yet we must observe and work through these effects, because our view is formed, indeed even misinformed, by them. Therefore, from the effects let us attempt to go back to the word that has brought about these effects – indeed, to Luther's work itself as it is disclosed from its sources.

These sources – which in the Weimar Edition fill many volumes – are a whole library of various texts: lectures on the exposition of Old and New Testament books (Luther was indeed by profession a doctor and professor of Holy Scripture!), transcripts of sermons, polemical writings, writings of consolation, prefaces, letters, disputation theses, table talk, fables, and songs. They delight, teach, exhort, comfort, rebuke, and attack. They are gross, biting, extremely ironical, but also offer tender tones – depending upon to whom the word is addressed: the hardened or the one whose conscience is ridden with *angst*,[5] the scholar, "councilors of all cities in Germany,"[6] the "Christian nobility of the German nation,"[7] or on the other hand the "papacy of Rome, founded by the devil."[8] Luther knew how to distinguish.

So many different addressees, so many different types of speech and address, so many different literary forms! Can one in all this discern a leading note? Can we at the same time recognize why Luther wrote such good German as no other, why for him German was really a language (and not a script) which was first of all to be spoken and not written, to be heard and not read? Why did he want the Bible so to be translated that it "pierces and rings through the heart, through all the senses," as he states it in his *On Translating: An Open Letter*?[9] Why for him was the word embodied, vocal, not first of all inward, but oral and public: voice and sound? Why for him was the word not a sign of a meaning, but the reality itself that affects – that kills and makes alive?

### THE SPEECH-ACT OF PROMISE

Because Luther knew that spoken language deals with death and life, being and non-being – without word no world –, he pushed for unequivocalness and clarity. He himself took care that in everything that he thought, researched, spoke, and wrote a single tone could be heard: the freedom of faith which is indebted to the reliable word, the promise of God.[10]

God's promise is the source of Luther's new understanding of language and the world. What is meant by it results from the toilsome way in which Luther arrived at its understanding. His "Reformation Discovery" happened in the wake of a deeply profound reflection on the sacrament of penance, which had been required of him by the monstrosity of indulgences. At first, Luther understood the priestly word of absolution: "I absolve you of your sins!" as an activity of declaration, which states something already present. The priest sees the remorse, takes it as a sign of the divine justification – the divine absolution occurring already in the one being absolved but unknown to him – and lets this appear as such. He states it for the assurance of the one being absolved. By this means the word of absolution is understood as a judgment in the sense of a statement.

Luther initially remained within this ancient understanding of language that was still wholly framed by the milieu which Augustine inherited above all from the Stoics and which still widely dominates today. According to this ancient understanding, language is a system of signs that refer to objects or situations or of signs that express an emotion. In either case the sign is – as a statement or as an expression – not the reality itself.

That the linguistic sign is itself the reality, that it represents not an absent but a present reality,[11] was Luther's great hermeneutical discovery, his "Reformation Discovery" in the strict sense. He made it first (1518) in reflection on the sacrament of penance. That the sign itself is the reality means, with reference to the absolution, that the sentence "I absolve you of your sins!" is no judgment which only ascertains what already exists, therefore assuming an inner, divine, proper absolution. Rather, the word of absolution is a speech-act that first establishes a state of affairs, first creates a relationship – between the one in whose name it is spoken, and the one to whom it is spoken and who believes the promise.

This speech-act is an effective, active word that establishes community and therein frees and makes certain. It does what it says. It says what it does. In the institutions of Baptism and the Lord's Supper, too, Luther discovered such an effective word – just as in the story of Christmas ("Fear not!"), in the story of Easter, and indeed in the whole Bible, including the story of creation, which Luther understood as a promise, as his translation of Psalm 33:4b indicates, "what he promises, that he certainly does." God's promise is the concrete manner in which he introduces himself: "I am the Lord, your God!" and in which Jesus is present as God's Word: reliable and clear – clearly liberating and making certain. One cannot remind oneself of such freedom and certainty in a solitary, inner monologue. It is guaranteed and constitutes itself only by means of the promise of one other person (not only that of the officiating priest or preacher!), who gives it to me in the name of Jesus. I cannot give the promise to myself. It must be given to me. For only in this way is it true, bringing freedom and certainty.

What this certainty involves becomes clear in a later text from the *Lectures on Genesis*, which precisely gives Luther's theological bequest:

I have been baptized. I have been absolved. In this faith I die. No matter what trials and cares confront me from now on, I will certainly not be shaken; for He who said: "He who believes and is baptized will be saved" (Mark 16:16) and "Whatever you loose on earth shall be loosed in heaven" (Matt. 16:19) and "This is My body, This is My blood, which is shed for you for the remission of sins" (cf. Matt. 26:26, 28) – He cannot deceive or lie. This is certainly true.[12]

In another place, in the *Large Commentary on Galatians*, he said: "And this is the reason why our theology is certain: it snatches us away from ourselves and places us outside ourselves, so that we do not depend on our own strength, conscience, experience, person, or works but depend on that which is outside ourselves, that is, on the promise and truth of God, which cannot deceive."[13]

Accordingly, in distinction to every metaphysical construction of the doctrine of God, God's truth and will are not abstract attributes, but that which is orally and publicly related as concrete words of comfort to a particular hearer in a particular situation. "God" is grasped as the one who in the oral word promises himself to a person in such a way that this one can rely on him. God's truth lies in his faithfulness, with which he stands to his given word. God has so bound himself in the baptismal promise given once and for all that the conflict-ridden person, strengthened and encouraged by the oral word of preaching, may subject God ever anew to the one, specific promise: He can, as Luther drastically says, "hold" this promise "up" to God[14] – rub it under his nose – and in such "defiance" of faith one is torn away from presumption as well as from despair and anxiety. "For this is our assurance and defiance... that God wishes to be our Father, forgive us our sin, and bestow everlasting life on us."[15]

### SALVATION EXPERIENCED

To perceive for the first time such a promise which one can "hold up" to God denotes the reformation change in Luther's life and theology. With the promise, with the reliable word, and with trust in it is at once named the source of the experience from which flows what Luther had to say.[16] Word and faith are the core of his theology.

"Theology" is not only that which a doctor and professor of Holy Scripture must practice but what everyone must practice. By experiencing the confrontation of the heard promise with his experience of the world and the self, everyone comes upon that temptation for which one can only be sustained by prayer. Thus Luther finds three characteristics of theology: *oratio, tentatio, meditatio* – prayer, temptation, and the continual intercourse with the biblical word, from which God's promise is to be heard.[17] Faith in this promise is nothing other than prayer. In what it consists, Luther emphatically said in the first of two sections of his *Sermons on Prayer* (1519), the first comprehensive attestation of his reformational understanding of prayer:

> To begin with, two things are necessary so that a prayer is good and so that it is heard. First, we must have a promise or a pledge from God. We must reflect on this promise and remind God of it – hold it up to him – and in that way be emboldened to pray with confidence. If God had not enjoined us to prayer and if he had not promised fulfillment, no creature would be able to obtain so much as a kernel of grain despite all his petitions.
>
> It follows from this that no one obtains anything from God by his own virtue or the worthiness of his prayer, but solely by reason of the boundless mercy of God, who, by anticipating all our prayers and desires, induces us through his gracious promise and assurance to petition and to ask so that we might learn how much more he provides for us and how he is more willing to give than we to take or to seek [Eph. 3:20]. God wants to encourage us to prayer with confidence, since he offers us more than that for which we are able to ask.
>
> Second, it is necessary that we never doubt the promise of the truthful and faithful God. He promised fulfillment, yes, he even commands us to pray, so that we will be filled with a sure and firm faith that we will be heard. Thus God declares in Matthew 21 [:22] and in Mark 11 [:24], "Therefore I tell you, whatsoever you ask in prayer, believe that you receive it, and you certainly will." . . . We should cheerfully rely on these and similar promises and commands and pray with true confidence.[18]

In such confidence, such reliance on the promise – on the reliable word – anxiety is overcome. This anxiety is that of sin in the face of death and the devil, and in the face of the last judge, the Christ of the Last Judgment, whose voice is heard in all worldly demands that afflict me, requiring my accountability and threatening me with punitive righteousness. The liberation that Luther came to share was not first of all from earthly authorities and institutions, not even the restricting rites of the ecclesiastical hierarchy, including that of the papacy, but it was the forgiveness of sins occurring unambiguously in the word of absolution as a pronouncement of eternal salvation: "where there is forgiveness of sin, there is also life and salvation,"[19] eternal community.

Luther has something to say about this experienced salvation and liberation, something unheard of and incomparably new, "good news," and "of it I must both speak and sing."[20] He said and sang this story of liberation in a dramatic song:[21]

Fast bound in Satan's chains I lay,
Death brooded darkly o'er me,
Sin was my torment night and day...
But daily deeper still I fell;
My life became a living hell,
The pangs of hell I suffered.

To me he said: "Stay close to me,
I am your rock and castle.
Your ransom I myself will be;
For you I strive and wrestle;
For I am yours, and you are mine,
And where I am you may remain;
The foe shall not divide us."[22]

What a promise! About it one must sing. For "God has cheered our hearts and minds through his dear Son, whom he gave for us to redeem us from sin, death, and the devil. He who believes this earnestly cannot be quiet about it. But he must gladly and willingly sing and speak about it so that others also may come and hear."[23]

The story narrated in the song and the promise of the one who speaks: "Stay close to me!" is not only Martin Luther's story. Many others agreed with it and saw in Luther's change of life their own change of life. Albrecht Dürer confessed that Luther had helped him "from greatest anxiety"[24] with his reformational word.

That was the anxiety of a whole epoch. Consequently, it is understandable that the liberation worked epochally. The answer to the question of grace from an individual who suffered in deepest anxiety in the face of God's judgment became for many others the basis and confession of their faith. Of course, this answer became twisted and misused. Scarcely had Luther begun to preach about the freedom of a Christian than he had already to fight against its misuse.

## THE ADDRESSED PERSON IN ITS KNOWLEDGE OF THE WORLD AND THE SELF

The echo which Luther's voice found cannot sufficiently explain its power and authority. For that one must pursue its self-understanding.

In this way, one is led deeply into the Bible – into the history between God and humanity witnessed by it and in turn formed by it. It is not only the history of Israel and the church, but – reflected in it, but reaching far beyond it – the whole history of nature and humanity: of the creation fallen, redeemed, and sighing for fulfillment. Hence, the Bible is for Luther in fact, as Goethe said, a "mirror of the world."

The Bible is a "mirror of the world" in a quite specific way. It can best be recognized from the Psalms, which Luther regarded as containing the whole Bible in a kernel and therefore designated a "little Bible."[25] In the *Preface to the Psalter* (1528) Luther, immediately addressing the single reader as he so frequently did, wrote: "...if you would see the holy Christian Church painted in living color and shape, comprehended in one little picture, then take up the Psalter. There you have a fine, bright, pure mirror that will show you what Christendom is. Indeed you will find in it also yourself and the true *gnothi seauton*, as well as God himself and all creatures"[26] – the whole creation and history of the world.

The little Bible, the Psalter, like the entire Bible does not lead one away from the world, but instead deeply into it. It leads to knowledge of self by leading to knowledge of the world. There is no knowledge of self apart from knowledge of the world! But both are embraced and penetrated by the knowledge of God who justifies the sinner.

This experience, which is the most individualizing one because it individuates my own self to the greatest depths as a sinner who lives through and by faith in the promise of the forgiveness of sin, is at the same time that experience which I can have only in the worldwide communion of saints, in a community which reaches through all times. The Psalter, Luther said, leads you into the communion of saints, "For it teaches you in joy, fear, hope, and sorrow to think and speak as all the saints have thought and spoken."[27] The true universal community of communication is that of the justified sinners who pray the Psalms. A double "earnestness and life" are "in the words" of the Psalter, which the saints "speak to God and with God."[28]

If we hear Luther's further exposition of this twofold earnestness of life from the language of the Psalter, then it discloses fully for us his understanding of language and the world. Luther's use of the Psalter is the key in general to the understanding of his use of language, his linguistic power, as well as his experience of his world and life.

Where does one find finer words of joy than in the psalms of praise and thanksgiving? There you look into the hearts of all the saints, as into fair and pleasant gardens, yes, as into heaven itself. There you see what fine and pleasant flowers of the heart spring up from all sorts of fair and happy thoughts toward God, because of his blessings. On the other hand, where do you find deeper, more sorrowful, more pitiful words of sadness than in the psalms of lamentation? There again you look into the hearts of all the saints, as into death, yes, as into hell itself. How gloomy and dark it is there, with all kinds of troubled forebodings about the wrath of God!

Likewise, "when they speak of fear and hope, they use such words that no painter could so depict for you fear or hope, and no Cicero or other orator so portray them."[29]

A reflection on the rhetorical means also used by Luther allows one to recognize only insufficiently how Luther's feeling for life and the world is conceived linguistically. It is the language of the Bible that discloses for him the world and does so in a wholly specific way. By means of the word of the Bible he finds himself as one addressed in the world and as one who answers – either this or that way. For with God's self-introduction: "I am the Lord, your God" we are addressed in a way that cannot in any way be revoked. With this self-introduction of God in his address to us it is said "that we are such creatures with which God wants eternally and undyingly to speak," "whether it should be in wrath or in grace."[30]

The humanity of the person consists in that he or she is addressed and therefore can hear, answer, and even speak himself or herself. Therefore, in distinction to the Western philosophical tradition, which sees the person distinguished through its intellect from the other living creatures, Luther by contrast sees "nothing more powerful, or nobler work of a person . . . than speaking," since "through speaking the person is most distinguished from other animals, more than through character or other works."[31]

## WITHOUT THE WORD NO WORLD

God rules the world with his reliable and loving word.[32] Whoever shuts himself off to this word, for him heart, mouth, and hand are closed. The entire world becomes too narrow for him. He experiences anxiety and suffers God's wrath.

Whoever shuts himself off to the reliable word, the promise, loses the world as a home and trades it in as a wasteland. The world is then no longer the medium of a promise to me by which I am addressed by God, and in which I am set within a space granted for living that is governed by the rhythm of day and night, summer and winter, youth and old age, and in which I can enjoy my life. If the world is not believed in as something promised, then it is experienced as a "terrible naturalness,"[33] as inexorable law – inexorable, compulsive necessity which says: you must wrest a meaning from this chaos, this fearful naturalness in its whole indeterminateness;

you must first give a meaning for this chaotic world from out of itself; you must establish order. If the world is not believed as something promised, then it becomes, as Nietzsche appropriately said, "a thousands wastes, silent, cold."[34] In such silence and such coldness Luther experiences the wrath of God. All creatures around me – even if it were only a rustling leaf that frightens me[35] – make me know and speak of this wrath, but mostly it is spoken in my own heart in its spite and in its despondency. Luther does not recognize anything neutral beyond wrath and grace. Wrath and grace – therein lies the fundamental dual focus of his feeling of the world, his language, and his understanding of history. In this is founded the struggle which is to be carried out and which Luther did carry out his whole life long.

Luther has not been trapped by the temptation to seek another clarity than the one of the reliable word of promise. Therefore the world is not transparent for him, not wholly calculable and intelligible. His theology is devoid of any historical-philosophical speculation of unity. To the degree to which it contradicts such speculations – for instance, the illusion of invariable progress within the history of the world – it is reasonable, realistic, and fully cognizant of the experience of the concrete world.

The much referred to, although frequently misunderstood, "secularity" of Luther is to be understood as theological through and through. For with it, the world is perceived as created by God's reliable word and as sustained despite persistent threats. Its perception is that of justice and grace.[36]

### Notes

1. Friedrich Nietzsche, *Beyond Good and Evil* (1886), #247 in *Basic Writings*, trans. Helen Zimmern (New York: Modern Library, 1947), 560–61 (*Werke Kritische Gesamtausgabe*, ed. G. Colli and M. Montinari [Berlin: Walter de Gruyter, 1968], VI-2, 199): "The preacher was the only one in Germany who knew the weight of a syllable or a word, in what manner a sentence strikes, springs, rushes, flows, and comes to a close; he alone had a conscience in his ears . . . The masterpiece of German prose is therefore with good reason the masterpiece of its greatest preacher: the *Bible* has hitherto been the best German book. Compared with Luther's Bible, almost everything else is merely 'literature' – something which has not grown in Germany, and therefore has not taken and does not take root in German hearts, as the Bible has done."
2. "Letter to Zelter," November 14, 1816 (*Artemis-Gedenkausgabe der Werke, Briefe und Gespräche* [Munich: Artemis, 1949], vol. XXI, Letters for the years 1814–32; 195–98, 196).
3. Fr. G. Klopstock, *Die deutsche Gelehrtenrepublik*, Part 1 (1774), 170.
4. J. Cochlaeus, *Commentaria de Actis et Scriptis Martini Lutheri Saxonis* (1549), 55 (translated from Latin).
5. Compare "Pro veritate inquirenda et timoratis conscientiis consolandis" (1518), WA 1, 629–33.

6. *To the Councilmen of All Cities in Germany That They Establish and Maintain Christian Schools* (1524), LW 45, 341–78 (WA 15, 9–53).

7. *To the Christian Nobility of the German Nation Concerning the Reform of the Christian Estate* (1520), LW 44, 117–217 (WA 6, 381–469).

8. *Against the Roman Papacy: An Institution of the Devil* (1545), LW 41, 257–376 (WA 54, 195–299).

9. LW 35, 192 (1530) (WA 30/ii [627–46] 639, 2).

10. The following is a synopsis of Oswald Bayer, *Promissio: Geschichte der reformatorischen Wende in Luthers Theologie*, 2nd edn., 1989 (1974) (Darmstadt: Wissenschaftliche Buchgesellschaft) in various places, especially 68f. and 249–53. Compare Oswald Bayer, *Theologie* (Gütersloh: Gütersloher Verlagshaus, 1994), 438–53. The methodological and material issues that arise in connection with the question about Luther's "Reformation Discovery" in his life and theology are solved if attention is paid to the multiple meanings of "Reformational." Its essence lies not in the discovery of a *iustitia dei* that can be separated from the manner and medium of the self-disclosure of God's righteousness in the trustworthy message of the promise of salvation (*promissio*). Compare Oswald Bayer, "Die reformatorische Wende in Luthers Theologie" (ZThK 66, 1969, 115–50); 115–22, particularly 119 ("To my knowledge adequate attention until now has never been paid to a third series of retrospective autobiographical remarks that are characterized by the term 'promissio'") and the conclusion (121): "The materials we have examined so far indicate the necessity, first, of viewing the content of Luther's idea of 'Reformational' as having been influenced by the '*promissio*' interpretation of '*De captivitate*', and second, of interpreting the formulas of the retrospective remarks that are not characterized by use of the term '*promissio*' from this very perspective."

11. "Signum philosophicum est nota absentis rei, signum theologicum est nota praesentis rei": WA BR 4, 666 (Nos. 5106, 1540).

12. LW 8, 193–94 (1545) (WA 44, 720, 30–36 [on Gen. 48:21]); translated from Latin.

13. LW 27, 387 (1535) (WA 40/i, 589, 25–28 [on Gal. 4:6]); translated from Latin.

14. The *Large Catechism* (1529) in *The Book of Concord: The Confessions of the Evangelical Lutheran Church*, ed. Robert Kolb and Timothy J. Wengert (Minneapolis: Fortress Press, 2000), 443, 21 and 444, 28 (*Die Bekenntnisschriften der evangelisch-lutherischen Kirche*, 3rd rev. edn. [Göttingen: Vandenhoeck & Ruprecht, 1930] 667, 1f. and 669, 3, see also WA 30/i, 196, 2 and 197, 9). For further references that emphasize the importance of faith as "holding up" the promise to God, see WA 10/ii, 295, 5 ("Vom ehelichen Leben," 1522) and WA 17/ii, 202, 22.

15. *Confession Concerning Christ's Supper* (1528), LW 37, 366 (WA 26, 505, 35–37); translation slightly altered. The word "assurance" (*Trotz*; in German the same as "defiance" and "contrariness") which appears to signify a subjective affect in contemporary idiom said, for Luther, that which the trustworthiness and strength of the word mediates. The "assurance" of faith is the promise on which faith may boast. With reference to Matt. 11:28 Luther said: "Therefore one must approach with a 'presumptuous' confidence in these words, and those who approach in this way will not be confounded." See *Lectures on Hebrews* (1518), LW 29, 173 (WA 57/iii, 171, 7f. [on Heb. 5:1]); translated from Latin. Compare Bayer, *Promissio* (see endnote 10), 208f.

16. On the relation between the experience of faith and theological writing compare, for example, the (Latin) prologue to *The Freedom of a Christian* (1520), LW 31, 343 (WA 7, [40–73] 49, 7–19).

17. Compare especially WA 50, 658, 29–661, 8. See the interpretation: Bayer, *Theologie* (see endnote 10), 55–106.

18. *On Rogationtide Prayer and Procession* (1519), LW 42, 87–88 (WA 2, 175, 4–32); translation slightly altered.

19. The *Small Catechism* (1529) in *The Book of Concord*, ed. Kolb and Wengert, 362:5–6 (*Die Bekenntnisschriften der evangelisch-lutherischen Kirche* 520, 29f. [WA 30/I, 317, 25–27]).

20. "From Heaven Above," LW 53, 290–91 (WA 35, 258–63) and also *The Lutheran Book of Worship* (Minneapolis: Augsburg, 1978), #51 (*Evangelisches Gesangbuch* 24, 1); translation from the latter source.

21. "Dear Christians, One and All," LW 53, 219–20 (WA 35, 422–25) and *The Lutheran Book of Worship* (Minneapolis: Augsburg, 1978), #299 (*Evangelisches Gesangbuch* 341, 2.3); translation from the latter source. On the character of this hymn, see WA 35, 133–35.

22. Ibid. (*Evangelisches Gesangbuch* 341, 3.4.7). One needs to hear the whole hymn. Nevertheless, by omitting two stanzas, it becomes clear that the liberation happens by means of the promise.

23. *Preface to the Babst Hymnal* (1545), LW 53, 333 (WA 35, 477, 6–9), text slightly altered. In the eyes of the Jesuit Adam Contzen (1571–1635) the Lutheran hymns have killed more souls than writings or speeches are capable of doing: A. Contzen, *Politicorum libri decem . . .*, Moguntiae 1620, Lib. II., c. xix, 2 (p. 100).

24. Albrecht Dürer in a letter to Spalatin from the beginning of 1520 (Dürer, *Schriftlicher Nachlass*, ed. H. Rupprich [Berlin: Deutscher Verein für Kunstwissenschaft, 1956], vol. i, letter 32, [86f.]); citation modernized.

25. The Psalter "might well be called a little Bible. In it is comprehended most beautifully and briefly everything that is in the entire Bible. It is really a fine enchiridion or handbook. In fact, I have a notion that the Holy Spirit wanted to take the trouble himself to compile a short Bible and book of examples of all Christendom or all saints, so that anyone who could not read the whole Bible would here have anyway almost an entire summary of it, comprised in one little book." See *Preface to the Psalter* (1528), LW 35, 254 (WA DB 10/i, 98, 22–100, 2).

26. LW 35, 256–57 (WA DB 10/i, 104, 5–9). In his letter to Zelter (see endnote 2) Goethe himself based his understanding of the Bible as a "mirror of the world" on Luther's *Preface to the Psalter* (1528) (ibid., 198: "Above all, read the wholly invaluable Preface to the Psalter").

27. LW 35, 256 (WA DB 10/i, 104, 2–4).

28. LW 35, 256 (WA DB 10/i, 102, 19f.).

29. LW 35, 255–56 (WA DB 10/i, 102, 8–18).

30. *Lectures on Genesis* (1541), LW 5, 570 (WA 43, 481, 32–35 [on Gen. 26:24]); translated from Latin.

31. WA DB 10/i, 100, 12–14 (see endnote 25). In the same sense Luther speaks in his writing *A Sermon on Keeping Children in School* (1530) of "speaking" as the "highest work" which is "love of humanity": LW 46, 249 (WA 30/ii, [508–88]

574, 17). For such a critical reception of the definition of the human as "rational animal" compare also WA TR 1, 565 (No. 1148).

32. "Without the *Word* . . . – no world. Here is the source of the creation and government." Johann Georg Hamann to Friedrich H. Jacobi on November 2, 1783 (Hamann, *Briefwechsel*, ed. W. Ziesemer and A. Henkel [Wiesbaden: Insel-Verlag, 7 vols., 1949–79], V:95, 21f.). Here in Hamann's expression Luther's understanding of language and the world is concisely conceived together and made valuable.

33. Arnold Gehlen, *Anthropologische Forschung: Zur Selbstbegegnung und Selbstentdeckung des Menschen* (Hamburg: Rowohlt, 1961), 68.

34. Friedrich Nietzsche, "Der Freigeist," Part 1, stanza 3 (*Werke Kritische Gesamtausgabe*, ed. G. Colli and M. Montinari [Berlin: Walter de Gruyter, 1974] VII-3, 37 ["Aus den Nachgelassenen Fragmenten," autumn 1884; *Werke Kritische Gesamtausgabe* VII-3, 28 (64)]).

35. Lev. 26:36 was often cited by Luther. Compare for example LW 9, 267 (WA 14, 724, 33f.) and WA 8, 677, 3f. (LW 45, 58) (*A Sincere Admonition* . . . , 1522): "Es soll sie auch eyn rauschend bladt erschrecken."

36. A further discussion of the literature cited in this text can be found in Oswald Bayer, *Schöpfung als Anrede*, vol. II. Enlarged edn. (Tübingen: J. C. B. Mohr [Paul Siebeck], 1990), 33–45.

# 6 Luther's theology

MARKUS WRIEDT

Translated by Katharina Gustavs

## INTRODUCTION

With Martin Luther a parting of the ways is inevitable. To some he was a religious genius or German hero, others saw in him the destroyer of the Western church and with it the associated inseparable unity of empire and nation. Curiously enough there is no firm historical verification of Luther's self-understanding that could possibly be condensed into one characteristic keyword – despite a multitude of self-statements and a deep reflection on his own thoughts and actions going far beyond the usual measure. Luther pictures himself in various positions and taking on many different tasks.[1] Thus the programmatic change of his name already reveals a fundamental insight behind it: Luder – in late medieval High German bearing the connotation of such words as "dirt" and "garbage" – is changed into *eleutherius* or Luther – "the liberated and at the same time Christ's servant and prisoner."[2] This gives us a hint of his future insight – extensively formulated in a style of paradox later on – into God's justifying action and the resulting knowledge of the complete inability of humans to act independently in accord with a requisite obedience to God and love for one's neighbor. At the same time Luther stresses over and over again his dignity and position as a Master of Holy Scripture, which to him embodied the ultimate authority and therefore also served him as the unquestionable basis for any theological argument.[3] From 1521 another title takes center place: Luther refers to himself as ecclesiast, preacher, or even evangelist.[4] All three self-designations have this in common, they make central Luther's self-awareness of being an interpreter of Holy Scripture as well as a preacher of the promise of God's reconciliation with and redemption of humanity through Jesus Christ. In Luther's understanding this task is rooted in baptism, manifesting itself in his own individual person as the common priesthood of all believers.

In our quest for a systematic key to Luther's theology, these self-designations may serve as guides. Luther saw himself as a preacher, as a Scripture interpreter. All that can be summarized in one single term, which he helped shape and which in our modern language is referred to as a pastor.[5] Here we see the first problem surface awaiting those trying to systematize Luther's theology: Martin Luther was not a systematic theologian. He did not develop and present his "teachings" in concise treatises, logically arranged and secured to all sides. Luther's theology rather grew out of a concrete situation. As much as he favored reliable and clear statements on the one hand,[6] so little would he have himself tied down to specific doctrinal formulations on the other. The lively, situation-centered and context-related style of Martin Luther's Scripture interpretation cannot and could not be pressed into a Procrustian bed of orthodox confessional and doctrinal writings.

Frequently enough the situation in which Luther was asked for his interpretation of Holy Scripture, be it in the form of an ethical evaluation, a pastoral counsel or even a report for the electoral government, turned out to be one of conflict. If you will, Luther was also a theologian of conflict or controversy. Never, of course, would he be involved for the sheer confrontation itself or for the sake of the conflict, but he would always keep his eyes on a true-to-life interpretation and on the judgment of Scripture itself.

How then can we present and describe Luther's theology? Numerous attempts have been undertaken to this end which remain unsatisfactory because they do not hit on the power and significance of Luther's teachings or his charisma for teaching and preaching.[7] Luther's statements were either placed into the framework of dogmatics, following the old Protestant pattern of orthodoxy, or they were assembled in the order of their appearance with reference to their historical occurrence. In the end the attempt to fuse the historical and the systematic exposition also remains disappointing because it invites too systematic an inquiry into Luther's texts. They were never intended to answer such inquiries.[8] Furthermore the systematically initiated approach does not do justice to the human gap between today's readers and those who were part of the originating situation – despite all asseverations to the contrary.[9] There have already been several other attempts made in times past to base theological explorations of Luther on his vocation as a pastor,[10] a preacher[11] or a professor.[12] As with many studies, hard to keep up with, on various individual topics of Luther's theology, those too still lack the overall view that we hope for.

In the following essay I will try to make a virtue out of this necessity. That is, I will not even try my skills at a systematic overall view. There are solid and particular historical arguments at hand to prove my point. Luther develops his theological view out of existentially troubling spiritual trials. This of course forms his theological reflection. To the degree to which he tries to pin down the causes of his theological temptations, in search of a way out, he causes some parts – or in his opinion even the core – of the theological system of his time to totter and even partly to collapse.[13] Given this background and the necessity of dealing with further controversies coming his way, Luther is more and more frequently forced to state his one concern, which is the gospel, in the shortest time possible and in a condensed, sometimes polemically exaggerated, style. Distinctions, polemics, and corrections rule his writings far more than the peaceful development of individual thoughts. In retrospect Luther observes that he "had been dragged into that matter" and that he had sought neither controversy nor conflict out of himself.[14]

Yet we will have to question which principle unifies this multitude of disparate and even contradictory statements. In the first part of the following essay, I will explore this question under the heading: Luther's Reformation Discovery. Throughout the subsequent five points, I will present some typical historical situations, in which Luther proves his Reformation Discovery using the form of theological statements and doctrines. The final question will be to discover whether Luther's approach was "spoiling the system" (Hamm) and as a result legitimately led to church separation.

## LUTHER'S REFORMATION DISCOVERY

In the preface to the first edition of his Latin writings in 1545, Luther writes about his theological development:

> I had conceived a most unusual, burning desire to understand Paul in his letter to the Romans; thus far there had stood in my way not a cold heart but one single word that is written in the first chapter: "In it the justice of God is revealed" (Rom. 1:17) because I hated that word "justice of God." By the use and custom of all my teachers I had been taught to understand it philosophically as referring to so-called formal or active justice, that is, justice by which God is just and by which he punishes sinners and the unjust. – But I, impeccable monk that I was, stood before God as a sinner with an extremely troubled conscience and I could not be sure that my merit would assuage him. I did not love, no, rather I hated the just God who punishes sinners. In silence if I did not blaspheme against God, then certainly I grumbled with vehement anger against him. As if it isn't enough that we miserable sinners, lost for all eternity because of original sin, are oppressed by every kind of calamity through the Ten Commandments. Why does God heap sorrow upon sorrow through the gospel and through the gospel threatens us with his justice and wrath? This was how I was

raging with wild and disturbed conscience. Thus I continued
badgering Paul about that spot in Romans 1 seeking anxiously to
know what it meant.[15]

At first Luther had experienced Christ as the angry judge who would
judge him according to his deeds. The fear of the Day of the Last Judgment
was at the same time connected with an extreme fear of hell's punishment
and eternal fire. For the young monk the presence of the judging Christ
became especially acute during mass. In his early sermons Luther conveys
a very impressive image of the pious supplicant who is very well aware
of this judge. Equally clear is that Christians are not subject to arbitrary
judgment. Therefore the late medieval practice of devotion is sometimes
aimed at bringing about a predictable judgment and at attracting a more
favorable decision with the help of pious works.

The central term, to which Luther's deep spiritual trials can be pinned
down, is the "justice of God" that Luther understood as an active pursuit: the
just God pursues the lawbreaker with wrath and punishment. The tested
monk becomes more and more tangled in a vicious circle of exaggerated fear
of sin and of works of repentance, which become perceived of as futile. This
culminated in the question as to whether salvation was at all possible or if
Luther had not already been forgotten by God's grace, being condemned for
all eternity. The study of the core tenets of the doctrine of grace, that is, the
teachings about God's eternal providence and predestination, fling Luther
into deepest despair. No wonder then that in retrospect Luther accused
his monastic teachers and ecclesiastical theologians of the way they spoke
of Christ exclusively as the judge to whom account had to be given and
good works had to be shown. Christ was not shown to his advantage as a
comforter, savior, and redeemer but as a tyrant.

A decisively new direction for his devotion Luther received from his
fatherly friend and vicar general of the order, Johannes von Staupitz
(1465–1524). The Saxon nobleman did not exactly distinguish himself by
systematically outlining a theological system of his own, but he certainly
knew how to provide outstanding pastoral counsel guided by the language
of the Bible and moved by the individual sorrows of the tested believer.
He referred Luther to the merciful God and the representative atonement
gained through Christ in his suffering and dying. It must have been Staupitz
who untangled Luther from the spiritual knots that constrained the Christian to be completely obedient to God out of one's own power, love him
perfectly out of one's own heart. He points to the suffering Christ revealing
the love and mercy of God, in whose light the question of our eternal election or condemnation loses its meaning. We can be certain that Staupitz

counseled Luther mainly along the lines of late medieval devotional practices strongly influenced by mysticism and a meditation on Christ's wounds
by Bernard Clairvaux. The deeply humane exhortation by the vicar general
not to become lost in the examination of one's own sinful nature, but to put
confidence in God's love and mercy, certainly touched Luther so deeply that
he came to interpret numerous hitherto dark passages of Scripture anew in
the light of these sentences. This talk with Staupitz, which defies precise
dating, impressed Luther so deeply that later he could claim that it had been
his fellow friar who started the new teaching.[16] Looking back on it, the light
of the gospel lit by Staupitz shines especially brightly in the term that at
first had landed Luther in such deep spiritual despair:

> Night and day I meditated on those words until at last, by the mercy
> of God, I paid attention to their context: "The justice of God is revealed
> in it, as it is written: The just person lives by faith." Then I began to
> understand the justice of God by which the just person lives by a gift
> of God, that is by faith. The meaning of this verse started to open up
> to me: The justice of God is revealed through the gospel but it is a
> passive justice by which the merciful God justifies us by faith, as it is
> written: "The just person lives by faith." All at once I had the feeling of
> being born again and entering into paradise itself through open gates.
> Immediately the whole of Scripture shone in a different light. I ran
> through the Scriptures from memory and found that other terms also
> had analogous meanings: e.g. the work of God, that is, what God works
> in us; the power of God, by which God makes us powerful; the wisdom
> of God, by which he makes us wise; the strength of God, the salvation
> of God, the glory of God. – I would exalt this sweetest word of mine
> "justice of God" with as much love as before I had hated it with hate.
> Thus this phrase of Paul was for me the true gate to paradise.[17]

The discovery of God's passive justice, that justice with which sinners
are clothed and justified, turned for Luther into the opening key to the
complete revelation of Holy Scripture.[18] The insight that God acts "for me –
for us (*pro me* – *pro nobis*)" turns Luther's past religious experience and
theological thinking upside down, though he would call it being "back on
his feet." In view of God's free and necessarily given gift of grace, Luther's
striving for perfection, for pure love to God, for justification and holiness,
proves to be absolutely wrong, even blasphemous. It appeared that he had
rejected the caring love of the merciful God in favor of overconfidence in
his own power to find happiness, that is, to acquire eternal salvation.

This fundamental conviction lasts through all controversies with and
about Luther: He lays emphasis on the free, absolute sovereignty of God and

his merciful acts of grace toward creatures full of sin and separated from him. Theological dispute always crops up when one of these two fundamental statements is narrowed down or leveled out. And Luther is certainly not after a rendition of a precisely stated doctrine or even the repetition of certain doctrinal formulations, such as would soon become the case with the claims made by early orthodoxy, but he was after the theological path of knowledge behind it. Luther's Reformation Discovery was first of all a hermeneutic insight,[19] which he had gained from the (re)discovery of Paul's message on justification through the analysis of the term "justice of God." The term itself actually does not play such an important role. Rather more important is the "new method" used to grasp its meaning in the light of Holy Scripture. This is all about a new or, as Luther would say, different way of reading Scripture through the gospel, which remains uninfluenced by human influence or, to put it in modern words, free from pre-understanding and anticipated results being read into the text.

During the following years (in good company with senior researchers I still assume an early date of 1514 for the Reformation breakthrough[20]) Luther unfolds his new line of thought within the rather sheltered world of the monastery and university. The writings of the young Luther up to about 1521, sometimes even much longer through to 1530, show clearly how much the young monk struggles with the consequences of his (re)discovery of the gospel's message of God's righteousness, which he perceived as liberating. Small wonder then that the systematically matured reflections of later years cannot be found in his early writings, neither with regard to the terminology nor the contents. As an example we refer to the justification of sinners and what a marginal mention it received in his lectures on Romans in 1515/16. The relevant passages bear no hint of Luther's Reformation Discovery. However, the exposition of other topics is worked very meticulously following patterns of contemporary devotion and this only makes sense if seen against the backdrop of a Reformation Discovery already having taken place.[21]

There is another peculiarity, which deserves mention here. Only of late could this reference be applied more generally to an interpretation of the developmental lines of young Luther's theology: A comparison between Luther's own notes of his lecture on Romans (WA 56) and the student's notes from dictation (WA 57) reveals how carefully Luther chose words describing his new insights and the resulting criticism of then current theological doctrines, criticism as well of the church as of devotional customs of his time, which was based on the latter notes. Numerous passages from his lecture on Romans, which former researchers have quoted as evidence for Luther's presumably already developed anti-scholastic and especially critical thinking about the pope and church reformation theology, these he had actually withheld from his students. Obviously he showed consideration for those who had not yet fully developed such a deep insight into Paul's theology and from whom at the same time he could also conceal the corresponding immaturity of his own approach.[22]

Over the next two years Luther comes across other sources of late medieval (reform) theology – superseded by scholasticism but still persistent in common devotional practices – such as the mystic writings of Tauler and the *Theologia Deutsch*. Thus Luther, confirmed in his own thinking,[23] dares to go public in a few disputations with preliminary thematic theses of his "new theology" geared toward academic discussion, even though the public would only comprise the small world of his own university.[24]

When we take a systematic theological look at those theses, a rightful claim can be made that they form the backbone of Luther's theology. In the center we have the absolute sovereignty and freedom of God – expressed in such terms as grace, mercy, and righteousness – and across from him humans who are caught in their sin, completely incapable of taking any saving action. Sin hereby takes the expression of humans' perpetual attempt to place themselves in God's position and the desire to create and fulfill their lives out of their own power and responsibility. This human overconfidence becomes most manifest in relationships with authorities from outside the Bible such as Aristotle and a Scripture interpretation led astray by church traditions lacking true theological back-up. Here we see again Luther's fundamental theme shine through most brightly: Poor interpretation of Scripture leads inevitably to the introduction or maintenance of biblically unfounded doctrines and thus illegitimate devotional practices. Only where a biblically legitimized Scripture interpretation provides orientation and foundation for human action can the required obedience to God's law be fulfilled. Such interpretation certainly cannot be achieved through human power. The gift of the Holy Spirit and the grace of God, not owed but given freely, are needed for that.

This summary is of course the result of interpreting the young Luther in the light of the mature statements in his later writings. At that point, Luther himself is still in search of those relationships, unable to relate them in a concise form. Thus the *Disputatio contra scholasticam theologiam*,[25] for example, starts out not with a thematic formulation of the doctrine of righteousness, but with a not particularly exciting comment on the contradictory interpretation of Augustine, as can be found throughout all of the late Middle Ages. In his line of argument Luther is exemplary in proving that the theologians of his time have neither worked methodically and cleanly within their system of assumed categories nor proven a solid reference base of appropriate Scripture interpretation, but instead base their conclusions on unproven *axiomata*. At first only the generally held opinion appears to him to be an expression of this discrepancy (thesis 5). Thereafter he proceeds through questions of anthropology, doctrines of grace and predestination to issues of righteousness (thesis 40) and shows that behind all of those statements of contemporary theologians contested by him there is a fundamental theological problem hiding, which he is prepared to solve. It is only throughout the last third of the quite comprehensive series of theses that he develops his own position by formulating theses without the philosophic-theological burden of scholastic traditions, but rich with his own understanding of grace and God. The explosive force of those sentences is very clear to theologians of later times with their knowledge of Luther's further theological development. For his contemporaries, however, who do not even know where the journey of Luther's theology will take them in the end, it is just another disputation among many others, which once again criticizes incongruencies and contradictions in scholastic theology. Toward the end of the late Middle Ages this was not a scandal at all, especially not at a university in Electoral Saxony founded on a reform impetus of highly varied origins. It does not come as a surprise then that hardly anybody took note of this theological dispute within the university.

Even the later and powerful *Ninety-five Theses* [26] were at first initiated as an inner academic disputation about theology and the then current understanding of unresolved questions about the grounds and workings of the sacrament of penance and in particular of indulgence practices, things also highly controversial among Luther's contemporaries. Here Luther analyzed first of all the inner stringency of the theological grounds of indulgence practice. While exposing major gaps in reasoning, the contemporary church doctrine appears to him as a human doctrine.[27] At that point, of course, it must have begun to dawn on Luther that his criticism is landing a fundamental attack on the decision-making authority of the church. Even though he only gives advice to be especially careful about announcing papal indulgences (thesis 41), his intention in so doing makes it very clear that he doubts the theological grounds of indulgences, including the method of the dogmatic decision-making process. It was probably for the exact same reason that Luther had sent his theses to the responsible bishop, Archbishop Albert of Brandenburg located at Mainz, and asked him for theological evaluation or approbation.[28]

During his work on this disputation it must have become clear to Luther that his exegetical insight and its fundamental theological reasoning allow for no other authority beside Scripture and radically call the structuring of the church's own authority into question. Thus far Luther's battle against scholastic theology is actually a fight between the super-revelation of Aristotle's pagan authority and the genuine Christian authority of Holy Scripture. The exegetical rediscovery of Paul, confirmed among others by the anti-Pelagian writings of St. Augustine, turns into the fundamental question of ultimate authority[29] within the church and consequently the question of the unity of the nation state and the institution on which Western culture is founded.

Whether Luther himself saw this last dimension of his approach clearly remains to be left unanswered. His hesitation to go public with his "new theology" is probably founded on the fact that he did not fully comprehend the consequences of his Scripture interpretation. The more he became involved in conflict with the ecclesiastical and secular authorities over the next years, the more he felt himself forced to lay open the hermeneutic foundations of his exegetical discovery.

To illustrate this highly complex process of clarification, separation, and retraction, spanning almost thirty years, I have chosen five exemplary situations for the second part of this essay.

## THE FORMATION OF LUTHER'S THEOLOGY IN THE CONTEXT OF CONTROVERSIES

### Argument over traditional devotional practices

When Albrecht of Brandenburg assumed his office as archbishop in Mainz an installation fee to Rome became due, which Albrecht was unable to pay out of his own pocket. In conjunction with the Fugger bank a complex financial strategy was agreed upon, as a result of which among other things the plenary indulgence was sold throughout Albrecht's diocese to raise the necessary funds.[30] It was not for the circumstances that brought about the sale of indulgences that Luther's opposition was stirred, but, as mentioned above, rather for its unresolved theological grounds.

In addition to his academic, theological line of thinking, there may also have been pastoral considerations. It was not least his own existential anxiety, brought about by the church's offer of the sacrament of penance and his own spiritual trials, that caused Luther to nail his colors to the mast of theology. In his letter of October 31, 1517, which Luther sent along with the theses to his bishop, he emphasized that nobody could be made sure of his or her salvation by a gift from a bishop. Church authorities are rather called to teach the people the gospel and love of Christ.

Luther opens his series of theses with a radical new understanding of repentance, guided by the New Testament and Paul's letters in particular: "When our Lord Jesus Christ said, 'Repent' (Matt. 4:17) he wanted the whole life of a believer to be nothing else than repentance" (thesis 1). In Luther's opinion Christ's call for repentance stands in contradiction to the current church practice of repentance: "This word cannot be understood from sacramental repentance (that is, from confession and acts of satisfaction administered through the office of the priest)." Luther shows the tension between an understanding of repentance rooted in Scripture and the actual church practice of repentance. For him repentance and faith become almost synonymous: a faith that does not include repentance ignores the radicalism of being a sinner; a repentance that is not inseparably united with faith is at once degraded to a "satisfaction," finally leading to a "righteousness of good works."

It does not seem to be Luther's intention to call the instrument of indulgences completely into question, but he tries to contribute to its theological clarification. The wording of his theses, however, already hints toward a future radical questioning. For instance, in thesis 36 Luther writes: "Every Christian who feels true contrition has of right plenary remission of punishment and guilt, even without letters of indulgence." Generally speaking, the Ninety-five Theses are by no means the ultimate treatise on all questions concerning indulgence. Yet its fundamental importance for the future development of this controversy is obvious: First of all, Luther felt himself called upon as a theologian to name a question of theological dispute and also to contribute to its clarification. His line of argument is not based on the abuse of indulgences, but rather on his theology learned from Paul and Augustine. In the end it becomes obvious, as the fundamental importance of the theses manifests itself, that the authority of Scripture and the authority of the church, especially the papal primacy of teaching and discipline, cannot be brought to agreement any more. Luther is trying to make it clear that the word of Christ should be the sole guide and yardstick for all teaching and acting in the church. The further course of events in this conflict shows clearly that it is the ultimate question of authority over which the opponents break up and accuse one other.

This was not what Luther was aiming at, and he showed himself surprised about the reaction from the other side of the old faith. Many an author did not bother at all with the central issue of indulgences, but most of them focused their refutation of indulgences on questions of papal authority. Archbishop Albrecht of Mainz himself did not take the whole affair too seriously. Because of his own lack of interest in theological matters, he passed the theses on to Rome and asked for Luther to be rebuked. A conviction or even excommunication was not something he would have had in mind. Yet this was certainly the opening to the Roman trial, during which event the conflict escalated quickly. In Germany certain statements of theologians from the old faith also saw to that.[31] Based on the 106 theses by Tetzel and Wimpina, the German chapter of Dominicans decided to take Luther to trial in Rome on suspicion of heresy. In the person of Johannes Eck from Ingolstadt, one of the most highly profiled and educated theologians of Germany accused Luther of spreading the "Bohemian virus." For clarification of his own standpoint Luther himself published the *Resolutiones*,[32] in which he not only stated his exegetical insights more clearly, but also pushed forward into the question of papal authority: "It is not the task of the pope to set up new articles of faith, but rather to evaluate and decide issues of faith in accordance with the already existent articles of faith." Anyway, Luther continued:

> The church is in need of a reformation. This is not something to be undertaken by one person, the pope or many cardinals, but by God alone. Yet the timing for this reformation knows only he who has created time itself. In the meantime, however, we cannot deny such obvious errors. The power of the keys is being abused and is forced to serve money and ambition. The flood has begun to rise, it is not in our power to make it stop now. "Our iniquities testify against us" (Jer. 14:7) and each of us is incriminated by his own words.

Even though Luther reduces the pope's authority to canonical matters, he does not deny it in principle. This he makes clear in his accompanying dedication, in which on the one hand he emphasizes that he could not take anything back, but on the other hand he is also prepared to submit himself completely to the pope:

> Most Holy Father, prostrate at the feet of your Holiness, I offer myself with all that I am and have. Bring to life, put to death, call, recall, approve, reprove, just do as it pleases thee: I will acknowledge thy voice as the voice of Christ, reigning and speaking in thee. If I have deserved my death, I will not refuse to die. The earth and its fullness are the Lord's, He be praised forever and ever. Amen.[33]

In spring 1518 Silvestro Mazzolini, named after his place of birth Prierias, was entrusted with the initiation of the canonical process against Luther. His *Dialogus* reflects the common – in Rome, predominant – view of the matter. The four fundamental sentences about the church culminate in the thesis: "He who says that the Roman church cannot do with regard to indulgences what she is doing is a heretic." In the past Prierias had already been known for emphasizing the infallible authority of the pope in questions of interpretation, thereby raising it above Scripture, yet with this last sentence the judgment on Luther was pronounced, laying the basis for the future conflict.

When in August 1518 Luther received the subpoena summoning him to Rome and at the same time also took note of the *Dialogus* by Silvester Prierias (Mazzolini), he felt confirmed in his suspicion, until then only cautiously voiced, that Antichrist would rule in Rome. The conflict with Rome finally escalated because an average theologian in his attempt to protect the pope and with his responsibility to settle a question of doctrine left behind the foundation of Scripture and formulated an extremely explosive statement that was no longer theologically tenable. From a not quite unfounded historical perspective, Luther on the contrary saw in Prierias a representative of the predominant view not recalled by the pope or any other theologian, inferring from this that the theological corruption of the church in Rome must be huge.

From spring 1518 the conflict between Luther and Rome was played at several levels. At first various replies to Luther's theses and his subsequent *Resolutiones* were written – the level of literary-academic dispute. The arguments on both sides were double-checked and formulated more precisely. Thereafter the preparation of the canonical process started a canonical dispute rolling which became increasingly narrowed down to the intense question of the church's ultimate authority. Finally, in summer 1518, the secular authority also began to deal with "Luther's case." On August 5, 1518 Emperor Maximilian informed the pope in writing about the Diet and in this letter expressed his worries that Luther represented a danger for the unity of faith and promised that he would be prepared to help enforce church laws against Luther in the German empire. At the same time Elector Frederick III, also called the Wise, from Saxony stood up for Luther after his appellation and asked to have the trial of this theologian from Wittenberg moved to Germany, thus ensuring a fair and due process.

In the course of the canonical controversy a most memorable interview took place at Augsburg in October 1518.[34] Thoughts were exchanged between Luther and probably the best theologian of his time, the papal cardinal legate Thomas de Vio Cajetanus (Cajetan), by profession a foremost expert and commentator on Thomas Aquinas and one of the most intelligent representatives of scholastic theology in the sixteenth century. For a long time the Italian Dominican had already belonged to those defending papal infallibility and had harshly criticized the conciliaristic reform movement of his time. With regard to Luther's question he was generally open because he himself had already published a treatise on the issue of indulgences in December 1517. Contrary to numerous of his contemporaries Cajetan had chosen his words cautiously and carefully.[35]

Though Cajetan kept to his promise to treat Luther with fatherly mildness, the course of the talk also showed the principal difference in their opinions and theological motives. Ecclesiology and papal authority were the hot issues. However, there seemed to be no rapprochement possible. While Luther emphasized the potential fallibility of the papacy and the church councils, particularly in view of the controversial doctrine on the treasure of the church, whose doctrinal tenets he wished to see subjected to the ultimate judgment of Scripture, Cajetan pointed to the pope's fullness of power in questions of teaching and tried to put Luther closer to the conciliaristic theologians of the fifteenth century. For Cajetan the dispute finally boiled down to the issue of papal authority, criticism of which was, on principle, worthy of condemnation for a Dominican. In this conviction Prierias had preceded him.

One more time the question of the pope's ultimate authority was to be discussed. In spring 1518 the theologian Johannes Eck from Ingolstadt had replied to Luther's theses on indulgences with his *Obelisci (Skewers)*. In turn Luther answered with his *Asterisci (Stars)*, pointing out: "That the Roman church stands high above all others is proven by the harsh decrees issued by the Roman popes throughout the last four hundred years. The proven track record of the first one-thousand-and-one-hundred years of Holy Scripture as well as the decision of the Nicean council are put against it."[36]

Luther's way of doing theology takes on a new quality in the literary-academic dispute with Eck. Having started out as an exegete and a co-reformer of the course of studies at the University of Wittenberg, in his dedicated search for theological clarification of open and controversial questions Luther soon moved from the small academic audience to the broader public of the church. Yet with his *Resolutio* against Eck he presented a polemic which attacked the foundations of the late medieval church. It seems as if Luther would have liked to have avoided such a confrontation. Because of the positions declared by Prierias, Cajetan, and Eck, however, he felt compelled to push further with his criticism than was his original intention. Armed with arguments from exegesis, church history, and common knowledge, he went on to refute the pope's claim of divine canon law. The fact that Luther recognizes the office of the pope as a human category shows how hard he tried to moderate – as much as he could help it – the consequences of his critical inquiry. Though it does not change a single bit of the radical consequence going hand in hand with his Reformation Discovery.

Beside its significant role in the canonical process, the Leipzig Disputation also turned out to be of great importance to Luther himself. First of all,

Luther seized the opportunity to become more precise in his wording with regard to the Bohemians. In 1521 he had demanded from secular authorities in his "nobility treatise" that they make contact with the Bohemian church. The issue of Scripture authority also needed further clarification.[37] To this of course he would find a more final answer only during the future course of the inner Protestant discussions, to which we will return later. For now, the Leipzig Disputation prompted him to refine his definition of the church more precisely.[38] The emphasis on the spiritual aspect of ecclesiology as well as the distinction between a spiritual and a bodily church move to the background. Instead, the distinction between a true and a false church grows in importance after 1519. With the revision of his opinion on the Hussites it becomes even more problematic for Luther naturally to equate the Roman Catholic Church with true Christianity. Luther cannot close his eyes to the insight that there are true Christians outside the church of Rome and that some of those Christians have been excommunicated even though they appear to have the greater right to call themselves Christians.

With a growing conviction that the papacy is actually an instrument of the antichrist, Luther states his ecclesiological arguments ever more pointedly. The apocalyptic tone of his style becomes more pronounced.[39] He feels himself being increasingly dragged into the battle between God and Satan for the ultimate rule. This apocalyptic atmosphere of course leads Luther into making statements which in this form are no longer tenable in our modern ecumenical dialogue and which for that reason should not be repeated at all.

During his early years Luther's criticism of the current church practice of the sacraments as well as the foundation of their authority for dogmatic decision-making takes center stage in his theological reflections. It should also be noted here that though Luther bases the development of his criticism on the (re)discovery of Paul's message of God's righteousness, the ecclesiological discourse certainly forms the center. Luther's characteristic and mature statements of the priesthood of all believers, which turn the hierarchy of the church upside down and plant a biblical theological foundation, can only be found in his later ecclesiology after he had been provoked by the failed talks with Rome and his order to think his alternative approach through to the end. The relative peace of the years prior to and after Charles V's election to be Emperor of the Holy Roman Empire of the German Nation in 1519 provided Luther with the necessary opportunity. Because of the numerous negotiations associated with the imperial election, the curia's activity regarding Luther's trial was more or less put to rest. During the course of 1520 this process was continued again.

### First contributions to the consolidation of an evangelical Lutheran theology

In his early academic publications Luther focused mainly on negating wrong developments within the church and its devotional practices based on his understanding of Scripture, but now he turns to creatively formulating new teachings. It is important here again to draw attention to the fact that with only a very few exceptions Luther was not accustomed to come out with programmatic treatises, but rather presented them in a rich variety of occasional publications, sermons and writings of comfort, catechism treatises, polemics, and disputes. Several times Luther complained that polemics and disputes were hindering him from his own constructive work. In contrast to academic disputations, the theologian from Wittenberg now made extensive use of the German language, which furthered the widespread impact of his writings enormously. Supported by the picture material from the associated Cranach house and other workshops, Luther's writings became especially popular with educated lay people.

First of all Luther contributed to the creation of a new form of devotion in his *Sermon von der Betrachtung des heiligen Leidens Christi* (*A Sermon on the Meditation on Christ's Passion*).[40] Contrary to the common superficiality of passion devotions, it was dear to Luther's heart that a passion meditation may lead to the recognition and confession of one's own sin, the sin that is partly responsible for Christ's suffering. This insight of course cannot be acquired through the sinner's own power, but can only be granted by God himself.

This line of thought closely ties in with Luther's criticism and the resulting change caused in the common practice of prayer, as outlined by Luther in his interpretation of the Lord's Prayer in 1519.[41] The theologian from Wittenberg urges people to internalize their praying. In his interpretation of the Lord's Prayer the central threads of the confession of sins and righteousness star again: Prayers are addressed to the merciful father and not to the angry judge, rising above human trouble to God. The seven requests are a showcase of human misery and thus include the recognition of one's own sin. The hope of being heard is at the same time the confidence in God's merciful and redeeming will, whose consent and promise form the first and foremost prerequisite for true prayer.

Earlier publications already gave a hint of Luther's own understanding of the sacraments, which he states more strongly now in three sermons on penance, baptism, and the Lord's Supper[42] as well as in other writings: for example, providing comfort to Elector Frederick,[43] who fell seriously sick after his return from the imperial election in September/October 1519, and to his minister Markus Schart in the *ars moriendi*[44] on how to die, or answering questions on work[45] or marital ethics.[46] In those sermons Luther borrows a scheme from Augustine, who distinguished between visible signs (*signum*) and their meaning (*res*). New of course is Luther's addition of faith, which functions as a unique mediator for connecting the two. Reducing his definition of the sacraments to the Augustinian formula "accedit verbum ad elementum et fit sacramentum"[47] prompts Luther to criticize the commonly used number of seven sacraments offered through the church since the thirteenth century. To Luther a sacrament is constitutively characterized by the divine promise. After all, our relationship with God is formed through his promising word, received by faith. The other sacraments, however, do not fulfill this condition.

Again and again Luther is asked for an ethical exposition which would explain how he understands righteousness. In his *Sermon on Good Works*[48] he presents a short draft, which is later combined with the concrete societal and political situation of the nation in his programmatic writing *To the Christian Nobility of the German Nation Regarding the Reform of the Christian Estate.*[49] The point of departure for Luther's reflections is the First Commandment. From that it follows for Luther that there are no other good works of obedience in faith than those which have been commanded by God. This had to have a most reducing effect on all extra satisfactions. Contrary to common belief faith is the first and foremost work. Apart from faith no good works exist. Anything that is done without faith is rather sin. This basic concept is shortly applied to all other commandments.

Among Luther's writings the "nobility treatise" occupies a special place insofar that it did not present Scripture interpretation and theological teaching as usual, but offered practical advice to the German nobility in the form of a "fool's speech." By means of a literary alienation technique, Luther slips into the role of a fool, maybe also owing to the fact that he does not feel too comfortable in the role of a political advisor, and makes himself the speaker of the German Gravamina movement.[50] Luther's relevant matters concerning reform are of course tied into some fundamental theological reasoning.

Luther starts from the assumption that papacy is surrounded by a threefold wall, since it would lay claim on, first, the supreme rule over secular authorities, second, the monopoly over the normative Scripture interpretation, and, third, the supreme rule over the council. In contrast to this claim of universal supremacy, Luther develops his theory of the common priesthood: According to 1 Peter 2:9 all Christians are chosen to be kings and priests. The office bearers elected from among them by an unspecified method of election are only the servants and do not feature any superior qualities. This not only implies the negation of the formerly stated qualitative difference between priests *(character indelibiles)* and laity, but the incredible enhancement of the status of the latter and the total abolition of any type of hierarchy in the church. Though this line of argument reveals a tremendous emancipatory claim, Luther never called the medieval order of imperial estates into question. Therefore it is not an anti-authoritative democratism, but a theological-exegetical reasoning, which leads Luther to such a radical formulation of the common priesthood of all believers. This in turn offers him the opportunity to revolutionize the papal primacy completely. In numerous, far-reaching, individual demands and exemplary criticism Luther then develops his reform program. Generally speaking, he had the thorough decentralization of the church at his heart combined with a drastic reduction in Roman central power and the resulting greater independence of the German church. At the same time Luther hopes for intensification of individual devotion as outlined in his early writings.

Based on his newly found understanding of the sacraments, Luther summarizes and to a certain degree also finalizes his criticism of the current practice of devotion as manifest in worship services in an equally powerful writing, *On the Babylonian Captivity of the Church. Prelude.*[51] What is headed as a preface turns out over many long years to be the matured and ultimate convictions of the theologian from Wittenberg. Christ's words of institution become for him the center of the mass:

> When man is to deal with God and receive something from him, it will be inevitable that no man will start and lay the first stone, but rather God alone will be the first to make a commitment without any desire or request on the part of humans. It is this word of God that is the first and foremost, the foundation and the rock onto which all other works, words and thoughts of man are going to be built.[52]

The pattern of promise and faith again forms the dominant force for all further conclusions. It must be for that reason that Luther criticizes the quiet voice with which the words of institution are spoken, and the sacrificial understanding of the eucharist, as well as the removal of the cup from the laity. The sacrifice offered by humans should rather be lived in prayer, praise, and gratefulness. Faith focuses on Christ's sacrifice for humanity. Insofar as it is faith that performs the sacrament, then as a result the function of the sacrificing priest is abolished. Thus Luther once again reaches the notion of the common priesthood of all believers, with his understanding of the Lord's Supper revolutionizing the doctrine of the church in a shockingly new way, and consequently the foundations of late medieval ecclesiology itself. In numerous disputations and sermons Luther, supported by Melanchthon, continues to develop his theology of the sacrament.

More frequently Luther ends up between the fronts of old believers and representatives of Rome on the one hand and the reform forces of highly different provenance calling upon him on the other hand. Beginning in his "liberty treatise"[53] but also in numerous later writings, Luther sees himself forced to be more precise in his wording, protecting and dissociating himself from arguments of both sides. The tension between evangelical freedom and politically advisable caution had begun its endless build-up. For Luther, Christian freedom is certainly not about doing what pleases you, but rather what pleases God alone and is invisible, while believing in Christ and having a clear conscience. In the outside world, however, before the people this freedom is to give way to the service of one's fellow humans:

> "Therefore, dear friends, because God has shown his grace so that we could grasp the gospel and begin to understand some of its freedom, let us make any effort to again honor it faithfully and not to dishonor it unfaithfully."[54]

Through these few sentences runs a basic pattern, which is typical for Luther's theology: Since positive statements often turn out to seem quite unclear or even contradictory, he makes conscious use of the style of opposites or paradox. Speaking in opposites or word pairs is very much preferred by Luther over making definite individual statements: freedom and service, external and internal, before God and before people, hidden and obvious, flesh and spirit, law and gospel, promise and fulfillment, justified and sinner at the same time, etc. Not the individual statement itself, but the space of tension related between the two extremes or even contradictions is the content of his theological concept. Therefore if we were on the lookout for a term specifically to describe Luther's theology, I feel inclined to speak of a "relational theology."[55] After all, this seems to be the reason why Luther's theology eludes the organizing power of classical dogmatics so persistently. Instead of God he speaks of God's relationship with humans as documented in his almighty power of creation, his bottomless mercy, his perfect will of redemption and atonement. Instead of speculating about the double nature of Christ's existence Luther speaks of his suffering, dying, and resurrection and the service of the resurrected in the threefold office of king, priest, and prophet. Instead of a doctrine of righteousness Luther presents numerous situations in which the justification of humans becomes reality in the tension between the current promise of Scripture and its eschatological fulfillment at Christ's return (*simul iustus et peccator*). Instead of a doctrine of the church Luther develops a guiding formula based on the biblical understanding of the Lord's Supper, with which he also turns late medieval ecclesiology back on its feet, and so forth. This basic pattern starts to gain momentum at a time when Luther, placed under the imperial ban following the decisions of the Diet at Worms and therefore bereft of the power to act at church or state level, is forced to create the alternative model of a Scripture-based, evangelical theology and to give guidance for its practical application in a new church and devotional practice.

Certainly this holds a great deal of tension, which in its final consequence has Luther's ecclesiology appear contradictory: Luther always assumed that it would be possible to win the Roman bishops – at least those of the German empire – for the truth of the gospel, as it was evident to Luther, so that a "system-conforming Reformation from above" could be carried out.[56] It was a fact, however, that his criticism of the Roman system was of such a fundamental nature that it would destabilize the system to the extent that the desired reformation of head and limbs could not be achieved any longer. This inner conflict worsens to a point of confrontation where Luther is finally forced – against his own will – to "build a new church." Designed by him as an interim solution, it always remains a half-hearted endeavor and sows the seeds for the constant self-inquiry of future Lutheran churches, which refer to Luther though in fact they should no longer be in existence according to their founder's own Reformation approach.

### Disputes within the Reformation movement

Probably also due to those never explicitly discussed relations, it soon came to separations and differences within the Reformation camp after the publication of Luther's major treatises in 1520/21. In the first years the common interest in a comprehensive reform of Western theology and church in its head and limbs united numerous, highly different, groups and individuals. To the extent that it became manifest in the person of Luther that resistance against encrusted structures in church and society could be possible and even successful, the original arguments and intentions would surface again. After 1521 Luther had to deal not so much with the church representatives of Rome and the papacy, but rather with dissidents from his own side, regarding Holy Scripture as the norm and measure of church life as well as justification and salvation. In Luther's opinion it was necessary to defend the preaching of the gospel and the freedom thus acquired from human rules against any form of legalism. Luther himself refers to it as "work holiness."

### *Andreas Bodenstein von Karlstadt and the authority of the Spirit*

With logical consequence the first conflict was ignited over the legitimacy of Luther's theological teachings on reform, his concept of Scripture interpretation. Delicately enough this conflict arose with his doctor father, the comprehensively educated former lawyer and representative of the *Via antiqua* Andreas Bodenstein von Karlstadt,[57] who at first supported scholastic theology. The controversy developed around the acceptance of the thoughts and notions of the African church father Augustine. In his writings Luther had found his own understanding of God's passive righteousness and the grace-given justification of human beings remarkably confirmed, sometimes taking the interpretation beyond the wording of Augustine's own writing, his main authority. Karlstadt however kept closer to the formulations of Augustine's original works and developed his concept of the Holy Spirit further. Unlike Luther he did not emphasize the allowance for an external justification, but the fulfillment of the law as made possible through the gift of the Spirit.

The arguments escalated after Karlstadt had taken over the Reformation movement in Wittenberg while Luther stayed put at the Wartburg in 1521/22. Karlstadt held on to the conviction that the Old Testament law should also apply to Christians and for its fulfillment called in a peculiar fashion upon the help of the Holy Spirit. In the process of reforming church and society he would apply the rules of the Law of Moses literally to the circumstances in Wittenberg. Thus, for example, Karlstadt took the prohibition of images in the Old Testament literally. To him it was of utmost importance that the Christian faith should also be preserved in externally visible obedience to God's law. Theologically speaking, righteousness must lead to salvation and Christian freedom must express itself in new forms, including social life. Karlstadt basically stands for a "puritan" form of Reformation Christianity. In any case, the difference between Karlstadt and Luther not only touched on the question of a different strategy as to how to translate evangelical insights into action, but also on fundamental aspects of Reformation theology.

At the beginning Luther agreed totally with the reforms carried out under Karlstadt's leadership in Wittenberg. That Luther, over the course of events in Wittenberg, became increasingly critical toward the Wittenberg movement, and that in the course of the arguments this generated he even modified some parts of his theology, had several reasons.

First of all the appearance of the so-called "Zwickau Prophets," who referred to an immediate revelation of the Spirit as the basis of their demands for reform, should be mentioned here.[58] Regarding their claim, Luther pointed out that the Holy Spirit has bound itself to the external Word of Scripture. For the evaluation of true teachings, this new approach becomes crucial. Revelations of the Spirit need to be checked against the examples in Holy Scripture. Furthermore Scripture already contains the complete revelation of God established in Christ. Statements reaching beyond this truth are simply impossible. After having defended the supreme authority of the Bible (*sola scriptura*) against all competition, which might suggest consulting ecclesiastical and theological traditions for the interpretation of controversial Scripture passages as the Romans do, he finds a new front here. The binding of the Spirit to the external Word, however, protects from spiritualistic and enthusiastic concepts.

### Law and gospel

Even more poignantly than in the past, Luther brought out the difference between law and gospel.[59] By law Luther understands all statements of Scripture that uncover the sin of humans and accuse them. In contrast, the gospel includes all statements that promise comfort, redemption, and the grace of God. The gospel cannot be limited to the body of text laid down in the New Testament, nor can every single Scripture verse be exclusively assigned to either gospel or law. Their respective functions are revealed in the context of complex relationships, the personal situation of the listener or reader, and God's plan of salvation as a whole. The literal translation of demands from the Old Testament into new action harbors the danger of turning Christian freedom, for example toward pictures in churches and on altars, into a law. At the same rate faith would be externalized in this way. After all, Luther continues to point to the fact that the law is an office of punishment here to stay, through which a believer is continuously made aware of his or her sin and the judgment of God is proclaimed. The reformers in Wittenberg, however, had denied the exact same fact.

The struggle for the appropriate relationship between law and gospel flares up within the Reformation camp on a regular basis. Even though everybody would agree on rejecting the supposed or actual Roman "work holiness," it continued to remain controversial as to whether the sermon of repentance belonged theologically to the interpretation of the law or if it had better be seen from the interpretation of the gospel. Another contentious issue also surfaced again: if, in what sense, and to what extent the preaching of the law should remain the task of the church. Luther owed the crucial insight that true repentance starts with love for righteousness and God to Johannes of Staupitz. Melanchthon, however, laid emphasis on the need for the law first to reveal sin so that grace could then be mediated by the gospel. To him the process of salvation was divided into several succeeding stages designated by the law, the gospel, and the necessary renewal through the Holy Spirit. Luther, however, saw humans in the dialectic between judgment and grace or law and gospel. This distinction was further intensified by Johann Agricola (1499–1566) who stressed that penance was the fruit of the gospel because the law could never lead to faith. Christ fulfilled the law; therefore it is excluded now from the path of salvation. The controversy broke out again over the writing of the visitation articles for Electoral Saxony in 1527 on the issue of whether the law should still have its place in the Protestant sermon.[60] Despite repeated declarations of consensus from all sides, this argument continued to smolder at the root of the Reformation movement, flaring up from time to time.

During the 1530s and 1540s, the conflict with the Antinomians became a huge burden for Luther.[61] At first he had emphasized the gospel as the merciful turning toward humans against the Roman position; he now only stressed the lasting importance of the law. Luther saw Agricola as representative of all Antinomians, in danger of abolishing the dialectics between law and gospel only to form a new law out of the gospel. The lasting importance of the law lies in its exposing humanity's sinful nature. Essentially, the meaning of the salvation of Christ's cross cannot be understood at all without the law. The law itself is not an efficient cause (*causa efficiens*) of righteousness, but is certainly its prerequisite.

The externalizations of faith, as well as the tendency toward legalism, toward restrictions of Christian freedom, grows into the central issue of numerous controversies within the Protestant movement. The accusation of "lawlessness" and "work holiness" is no longer exclusively reserved for Roman theologians, but is also raised in particular against the radical reform forces (spiritualists, peasants, "enthusiasts").

### Attitudes toward authorities

In the end, Luther rejected uproar and resistance against the imperial forces in any shape or form for the reason mentioned above, and also rejected the establishment of God's Kingdom through human, or even armed, forces. In January 1522 a mandate was adopted to fight the *Neuerungen wider den hergebrachten christlichen Brauch* (New Developments Against the Old Christian Custom). Luther was worried that out of consideration for his position within the empire the elector might withdraw his policy of toleration and silent support. In this context Luther developed his notion of God-given authority, to which the subjects owe obedience for the sake of God's will.[62] Temporal authority is necessary for maintaining external order; without it the church could not continue to exist. At this point Luther voiced for the first time his convictions that in special emergency situations Christian authorities are called to carry out a church reform based on the gospel, even against the official church government. In his famous writing *To the Christian Nobility of the German Nation Regarding the Reform of the Christian Estate* he had earlier pleaded with them to push comprehensive reform efforts through at the church as well as state level because of the obvious failure of the ecclesiastical authorities to do so. In the background of Luther's reasoning, secular authority is independent, having received its special mandate from God and not being subordinated to ecclesiastical authority.

The fact that Luther, since his move to Wittenberg, received ongoing support and the promise of secular protection by his electoral ruler cannot be overestimated for the development of his understanding of authority. In reply to Rome it had been Luther's main concern to emphasize the independence of secular powers. But in face of the more radical reformers he now had to place more emphasis on the necessity of a secular order. This change of fronts set in while the Wittenberg Reformation began to unfold under the leadership of Karlstadt in 1521/22, but soon it gained even more momentum when revolutionary forces tried to change conditions through violence and to establish an allegedly divine rule.

### Controversy about the understanding of the Lord's Supper

Without discussing this dispute in great detail, the controversy about the understanding of the Lord's Supper deserves mention in this context.[63] From the start a great variety of opinions came together in the Reformation movement. These were initially covered up by their united forces against the Roman doctrine of the sacraments. Together they had attacked the notion of the mass as a sacrifice, attaching great importance to the uniqueness of Christ's sacrifice on the cross and the necessity of faith. Within the Reformation movement the words of institution, however, had already been interpreted in different ways during the first years of the controversy about the understanding of the Lord's Supper (1517–21). In subsequent years the issue of the real presence versus the symbolic character of the sacramental actions moved more and more to the forefront, owing to a long history of divergent interpretations of Augustine.

Luther's own position undergoes a change over the course of the controversy. Having first focused on the concept of communion, he now gave the words of institution and the quality of the participation regarding the forgiveness of sins more prominence. In contrast Ulrich Zwingli, Luther's equal in Zurich and main opponent in this controversy, set out with a similar notion of Christ's presence in bread and wine. However, over the course of the argument he increasingly stressed the spiritual nature of the sacrament.

Interestingly enough it was Karlstadt again who was the first to present publicly a different view of the doctrine of the sacraments than Luther. According to his point of view, Jesus refers to his body while speaking the words of institution. Therefore the spiritual aspect takes center place in his understanding. He is not alone in his opinion but in good company with former theologians, dogmatics, contemporary humanists, and the so-called "Bohemian Brothers," who all preferred the spiritual meaning of the Lord's Supper. Yet he is certainly the first one to voice such an opinion within the Reformation camp, drawing attention to the inner pluriformity of the Reformation movement in Wittenberg.

Luther has a good look at those positions in his writing on the Lord's Supper *On the Worship of the Sacrament of Christ's Holy Body*, 1523,[64] stressing the real presence of Christ in bread and wine as he had already done in earlier years. During the first years of his teaching activity the emphasis had mainly focused on "for you" (*pro nobis*). Now the "is" of the words of institution moved to the center.

The dispute, of course, continued with Zwingli. Zwingli was convinced that faith could not possibly be based on something of creation. Jesus' word that the flesh was of no use (John 6:63) should also be applied to the Lord's Supper. For that reason Zwingli rejected the idea of the real presence as well as the transformation of bread and wine. Those who would eat Jesus' flesh and blood in bread and wine could only be called "men or flesh eaters." The Lord's Supper was rather a supper of commemoration, "through which those who strongly believe that they are reconciled with the father through Christ's death and blood proclaim his life-giving death." Over the course of the controversy Zwingli tends increasingly to rely on Jesus' words, "Do this in remembrance of me," thus accentuating a position he had already established in his argument against Rome. The death of Christ has worked redemption for now and all times. The remembrance is not a mere commemoration, but the saving significance of the unique act at Cavalry reaching into the present.

In Zwingli's background we can also find a fundamental decision regarding Christology: He distinguishes strictly – in line with the Antioch school – between the divine and human natures of Christ. Over and above that he also differentiated between Jesus' fleshiness before and after his resurrection. In his words of institution Jesus refers to his earthly body, not his raised one that since his ascension sits at the right hand of God in heaven. The reunion with his human nature will only take place at his return for the Last Judgment. To claim that Christ was also present in his human nature in the sacramental elements would mean offending the majesty of God.

Luther for his part refused to apply the words of Jesus from John 6 to the interpretation of the words of institution. He sticks to the simple meaning of the words of institution: the word "is" cannot be interpreted as "means." Luther views this not only as a specific problem of the teachings regarding the Lord's Supper. For him it is also about the fundamental question of God's presence in the Christ who became flesh. Between the revelation of God in Jesus of Nazareth and the presence of Christ's body and blood in bread and wine runs an inseparable connection because in both cases we are dealing with the paradox of God's presence in the flesh. Or, put in the traditional terms of Christology, with the union of divine and human nature.

The Lord's Supper is all about the communion with the flesh and the suffering of the God who became flesh and about human salvation. Whoever calls that into question causes the foundation of Christianity to collapse. The idea of moving the raised Christ into heaven contradicts Luther with his doctrine of ubiquity, according to which Christ's body and blood is also always present in the elements of communion at all places in historical reality. Even though Luther draws on sophisticated scholastic theories about the (circumscriptive) spatial or definitive presence in his line of argument, for modern thinking he unfolds thoughts of an existential nature. We see this, for example, when he sees the right hand of God as just that place which guarantees the presence of Christ, and when he moves heaven into the human heart and suspects hell to be also found there. Thus there is no longer a fundamental dissent and there does not need to be an interpretive shift of emphasis in the words of institution, something which would have justified an opponent's accusation. This of course holds true not only for the reform tradition in upper Germany, but also for a potential consensus with those of the old faith who hold on to the doctrine of the Eucharist.

### Controversy about human free will

While the controversy about reform options was in full swing, the next real conflict about another essential point in Luther's Reformation theology gathered force. This was about Luther's radical notion of sin and the un-freedom of human will with regard to grace. Erasmus of Rotterdam, the uncrowned king of the humanists north of the Alps, was the opponent. The reformers in Wittenberg owed a great deal to the humanists' endeavors in promoting philological studies and editing the publications of the church fathers.[65] As much as the humanist movement agreed with numerous statements of Luther, the differences sleeping in the background were very great and now began to break loose in argument about the freedom of the will. Erasmus writings since 1524 had defined free will as that power with which humans can turn either toward or away from what leads them to eternal salvation. Contrary to Luther he stressed that the denial of human free will or choice would easily open the gate to godlessness. The notion that God could harden a human's heart is particularly foreign to him. Erasmus specially emphasized the fact that humans owe the entire work to God and without him are capable of nothing. Indeed, even free will itself with its rather limited effect is also a gift of God. However, it is very dear to his heart that the human response toward God's offer should be interpreted as an act of free will.[66]

Luther's reply of 1525[67] is written with a passionate desire to bring the abyssal experience of spiritual trials on the one hand together with the promise of divine mercy and grace on the other. He reproached Erasmus for having explored the question of human free will without any reference to Christ. Therefore the image of a Christian is conjured up that pictures him as a human who should subject himself with all his might to repentance and place all his hope in the mercy of God, without which the human will could achieve nothing at all. Erasmus seems to try to avoid making a statement on the question of what humans are actually capable of achieving from their own power and how far their possibilities may reach. In contrast, Luther makes use of hard-hitting sentences pointing out that humans caught in their own sin are totally dependent on the merciful attention of God. The loss of free will is a consequence of the fall of humanity. Luther almost falls prey to determinism, only on the sidelines conceding the freedom of the human's choice with regard to those things which are below him. To Luther the emphasis on the radical sinfulness of the whole human being is only natural because of God's exclusive and universal act of salvation in the suffering and dying of Jesus Christ: "When we believe that Christ has redeemed humankind through his blood, then we will have to admit that the whole human body must have been lost; otherwise we would be making Christ superfluous or the redeemer of the lesser part, which would be blasphemous and sinful." The statements concerning the total forlornness of humans can only make sense in the light of the equally total redemption of the sinner through Jesus Christ.

## CONCLUSIONS: CONFLICT-AWARE (ASSERTORIC) THEOLOGY

We started out with Luther's discovery of Paul's message of righteousness because of which Luther developed a new method of exegesis, the evangelical interpretation of the gospel (Ebeling). As a result he came to criticize radically and creatively rethink a biblically founded way of church teachings as well as the associated devotional and church practices rooted in them. With persistent and uncompromising theological statements as well as sharp polemic, certainly not sparing his opponents, Luther unfolded the fundamental lines of his theology in the diversity of challenging arguments and conflicts. The *assertio* becomes the expression of choice for the Christian faith and finds its premise in the clarity of Holy Scripture. To make his point Luther refers to the central message of the Bible: the revelation of Jesus Christ. "If you take Christ out of Scripture, what are you going to have left in it after all?" Luther hereby distinguishes between a double clarity and a double darkness in Scripture:

> We find a double clarity in Scripture as well as a double darkness, one put in the external service of the Word and the other placed in the knowledge of the heart. Now when you speak of inner clarity, no man will ever grasp only one single iota in Scripture if it was not for the Holy Spirit... However when you speak of external clarity nothing will be left in the dark or ambiguity, but all of what is written in Scripture is revealed through the word placed in the most certain of lights and publicly preached to the whole world.[68]

External clarity stresses the non-ambiguity of Christ's witness, whereas the inner clarity highlights the receiving of the gospel message in the human heart. With this teaching, including the statement of the self-interpreting Scripture (*sacra scriptura sui ipsius interpres*), Luther declares the independence of Reformation theology from any central doctrinal office on the one hand and the tight bond of all faith statements to the witness of Scripture on the other. Outside of biblical statements there is no true tenet of faith possible.

It is right here that Luther's greatest work, the continuously revised and improved translation of the Bible, has its systematic-theological place. The translation of course is determined by his theological approach. The Bible interprets itself and all topics point to the one message whose center is established in human salvation solely through Christ's suffering and dying, human reconciliation with the angry God and human justification through the God-given gift of faith in eschatological completion. It is indeed this center that guides the translation. This is also the central message to be brought out and at the same time the presence of God to be witnessed. Accordingly creative, Luther sets out on his translation work, leaving behind traditional methods of translating word for word and letter for letter in favor of a gospel-centered translation in the language of his time.[69]

Against this backdrop it becomes clear why any controversy coming Luther's way was reduced by him to the question of Scripture interpretation and the relation of law and gospel on the one hand and fought with such great enthusiasm and an almost shocking ruthlessness toward his theological opponents on the other. For Luther everything is at stake, the rediscovery of the gospel and the message of the free and absolute gift of God's grace.

Was this type of theology new? Did it break with or spoil the "system" of the late medieval church and piety so fundamentally that apart from all historically conditioned contingencies the church separation would be justified? And if so, should we be forced to continue doing so? Was and is Luther's approach, as Berndt Hamm put it,[70] so "spoiling the system" that in it the onset of a new era could be seen?

For the ultimate answer to this question much more detailed research is required. From the background of the highly intensive studies on the different strands in late medieval theology, especially those done during the last couple of years, this much can be said with certainty: Luther was a child of the late Middle Ages and also remained one throughout his whole life. On the one hand we have his explosive approach, which gathered force to break the system over the course of his lifetime and also worked forcefully against influences of contingent historical implications from outside of theology and church. On the other hand we have his demand for reform rooted in theological reasoning, which took on its own life independent from other reform endeavors of the sixteenth century that he would draw on for resources. All his efforts make Luther – against his will! – one of the founders of a new epoch, which we now call the era of confessionalism. A systematization of Luther's theology according to a normative doctrine of how to interpret the gospel is made impossible because of the inner conflict going back to the sources. But at the same time it is impossible for us actually to be able to turn back time or to preach the gospel without the challenging structures, if not of a new era, then certainly of a time essentially different from that of the first church. Furthermore this time-dependent way of preaching should also offer something new. It is this systematic tension that makes for a constant contrast in the Protestant Scripture interpretation and church teachings following Luther. Here we can see the opportunities and limits offered by such theology for today: A gospel-centered theology can only be pursued as a concrete announcement in real time here and now in the light of the message of the merciful God, in the tension between law and gospel. The historical development, which in faith is understood as the unfolding of God's all-encompassing will of salvation, will always overtake all things.

Thus we have reached the end of our reflections on Luther's theology. In view of bygone anniversaries and numerous denominations named after the theologian from Wittenberg as well as the issues surrounding our own Protestant identity, the following question presents itself: What has Luther and his theology to tell us today?

1. The above essay has shown to what a large extent Luther developed and formulated his theological statements in concrete conflicts, sometimes provoked by a deplorable state of affairs or an opponent's position. Luther can only be understood through his time and in his time. Thanks be to God, time has changed. As a result numerous occasions that prompted Luther to make hard-hitting statements are also gone. To this extent any single criticism, idea, or statement of Luther should always be carefully checked for whether it stands up to the test of our modern time.

2. No one disputes that Luther was a great theologian, a brilliant rhetorical speaker and in many regards a highly successful reformer. If we would like to keep his legacy alive, it will be our foremost task to zero in on his theology as a whole and to analyze his patterns and processes of argumentation to unearth his unique way of "doing theology." It is not about individual arguments, but an entire line of argumentation; not about biblical fundamentalism, but an ongoing relationship with Scripture; not about systematic Lutheran dogmatics, ethics, or the like, but his dynamic way of reaching answers and statements which are both worth keeping for future generations and worthy to be gathered into the wealth of ecclesiastical and spiritual traditions. In addition to the fundamental reconnection to Scripture (*sola scriptura*), we can also treasure the hermeneutic distinction between law and gospel, the teaching of the Holy Spirit as the Spirit is bound to Scripture, the evaluation of human freedom as it is bound to God's Word and commandments, the teaching of unconditional justification out of grace alone, the view of the church as a communion of sinners called and redeemed by God, the highlighting of the church's office of comfort, the common priesthood of all believers, and last but not least the spiritual approach to the question of authority.

### Notes

1. See Bernhard Lohse, "Luthers Selbsteinschätzung," in *Martin Luther: Reformator und Vater im Glauben*. Referate aus der Vortragsreihe des Instituts für europäische Geschichte Mainz, ed. Peter Manns (Stuttgart: Steiner-Verlag-Wiesbaden-GmbH, 1985), 118–33. Reprinted in *Evangelium in der Geschichte: Studien zu Luther und der Reformation*. In honor of the 60th birthday of the author, ed. Leif Grane, Bernd Moeller, and Otto Hermann Pesch (Göttingen: Vandenhoeck and Ruprecht, 1988), 158–75).
2. WA BR 1, 56f. (No. 52 from November 11, 1517 to Johannes Lang); compare also Bernd Moeller and Karl Stackmann, *Luder – Luther – Eleutherius: Erwägungen zu Luthers Namen* (Göttingen: Vandenhoeck and Ruprecht, 1981).
3. See for example WA BR 1, No. 48, 69–71; WA BR 2, No. 371, 46–59 (from January 25, 1521); WA 6, 404, 31–405, 1.
4. WA 10/II, 105, 2–106, 14; WA BR 2 No. 455, 39–45 (from March 5, 1522); WA BR 3 No. 567, 31–33 (from January 3, 1523); WA 18, 327, 30f.

5. Gerhard Ebeling, "Luthers Gebrauch der Wortfamilie 'Seelsorge,' *Lutherjahrbuch* 61 (1994), 7–44.

6. "It is not the way of a Christian heart not to rejoice in reliable statements (*assertiones*). To the contrary a Christian must rejoice in reliable statements or he would not be a Christian. I call a reliable statement – not to play with words any further – a statement you can constantly hold on to, approve of, bear witness to, keep in your heart, in short an unsurpassed perseverance." (*De servo arbitrio*, 1524; WA 18, 603); Dietrich Kerlen, *Assertio: die Entwicklung von Luthers theologischem Anspruch und der Streit mit Erasmus von Rotterdam* (Wiesbaden: Steiner, 1976).

7. See most recently Volker Leppin, "Luther-Literatur seit 1983," *Theologische Rundschau* 65 (2000), 350–77; 431–54; Scott Hendrix, "American Luther Research in the Twentieth Century," *Lutheran Quarterly* 15 (2001), 1–23. For the older research see George W. Forell, "Lutherforschung in den USA," in *Lutherforschung heute. Referate und Berichte des 1. Internationalen Lutherforschungskongresses Aarhus, 18.–23. August 1956*, ed. Vilmos Vajta (Berlin Lutherisches Verlagshaus, 1958); Lowel C. Green, "Luther Research in English-speaking Countries since 1971," *Lutherjahrbuch* 44 (1977), 105–26; Scott H. Hendrix, "Martin Luther und die 'Confessio Augustana' in der englischsprachigen Forschung seit 1977," *Lutherjahrbuch* 50 (1983), 166–80; Karl-Heinz zur Mühlen, "Zur Erforschung des jungen Luther seit 1876," in *Lutherjahrbuch* 50 (1983), 48–125; Lewis W. Spitz, "Luther in America: Reformation History Since Philip Schaff," in Bernd Moeller, ed., *Luther in der Neuzeit* (Gütersloh: G. Mohn, 1983),160–77; James M. Kittelson, "Luther the Theologian," in *Reformation Europe: A Guide to Research* (St. Louis: Center for Reformation Research, 1992), II:5–46; Hartmut Lehmann, *Martin Luther in the American Imagination* (Munich: Wilhelm Fink Verlag, 1988).

8. Bernhard Lohse, *Luthers Theologie in ihrer historischen Entwicklung und in ihrem systematischen Zusammenhang* (Göttingen: Vandenhoeck and Ruprecht, 1995). ET *Martin Luther's Theology: Its Historical and Systematic Development* (Minneapolis: Fortress Press, 1999).

9. "I wish we would put Luther back into the sixteenth century – and leave him there." Bernhard Lohse, *Eine neue Darstellung der Theologie Luthers* (Hamburg: Kath Akad, 1996), 23.

10. Gerhard Ebeling, *Luthers Seelsorge an seinen Briefen dargestellt* (Tübingen: Mohr, 1997).

11. Ulrich Asendorf, *Die Theologie Martin Luthers nach seinen Predigten* (Göttingen: Vandenhoeck and Ruprecht, 1988).

12. Ulrich Asendorf, *Lectura in Biblia. Luthers Genesisvorlesung (1535–1546)* (Göttingen: Vandenhoeck and Ruprecht, 1998).

13. New studies have shown that the evaluation of Luther is in desperate need of correction. It is true that scholasticism was the dominant thought and knowledge system at the universities in Luther's time, especially at the universities known to him. Yet the term "scholasticism" is a question in itself. Over the course of the late Middle Ages numerous and highly different ways of scholastic thought had developed that denied one another's authorization. Though this scholastic controversy abated toward the end of the fifteenth century, it still continued to shape the propaedeutic education in the *artes liberales*. In addition, some

explicitly anti-scholastic approaches to education and knowledge systems began to gain influence, which made for an evermore diverse and colorful theological landscape toward the end of the late Middle Ages. Only some reform efforts representative of the great variety will be mentioned here: the diverse movement of humanism and its highly varied proponents in Erfurt; numerous theologies in various orders, which did not draw on Thomas Aquinas and the Dominican scholasticism referring to him but, for example, on Augustine who generated many a reform movement or "theology" during the fourteenth and fifteenth centuries; the *Devotio Moderna* and its movement of the Brethren of the Common Life as well as many other reform efforts spawned within the monastic orders with the goal of returning to the original observant way of their founding time. Yet an overview summarizing the diversity of these movements did not exist – until now.

14. Cf. WA 54, 179–87.
15. Cf. ibid.
16. See Markus Wriedt, *Gnade und Erwählung* (Mainz: P. Von Zabern, 1991).
17. LW 34, 336–37.
18. Martin Brecht, "Iustitia Chrsiti. Die Entdeckung Martin Luthers," *Zeitschrift fur Theologie und Kirche* 74 (Tubingen: Mohr, 1977), 179–233; and "Der rechtferigende Glaube an das Evangelium von Jesus Christus als Mitte von Luthers Theologie," *Zeitschrift für Kirchengeschichte* 89 (1978), 45–77.
19. Cf. Gerhard Ebeling, *Evangelische Evangelienauslegung: eine Untersuchung zu Luthers Hermeneutik* (Darmstadt: Wissenschaftliche Buchgesellschaft; new edn. with an Afterword by the author, 1991); Gerhard Ebeling, *Lutherstudien* (Tübingen: Mohr, 1971–89), I:1–220.
20. Compare the overview to the current research in Bernhard Lohse's two volumes *Der Durchbruch der reformatorischen Erkenntnis bei Martin Luther* (Darmstadt: Wissenschaftliche Buchgesellschaft, 1968) and the edition with the subtitle *Neue Untersuchungen* (Stuttgart: Steiner-Verlag Wiesbaden, 1988).
21. For an example compare the marginal notes of Rom. 1:17 or those in chapter 3 with the finished commentary on 4:7 or 8:25–35. LW 25, 36 (for Rom. 1:17), LW 25, 74 (for Rom. 8:25–35).
22. Gabriele Schmidt-Lauber, *Luthers Vorlesung über den Römerbrief 1515/16* (Cologne: Böhlau, 1994).
23. See Karl Heinz zur Mühlen, *Nos extra nos: Luthers Theologie zwischen Mystik und Scholastik* (Tübingen: Mohr, 1972) and Volker Leppin: "Zur Aufnahme mystischer Traditionen in Luthers erster Ablaßthese," *Archiv fur Reformationsgeschichte* 93) (Gutersloh: Mohn, 2003), 7–25; Markus Wriedt: "Martin Luther und die Mystik," in: Anne Baumer-Schleinkofer: *Hildegard von Bingen . . .* (Wurzburg: R&K Verlag, 2001), 249–273." The appeal of this so radically different way of theological reasoning and arguing is most probably to be found in the mystic's tradition of allowing no other authority next to God himself or his Word and for interpretations only accepting one's own personal experience of God or the one made possible through Scripture. For the young Luther the so-called spiritualistic way of mystic thinking seemed to harbor no danger. Only over the course of later controversies with spiritualistic opponents did he see himself faced with the necessity of acknowledging the working of the Spirit in its relationship to Scripture. While he is successful in warding off the danger

of spiritualism from Reformation theology, he falls victim to dogmatizing and reducing Reformation theology to confessional formulas as well as a doctrine to be preached in the same conformist way in all places at all times. The developing deficit in the spiritual realm of the Reformation from Wittenberg is at first filled by so-called "enthusiasts" and later by non-conformists and dissident groups, which either have not been recognized as legitimate preachers of the Protestant teachings or, if so, only much later. Markus Wriedt, "Mystik und Protestantismus-ein Widerspruch?" in Johannes Schilling, ed., *Mystik-Theologie-Religion* (Leipzig: Evangelische Verlagsantalt, 2003).

24. See e.g. *Disputatio contra scholasticam theologicam* (WA 1, 224–28); the *Heidelberg Disputation* (WA 1, 353–74); *Ninety-five Theses* (WA 1, 233–38). That this small circle of his first audience cannot remain that closed for long, how Luther's Reformation hermeneutics finds its way to a broader public, and what implications are involved for the University of Wittenberg, as also of course for Luther's own person and the formation of a Reformation movement, was shown only recently by Jens Martin Kruse, *Universitätstheologie und Kirchenreform: die Anfänge der Reformation in Wittenberg 1516–1522* (Mainz: von Zabern, 2002).

25. WA 1, 224–28.

26. WA 1, 233–38.

27. Thesis 27: They preach only human doctrines... (LW 31, 27).

28. Cf. WA Br 1, 108–12 (No. 48).

29. Cf. Kurt-Victor Selge, "Normen der Christenheit im Streit um Ablaß und Kirchenautorität 1518 bis 1521." Typescript, University of Heidelberg, 1968.

30. Friedhelm Jürgensmeier, Erebishof Albrecht von Brandenburg 1490–1545 (Frankfurt/main: Knecht, 1991): 88–91.

31. Compare *Dokumente zur Causa Lutheri (1517–1521)*, ed. and comm. by Erwin Iserloh and Peter Fabisch (Münster Aschendorfische Verlagsbuchhandlung, 1988).

32. WA 1, 525–628.

33. WA 2, 28–33.

34. WA 2, 5–26.

35. Bernhard Alfred R. Felmberg, *Die Ablasstheologie Kardinal Cajetans (1469–1534).* Studies in Medieval and Reformation Thought. Vol. LXVI (Leiden: Brill, 1998), cited in *Revue Thomiste* 100 (2000), 138–41.

36. WA 1, 281–314.

37. Friedrich Beisser, *Claritas scripturae bei Martin Luther* (Göttingen: Vandenhoeck and Ruprecht, 1966); Walter Mostert, "Scriptura sacra sui ipsius interpres: Bemerkungen zum Verständnis der Heiligen Schrift durch Luther," *Lutherjahrbuch* 46 (1979), 60–96; Albrecht Beutel, *In dem Anfang war das Wort. Studien zu Luthers Sprachverständnis* (Tübingen: Mohr, 1991). For the later years see Kenneth Hagen, *Luther's Approach to Scripture as seen in his 'Commentaries' on Galatians 1519–1538* (Tübingen: Mohr, 1993).

38. Carl Axel Aurelius, *Verborgene Kirche: Luthers Kirchenverständnis aufgrund seiner Streitschriften und Exegese 1519–1521* (Hanover: Lutherisches Verlagshaut, 1983; Tarald Rasmussen, *Inimici ecclesiae: das ekklesiologische Feindbild in Luthers "Dictata super Psalterium" (1513–1515) im Licht der theologischen Tradition* (Leiden: E. J. Brill, 1989).

39. Cf. Bernard McGinn, *Antichrist* (San Francisco: Harper, 1994); Volker Leppin, "Antichrist," II.1, RGG⁴ 1 (1998), 532f.; Volker Leppin, *Antichrist und Jüngster Tag: das Profil apokalyptischer Flugschriftenpublizistik im deutschen Luthertum 1548–1618* (Gütersloh: Gütersloher Verlagshaus, 1999).

40. WA 2, 136–42.

41. WA 2, 80–130.

42. WA 2, 685–97; 713–23; 727–37; 742–58.

43. WA 6, 104–34.

44. WA 2, 685–97.

45. WA 6, 3–8; 36–60; cf. WA 15, 293–322 and WA 51, 331–424.

46. WA 2, 166–71; cf. WA 10/II, 265f. and WA 30/III, 205–48.

47. Karl Heinz zur Mühlen, "Zur Rezeption der augustinischen Sakramentsformel 'Accedit verbum ad elementum et fit sacramentum' in der Theologie Luthers," ZThK 70 (1973), 50–76.

48. WA 6, 202–76.

49. WA 6, 404–69.

50. At the imperial diets demands for reform and criticism of prevailing injustices were again and again presented under the *gravamina germaniae nationis*. Cf. Bruno Gebhardt, *Die Gravamina der deutschen Nation gegen den römischen Hof* (Breslau: Koebner, 1895); Heinz Scheible, "Die Gravamina: Luther und der Wormser Reichstag 1521," in *Melanchthon und die Reformation* (Mainz: P. von Zabern, 1996), 167–83; Hans Christoph Rublack, *Gravamina und Reformation. Städtische Gesellschaft und Reformation* (Stuttgart, 1980).

51. WA 6, 497–573.

52. WA 6, 356, 3–8.

53. WA 7, 20–38 (German); 42–73 (Latin).

54. WA 9, 582, 31.

55. Cf. Gerhard Ebeling, *Luther: Einführung in sein Denken* (Tübingen: Mohr, 1981). ET *Luther: An Introduction to His Thought*, trans. R. A. Wilson (Philadelphia: Fortress Press, 1972).

56. Cf. Eike Wolgast, *Die Religionsfrage als Problem des Widerstandsrechtes im 16. Jahrhundert* (Heidelberg: Winter, 1980); Eike Wolgast, *Hochstift und Reformation: Studien zur Geschichte der Reichskirche zwischen 1517 und 1548* (Stuttgart: Steiner, 1995).

57. Cf. Markus Matthias, *Andreas Bodenstein von Karlstadt (1486–1541), ein Theologe der frühen Reformation*. Beiträge eines Arbeitsgesprächs vom 24.–25. November 1995 in Wittenberg (Lutherstadt Wittenberg: Drei Kastanien Verlag, 1998).

58. On the Zwickau prophets see Lohse, *Martin Luther's Theology*, 146–47.

59. Cf. Albrecht Peters, *Gesetz und Evangelium* (Gütersloh: Gütersloher Verlagshaus Mohr, 1981).

60. Timothy Wengert: *Law and Gospel: Philip Melanchthon's Debate with John Agricola of Eisleben over Poenitentia* (Grand Rapids: Baker, 1997); Timothy Wengert, "Gesetz und Buße: Melanchthons erster Streit mit Johannes Agricola," in Günter Frank, ed., *Der Theologe Melanchthon* (Stuttgart, 2000), 375–92.

61. Matthias Richter, *Gesetz und Heil: Eine Untersuchung zur Vorgeschichte und zum Verlauf des sogenannten Zweiten Antinomistischen Streits* (Göttingen: Vandenhoeck and Ruprecht, 1996).

62. In research papers the interpretation of Luther's understanding of authority has been discussed controversially. Compare an overview of different positions at Gunter Wolf, ed., *Luther und die Obrigkeit* (Darmstadt: Wissenschaftliche Buchgesellschaft, 1972).

63. Cf. Walther Köhler, *Zwingli und Luther: ihr Streit über das Abendmahl nach seinen politischen und religiösen Beziehungen* (Leipzig: Verein für Reformations geschichte, 1924–53); Eberhard Grözinger, *Luther und Zwingli: die Kritik an der mittelalterlichen Lehre von der Messe als Wurzel des Abendmahlsstreites* (Zurich, Cologne, Gütersloh: G. Mohr, 1980).

64. WA 11, 431–56.

65. Maria Großmann, *Humanism in Wittenberg 1485–1517* (Nieuwkoop: De Graaf, 1975); Helmar Junghans, *Der junge Luther und die Humanisten* (Göttingen: Vandenhoeck and Ruprecht, 1985); Helmar Junghans, "Die Worte Christi geben das Leben," *Wartburg Jahrbuch 1996*, 154–75.

66. Manfred Hoffmann, *Erkenntnis und Verwirklichung der wahren Theologie nach Erasmus von Rotterdam* (Tübingen: Mohr, 1972); ET, *Rhetoric and Theology: The Hermeneutic of Erasmus of Rotterdam* (Toronto: University of Toronto Press, 1994).

67. WA 18, 600–787.

68. WA 18, 609, 4–14.

69. See also Eric W. Gritsch, "Luther as Bible translator," chapter 4 of the present volume.

70. Berndt Hamm, "Was ist reformatorische Rechtfertigungslehre?," ZThK 83 (1986), 1–38; Berndt Hamm, "Einheit und Vielfalt der Reformation – oder: was die Reformation zur Reformation machte," in Hamm, et al., *Reformationstheorien: ein kirchenhistorischer Disput über die Einheit und Vielfalt der Reformation* (Göttingen Vandenhoeck and Ruprecht, 1995), 57–127. Most recently, Volker Leppin, "Wie reformatorisch ist die Reformation?," ZThK 99 (2002), 162–76.

# 7 Luther's moral theology

BERND WANNENWETSCH

## APPROACHING LUTHER'S ETHICAL THOUGHT

A proper understanding of Luther's ethical thought is hampered in two ways. First, contemporary ideas of ethics as a discipline in its own right, when projected back on to Luther, are likely to fail, as his ethical thought cannot be separated from doctrinal considerations within the whole scope of his theology. Instead of singling out his "ethics," then, we must rather explore his "moral theology," the web of theological thought of which the texture of his moral ideas is composed.

The second complicating factor is that Luther's ethic has elicited a degree of passionate apologetic and repudiation rare among theological ethics, and thereby has been exceptionally exposed to one-sided and distorted interpretations. Consequently, no account of his moral theology can be given without some engagement with those interpretations and their problematic claims.

A look at the history of the reception of Luther's theology arouses our suspicion of monistic accounts such as Hegel's Luther of "freedom," Karl Holl's Luther of "conscience" or many a theologian's Luther of "justification." These fall short not because they overemphasize one aspect of Luther's thought to the disadvantage of others, but because they fail, in most cases, to do justice to the very concept focused on. Hegel, for example, was not wrong to present Luther's theology as a theology of freedom; rather, his account of freedom was flawed because his portrayal of Luther as the founding father of modern individualism by virtue of his superseding traditional authority could not be reconciled with Luther's strong theological concept of authority.

Over against monistic explanatory schemes, we are assuming that Luther's theology must be understood as having its unity, or (to hazard a musical metaphor) its harmony, at the grammatical level. Its coherence lies less in the formal domain, in terms of a systemic relation of parts, and more in the harmonious way in which the different language games it engages resonate with one another. Hence, if we allow for a variety of appropriate accounts of Luther's moral theology, we are bound to require that each be harmonically rounded enough to comprise *the whole* of Luther's ethics, not by muting but by integrating the overtones produced by the other accounts.

## THE FIRST COMMANDMENT AND THE SECOND TABLET

The grammatical coherence in Luther's moral theology can be grasped initially by attending to his concern for the commandments.[1] Although Christian moral theology has always taught the divine commandments, it was only in the Reformation that the Decalogue took center stage in moral instruction. Before that time, it had gradually emerged from a shadowy existence to assume, by the high Middle Ages, an important role as a mirror of sin in confession, therein almost absorbing other concepts such as the double love command. In a typical move, Luther did not merely take over this tendency but redirected it toward a focus on the First Commandment. For this reason his ethics cannot simply be understood as a version of "divine command theory." Rather, his handling of the issue of commandment, law, and obedience mirrors his theological imagination, which revolves around the primacy of God's efficacious word that creates its own response in faith.

### The oneness of God's command

Luther insisted on the oneness of God's command over against the in-herited tradition of distinguishing the Decalogue as a merely moral code from other codices in the Old Testament of a ceremonial or a legal nature. The reformer rejected this distinction by pointing out that the Decalogue itself encompasses a cultic order (inherent in the Second and Third Commandments) as well as a legal order (inherent in the Eighth Commandment which presupposes and reinforces judgment in the gate). His most important shift, however, was the straightforward christological focus that he brought to bear on interpreting the commandments. In both forms, as natural law engraved in every human heart, and in their revealed Mosaic version, the divine commands suffer from the distorting eyesight of fallen humankind. Therefore the content of God's law in its original purpose and scope is only really intelligible in Jesus Christ.

This christological focus issued in a twofold movement. First, fulfill-ment of the divine commandments is construed as moving from outside to within the agent. Luther gathers from Jesus' antitheses in the Sermon of the Mount that it is not enough to act externally in accordance with what is demanded if the inner motives are not in concert. Thus, in a physico-theological image, Luther envisages a necessary movement from the hand (of action), by way of the mouth (of words), up to the heart (of inward thought and affect, WA 30/I, 30–32).

Second, corresponding to this is a movement toward the positive implications of negatively formulated commands. So, for example, the prohibition of adultery is extended toward the positive command to live a chaste life and to "help others to live likewise." Similarly, Luther comments on the Fifth Commandment: "... we should not endanger our neighbour's life, nor cause him any harm, but help and befriend him in every necessity of life" (BoC, 343).

From his theological concern for the oneness of God's command sprang Luther's resistance to the tradition of the "evangelical counsels" that had served as a map for the moral life over centuries in Christendom. In opposition to this tradition, which contrasted "mere" obedience to the commandments (in the literal sense of avoiding certain actions) as the morally required, bottom-level performance of the ordinary Christian with a higher calling to supererogatory works associated with the monastic life, Luther insisted that, in following the route of the commandments, the *whole* of the Christian life and vocation was at stake.

The deeper theological reason for his insistence is brought out in his explanation of the Decalogue in both *Small* and *Large* versions of his *Catechism*, a literary genre intended to "instruct beginners in the Christian life on how to believe, to perform and to avoid certain actions" (WA 19, 76, 2). Here, the close connection between the First Commandment and the others becomes the theological clue to the whole. Luther was by no means the first to emphasize this connection. Late medieval theologians such as Gerson had held that only he who keeps the individual commandments is a true keeper of the First. Yet Luther significantly reverses the order: "... *primum mandatum omnia alia in se continet. Qui enim hoc servat, omnia servat, et qui aliquod non servat, hoc non servat, quia cor eius aliud quam solum deum respicit.*" ("The first commandment contains in itself all the other commandments. Whoever keeps it, keeps them all, and who does not keep it, neither keeps them, for his heart clings to something other than God alone," WA 1, 438, 7). He sees the First Commandment as the "chief source and fountainhead," the light which is to "illuminate ... all the others" (BoC 409f.), not only the other commandments, which are seen as "exercises" of the first, but also "all doctrines of the prophets and Psalms, all curses ... and promises" (WA 28, 601, 21).

Luther's insight is mirrored in the organization of his series of short explanations in the *Small Catechism*, where each individual commandment is introduced by the same wording that echoes the Sch'ma Israel (Deut. 6:4): "We should fear and love the Lord so that we ..." Yet his construction does not introduce a clause of intention but a clause of result: it introduces a theological consequence rooted in his conviction that there is only one way in which the First Commandment is to be fulfilled: faith.

### Faith as fulfillment of the commandments

In explaining the First Commandment, "I am the Lord your God, you shall have no other gods except me," Luther says: "We should fear, love and trust in God above all things" (BoC 342). And the question "What is it to have a god?" is answered: "A god is that to which we look for all good and in which we find refuge in every time of need...The trust and faith of the heart alone makes both God and an idol...That to which your heart clings and entrusts itself is, I say, really your god." Hence it becomes clear what the First Commandment calls for: "The purpose of this commandment, therefore, is to require true faith and confidence of the heart" (BoC 365).

At the same time, Luther's emphasis on the First Commandment is the strongest possible guard against the assumption that fulfilling the commands could be an achievement. For faith is a gift in the light of which the preamble of the Decalogue ("I am the Lord your God who...") reads as gospel; and this allows Luther to draw on the philological coincidence of imperative and future tenses in the Hebrew wording of "you shall": "Where the heart is right with God and this commandment is kept, fulfillment of all the others *will follow* of its own accord" (BoC 371, emphasis mine).[2] The oneness of God's command is rooted in faith, which holds together the first and second table of the Decalogue. Even though Luther can follow Augustine in adopting a triadic interpretation of the first tablet, according to which the First Commandment directs the heart, the Second the mouth, and the Third the whole body in its works (WA 6, 229, 21), it is nevertheless true that the very way in which the individual commandments are fulfilled – by hand and mouth and body – is to be, in the first place, a matter of the heart (i.e., of faith). This is why the Christian life does not fall apart into a "spiritual" sphere on the one hand and a "worldly" sphere on the other.

### Natural law

The primacy and permeating power of the First Commandment leads to another consequence that distinguishes Luther's moral theology from the medieval mainstream characterized by recourse to the idea of an innate moral knowledge. While "to know that there is a god" is implied by natural law, it makes a world of difference, argues Luther, "to know who God is. The first is known by nature and written in hearts, the second is taught through the Holy Spirit alone" (WA 19, 207, 11).

Furthermore, for the second table of the Decalogue, medieval theology usually identified the content of natural law with the golden rule, thereby interpreting the demand to love the neighbor as oneself in terms of reciprocity. Luther, by contrast, arrives at a sharp alternative: either self-love or love of neighbor. His reading of Leviticus 19:18 is again driven by a christological consideration, drawing on Philippians 2:4–11 and Christ's condescension (WA 2, 147, 19–150, 31). In the light of Christ's self-less love, neighborly love cannot but become self-disinterested. The "as yourself" may serve as a pointer toward the rationality of natural law – everyone can see that what the golden rule says is just and true. But now, in the light of Christ, all the fervor that is naturally directed toward the safeguarding of one's own interest is now free to turn to the neighbor – without return. This non-reciprocal understanding of what Luther can now term "Christian and evangelical law" (WA 18, 308, 34) is conceived as being essentially participation in Christ's sacrifice: "Suffering, suffering, cross, cross, is the right of a Christian, and none other" (WA 18, 310, 28).

## LAW: THE WHOLE STORY

If we are to expand our discussion of the Decalogue to Luther's wider theology of the law, we are well advised to approach it from his mature account in the commentary on Genesis.[3] Luther's theology of law has often been less than fully understood, as interpreters have tried to expound his ideas in terms of a systemic relation – a system of ideas on "law" where one idea is defined and circumscribed by the adjoining one. While the systematization of Reformation theology according to the notion of different "uses" of the law – political, theological (convicting, accusing), and a "third" use (controversial in Luther) as guidance for the Christian moral life – has its value, Luther's own account as laid out in the commentary has deliberately adopted not a systemic but a *narrative dramatic* perspective from which it cannot be abstracted without losing substance.

The most important hermeneutic implication is that Luther's theology of law cannot be equated with the infamous law and gospel antinomy. As much as Luther stresses this antinomy in the context of salvation – the law mortifies while the gospel resurrects – it is not meant to function as an all-encompassing category that absorbs every other theological *topos*. The narrow focus on this antinomy as the formal principle of modern Protestantism[4] has led to a variety of antinomian accounts of law's fundamental opposition to grace and gospel, in which law is either flatly rejected as altogether "heteronomous" or, by way of a second-order antinomy, reduced to its (formally) negative impact as a mirror of sin or a barrier against anarchy. Whatever sophistication those concepts display they are incapable of helping us discern what different theological language games require. Apart from the soteriological language game, in which the most extreme contrast of law to gospel is required to convey the radical nature of grace, when it comes to moral theology, the law plays a more complex role that can only be fully understood dramatically, i.e., in terms of what *becomes* of the law in various chapters of the history of salvation.

In contrast to the antinomian tendency in modern Protestantism, what is striking in Luther's reading of Genesis is that the law is already there in the garden at the very moment when God explicitly calls on Adam to eat and not to eat (Gen. 2:16f.). Surprisingly, the law is not envisaged as a postlapsarian device, a makeshift repair provoked by the fall, but rather as belonging to Adam's original righteousness, and as such, it could not be opposed to his spontaneous love of God. Indeed, Luther understands the original purpose of the law as being to provide Adam with a means of giving concrete form to this love through his responsive obedience to God's explicit command.

"And so when Adam had been created in such as way that he was, so to speak, drunk with joy towards God, and rejoiced also in all other creatures, then a new tree was created for the distinction of good and evil, so that Adam might have a definite sign of worship and reverence towards God" (WA 42, 71). Ultimately, for Luther, the meaning of the law is worship in its fullest sense, and this meaning requires at the same time a social setting proper to it. Therefore, the promulgation of law is deemed to be identical with the foundation of the church (in the universal sense): "*Haec est institutio ecclesiae*: this is the foundation of the Church" (WA 42, 79). Such is Luther's comment on the divine command to abstain from eating from the tree of knowing good and evil; and he imagines that Adam, Eve and their family would have gathered under this tree to delight in God's presence and praise.

We see the reformer emphasizing that the existence of the law presupposes grace and not sin. Its purpose could not be to attain righteousness, for Adam is already drunk with joy toward God; nor to accuse of sin, when there was none; nor to prevent anarchy, which it did not do, as the further plot of the biblical story reveals. Even the fall, moreover, does not do away with the law's original identity: "Adam after sin is not the same person as before sin in the state of innocence, and yet no distinction is made between the law promulgated before and after sin" (WA 42, 82). The fall changes the meaning of the law precisely as Adam changes. Together with its subject, the law becomes different: it becomes an "*alia lex.*" Luther describes this alienation of the law essentially as "letter" (*lex litterae*). The law becomes an external code; it becomes a "mere law" as opposed to its spiritual, life-giving, original meaning as both "gospel and law." The result is twofold: As a mere external code, the law is either received as an arbitrary imposition from outside, or it is up for objectification, to become circumscribed and defined as a precise list of demands. Only now and as such does the law turn into a "merely moral matter" ("*tantum rem moralem*" WA 40/I, 413) and, consequently, a means of attaining righteousness in one's own right.

But for Luther, as we have already seen, God's law demands not only just action but that the person be just: it calls forth the heart that "fears, loves and trusts God above all things." And it is precisely in this spiritual sense, which aims at the heart of the agent, that the accusing use of the law (*usus elenchticus*) shines out. Only when the law is understood in these terms can it be said truly to terrify and accuse, in that it demands a subject which is no longer there. In opposition to the false use of the law as means to self-justification made by the sinner in his or her desperate striving after righteousness, there is another use which God makes of the law that now acts as accuser, convicting of sin.

It is in this chapter of God's salvific history – and only in this – that the law must take on "alien cloth" as utterly mortifying. At the same time, it calls forth the gospel, as it requires another person. "That is, it calls for Christ, and pushes us towards him, so that we first become different people through his grace in faith, and become like him, and then do genuinely good works" (WA 17/II, 70). Only in our being conformed to Christ, in our being made a Christ-like person, is the accusing function of the law overcome.

In the light of this account, the Pauline imagery of dying and rising with Christ, seen from the perspective of Christ's double function as both the fulfiller of the law and the one who overcomes it (Rom. 10:4), takes on a precise meaning. It means dying to the external code, to its pride and desperation, and rising again to the law in its original sense, as that which gives concrete form and order to the joy of a life in Christ. The restitution of the law that accompanies the mortification and resurrection of its subject leads to knowing God's law in a new form, as the "law of the spirit of life in Christ" (Rom. 8:2).

## INNER AND OUTER MAN

The foregoing considerations allow us to glimpse why the widespread understanding of Luther's ethics as dualistic or polarizing is bound to fail.

This understanding is typically associated with Luther's distinction between the "inner" and the "outward" man, famously employed in his treatise on *The Freedom of a Christian* (1520).

In the view of interpreters such as Max Weber, Ernst Troeltsch, Herbert Marcuse and others, this distinction within Luther's theological anthropology comes down to a separation between the religious and worldly spheres – a separation that resurfaces again in Luther's social and political thought in the parallel distinction of the Two Kingdoms. The charge brought by these authors against Luther amounts to this: The distinction between the inner and the outward man promotes a schizophrenic character in the human agent – a disease that leads finally to the annihilation of ethics altogether. For the really important man is the inner: he is said to be a "perfectly free lord of all, subject to none," as Luther's quotation goes, while the outward man is a "perfectly dutiful servant of all, subject to all" (LW 31, 344). This seems to suggest that what the outward man does or leaves undone is relatively unimportant, as it cannot possibly touch the identity and the freedom of the inner, which is of a purely religious and spiritual nature, unaffected by any worldly circumstance. What is left then for the outward man engaged in worldly relations is twofold: Either he will be the perfect "subject," as the second part of Luther's saying seems to imply – the political quietist, easy to rule and manipulate (Marcuse). Or alternatively, his kind of engagement with the world will become the prototype for what Ernst Troeltsch has called "cultural compromise."

The fundamental misunderstanding of such interpreters lies in their supposition that "inner" and "outward" represent anthropological provinces *within* "man." Yet Luther thought of both those designations as assignable to man *as a whole*, only in different perspectives, either facing God (*coram Deo*) or facing the world (*coram mundo*). Likewise, freedom and bondage are not to be divided between the inner and the outer man, but belong to both. Liberated from the bondage of sin, the inner man is the slave of God and the outer is the slave of his neighbor; yet both bondages amount not to a new antinomy to freedom, but to its proper *Gestalt*.

In spite of its misconception, the dualistic reading of Luther has made its way into the self-perception of the Lutheran tradition with the help of Kantian moral philosophy. From the Neo-Protestant point of view, there is actually a way in which the inner man is capable of relating positively to the outward man, namely by supplying the "motivation" for the good works that the outward man is destined to do. The inner man of faith motivates the outward man to do what the outward man has rationally identified as the good thing to do, and insures that he does it with a happy mind.

## FAITH AND LOVE

The Neo-Protestant account typically involves the idea of an autonomous relationship between faith and love,[5] finding a warrant in Luther's other famous saying from the same treatise: "A Christian lives not in himself, but in Christ and in his neighbour ... He lives in Christ through faith, in his neighbour through love" (LW 31, 371). This saying seems to ascribe at least a relative autonomy to love. In dealing with the world, the Christian, motivated by faith, is to discover the right ways to act by virtue of the creative potential of love. While faith is good for motivation, love is the formative power in the Christian life.

But can this relative autonomy of love really derive from Luther? It sounds altogether different when the reformer says: "Therefore, faith remains the agent, love remains the act" (WA 17/II, 98, 25). Luther obviously conceives of faith and love in terms of a quasi-personal relationship and not in terms of an impersonal schema such as cause and effect, potentiality and realization, indicative and imperative, etc. This is related to his rich concept of faith, which he set against the scholastic notion that culminated in the formula "*fides caritate formata.*" The scholastic concept held that unless love has come to perfect faith by bestowing on it the right form and activity, faith is "mere faith" which neither saves nor makes for a life of holiness.

By contrast, Luther understood faith not as a cognitive or "inner" state of affairs but as a "work" in its own right: an inner movement that cannot rest. "As faith provides you with beatitude (*Seligkeit*) and eternal life, so it provides you with good works and it cannot be obstructed. For as a living human being cannot abstain, but must move, eat, drink and work," so it is with faith: "Just have faith and every work will flow from you naturally" (WA DB 7, 10).

Though faith and love must surely hang together in an organic way, there must still be a certain thrust: Are the good works meant to be ultimately works of love or of faith? What is at stake here is the correct interpretation of Galatians 5:6: "faith that is effective through love." In his commentary on Galatians, Luther dismisses the scholastic interpreters as "bad students of grammar" when they understand love as the formative power and faith as mere "raw material" or a "shapeless chaos" (LW 27, 29). In his close reading of Paul, Luther turns this account on its head: In fact, faith is always efficacious, and love is the instrument through which it works. Hence one can paraphrase the reformer's view as an exact reversal of the scholastic formula: *Caritas fide formata*; love is in need of being oriented and formed by faith.

It was because the term "love" had become so problematically charged with psychological and activist connotations (as a virtue) that Luther insisted on the centrality of faith rather than love. Having been a somewhat pale concept in medieval Christianity, faith was all the more suited to capture the radical nature of justification by grace as exclusively God's work without any human contribution. Consequently, love, when formed by faith, could no longer be understood as a human faculty; rather, a refined theological anthropology was brought to bear on the moral quality of love, which was given a highly compressed formulation in article XX "On Faith and Good Works" of the Augsburg Confession: "... *corda renovantur et induunt novos affectus, ut parere bona opera possint.*" In the power of the Spirit, faith renews the heart, and the renewed heart is clothed with new affects, which, in turn, enable good works (BoC 45, translation altered). Faith is the *"genitrix,"* the fertile soil of good will and just action, in that it gives a specific shape to love by transforming the affective existence of the believer, from the "impious affects" toward the affects of the Spirit.

## GOOD WORKS

This relationship bears on Luther's understanding of good works in a crucial way. If the heart is set right and the affects are renewed, the resulting works must be good in the fullest sense. "Through faith, every deed is good without distinction." They are indeed "perfect," not for their phenotypic splendor (as in the sense of supererogatory works) but in that they are works of faith. This Luther takes to be a legitimate positive conclusion from the Pauline statement that "everything that does not come from faith is sin" (Rom. 14:23). In turn, faith as the hidden agent of the works makes them perfect, i.e. whole, undivided (Greek *teleios*), even though it may be just a small and unspectacular gesture. "In this faith, all works become equal and one work is like the other; all distinctions between works fall away whether they be great, small, short, long, many or few" (LW 43, 26).

In this light, good deeds have to be of a significantly "external" character. They exist, as it were, "enhypostatically" in faith, which is God's work in his people. Faith creates and implants a new *telos*, which is identical for every deed that comes from faith: the praise and glorification of God. Therefore, it can fairly be said that Luther's ethic does not represent another version of an ethic of "the good" but very specifically an ethics of "good works." The good is not brought into view in eudaemonist terms as the aim of man's striving nor in consequentialist terms as the desired end that justifies the means, nor in liberal-procedural terms as the common denominator of public consent. Rather, in God's economy, Luther reckons with a rich surplus of good works in their full scope and perfected form "that God has prepared beforehand that we may walk within them" (Eph. 2:10).

But given the hidden character of faith, how can those works be identified and how can they be assured of their divine nature? Where can one learn to discern the good works when one encounters them? Luther came to formulate an answer to these questions especially in his conflicts with the Spiritualists of his day who claimed an inner disclosure of the goodness of their acts.

Luther's skeptical answer to them is twofold: Instead of private revelation, assurance of good works may be found in the created orders of political, economic, and ecclesial life on the one hand and, on the other, in the "lovely means" that believers experience by participating in worship: word and sacrament. Let us consider the first location as expounded in Luther's teaching on the Three Estates.

## THREE ESTATES

### Politics, economics and church

"Firstly, the Bible speaks of and teaches about the works of God without any doubt; these are divided into three hierarchies: economics, politics and church" (*oeconomia, politia, ecclesia*, WA TR 5, 218, 14ff.). In addressing "hierarchies," "estates," "orders," "foundations," "stations" or whichever of the various terms is applied, Luther does not employ a sociological concept (as though he were referring to the different levels of his own society), but refers to the elementary and paradigmatic forms of social life that are appropriate to creaturely existence from the beginning.[6] He conceived these estates as "con-creatures" of humankind ("*concreatae sint*," WA 40/III, 222, 35f.), created together with man in order to provide the social spheres that are necessary for a flourishing and obedient life.

As we have seen in his commentary on Genesis, Luther identified the issuing of the commandment to eat and not to eat as the foundation of the church "without walls"; and in the divine mandate to the first human couple toward reproduction ("be fertile and multiply") he detected the institution of "*oeconomia*" (literally the household rule). As for the institution of *politia*, he seems to be somewhat inconsistent. On the one hand, he sees it as a postlapsarian function of God's providence against the anarchic power of sin (*usus politicus*); but on the other, he entertains the existence of politics in a prelapsarian sense: namely as an ordered way of living together harmoniously under God's rule without the coercive feature that marks political authority after the fall.

As later developments in Lutheranism have pushed the notion of created social orders into a twilight zone – it would be used to legitimize political measures such as the *"völkisch"* purification policies in Nazi Germany, and the reaction to these abuses in recent (especially German) Lutheranism would swing to the other extreme of completely discrediting the doctrine – it is important to note that Luther himself did not conceive of those estates in an idealistic manner. Neither did he conceive of them as (some type of Kantian) "pure forms" existing *prior* to humankind, into which men and women must be squeezed to fit, nor as mere functions of cultural history *subsequent* to the creation of man, as arbitrary developments at man's disposal. Against those right- and leftwing idealist accounts, Luther's notion of "con-creatures" exactly provides us with a way of steering clear of the infertile alternatives of either upholding timeless static orders that are external to human nature or casting all social forms of life as mere inventions of human prudence.

### Sanctification

For the reformer, these stations are "holy" in that they are instituted by God and sanctified through his word – holy though not *media salutis* or means of salvation. Rather, they are like the elements in sacramental theology: "natural material" created by God and entrusted to humankind, always in danger of being misread. Therefore the word has to come in addition (*"accedit verbum ad elementum…"*) and qualify them as "holy" (*"…et fit sacramentum"*). The moral meaning of the three estates is further brought out with the help of another of Luther's distinctions: between holy (*heilig*) and saved (*selig*): "For to be holy and to be saved are two entirely different things. We are saved through Christ alone; but we become holy both through this faith and through these divine foundations and orders. Even the godless may have much about them that is holy without being thereby saved" (WA 50, 643).

Only with this distinction in mind is Luther's famous characterization of marriage as a "worldly thing" saved from misunderstanding. While this characterization was meant to reject the idea of marriage as a sacrament (a means of salvation), it does not divorce marriage from faith and does not rule out Luther's other characterization of marriage as a "most spiritual order" (WA 12, 105, 29). This theological dignity Luther deems valid for marriage because it is an institution of God's purposing and because, owing to the manifold hardships and temptations it entails, especially when there are children, it almost "compels" faith (WA 12, 106, 126f.), as it is clearly too difficult to manage marriage and a family without the assurance of God's

word ("it is good to live the married life, this and no other is your spouse...")
and without God's further help.[7]

Here we note an important ethico-theological point: Sanctification for
Luther is not just a matter of faith, but a matter of faith *and* created orders, or
more precisely of *faith that is exercised in love within the divinely assigned
spheres of social life*, politics, economics, and religion (cf. WA 16: "...*in
talibus ordinationibus exercere caritatem*"). Of course, when faith and the
elementary forms of life work together toward human sanctification, they
cannot be juxtaposed. Consequently, Luther spoke out against the various
forms of religiously motivated "desertion" of those orders. Of such flight
from economic and political life ("*deserere oeconomiam, politiam*," WA 20,
7, 35f.) he held not only the Spiritualist movement of his day guilty, but
also the Friars who lived their lives as "parasite" existences at the cost of
others who cared for those institutions which, in their zeal for a better
justice and their claim of perfect obedience, the religious presupposed but
devalued.

### The permeating power of faith

Therefore, when Luther highlights faith as the station "above all stations,
in all stations and through all stations" (WA 12, 126, 17f.), a twofold polemical thrust is involved. First, in that through baptism, the primal Christian
station of faith as a station *above all stations* is assigned to every believer, the
class distinctions within medieval Christianity of lower and higher stations
are ruled out. Second, the primacy of this one station *in all stations* ensured
that the gospel permeated every aspect of human social life. In contrast to
the doctrine of the Two Kingdoms, which served a merely emancipative
purpose in Luther's theology, directed against the conflation of secular and
ecclesial authority and illegitimate borrowings of one side from the other,
his revision of the traditional doctrine of the Three Estates featured in his
own summaries of his theology. Obviously, this revision is to be understood
as the framework within which the doctrine of the Two must be theologically embedded lest it be misunderstood in terms of a separation of spheres.
Whereas the "Two" was bound to distinguish the different ways in which
God is exercising his rule: through worldly authority (often symbolized
through the sword, though by no means reducible to its coercive aspect)
on the one hand, and through the free power of the word on the other, the
teaching of the "Three" is a way of expressing how God's rule and faith
*penetrate* the elementary forms of social life alike, bringing the worldly
(politics and economics) and the spiritual (religion) into line.

Yet, within the affirmation of politics and economics, Luther also reckons with a serious danger. Commenting on Psalm 127: "Unless the LORD

builds the house, those who build it labor in vain. Unless the LORD guards the city, the guard keeps watch in vain," he describes the most destructive attitude to which those who actively care for the worldly stations might fall victim. While Luther knows how to sing the praises of the worldly prudence of rulers and merchants, he makes it clear (by applying the Aristotelian schema of the four causes) that the scope of such prudence must be confined to the handling of material and formal causes: to the intelligent discernment of means to ends and how best to work with them. Yet, politics and economics cannot but be corrupted by those who are engaged in them, when they say "*ego feci*," conceiving of themselves as determining the final and efficient causes and imagining themselves to be the creators and fulfillers of political and economic life.

Luther does not entertain the idea of the autonomy of professional reason. To the contrary, he maintains: "God has created domestic and civic life not in the way a builder or carpenter builds a ship, who, after completing it, leaves it behind and hands the authority over the ship to the boatman. Instead, God remains with his creatures, rules and keeps them all: house, land and people."[8] In fact, Luther's moral theology provides an alternative to the various versions in which modernity has mapped Christian ethics. Accounts such as that of Ernst Troeltsch would typically draw a sharp line between a (compromising) ethics of the "household codes" and a (radical) ethics of "discipleship," between "personal ethics," and "social ethics," or between "merely religious" and "universalizable" features of Christian ethics – antinomies which, when projected back on to Luther, spring from the misconceived separation of an "inward sphere" of faith from the outward sphere of worldly engagement (love) and the subsequent error of taking the teaching on the Two Kingdoms as the key to open every door in Luther's social ethics.

### SACRAMENTAL ETHICS

As we have tried to show, there is no single key to Luther's moral theology. There are, however, paradigmatic theological language games which best characterize it, such as the specific ways of relating faith and love, the First and subsequent Commandments, justification and sanctification, and so on. If one should attempt to formulate a common rule in terms of a grammar that governs the various language games, it would perhaps be ideally expressed in what Luther himself called "*vita passiva*" – a concept that could be rendered "living a receptive life." Christian ethos and ethics should conceive of everything that is to be done and left undone as being shaped by God's own activity: marked by a passivity that can be highly active, transcending the inherited antinomy between the active and contemplative lives.

Although Luther meant *vita passiva* to describe the whole Christian life, he does, however, assign a specific time-space where this "active passion" or "passive action" can be experienced and exercised in a paradigmatic way. It is in worship where the "works of God that are prepared beforehand" can be entered and explored by human action in the most assured and assuring way. Though it tends to be notoriously overlooked in Luther studies, we find it hardly surprising to encounter in Luther another way of addressing the roots of the Christian moral life. In his treatise on the Eucharist from 1519 *The Blessed Sacrament of the Holy and True Body of Christ and the Brotherhoods* (WA 2, 742–58) Luther makes clear that celebrating the Eucharist is nothing less than a political act in which the communicants actualize and suffer the citizenship that has been bestowed on them by baptism.

> The significance or purpose of this sacrament is the fellowship of all saints... because Christ and all the saints are one holy body, just as the inhabitants of a city are one community and body, each citizen being a member of the other and a member of the entire city. All the saints, therefore, are members of Christ and of the Church, which is a spiritual and eternal city of God.

Luther then proceeds to explain the inner logic of this citizenship by the means of a communication of goods:

> This fellowship is of such a nature that all the spiritual possessions of Christ and his saints are imparted and communicated to him who receives this sacrament. Again, all his sufferings and sins are communicated to them... like in a city where every citizen shares with all the others the name, honour, freedom, trade, customs, usages, help, support, protection and the like, of that city, and on the other hand shares all the danger of fire and flood, enemies and death, losses, imposts and the like.[9]

In order to capture the true character of social relationships among Christians as a sacramental body, Luther employs the same (originally christological) logic of the *communicatio idiomatum* through which he would depict the "happy exchange" of the believing bridal soul with the bridegroom Christ in his treatise on *The Freedom of a Christian*. In this perspective, the whole of our Christian lives as agents is rooted in Christ's action, which not only provides a model (*exemplum*) or an impulse (*motivatio*) or a mere "foundation," but precisely the proper "form" (*sacramentum*) of the Christian life. Hence, for Luther, there is no prior "relationship with God" or a priori *"Glaubensbewußtsein"* (Schleiermacher) that would "set free" the believing individual to engage *then* in social relationships of a political kind. Instead, there is only political worship, which *simultaneously* relates the believers to God and their fellow citizens.

### Notes

1. See for this paragraph A. Peters, *Kommentar zu Luthers Katechismen*, vol. I: *Die Zehn Gebote* (Göttingen: Vandenhoeck & Ruprecht, 1990), 53–144.
2. "Thus it is a blind and dangerous doctrine which teaches that the commandments are fulfilled by works, since it is necessary for the commandments to be fulfilled before all works and for the works to follow the fulfilment" (WA 7, 56).
3. This paragraph draws on D. Yeago, "Martin Luther on Grace, Law and Moral Life. Prolegomena to an Ecumenical Discussion of Veritatis Splendor," *The Thomist* 62 (1998), 163–91.
4. On the "Protestant fallacy" as misconstrued relationship between freedom and gospel, see R. Hütter, *The Twofold Center of Lutheran Ethics: Christian Freedom and God's Commandments*, in Karen L. Bloomquist and John R. Stumme, eds., *The Promise of Lutheran Ethics* (Minneapolis: Fortress Press, 1998), 31–54.
5. See for this paragraph Bernd Wannenwetsch, "Caritas fide formata. 'Herz und Affekte' als Schlüssel zu 'Glaube und Liebe,'" *Kerygma und Dogma* 46 (2000), 205–24.
6. See for this paragraph O. Bayer, "Nature and Institution. Luther's doctrine of the three estates," trans. C. Helmer, *Lutheran Quarterly* 7 (1998), 125–59.
7. See Luther's treatise on Marriage (1522), WA 10/II, 275–304 and *On Marriage Matters* (1530), LW 46, 259–320.
8. *Luthers Psalmenauslegung*, ed. Chr. Eberle (Stuttgart: Evang. Bücherstiftung, 1987), II:315 (translation mine).
9. Cited after *Works of Martin Luther*, The Philadelphia Edition (Philadelphia: Muhlenberg Press, 1943), II:10f. See for this paragraph Peters, *Kommentar*, I:53–144.

# 8 Luther as preacher of the Word of God

FRED W. MEUSER

Martin Luther is famous as reformer, theologian, professor, translator, prodigious author, and polemicist. He is well known as hymn-writer, musician, friend of students, mentor of pastors, and pastor to countless clergy and laity. Yet he saw himself first of all as a preacher even though his only income came from his professorship at the University of Wittenberg.

No matter what else he was involved in, Luther preached, usually in Wittenberg's Stadtkirche. Unless he was away from home, he was in the pulpit at least as often as the congregation's pastor. Wherever he traveled, the local clergy insisted that Doktor Martin deliver the sermon.

Luther's preaching ministry was remarkable, his productivity prodigious – almost miraculous. In the midst of lecturing, protesting against churchly abuses, translating, writing scores of theological treatises, adjusting to marriage and children, carrying on a voluminous correspondence, and attending almost endless meetings and conferences, in 1528 he preached nearly two hundred times in spite of severe headaches and dizzy spells. On forty days that year he preached twice; most years he preached over a hundred times. Among the slower years were 1522 with only forty-six sermons, and 1540 with forty-three. Of the approximately 4,000 sermons he preached in his lifetime, about 2,300 have been preserved in some form.

When in 1511 Father John Staupitz, his spiritual advisor, assigned him to teach Scripture and preach in the monastery, Luther protested, "It will kill me. I won't last three months." How much more plaintive might his protest have been if Staupitz had said what Luther said later about the preaching office: "When the preacher speaks, God speaks!" If the pastor is not sure that God speaks through his mouth he should leave preaching alone for he surely denies and blasphemes God.[1]

## THE MESSAGE

For Luther, preaching was not a preacher's ideas stimulated by the prod of a text. It was not the preacher's reflections about God and life. Christian

136

preaching, when it is faithful to the Word of God in the Scriptures about our need and God's response to it, is God speaking. When it presents Christ so that faith becomes possible, it is God speaking. It is God's very own audible address to all who hear it, just as surely as if Christ himself had spoken it.

"This," said the German Luther scholar Emanuel Hirsch, "is the most characteristic and profound thing Luther said about preaching... The boldness with which Paul speaks of his preaching office in 2 Corinthians 3 and 4 comes to life again in Luther."[2]

Luther set the preaching of the apostles and our preaching, if centered in Christ, on precisely the same level. If the message is the same, then it is the same Word of God. In fact, he said that our preaching and Christ's preaching are the Word of God in the same sense. In a way, ours even exceeds Christ's because God has graciously given to the preacher's words an effect in numbers and outreach that even Christ's words did not have in his day.

Such confidence did not come easily to Luther and was not easy for him to retain. But inherent in such confidence is the trust that God is saying, "Just go on preaching; don't worry about who will listen... You preach and let me manage."[3] Luther said that he himself preached as a wanderer sings in the woods: the trees hear and the echo answers. That was enough. "Whom it hits, it hits."[4]

Luther's great insight was that God is present primarily through the message about God. If we are touched by that message, God has touched us. We need not go beyond the Word to find God. The proclaimed Word of God is not just preliminary to the sacraments, a lower stage of God's grace that we "really" get through sacramental action. Rather, the apostolic message brings God and all God's gifts. The sacraments are another form of the gracious and powerful word of God's promise. If the sermon is God's message of judgment and grace, one actually encounters God. That makes preaching and hearing a most dangerous business.

Though Luther often said that a sermon is simply composed of teaching and exhortation, he did not preach that way. He preached as if the sermon were not a classroom but a battleground! Every sermon was a battle for the souls of the people, an apocalyptic event that set the doors of heaven and hell in motion, part of the continuing conflict between the Lord and Satan. The Word is God's sword in this cosmic warfare through which the power of Christ invades life today.

The sermon itself is, therefore, a saving event. When God speaks, things can never be the same again. God's Word touches the hearer, condemns, offers forgiveness, appeals and draws. No one can listen in cool detachment on the perimeter in a neutral stance. One cannot go away from preaching in the same relationship to God as before. Neutrality means that the devil has won that skirmish. When the word about Christ is preached, God has spoken and one answers yes or no. There is no alternative.

But will preachers who think their words are the Word of God not become arrogant and domineering? Won't they forget that God's thoughts are higher than our thoughts and God's ways than our ways? Well aware of that danger, Luther one day said to students that the people are afraid of the tyranny of the preachers, and the preachers are always trying to play God over the hearers.

Luther's answer to the problem was simple enough – nothing except Christ is to be preached – Christ as Savior, the one in whom God shows his own face, in whom God has done a once-for-all deed and spoken a once-for-all definitive word to the world. When Christ is preached as the prophets and apostles present him, then when the preacher speaks, God speaks and the Holy Spirit produces faith, hope, love, and a joyful new life. "The poor Holy Spirit," said Luther, "doesn't want anything else to be preached." Such preachers will know themselves to be servants of the Word of God and of its hearers, for Jesus' sake. They will know their subservient place in God's scheme of things and will be content with it. "The preachers have no other office than to preach the clear sun, Christ. Let them take care that they preach thus or let them be silent."[5]

Critics have accused Luther of being so prejudiced in favor of Paul that he almost ignored the rest of the New Testament. They have implied that, because Romans and Galatians were basic to his doctrine, he pushed the Gospels aside in favor of a few favorite epistle texts. Those who have read his sermons know better. Luther loved the Gospels, immersed himself in them, lived and relived Christ's words and deeds as the Gospels present them. He has about thirty sermons on Romans, but more than 1,000 on the synoptic Gospels plus many hundreds on John. In 1531/32 he spent almost a year and a half on John 6, 7, 8. He preached more on John's Gospel in a year than on Romans in his whole life. The spirit of Romans and Galatians permeated all his preaching but the starting point and the focus was the human Jesus of the Gospels. "He pulled the Gospels from under the bench as much as he did Paul [and] he ... bound the whole life of faith into them."[6]

Preaching the Jesus of the Gospels always meant preaching his love for sinners. Notice how gently the Savior deals with wounded spirits, Luther said to the Wittenbergers, how friendly Jesus is to publicans and sinners, how patiently he bears with the disciples who misunderstood him, what compassion for lepers, for the widow whose son had died, for blind Bartimaeus, and for the woman taken in adultery. When Luther preached to people who, like himself, had been taught to think of God and Jesus as threatening and distant and to run to Mary and the saints as compassionate intercessors, Luther delighted in speaking of the Lord as one who made ordinary people feel at home in his presence. Comfort and assurance were high priorities for Luther, not only for the bereaved but for all who were burdened, tempted, or, like himself, crushed by their own sense of unworthiness. In the pulpit he spoke only rarely and then with great reserve about his own battles with doubt and despair but his empathy for others who had similar experiences shaped what he saw in every text. He deeply loved the beautiful, caring, human Jesus of the Gospels. Any sermon that failed to hold up that Lord so others could be drawn to trust in God's mercy did not meet his standard of preaching Christ.

In his later years, as people used the message of forgiveness to excuse sinful living, preaching to disturb the conscience became more frequent. Yet even then he never ducked the comforting texts in favor of the judgmental ones.

> If you preach faith people become lax. But if you do not preach faith, hearts become frightened and dejected... I would much rather hear people say that I preach too sweetly... than not preach faith in Christ at all for then there would be no help for timid frightened consciences. Christ himself had to hear that he was a friend of publicans and sinners... We shall not fare any better.[7]

To Luther, preaching Christ meant, above all, focusing on his death and resurrection. Prominent in the vast majority of his sermons is the human-yet-divine Jesus bearing our sin, its guilt, and its alienating power into death for us. Christ is our brother, atoner, deliverer, liberator, and victor. All the classic themes of the atonement appear side-by-side in his preaching. He did not, like many theologians of the atonement, pick out one theme as dominant or superior. He allowed each one to do its own work and bestow its own gifts. If a theme was in Scripture and was an expression of God's grace in action for us, he preached it. That may be one advantage that preachers have over systematic theologians.

One of the captivating and frustrating things about Luther is that everything he knew about Christ had a way of creeping into his treatment of almost any text. If you took his Christmas sermons as they stand, you could conclude that when the Son of God emerged from Mary's womb the whole task of redemption was finished. When Christ permitted himself to be baptized by John, his identification with sinners was so complete that he might have had nothing else to do when he stepped out of the Jordan. So with the temptation in the wilderness, the feeding of the 5,000, the healing of the paralytic, and most especially the Lord's agony in Gethsemane. Here,

Luther said, is the pinnacle of the passion. Here the Lord fought the supreme battle. Here he faced all the forces of terror and despair and conquered them. Luther did not regard the rest as a picnic, but in some ways Gethsemane was the climax. Of course, he said similar things about Jesus' trial, his bearing of the cross, and especially the experience of being forsaken which wrung "My God, my God" from his lips.

From this side of the resurrection, wherever Luther saw redemption he saw all of redemption. If he found more in a text than was there exegetically, at least he did not preach Christ in disconnected bits and pieces, expecting the hearers to connect them into a meaningful whole. He would much rather have too much of Christ in a given sermon than too little. It will not solve all of our exegetical and interpretive questions, but Luther's approach to preaching nothing but Christ is clear when he says, "If in a text I find a nut with a shell too hard to crack, I fling it on the Rock [Christ] and I get the sweetest kernel out of it."[8]

To Luther, preaching nothing except Christ also meant constant attention to the function and value of human effort. Luther was hung up on the subject. Were "good works" really so big a problem that no matter what the text, he had to go off on a tangent about their value in God's sight? Whether preaching on the Wise Men, the Magnificat, the stilling of the storm, "Peace I give to you," reception of the sacrament, miracles, or parables he made God's way of salvation crystal clear: not by our efforts but by God's gift.

Not only indulgences, pilgrimages, alms, repetitious prayers, and other so-called churchly good works felt Luther's lash, but also every innate human impulse to make God somehow indebted to us. Luther knew not only the Scriptures; he also knew people. From the way in which, year after year, he glorified God's undeserved grace despite our unworthiness, we can conclude that it was as hard for the Wittenbergers to say "Yes" to God's judgment on their lives and "No" to the urge to bargain with God as it is for us today. The frequency and clarity of Luther's words makes one wonder why he needed to say it so often, but they also give us a bit of comfort in our need to speak repeatedly to the perversions of the gospel in our day.

### FORM AND PREPARATION

With Luther came what many interpreters call a totally new form of the sermon: the expository sermon, *die schriftauslegende Predigt. Auslegen* literally means "to lay out," to exhibit, to make something evident or plain. Early on, Luther had come to the conviction that such laying out of Scripture's central message had top priority in the needed correction of the church's teaching and life. From the start of his preaching ministry he gave much greater place to Scripture than almost any of his contemporaries. After 1521 this switch was complete and permanent. Luther said:

> Some pastors and preachers are lazy and no good. They do not pray; they do not study; they do not read; they do not search the Scripture... The call is: watch, study, attend to reading... [Y]ou cannot read too much in Scripture, what you read you cannot read too carefully, what you read carefully you cannot understand too well, what you understand well you cannot teach too well, what you teach well you cannot live too well... Therefore dear... pastors and preachers, pray, read, study, be diligent... This evil, shameful time is no season for being lazy, for sleeping, and snoring.[9]

Preaching always meant setting loose the Word of God in the Scriptures by speaking it heart to heart. Through the spoken living word, not primarily the word read privately or publicly, the Holy Spirit leads people to Christ, works repentance and faith, and bestows the gifts of the Spirit. Without the word spoken by a believer, the Gospel cannot do its work. "Where the speaking of the Gospel ceases the people will revert to heathenism in a year's time... The devil cares nothing about the written word, but where one speaks and preaches it, there he takes to flight."[10] The command to the apostles was to preach, not to write, and Luther even tweaked their noses a bit for having written without an express command of Christ. They did it, he said (from his knowledge of early church history) only because the truth about Christ was in danger of being perverted or slipping away. "This is the sum of the matter: Let everything be done so that the Word may have free course instead of the prattling and rattling that has been the rule... We can spare everything except the Word... We profit by nothing as much as by the Word."[11]

By "Word" Luther meant Scripture, which he called a "great tree" which pours down beautiful, fresh, tasty fruit every time one shakes its branches. By "shaking the branches" of Scripture Luther meant study. Correct understanding is a gift of God we receive not through brooding over God's Word until the light goes on, but through serious study of the text. Personal faith and contemplation are necessary, of course, but never as a substitute for painstaking study. The best way to go to the Bible is in the original languages. Scripture, he said, is not obscure if one knows Greek and Hebrew. One should use other helps only when necessary. He even said he wished all his writings might be burned lest preachers rely on them rather than on their own study. "The languages are the scabbards in which the sword of the Spirit is sheathed."[12] If one does not study Scripture, people will soon tire of the preaching but "where the preacher is versed in the languages, there is freshness and vigor...and faith finds itself constantly renewed by a continual variety of words and illustrations."[13]

Proper preparation is hard mental and spiritual work, little appreciated by people who don't do it.

> Sure, it would be hard for me to sit in the saddle [as horsemen do]. But I would like to see the horseman who could sit still for a whole day and gaze at a book without... thinking about anything else. Ask a sermon writer...how much work it is to speak and preach...Three fingers do it all...but the whole body and soul have to work at it.[14]

Preachers should expect to have to work hard because listeners are to hear God speaking a gracious word through a text that has God's own authority behind it.

Luther's method is to take a given segment of Scripture, find the key thought within it and make that unmistakably clear. The text is to control the sermon. When the sermon is over, the people are to remember the text and its message more than the sermon itself. The sermon is to follow the flow, language, and dynamic of the text, and not impose its own direction or dynamic from without.

Luther's method has often but inaccurately been called that of the homily. A homily usually moves verse by verse, without tying the whole together. Luther insisted on finding the heart of the text. The kernel, as he called it, saves the preacher from getting lost in details or wandering off into self-chosen ideas. Every story has that kernel which the preacher must find and return to repeatedly. Every time he preached on Jesus' entry into Jerusalem, he landed feet first on "Behold your king comes to you!" even though no two sermons were alike.

The main point of the sermon is to be so clear in the preacher's mind that it controls everything that is said. Then the rest of the sermon may be allowed to flow with considerable freedom. "In my sermons I bury myself to take just one passage and there I stay so the hearers may be able to say, 'that was the sermon.' "[15] We have Luther's sermons on the Sunday Gospels over many years. No two are the same in structure or development. Yet every time he preached on the desire of the people to make Jesus their king, he stood face-to-face with the firm will of Jesus to lead the people past a faith dependent on miracles to trust in God's "naked word" and promise.

Luther rejected the art of fancy introductions in favor of a simple statement of the text's central thought. Preaching on a healing miracle, he begins: "In this Gospel our Lord tells us that God is merciful to those who suffer." On Matthew 11:25–30: The Lord here praises his heavenly Father for having made his gospel known to children rather than to educated adults.

Or, preaching on Christ's baptism, he refers to the beautiful glorious blessed exchange in which Christ changes places with us, takes our sin upon himself and gives us his innocence and purity. On special occasions such as weddings, baptisms, and funerals, there might be more of an introduction, but ordinarily he started with "What does the text want to tell us?" Then he went right into it.

Luther could not have been less interested in symmetry, external form, beauty of expression, alliterative phrases, plays on words, balance, polish, or other rhetorical arts. He had seen too much of that in the preaching against which he rebelled not to be deeply suspicious of it. Everything calculated or artful, he felt, tended to push the heart of the text and the natural flow of the Word of God into the background. Such playing around with words, as he would call it, is a toying with the proclamation and is unfitting to the appointed task. He also suspected that it masked an unworthy desire on the preacher's part to be popular, which he regarded as the preacher's death trap. "There is no greater evil or poison than vainglory," he said.

> It is the bride of the devil... [and] works great harm in a preacher. It moves him to... preach so that the people may say..."He is certainly a fine preacher; he knows how to hit the nail on the head; I have never heard anyone put it this way." And so the man is puffed up with pride, tickled with praise and imagines he is an ox when he is scarcely a toad. Then he must be very careful not to spoil things with the people. Because they praise him, he must, in turn, praise them. So they praise one another until one goes to the devil with the other.[16]

Luther's only device was to employ tensions, conflict, paradox: law/ gospel, sin/grace, God/Satan, free will/ bound will, and to use dialogue, at which he was a master. One finds dialogue in a high proportion of his sermons. Usually he spoke in the first person for both parties. There is conversation between Luther and the hearers, God and Adam, Jesus and the disciples, God and Satan, life and death, heaven and hell. This is as close as Luther came to a designed form of preaching, but he did it so naturally that there was never anything phoney about it. It was the way he saw life. "When I preach a sermon," he said, "I set up a conflict."[17]

That conflict is consistent with his sense that preaching the Word of God is part of the battle for the universe still going on between God and evil. It makes Luther's sermons vibrant, powerful, in touch with life as his hearers lived it. He could preach that way because he had come through great conflict, lived with conflict in his own soul, and knew the One whose victory in the greatest of all conflicts kept Luther from being exhausted or overcome by it.

## DELIVERY

What was he like in the pulpit? Strange how little his contemporaries, who tried their best to record his every spoken word, said about that. Never did he lose the holy awe of being allowed to speak for God. If it were not for the call of God, he said, he would never have courage to walk up the steps of a pulpit. His prayers before preaching are humble invocations that the Holy Spirit make it all turn out well. Never did he become blasé or self-confident.

Obviously people liked to hear him. It is said that he spoke slowly but with great vigor and often had a moving effect on the hearers. James Mackinnon refers to his "torrential speech alive with prophetic fire"[18] but his contemporaries say nothing like that. Luther said of Justus Jonas that the people didn't like him because he spit, sniffed, and cleared his throat too much. Either Luther had no idiosyncrasies or his contemporaries were too kind to mention them.

We may confidently say that everything about his preaching was genuine. The message was everything. Histrionics, calculated gestures, anything done for effect would have been regarded as a human intrusion on the Word of God. Although there was humor, there was never levity or anything calculated to produce laughter. Yet the congregation must have chuckled at his comment that God has chickens on earth who eat his grain and then lay their eggs elsewhere; or calling people who expect to prosper because they are Christians "knights of the belly"; or his comment that even asses would make it to heaven if good works were the key. Not everyone, however, was enthralled or Luther would not have said that the people sometimes sleep and snore during the sermon until the rafters crack or that they sleep and cough when "we preach the article of justification but prick up their ears as soon as we tell stories."[19]

To Luther, Christ himself was the great example in the way he tailored everything to his audience. Because his hearers knew about sheep and shepherds, wolves, vineyards, fig trees, reeds, fields and plowing, the Lord spoke about them. Similarly, speaking in the language of his people was more than just a tactic for Luther. Just as the Son of God humbled himself, became one of us and lived the life we live, so preachers, though they speak from high above the people, are one of them and should speak as one of them.

"In the pulpit," he said, "we are to lay bare the breasts and nourish the people with milk ... Complicated thoughts and issues we should discuss in private with the eggheads [*Klueglinge*]. I don't think of Dr. Pomeraneus,

Jonas, or Philip [Melanchthon] in my sermon. They know more about it than I do. So I don't preach to them. I just preach to Hansie and Betsy."[20] "He who teaches most simply, childishly, popularly...that's the best preacher. I like it to be easy and earthy. But now if it is debate you are looking for, come into my classroom! I'll give it to you plenty sharp and you'll get your answer however fancy your questions."[21]

## A SAMPLE OF LUTHER'S PREACHING ABOUT DEATH AND RESURRECTION

Luther preached often on death and probably just as often on the resurrection. The resurrection was a melody of his sermons even when it was not the theme. In 1532/33 he preached seventeen sermons in a row on 1 Corinthians 15. During the Easter season he could hardly tear himself away from the resurrection theme. Perhaps the difference from our age is that Luther's had not learned to hide from death as expertly as we have. Death was a visible and even an olfactory aspect of daily life that had to be faced.

Death's defeat was no mere figure of speech to Luther. The resurrection is as much *pro nobis* as the crucifixion. Here, as in all the great events of Christ's life, Luther spoke of the "great exchange" which God offers us in Christ. Christ exchanges all his beauty, purity, and strength for our ugliness, evil, and weakness; in his passion our guilt in exchange for his forgiveness; and in his resurrection our death – our ultimate defeat – in exchange for his life. This wonderful exchange is a theme he could find in almost every text. What it means is simply that nothing in life or death can really harm the person who is hidden in Christ. Christ's resurrected life begins in us now, will never cease, and will be fulfilled perfectly when he raises us up out of physical death.

In 1532, at the funeral of Duke John of Saxony, Luther preached on 1 Thessalonians 4:13–14: "We would not have you ignorant, brethren, concerning those who are asleep...for since we believe that Jesus died and rose again, even so, through Jesus, God will bring with him those who have fallen asleep." This is an excellent example of Luther's preaching. Here is a paraphrase of a few of his thoughts.

In comparison with Christ's death, Luther said, ours is but a sleep. His was so bitter, grandiose, and potent that it has baptized all the other dead, so that now they are not called dead but sleepers. Christ's death was the real death, ours only a sleep. No better comfort can be found than to contemplate Christ's death and see how it has devoured all other deaths. Do not look at the dead body of the prince before you, he said, but look at the death of

Christ through which our death is destroyed so that we see this prince, not lying smelly in the coffin and grave but in Christ.

Be thankful that God wrapped up our dear prince in the death of Christ and embraced him in his resurrection. The prince's real death occurred two years ago when at the Diet of Augsburg he openly confessed Christ's death and resurrection before the whole world and stuck to it, staking his land and people, indeed his own body and life on it. Christ's death and the death our prince suffered at Augsburg were "real death." Physical death, when we pass away in bed, is only a "baby death." (The word Luther uses, *Kindersterben*, makes one think of children playing dead.) So it was for our prince. He didn't labor, or struggle, or fear death. Fear of death – that is real death. But when one dies as our prince died, wrapped in Christ's suffering, that is a baby death, only half a death. Our real death occurs when we die with Christ and are raised up with him to new life. It is my hope, Luther said, that we too shall die this way. God will carry me and all other Christians through death and hell. So we shouldn't even call them dead people but sleepers, in such a deep sleep that they won't even dream. Without a doubt our prince has become a holy sleeper, not because he was a merciful, kind master but because he confessed Christ's death and clung to it. Let his death be a reminder of ours so that we may also be among those who suffer and die and are raised with Christ. May God grant this to us.[22]

## DISCOURAGEMENT AND RECOVERY

One would think that Luther's confidence in the Holy Spirit's power to make the preached word effective in the hearers would have kept him from what today we call "burnout." Not so. In 1528 he warned the Wittenberg congregation that he would stop preaching unless he saw more fruit of the gospel among them. In his New Year's sermon of 1530, he complained bitterly of their utter selfishness. A short time later he said he would rather preach to raving dogs than to them and that from then on he would confine himself to the classroom. He called preaching "an arduous office," a rotten office, whose misery is such that a person would rather be a swineherd. "The damned devil," Luther said, "and not a good man should be a preacher."[23] If he had known in advance what it would be like, twenty-four horses could not have drawn him into it. From January until the fall of 1530, Luther preached only three times in Wittenberg, two of those at the express command of his prince.

The fact that Luther preached in places other than Wittenberg during the spring and summer of 1530 shows that his disillusionment was with that congregation rather than with preaching itself, but some of his friends worried that he might never preach again. After the exhausting pace of the 1520s he was deeply disappointed that the restoration of the Word of God had produced little significant change in the people who heard it first. To the clergy assembled at Augsburg in 1530 he wrote that "no message would be more pleasing to my ears than one deposing me from the office of preaching... I am so tired of it because of the great ingratitude of the people, but much more because of the intolerable hardships which the devil and the world mete out to me."[24]

It was during Luther's extended stay at Coburg Castle, while the Augsburg Diet was meeting, that he found refreshment of spirit. From there he said that when we experience suffering because we hold to the Word of God, Christ will not only help us to bear it but will even "do something remarkable with it... Let him take care of it and fight it out... The Word of God puts us in a tight place, so that we learn... that the small weak miserable word is stronger than the devil and the gates of hell."[25]

When in the fall of 1530, following his return from Coburg, Luther again began to preach, it was almost as if nothing had happened. Consistent with not making his spiritual struggles prominent in the pulpit, Luther did not say anything more about it to the congregation. His friend Mathesius said that he "refrained from preaching until his zeal, that is, his holy wrath cooled, or rather until it [reignited] his own calling in his heart."[26] The closest Luther came to an explanation was his statement, "The poor souls [who are deprived of hearing God's word] will not let me rest. Then, too, there is a man whose name is Jesus Christ. He says no. Him I justly follow as one who has deserved more of me."[27] Never again did Luther take leave from preaching except for illness or travel. In 1531 he was back to 180 sermons.

To be sure, Luther was tempted on other occasions to quit. But, he said, the Scriptures overcame the temptation through their testimony that God has not yet tired of calling the fallen world back to himself. By sharing that tireless love with us, God restores our energies and our spirit. In his final sermon, just three days before his death, Luther rephrased Jesus' words, "Come to me all who labor and are heavy laden" to mean "Just stick with me, hold to my Word, and let everything else go. If you are burned or beheaded for it... if things go badly, I will give you the courage to laugh... Only come to me... It will not be heavy for you but light and easy to bear... [because] I myself am helping you."[28] That comforting conviction carried Luther through an incredibly difficult and demanding life which changed the face of Christendom in many ways, not the least of which was the office and practice of preaching.

If one's reading is always directed to the next Sunday's sermon, one shouldn't bother with Luther. But if one makes time for reading that waters the roots of faith, plumbs the depths of Scripture, nails the conscience, warms the heart, and frequently tickles the funny-bone, then one should read Luther's sermons. He was able to proclaim the wonderful news of God's amazing grace in Christ with simplicity and power. To this day Luther's preaching has not lost that refreshing power.

### Notes

1. WA 51, 517.
2. Emanuel Hirsch, "Luthers Predigtweise," *Luther: Mitteilungen der Lutherge-sellschaft* (1954), 16 (hereafter cited as *Luther: Mitteilungen*).
3. WA 10/I, 2, 51.
4. Cited in Hirsch, "Gesetz und Evangelium in Luther's Predigten," *Luther: Mitteilungen* (1954), 54.
5. WA 10/III, 361.
6. Hirsch, "Gesetz," 58.
7. WA 37, 394–95.
8. WA 3, 12.
9. WA 53, 218.
10. Cited in Hirsch, "Luthers Predigtweise," 19.
11. LW 53, 14.
12. Cited in Peter Meinhold, "Luther und die Predigt," in *Das Wort und die Wörter* Festschrift Gerhard Friedrich z. 65. Geburtstag, hrsg. von Horst Balz u. Siegfried Schulz (Stuttgart, Berlin, Cologne, Mainz: Kohlhammer, 1973), 118.
13. LW 45, 365.
14. Meinhold, "Luther und die Predigt," 113.
15. Cited in Martin Doerne, "Luther und die Predigt," *Luther: Mitteilingen* (1938), 40.
16. WA 27, 402.
17. Cited in Hirsch, "Luthers Predigtweise," 22.
18. James Mackinnon, *Luther and the Reformation*, 4 vols. (New York: Russell & Russell, 1930), IV:317.
19. TR 2, 2408.
20. TR 3, 3421.
21. TR 4, 5047.
22. LW 51, 334–43 *passim*.
23. LW 51, 222.
24. WA 30/II, 340–41.
25. LW 51, 203, 207.
26. Cited in Paul Glaue, "Der Predigtmuede Luther," *Luther: Mitteilungen* (1929), 72.
27. WA 30/II, 341.
28. LW 51, 392.

# 9 Luther's spiritual journey

JANE E. STROHL

From Luther's own day to the present, critics have raised questions about the distinctively personal stamp given by the reformer to his theology. Despite its claims to biblical fidelity and universal validity, they suspected that Luther's legacy was the projection of one man's neurosis on to the whole of human history and at the expense of the relative tolerance and unity of the Western church. There is no denying that Luther was himself a prime example of the desperately bound sinner whose terrified conscience, hungry for the assurance of God's grace and the experience of its transforming power, became *the* test case for Lutheran proclamation.

Without lionizing Luther as some spiritual "Everyman" for all generations, one can conclude that in the course of his spiritual journey he spoke persuasively to and for many of his contemporaries. Luther boldly articulated and responded to the acute anxieties of the age through his campaign for the liberation of the church from its latter-day Babylonian captivity, his demand for the freedom of the individual believer's conscience and the free reign of the Scriptures among the people, and his rejection of the ecclesiastical hierarchy in his appeal to the judgment of the common believer, that is, the baptized person who emerged from the waters of baptism the spiritual equal of priest, bishop, and pope.

Historians are fascinated by such fundamental shifts in the religious sensibilities of a society. Peter Matheson has suggested that the changes of the sixteenth century would be more fruitfully understood as a re-forming of the imagination, rather than as primarily a matter of doctrinal or structural innovations. Images, he points out, can and do burn out and have to be renewed continually, and in the imaginative architecture of the Reformation, the divine becomes more intimate and the human more earthly.[1] This essay will explore Luther's spiritual journey, recognizing that in its historical particularity it both reflected and shaped this new development of the life of faith.

## A BI-POLAR SPIRITUALITY

Erasmus of Rotterdam is famously quoted as asserting that he was not willing to burn for one of Luther's paradoxes. For Luther, the life of the Christian on earth is necessarily characterized by the presence and regular manifestation of a series of contrasting realities. His spirituality is built around these polarities that cannot be resolved. Luther's various opponents had, in his eyes, this in common: They tried one way or another to flatten out the paradoxes of life under the gospel and thus to rob discipleship of its relentless tension. In this respect Luther's theology is rightly described as acutely eschatological at its core: to live in paradox is to live in a state of crisis that cries out for resolution, a resolution that for Luther only God can effect. The work of those living in the time before the end is to manage the polarities and pray fervently for the coming of the Lord. Luther's own experience, in opposition first to Rome and then later to Zwingli and the radicals as well, caused him to defend these polarities ever more insistently, lest they be thrown out of balance by challengers from both sides.

## RELIGIOUS EXPERIENCE AND OBJECTIVE SIGN

Luther is well known for his disdain of the emphasis on direct, personal religious experience found among some reforming groups. He mocked them as having swallowed the Holy Spirit, feathers and all. The radical Thomas Müntzer, for example, whom Luther continued to demonize years after the former's death in the Peasants' Rebellion of 1525, insisted that the grace of Christ brought the spiritual gifts of visions, prophecy, and dreams to the saved, whose faith was thereby verified before others. Müntzer denounced Luther as a religious flunky, the court theologian of the Elector of Saxony, who denounced such gifts because he had never experienced them. Luther, on the other hand, feared greatly the spiritual chaos precipitated by such subjectivity. Over against it he insisted on the objective norms of the scriptural Word and, when in keeping with that Word, the church's tradition.

Yet one should not conclude from this that Luther was wholly dismissive of religious experience. His own spiritual life was characterized by *Anfechtung*, assaults of doubt and terror as to his standing before God. If one was to know the power of the gospel, one had also to feel the piercing condemnation of the law as it cut through the pretensions of self-righteousness to the core of sin's corruption. Luther could also speak out of an ebullient confidence and ecstatic joy. There has been considerable scholarly discussion about Luther's relation to Christian mysticism, and his own spirituality displays striking resemblances. He experiences both desolation and ecstasy;

*Anfechtung* is a true dark night of the soul. One notes also an acute awareness of the numinous quality of God. The miserable pygmy, as Luther describes himself, who dares to come before the Almighty One to offer his first mass, is overcome not just by the awareness of his sin before God's absolute righteousness but by the unfathomable otherness of the divine that separates it from human finitude and frailty. Luther marvels at how God has bridged the chasm and deigned to join humanity at its most vulnerable, as a helpless baby nursing at a woman's breast and finally as a forsaken man bleeding and dying on a cross.

## GOD HIDDEN AND REVEALED

It is against this backdrop that one can best understand the distinction Luther makes between the *deus absconditus* and the *deus revelatus*, that is, God hidden and revealed. For all that Luther does to restore Jesus to his preeminent place as Savior rather than judge, he does not domesticate the Christ into some kind of boon companion, nor does the revelation of the Father in the Son drain the godhead of its mystery and fearsomeness. Indeed, Luther experiences a twofold hiddenness, for the gospel itself, with its call to victory through the cross and power perfected in weakness, is a surprising and consequently deceptive revelation. In the company of Jesus, things are seldom what they seem and the saving truth is often hidden under its dispiriting opposite.

This is exemplified in Luther's 1530 *Sermon on Suffering and the Cross*, preached to the Saxon party on the eve of their departure for the Augsburg Diet. Using the legend of St. Christopher, he forewarns his cohorts that the freedom of the gospel inevitably proves to be onerous.

> When one receives the faith, one does not allow oneself to imagine that there will be difficulty in this. As was the case with Christopher, it appears to one as a tiny child, pretty and well formed and easy to carry. For the Gospel shows itself at first as a fine, pleasing, friendly and childlike doctrine, as we then saw at the start, when everyone seized upon it and wanted to be evangelical. There was such longing and thirst for the Gospel that no oven's heat could match that of the people then. But what happened? The same situation occurred as befell Christopher, who did not learn how heavy the little child was until he had entered the deepest water.[2]

The position of the believer is always an embattled one, and yet as one bears the Word through trial and suffering, as St. Christopher did the Christ child, one is borne up by it. Luther concludes the sermon by pointing out that as

Christians make their way through the deep, troubled waters, the current cannot carry them under because they have hold of a stout tree reaching out from the shore, "namely the Word and the fine, strong promises that we shall not be drowned by the breakers."[3]

In a remarkable sermon on the story of the Canaanite woman (Matthew 15),[4] Luther brings one face to face with the hiddenness of God in the most fearsome of places, the encounter of a trusting petitioner with an ungracious Savior. The woman, according to Luther, has heard the news about Jesus. She believes in his power and his compassion, and so, holding to that word, she goes to him, beseeching healing for her daughter. He rejects her outright; he has been sent only to the lost sheep of the house of Israel. She is an outsider and thus has no claim upon him. Indeed, it is not right to take bread from the children to throw it to dogs. She responds, "Yes, Lord, but even the dogs eat the crumbs from under the master's table." Luther concludes with relish that the woman has bested Jesus, caught him in his own word of promise so that he marvels at her faith and helps her. As she believes him to be, so she finds him. Luther offers this woman as a model for all Christians: they must hold to the Word, the proclamation of the merciful Savior Jesus Christ, in the midst of all contrary appearances and experiences, even the crushing suspicion that God has abandoned them and that the Word is a lie.

Luther's relationship with God is a remarkably volatile one. He cowers before God's wrath against sin; he takes sharply to heart God's unrelenting demand for righteousness; he knows God's love as both fierce and tender; and he makes bold to call God to account. A promise is a promise, Luther insists, writing in his Genesis commentary that if God appeared in majesty and announced that, having had second thoughts about human worthiness, God had decided to retract the promise of salvation, he would not yield but fight tooth and nail against the Creator.[5] The heights and depths of the soul's life, the cunning and courage required for such discipleship, are not, in Luther's view, the purview of a spiritual elite. Every Christian must develop the competence to make a good confession in the midst of temptation, fear, and obscurity. To do this one must be tireless in hearing the gospel.

THE EVANGELICAL GOSPEL

For Luther, the criteria for evaluating the integrity of any given proclamation are twofold: Does the gospel as it is offered here make the most of Christ, and does it console the doubting, troubled conscience? Making the most of Christ for Luther meant refusing to shoulder any of the burden that Christ had already borne for the sake of sinners. Christ's self-giving was all-sufficient; the grace he freely offers requires no human additive to become potent. To make the most of Christ was for Luther a matter of emptying the self of pious pretensions so that one could receive only what Christ gives. One might describe the condition of original sin, defined in the Lutheran confessional writings as the inborn inability to fear, love, and trust God, as manifesting itself as a kind of bi-polar disorder. In the manic phase the believer succumbs to delusions of self-righteousness that generate impenitence. In the depressive phase the believer is paralyzed by doubt and despair. In Luther's experience only the evangelical gospel, that is, the justification of the sinner by the grace of Christ through faith apart from works of the law, is able to rescue us from both perils. Therein lies the proof of its verity.

It is precisely because of the intensity of religious experience that engulfs the believer that Luther is so insistent upon the objectivity of the proclaimed Word and sacrament. How was one to know whether any given experience came from God or the evil one? And if one built upon a particular vision or event as the source of one's identity and the assurance of one's godliness, what was to preserve one's certainty when changing circumstances and demonic temptations undermined the original perception? Luther's own travail in the monastery derived from his uncertainty that God was gracious *for him*. The strategies of late medieval piety were no longer effective in his case. The balm of the nominalist dictum, *facere quod in se est*, do what is in you, that is, do one's best and trust that God's grace will meet you more than halfway and make up the deficit in righteousness, proved toxic to Luther's anxious conscience. How could one ever know if one had done enough of the right sort of things to trigger God's beneficent intervention? Relief and assurance could only come when one turned completely away from the self to behold Christ alone. For this reason Luther's spirituality was always intensely sacramental, not only in baptism and holy communion but in the proclamation of the gospel itself, the spoken human word functioning, as it were, as the earthly element bearing the divine into our midst. Behind the doctrinal quarrels about infant baptism and real presence lie this fundamental spiritual hunger and pastoral concern. This becomes clear when one looks at the specific issues that exercised Luther in the controversies about the nature and practice of the sacraments.

## BAPTISM

Baptism was for Luther the center of the Christian life. In contrast to the Anabaptists, who insisted that baptism required faith and should be administered only upon demonstration of conversion and repentance, Luther remained a vehement defender of infant baptism. This sacrament, given to an unwitting child, became for him the premier demonstration of the bountifulness of God's grace. God takes the initiative; God commits Godself before the needy human can do anything to prepare or respond. The gift of God's love as free and unconditional is clearly revealed. Of course, persons of any age may receive baptism, but the practice of infant baptism reminds all believers that even when one comes to the font as a person mature enough to understand and consent, this human condition is not what makes the sacrament valid.

Luther railed against what he saw as the Anabaptist perversion of a divine action into a human one. Here again one hears echoes of Luther's desperation at the prospect of relying on one's experience: how can one know if a person has faith strong enough to warrant baptism? Moreover, when one falters, and given the reality of *Anfechtung* one undoubtedly will, does the recurrence of sin and unbelief invalidate the first washing as premature? Does one need to be baptized again? Luther wrote:

> I would compare the man who lets himself be rebaptized with the man who broods and has scruples because perhaps he did not believe as a child. So when next day the devil comes, his heart is filled with scruples and he says, Ah, now for the first time I feel I have the right faith, yesterday I don't think I truly believed. So I need to be baptized a third time, the second baptism not being of any avail. You think the devil can't do such things? You had better get to know him better. He can do worse than that, dear friend. He can go on and cast doubt on the third, and the fourth and so on incessantly (as he indeed has in mind to do), just as he has done with me and many in the matter of confession. We never seemed able to confess sufficiently certain sins, and incessantly and restlessly sought one absolution after the other, one father confessor after the other. Just because we sought to rely on our confession, as those to be baptized now want to rely on their faith.[6]

The result for Luther was abhorrent: the very purpose and power of the sacrament, to lift one out of oneself and anchor one in Christ, were undermined. Luther insisted that the restless, anxious heart could not build with confidence upon its perceptions of its own faith and godliness. These were too fragile, too easily altered by circumstance in moments of weakness.

With baptism one enters a new and lifelong condition – one is constantly being killed and born anew, as Luther asserts, citing Romans 6:4, "We were buried with Christ through baptism into death, so that, just as Christ was raised from the dead through the glory of the Father, we, too, are to walk in a new life."[7] Baptism circumscribes the whole of life: through it one is joined to the body of Christ, in it one lives out one's salvation, and by it one passes securely from this world to the next.

Luther maintained the integral connection between baptism and confession, but he differed from his Roman Catholic heritage in his understanding of the relation of the two. Confession was not an additional, supplementary sacrament, necessary to restore the baptismal grace lost through subsequent sin. Confession was not a second plank rescuing the sinner after he had made shipwreck of the purity created by his baptism. Rather, for Luther confession was the continual enactment of one's baptism; it was the regular living out of the relationship between God and the believer according to the terms sealed in the sacrament. In the *Small Catechism* Luther provides the following answer to the question, "What then is the significance of such a baptism with water?"

> It signifies that the old creature in us with all sins and evil desires is to be drowned and die through *daily contrition and repentance*, and on the other hand that daily a new person is to come forth and rise up to live before God in righteousness and purity forever.[8]

Confession becomes the fundamentally defining act of the believer. It is the response of faith by which she grasps the gospel promise as her own; it is simultaneously the first fruit of God's grace in her life. To repent, to make confession and seek forgiveness, is to take God at God's word and thus to fulfill the first commandment, not by works but by faith.[9]

Luther's criticism of the Roman practice of confession is analogous to what he lodges against the Anabaptist use of baptism: it obfuscates the meaning of baptism itself and it perverts God's gracious gift into a required human work.[10] Luther is troubled on two counts by the requirement for the enumeration of all sins before the priest. It places a burden on the believer, suggesting that the reception of grace is conditional on his doing a thorough job. This is precisely the kind of demand that crushes the scrupulous conscience and makes of the good news a mockery. Moreover, it is based on the assumption that sin is contained in discrete acts and omissions after baptism, whereas for Luther sin continues to taint the whole of the believer and all that she does, for good and ill.

## SIMUL IUSTUS ET PECCATOR

The idea of the believer as saint (justified) and sinner is the most distinctive polarity of Luther's spirituality. It represents not a transitional state – one is partly sinner and partly saint at any given moment with the latter gradually expanding at the expense of the former – but a condition of simultaneous totality – wholly a sinner, a rebel and enemy of God, and wholly a saint, that is, a child made one with Christ in his righteousness, self-emptying, and love. This doctrine, along with Luther's emphasis on justification by faith alone, fueled his opponents' suspicions that the Lutherans were soft on good works and guilty, in their own way, of devaluing baptism, since it did not appear to have accomplished very much if sin remained so potent a reality.

Luther did not see baptism as effecting some ontological change in the recipient. Original sin was not something that could be excised, thus leaving the human will scarred but competent to act in its weakness with the assistance of divine grace. For Luther original sin was best described as a relational matter. It is how we regard God, our inability to fear, love, and trust, that produces sin. Our drive for self-assertion never deserts us. Our hostility toward those who interfere with it remains. But what has changed is our relationship with God, as God has made Godself known as God-for-us in Jesus the Christ.

> I believe that Jesus Christ, true God, begotten of the Father in eternity, and also a true human being, born of the Virgin Mary, is my Lord. He has redeemed me, a lost and condemned human being. He has purchased and freed me from all sins, from death, and from the power of the devil, not with gold or silver but with his holy, precious blood and with his innocent suffering and death. He has done all this in order that I may belong to him, live under him in his kingdom, and serve him in eternal righteousness, innocence, and blessedness, just as he is risen from the dead and lives and rules eternally. This is most certainly true.[11]

In baptism God's saving intent for particular individuals becomes a public reality. The celebrant begins with the command, "Depart, you unclean spirit, and make room for the Holy Spirit,"[12] who guarantees that the general promise of the Gospel is specifically *pro me*, "for me." For

> I believe that by my own understanding or strength I cannot believe in Jesus Christ my Lord or come to him, but instead the Holy Spirit has called me through the gospel, enlightened me with his gifts, made me holy and kept me in the true faith, just as he calls, gathers, enlightens, and makes holy the whole Christian church on earth and keeps it with Jesus Christ in the one common, true faith. Daily in this Christian church the Holy Spirit abundantly forgives all sins – mine and those of all believers. On the Last Day the Holy Spirit will raise me and all the dead and will give to me and all believers in Christ eternal life. This is most certainly true.[13]

For Luther, the post-baptismal condition of *simul iustus et peccator*, the only kind of Christian living possible, constituted something dramatically new, despite the continuing battle with sin: the transforming reality of divine forgiveness. It is a dynamic not a static condition.

Baptism places the individual within the church, where alone the means of the Holy Spirit's working are always and readily available. The mark of the cross, made upon one's brow in the sacrament, calls the believer to account, sometimes as blessed assurance, sometimes as brutal reprimand, until death finally grants the Christian's prayer for deliverance from temptation and evil. In both cases the objective sign of the sacrament is essential for revealing truth where one's own religious experience may deceive. We are as much sinners by faith as saints for Luther. We certainly have experience of sin in the world, but we are unable to recognize the insidious and pervasive depth of sin in ourselves. When we are brought face to face with its toxins, we fall into denial or despair.

For Luther the truth lies in being able continuously to name sin honestly and then face it down with the hope immovably grounded in Christ. In one of his more notorious letters, Luther brashly declares:

> If you are a preacher of grace, then preach a true and not a fictitious grace; if grace is true, you must bear a true and not a fictitious sin. God does not save people who are only fictitious sinners. Be a sinner and sin boldly, but believe and rejoice in Christ even more boldly, for he is victorious over sin, death, and the world. As long as we are here [in this world] we have to sin. This life is not the dwelling place of righteousness, but, as Peter says, we look for new heavens and a new earth in which righteousness dwells. It is enough that by the riches of God's glory we have come to know the Lamb that takes away the sin of the world. No sin will separate us from the Lamb, even though we commit fornication and murder a thousand times a day. Do you think that the purchase price that was paid for the redemption of our sins by so great a Lamb is too small? Pray boldly – you too are a mighty sinner.[14]

Extravagant statements like this one did not help clarify Luther's views to his opponents. He sounded like no friend to piety and moral probity. If sin is so rampant and grace so promiscuous, why struggle with discipline and the demands of good works? Yet as important as these are, for Luther true freedom could never come out of such efforts. Rather, it is the struggle of faith that is preeminent. The one bound to Christ in trust, as is the bride to her bridegroom,[15] is, as Luther famously put it, lord of all, subject to none, and servant of all, subject to all.[16] The human problem of sin is experienced in a new context, that is, the union with Christ in which the marriage portions, sin and death on our side, righteousness and life on his, are wholly shared. From this vantage point, the Christian's real challenge is to keep the faith, not to preserve a clean moral slate. In the realm of bold believing, both bold sinning and the rigorous pursuit of sanctification take their place as necessary but subordinate truths.

## HOLY COMMUNION

Concern for sustaining the believer in this ongoing struggle lies behind Luther's insistence on Christ's real presence in the Supper. Once again, Luther forges his sacramental spirituality against two opposing fronts, in this case the propitiatory sacrifice of the Roman Catholic mass on the one hand, which will be discussed more fully in the following section, and the memorial meal of the Zwinglians on the other. Here as before, he combats these interpretations as perversions of the sacrament that transform God's gracious act of self-giving into occasions for human performance.

At the heart of the christological controversy precipitated by Luther's doctrine of ubiquity stands his insistence on the objective certainty of the Word for the sake of the troubled conscience. Zwingli and his followers emphasized the faith of believers, who receive the bread and wine as salutary reminders of Christ's sacrifice on their behalf and are thereby spurred to grateful reflection. In this way they come into communion with Christ who is able spiritually to be present everywhere but whose body can be in only one place, as is the nature of human being, and thus remains at the right hand of God until the Lord comes again. Luther took the risk of transgressing the boundaries of the human as we know it in order not to violate what he deemed essential to Christology. After the incarnation there can be no human Jesus separate from the second person of the Trinity. Christ's ascension to the right hand of the Father means that wherever God's power is at work (and that is everywhere, i.e. ubiquitous), the Father acts in and through the Son. And the Son saves us and reigns over us as one fully human and fully divine; wherever he is present, he is necessarily present in both natures.

For Luther one does not rise up in faith to commune with the spiritual or divine Jesus who can be present everywhere. Rather, the crucified and resurrected Incarnate One comes to those gathered at the table and in the breaking of the bread makes himself known unequivocally as the One who saves. For Luther, the conscience in whatever condition it finds itself – impenitent, despairing, indifferent – requires this kind of in-your-face intervention to be convinced. Given the doctrine of ubiquity, there is no doubt one encounters Christ everywhere, but what is not certain is that these encounters will be experienced as saving. The Christ present in the sacrament allows for no ambiguity. Here by his own power and promise Jesus counters every human objection. If Zwingli emphasized the command to "do this in remembrance of me" in the narrative of the Last Supper, Luther revels in the specification "this is my body given *for you.*" The Supper is not a general announcement about the how of human salvation; it is the experience of one's personal salvation through the body (Christ's real presence and the church of which he is the head) in the here and now.

> Thus you must also say with regard to the Sacrament of the Altar, "If the priest gave me the holy body of Christ, which is a sign and promise of the communion of all angels and saints that they love me, provide and pray for me, suffer and die with me, bear my sin and overcome hell, it will and must therefore be true that the divine sign does not deceive me. I will not let anyone rob me of it. I would rather deny all the world and myself than doubt my God's trustworthiness and truthfulness in his signs and promises. Whether worthy or unworthy of him, I am, according to the text and the declaration of this sacrament, a member of Christendom. It is better that I be unworthy than that God's truthfulness be questioned. Devil, away with you if you advise me differently."[17]

This proclamation made individually to participants in the sacrament challenges, exhorts, and invites them simply to take the Savior at his word.

It is in these sacramental celebrations, when God, no longer ambiguously hidden behind the masks of creation, makes God's will to save manifest, that the driving tension of Luther's eschatology is temporarily released. When one looks at the eschatological understanding of the various Western Christian communities at the time of the Reformation, one finds that Luther and his followers were the most reserved.

The Roman Church regarded the church on earth as a beachhead of the Kingdom of God, the institution itself being sacramental in nature, the instrument and guardian of saving grace. In particular, the monastic orders, living under vows of poverty, chastity, and obedience, embodied a spiritual estate that was a foretaste of the life to come, in which "... they neither marry nor are given in marriage, but are like angels in heaven."[18] The imperfections that many within the Catholic Church acknowledged and sought to remedy notwithstanding, the splendor and power of the institution served as testimonies to its divine status.

Here one notes a fundamental difference in Luther's spiritual self-understanding. One could describe his reforming career as the lifelong prosecution of a pastoral malpractice suit against the Roman hierarchy. Rather than being confident of the church's sacral integrity, guaranteed by the action of God through the conferring of holy orders, Luther's experience led him to denounce as traitors to the gospel those claiming the authority of the magisterium. He lost the fundamental confidence that God would not allow the pope and the bishops to lead the faithful into error in matters crucial to salvation. In its place one finds a relentless hermeneutic of suspicion. Luther held that the gospel was indefectible, that is, at all times God has insured that somewhere in the world the Good News is being rightly proclaimed and received in faith. This is the true church, against which the gates of hell shall never prevail, but one cannot identify it on the basis of outer trappings or human claims to preeminence. Rather, one must test what happens in any given assembly by the criteria of Word and sacrament: What is being said and done here and what effects are these activities producing among the faithful? The earthly church itself becomes a far more ambiguous reality for Luther and can no longer be regarded as an inbreaking of the fullness of the Kingdom of God. This limits the experience of realized eschatology for him to the celebration of the sacraments and the preaching of the gospel, where the Lord is made manifest as victorious Savior *pro nobis*.

In contrast to other Protestant groups, such as the Reformed and the Anabaptists, Luther does not accord the justified sinner's pursuit of sanctification significant weight as evidence of the inbreaking of God's Kingdom. Luther recognized that the life of discipleship allowed for such moments of eschatological revelation, moments when one saw the neighbor's need and responded reflexively, emptying the self for the sake of the other without stopping to calculate the cost. This surrender to love is surely the work of God in us, but these fleeting experiences of perfect Christian freedom are not what faith builds upon.

There is considerable debate as to whether Luther embraced a third use of the law, which was for Calvin its chief use. In the life of the believer the law continues to make external demands curbing wickedness (first use) and condemning sin (second use), but it can also instruct, motivate, and encourage. Thus, it can be heard by believers as not threatening, and that is a measure of how far grace has already succeeded in redeeming the creation. This emphasis, so salient in Calvin's theology, is not a lynchpin of Luther's spirituality. He clearly expects good works and amendment of life to flow from the hearing of the gospel. But Luther remains

acutely aware that one's concern for moral betterment and ear'
can all too easily fill the places of the heart to which God alo
ful claim. In the controversy with the Anabaptists, he was as ɔ
rejecting their earthly pursuit of a distinctively Christian higher righteʋ
ness as he was in dismissing the monastics' efforts. For Luther, the life of
faith is surrender rather than accomplishment; it is regular exercise in self-
emptying, which is simultaneously apprenticeship in receiving the fullness
of God.

## VOCATION

The believer is called to imitate Christ by bearing the cross of the need
of others.

> See, according to this rule the good things we have from God should
> flow from one to the other and be common to all, so that everyone
> should "put on" his neighbor and so conduct himself toward him as if
> he himself were in the other's place. From Christ the good things have
> flowed and are flowing into us. He had to "put on" us and acted for us
> as if he had been what we are. From us they flow on to those who have
> need of them so that I should lay before God my faith and my
> righteousness that they may cover and intercede for the sins of my
> neighbor which I take upon myself and so labor and serve in them as
> if they were my very own. That is what Christ did for us. This is true
> love and the genuine rule of a Christian life. Love is true and genuine
> where there is true and genuine faith.[19]

The arena for this discipleship is the world, not a self-styled oasis of higher
righteousness, and the means are the commonplace vocations of family life,
civic duty, friendship, and work. If all the baptized emerge from the water
of the sacrament "priest, bishop, and pope," then a miner, a laundress, or a
parent is a member of the spiritual estate, serving and praising God in and
through their routine activities. The particularity of vocation was a great
comfort for Luther. He was called to be a doctor of Scripture in service
of the church; he was called to be the husband of one particular woman
and the father of her children. One need not go looking for crosses to bear
to prove one's godliness. One may be content with these unexceptional
responsibilities and relationships, for it is through them that the will of God
is done and we are brought to abundant life.

On one hand, then, we have the intensity of Luther's eschatological
expectation. Although he was never one to calculate the exact day and time

of the Lord's coming, his spirituality is characterized by a sense of living in the last times. The saving gospel had emerged with a clarity unparalleled since the age of the apostles. Now, as St. Paul puts it, is the acceptable time; now is the day of salvation, and Luther was as ardent as the apostle in urging his hearers not to accept the grace of God in vain.[20] Or, in words reflective of the commercial concerns of sixteenth-century Europe, in urging his fellow Germans to buy while the market is good. On the other hand, Luther insists that the business as usual of the world – politics, productivity, reproduction – is the matter of discipleship. He is reputed to have said that if he knew the world would end tomorrow, he would go out and plant an apple tree today. The saying has never been verified from his writings, but its currency shows that whether or not the actual words were his, there was no doubt that the sentiment was perceived as genuinely Lutheran.

## FAITH AND PRACTICE

The final polarity to be considered concerns the role of faith in Luther's spirituality. Over against the practice of believer's baptism or the celebration of the Lord's Supper as a memorial meal, Luther is adamant that the sacraments derive their power not from human faith but from the command and promise of God.

> Thus we do the same with infant baptism. We bring the child with the intent and hope that it may believe, and we pray God to grant it faith. But we do not baptize on this basis, but solely on the command of God. Why? Because we know that God does not lie. My neighbor and I – in short, all people – may deceive and mislead, but God's Word cannot deceive.[21]
>
> Our conclusion is: Even though a scoundrel receives or administers the sacrament, it is the true sacrament (that is, Christ's body and blood), just as truly as when one uses it most worthily. For it is not founded on human holiness but on the Word of God. As no saint on earth, yes, no angel in heaven can make bread and wine into Christ's body and blood, so likewise can no one change or alter the sacrament, even through misuse. For the Word by which it was constituted a sacrament is not rendered false because of an individual's unworthiness or unbelief.[22]

Yet at the same time, in his criticism of Roman Catholic sacramental practice Luther vehemently rejects what he judges to be an *ex opere operato* understanding, that is, that the sacrament is effective simply through the performance of it, particularly with regard to the celebration of the mass as a sacrifice. In this case, he objects, too little is made of faith, and the believer is thus defrauded of the gift rightly hers in the sacrament.

> ...because he offers and promises forgiveness of sins, it can be received in no other way than by faith. This faith he himself demands in the Word when he says, "given FOR YOU" and "shed FOR YOU," as if he said, "This is why I give it and bid you eat and drink, that you may take it as your own and enjoy it." All those who let these words be addressed to them and believe that they are true have what the words declare. But those who do not believe have nothing, for they let this gracious blessing be offered to them in vain and refuse to enjoy it. The treasure is opened and placed at everyone's door, yes, upon the table, but it is also your responsibility to take it and confidently believe that it is just as the words tell you.[23]

This double perspective on faith produces some conflicting exhortations from Luther, at the root of which lies his consistent pastoral concern for those troubled in conscience and haunted by doubt. One comes to the Lord's table not on account of any personal worthiness in terms of piety or virtue but precisely because of one's unworthiness and need for what is given there. However, "[t]hose who are impudent and unruly ought to be told to stay away, for they are not ready to receive the forgiveness of sins because they do not desire it and do not want to be righteous."[24] But what about those who feel unfit? Luther acknowledges that he shares this struggle, "...especially inherited from the old order under the pope when we tortured ourselves to become so perfectly pure that God might not find the least blemish in us."[25] Here one sees the sharp conflict between the objective sign that stands superior to any subjective religious feeling. "If you choose to fix your eye on how good and pure you are, to wait until nothing torments you, you will never go."[26] Yet "...it is true that those who despise the sacrament and lead unchristian lives receive it to their harm and damnation."[27] So the believer is obliged to know the difference between culpable avoidance and paralyzing weakness, the difference between being a person "...who desires no grace and absolution and has no intention of improving"[28] and a person who hears the Good News as too good to be true for him. "...We must examine our heart and conscience and act like a person who really desires to be right with God."[29] There is a tension here in Luther's spirituality. At what point does indifference or anxiety shade off into hostility and unbelief? At what point must faith stop scrutinizing the probity of its desire and simply open the mouth and stretch out the hand? In developing a new architecture for the life of faith, Luther and the Lutherans who followed him have always been wary lest the foundation in free grace degenerate into grace that is merely cheap.

## Notes

1. Peter Matheson, *The Imaginative World of the Reformation* (Edinburgh: T&T Clark, 2000), 6–7.
2. LW 51, 202. The translation is mine from the critical edition of Luther's works (WA).
3. LW 51, 204. My translation.
4. John Nicholas Lenker, ed. and trans. *Sermons of Martin Luther* (Grand Rapids: Baker), II:148–54.
5. LW 6, 131.
6. Martin Luther, *Concerning Rebaptism*, in Timothy F. Lull, ed., *Martin Luther's Basic Theological Writings* (Minneapolis: Fortress Press, 1989), 352.
7. Martin Luther, *Small Catechism*, in Robert Kolb and Timothy J. Wengert, eds., *The Book of Concord: The Confessions of the Evangelical Lutheran Church* (Minneapolis: Fortress Press, 2000), 360.
8. Ibid., emphasis added.
9. Ibid., 351: "You are to have no other gods. What is this? Answer: We are to fear, love and trust God above all things."
10. See the passage cited above at note 6 for the explicit comparison.
11. Luther, *Small Catechism*, 355.
12. Ibid., 373.
13. Ibid., 355–56.
14. LW 48, 281–82.
15. Martin Luther, *The Freedom of a Christian*, in Lull, 603–04.
16. Ibid., 596.
17. Martin Luther, *A Sermon on Preparing to Die*, in Lull, 650.
18. Matthew 22:30 (NRSV).
19. Luther, *Freedom of a Christian*, 623.
20. 2 Corinthians 6:1–2 (NRSV).
21. Martin Luther, *Large Catechism*, in Lull, 464.
22. Ibid., 468.
23. Ibid., 470.
24. Ibid., 473.
25. Ibid., 472.
26. Ibid., 473.
27. Ibid., 474.
28. Ibid., 473.
29. Ibid., 472.

# 10 Luther's struggle with social-ethical issues
CARTER LINDBERG

The crucial point to remember in discussing Luther's struggle with social-ethical issues is that he understood himself to be a theologian and pastor not a sociologist or economist or politician. Indeed, Luther's ethics may be understood as pastoral care.[1] For Luther, therefore, theology and ethics served the proclamation of the good news that salvation is received not achieved. Our justification before God "must be believed and cannot be obtained by any work, law, or merit."[2] In contrast to all pieties of achievement, then and now, Luther affirmed God's descent in Jesus to us rather than our striving to ascend to God. In opposition to the medieval renunciation of the world, epitomized by the image and metaphor of the ladder to heaven, Luther proclaimed that Christ could not be dragged too deeply into the flesh.[3] Hence Luther criticized the religion of the Turks, Jews, and papists for prescribing "heavenward journeys on which the travelers will break their necks."[4]

The subject of theology and ethics is not God in heaven, in his absolute majesty, the "naked God," but rather God "clothed in His Word and promises" for us.

> God says: "I do not choose to come to you in My majesty and in the company of angels but in the guise of a poor beggar asking for bread." You may ask: "How do you know this?" Christ replies: "I have revealed to you in My Word what form I would assume and to whom you should give. You do not ascend into heaven, where I am seated at the right hand of My heavenly Father, to give Me something; no I come down to you in humility. I place flesh and blood before your door with the plea: 'Give me a drink!... I do not need food in heaven. I have come all the way from Judea. Give me a drink!' I have had it announced to all the world that whatever is done to the least of My brethren is done to me" (Matt. 25:40).[5]

Thus Luther's struggle with issues of social ethics proceeded from his perceived vocation to proclaim God's promise and judgment. He wrote:

Let no one, therefore, ponder the Divine Majesty, what God has done and how mighty He is; or think of man as the master of his property, the way the lawyer does; or of his health the way the physician does. But let him think of man as sinner. The proper subject of theology is man guilty of sin and condemned, and God the Justifier and Savior of man the sinner. Whatever is asked or discussed in theology outside this subject is error and poison.[6]

Since for Luther salvation is not the process or goal of life, but rather the presupposition of life, his theology became a transvaluation of all values. Thus his orientation to social issues was not in the mode of the Aristotelian (and modern!) progress from vice to virtue.[7] Service to the neighbor is based neither upon self-development nor upon its results, but upon God's promise. Said Luther, "We do not become righteous by doing righteous deeds but, having been made righteous, we do righteous deeds."[8] Social ethics therefore does not depend upon success, but upon God's promise: faith is active in love.

The Bible has been put into your workshop, into your hand, into your heart. It teaches and preaches how you should treat your neighbor. Just look at your tools – at your needle or thimble, your beer barrel, your goods, your scales or yardstick or measure – and you will read this statement inscribed on them... "Friend, use me in your relations with your neighbor just as you would want your neighbor to use his property in his relations with you."[9]

Good works are not salvatory, but they do serve the neighbor. Since works are not ultimate but penultimate activities of the sinner saved by the justifying God, they are this-worldly rather than other-worldly, directed to the neighbor as a response to God's promise. Thus Luther's social ethics is aptly described as "the liturgy after the liturgy." "Now there is no greater service of God [*dienst Gottes*; *Gottesdienst* = worship] than Christian love which helps and serves the needy, as Christ himself will judge and testify at the Last Day, Matthew 25[:31–46]."[10] "The world would be full of worship if everyone served his neighbor, the farmhand in the stable, the boy in the school, maid and mistress in the home."[11]

## THE CONTEXTUAL NATURE OF LUTHER'S SOCIAL ETHICS

From the initial uproar over the Ninety-five Theses of 1517 to his death after mediating a dispute between the counts of Mansfeld in 1546, Luther remained center stage through the religious, economic, political, and social upheavals of the period. He could do no other, for "it is the most unvarying fate of the Word of God to have the world in a tumult because of it ... For the Word of God comes, whenever it comes, to change and renew the world."[12]

Throughout these upheavals and rapid social changes, people appealed to Luther for advice about every area of personal and social life. Since our focus is on social issues we shall leave to one side the more personal appeals that deluged Luther.[13] The multiplicity of social issues created as well as unleashed by Luther's initiation of reform may be approached under the rubric of the "three orders" or "estates": the church (*ecclesiam*), household (*oeconomiam*), and government (*politiam*).[14] According to Luther, these are the fundamental forms by which God's promise of creation constitutes human existence.[15]

> Above these three institutions and orders is the common order of Christian love, in which one serves not only the three orders, but also serves every needy person in general with all kinds of benevolent deeds, such as feeding the hungry, giving drink to the thirsty, forgiving enemies, praying for all men on earth, suffering all kinds of evil on earth, etc. Behold all of these are called good and holy works. However none of these orders is a means of salvation. There remains only one way above them all, viz. faith in Jesus Christ.[16]

It is important to bear in mind that a synthesis of Luther's responses to social-ethical issues under the heading of the Three Estates minimizes the historical development of Luther's social-ethical struggles. On the other hand, there is not sufficient space here to explore the messiness and complexity of his ethical struggles, nor the intertwining of ethical issues. Luther himself did not have the luxury of treating ethical issues in the abstract nor one at a time. Rather, once the reform got under way there was a deluge of social-ethical issues clamoring for resolution. Since other chapters in this volume focus on Luther's contributions to the estates of the church and politics, I shall focus on some of the issues within the estate of the household. It is also important to recognize that the borders between the three estates are permeable, and the concerns of one estate frequently relate to the concerns of the other. Further, the estate of the household (*oeconomium*) was broadly conceived to include not only marriage and the family, but also social welfare and local and national economic concerns.

## THE HOUSEHOLD: MARRIAGE AND FAMILY

The concomitant of Luther's proclamation of justification by grace alone apart from works was a "doxology of the ordinary."[17] Convinced that the finite is capable of the infinite (a motif that Luther developed in his Christology, eucharistic theology, and theology of creation), Luther rejected every form of flight from the world with its suspicion of creation including the human body. Humankind is not called to flee the world but rather to engage the world for the common good. The concrete demonstration of the new faith very soon became clerical marriage. This was not just a matter of breaking church law; rather, the public rejection of mandatory clerical celibacy encompassed the new evangelical understanding of the relationship to God and the world.[18]

Luther's confrontation with church authorities on this subject began with his *To the Christian Nobility of the German Nation Concerning the Reform of the Christian Estate* (1520). Every priest should be free to marry because "before God and the Holy Scriptures marriage of the clergy is no offense." Clerical celibacy is not God's law but the pope's, and "Christ has set us free from all man-made laws, especially when they are opposed to God and the salvation of souls . . ." Thus the pope has no more power to command celibacy than "he has to forbid eating, drinking, the natural movement of the bowels, or growing fat."[19] Luther was well aware that the abolition of clerical celibacy would entail "a very different kind of government and administration of church property; the whole canon law would have to be abolished . . ."[20] "No institutional change brought about by the Reformation was more visible, responsive to late medieval pleas for reform, and conducive to new social attitudes than the marriage of Protestant clergy. Nor was there another point in the Protestant program where theology and practice corresponded more successfully."[21] Luther's application of evangelical theology to marriage and family desacramentalized marriage; desacralized the clergy and resacralized the life of the laity; opposed the maze of canonical impediments to marriage; strove to unravel the tangled skein of canon law, imperial law, and German customs; and joyfully affirmed God's good creation, including sexual relations.[22]

The medieval church viewed the celibate life as a meritorious work for salvation, and perpetuated patristic suspicions of sexuality as the font of original sin. Jerome's view that virginity is the ideal state of Christian life ("Marriages fill the earth, virginity fills heaven") was repugnant and blasphemous to Luther.[23] To Luther, sex is an aspect of God's good creation. In contrast to the patristic and medieval tradition of asceticism, Luther and his colleagues "literally transferred the accolades Christian tradition heaped on the religious in monasteries and nunneries to marriage and the home . . . 'Faith, not virginity, fills paradise,' the Wittenberg pastor Johannes Bugenhagen retorted in the 1520s. 'Saint Jerome's unfortunate comment . . . must be corrected,' agreed the Lutheran poet Erasmus Alberus . . ."[24]

With marriage and the household estate came multiple responsibilities to the larger community and vice versa.[25] "Marriage does not only consist of sleeping with a woman – anybody can do that – but of keeping house and bringing up children."[26] Those who followed Luther saw in marriage not only a new joyous appreciation of sexual relations, but also a new respect for women as companions. Luther could not imagine life without women: "The home, cities, economic life and government would virtually disappear. Men cannot do without women. Even if it were possible for men to beget and bear children, they still couldn't do without women."[27]

Luther sought to redefine what his society thought appropriate for male and female behavior. For example, medieval society and theology sanctioned prostitution and civic brothels. Prostitutes were thought to purify a town by draining off excess male sexual energy as a sewer drained off waste.[28] The church tolerated prostitution because its gender values denigrated sex and also assumed that male desire was an anarchic, uncontrollable force that if not provided an outlet would pollute the town's respectable women. Luther's criticism of this rationale attacked his culture's gender presupposition concerning males. In asserting equal responsibility for males and females, Luther criticized the double standard of his day as well as the existence of brothels.[29] Luther attempted to redefine his culture's understanding of male gender from uncontrollable impulse to social responsibility.

Luther likewise opposed the medieval practice of clandestine marriage. The canon law that "consent makes the marriage" allowed abuses of minors who entered marriage without parental consent as well as deceptions of women. Luther spoke to this issue in his tract *That Parents Should Neither Compel nor Hinder Their Children and That Children Should Not Become Engaged without Their Parents' Consent* (1524). His concern was to increase the parents' role in the marriages of their children, not to constrict the children. Luther opposed secret betrothals without the consent of the parents and the public support of the community because he saw that it was the woman and her children who were at risk of being discarded with no rights. In these arrangements to live together, the woman could not file suit for her rights if the man left her. Luther stated clearly: "A secret engagement should yield to a public one."[30] "Marriages" without communal and legal validation, according to Luther, led to legal, economic, and pastoral problems.[31] Such arrangements undercut the communal stake in family life. Furthermore, the theological perspective that marriage is based in faith and trust makes "trial marriage" an oxymoron. Public marriage is difficult enough, secret marriages which lack legal and communal support are even more so. Every marriage is a risk, but a clandestine marriage based only on mutual attraction increases rather than minimizes the risk.

For Luther, marriage and family life are Christian callings. Luther's sermons and catechisms made it clear in contrast to the theology and laws of the medieval church that home and discipleship are not mutually exclusive. To the contrary, it is precisely in marriage that chastity is possible, and religious vocation finds its realization. To the medieval person, vocation was limited to priests, nuns, and monks. The thought that persons could serve God in marriage was revolutionary. Justification by grace alone apart from works liberated Christians from achieving salvation by renunciation of the world, and enabled service to the neighbor in the world. The neighbor here is the person encountered in the concrete situation, that is, parents, spouse, and children.

Luther rejected flight into self-chosen religious callings of clericalism, and called people to serve others in the web of relationships where they live. We are to do, Luther asserted, what God commands not what we fancy God would like. Here, again, Luther focused on "the ordinary." The perennial temptation of the religious person is the desire to do "important" things rather than sweep the floor, change diapers, and do the dishes. Luther's point, however, is that we are not called to self-chosen extraordinary tasks, but rather to service in the world.

> We err in that we judge the work of God according to our own feelings, and regard not his will but our own desire... Now observe that when that clever harlot, our natural reason... takes a look at married life, she turns up her nose and says, "Alas, must I rock the baby, wash its diapers, make its bed, smell its stench, stay up nights with it, take care of it when it cries, heal its rashes and sores, and on top of that care for my wife, provide for her, labor at my trade... and whatever else of bitterness and drudgery married life involves?... It is better to remain free and lead a peaceful, carefree life; I will become a priest or a nun and compel my children to do likewise."[32]

The center of Luther's ethic of vocation is not self-sanctification, but the neighbors' needs. "[E]veryone must benefit and serve every other by means of his own work or office so that in this way many kinds of work may be done for the bodily and spiritual welfare of the community..."[33] For Luther, the Christian is called to live and serve others wherever God has placed him or her. Thus "when a father goes ahead and washes diapers or performs some other mean task for his child, and someone ridicules him as an effeminate fool... my dear fellow you tell me, which of the two is most keenly ridiculing the other? God, with all his angels and creatures is smiling – not because that father is washing diapers, but because he is doing so in Christian faith."[34] For Luther, "vocation is the work of faith; vocation is worship in the realm of the world."[35]

## THE HOUSEHOLD: SOCIAL WELFARE AND ECONOMICS

A major social issue on the eve of the Reformation was widespread poverty exacerbated by the rapid, unrestrained growth of the profit economy and legitimated by the church's sanctification and idealization of poverty as the preferred condition of Christian life. Poverty was perceived as a kind of spiritual capital for poor and rich alike.

God's preferential option for the poor gave them a decided edge in the pilgrimage to salvation (the rich can no more squeeze through the eye of the needle into heaven than can a camel). On the other hand, the church had long emphasized that almsgiving atones for sin. Thus almsgiving provided the poor with some charity, enabled the rich to atone for their sins, and blessed the rich with the intercessions of the poor. This symbiotic relationship of rich and poor is succinctly expressed by the ancient line: "God could have made all men rich, but he wanted poor men in this world so that the rich might have an opportunity to redeem their sins."[36] The economy of salvation as well as the economy of the marketplace promoted the perpetuation of poverty. The poor were not only a large and inexpensive labor pool, they were also the object for the good works of the wealthy.[37]

Luther's doctrine of justification cut the nerve of the medieval ideology of poverty. Since salvation is God's free gift, both poverty and almsgiving lose saving significance. The de-spiritualization of poverty allowed recognition of poverty as a personal and social evil to be combated. Justification by grace alone caused a paradigm shift in the understanding of poverty. Poverty was no longer understood as the favored status of the Christian, but rather as a social ill to be combated.

> [A]ll who display, and boast of, external poverty are disciples and servants of Satan, who rage directly contrary to the Lord and His Christ . . . Poverty, I say, is not to be recommended, chosen, or taught; for there is enough of that by itself, as He says (John 12:8): "The poor you always have with you," just as you will have all other evils. But constant care should be taken that, since these evils are always in evidence, they are always opposed.[38]

The poor are no longer the objects of meritorious charity, but neighbors to be served through justice and equity.[39] Under the rubrics of justice and love to the neighbor, that is, the civil use of the law, Luther and his colleagues moved in alliance with local governments to establish and legislate government welfare policies.

The first major effort was the Wittenberg Church Order of 1522 that established a "common chest" for welfare work. Initially funded by medieval ecclesiastical endowments and later by taxes, the Wittenberg Order prohibited begging; provided interest-free loans to artisans, who were to repay them whenever possible; provided for poor orphans, the children of poor people, and poor maidens who needed an appropriate dowry for marriage; provided refinancing of high interest loans at four percent annual interest for burdened citizens; and supported the education or vocational training of poor children. The Wittenberg common chest was a new creation of the Reformation that transformed theology into social praxis. Its financial basis soon included sales of grain, public collections, and a primitive banking operation. These resources enabled it to exercise a broad spectrum of social welfare including care of the sick and elderly in hospitals, a medical office for the poor whose doctor, Melchior Fendt, established prophylactic measures in times of hunger and inflation, and support of communal schools.[40] Other communities quickly picked up these ideas. By 1523 there were common chest provisions for social welfare in the church orders of Leisnig, Augsburg, Nuremberg, Altenburg, Kitzingen, Strasbourg, Breslau, and Regensburg.[41]

These ordinances for poor relief were efforts to implement Luther's conviction that social welfare policies designed to prevent as well as alleviate poverty are a Christian social responsibility. While Luther's efforts to develop welfare legislation were well received in the cities and territories that accepted the Reformation, his efforts to encourage civic control of capitalism gained little support. Luther discovered it was easier to motivate assistance to the poor than to curb the economic structures and practices that created and fostered the conditions of poverty. The squalor of poverty calls out for redress, whereas the attractive trappings of business muffle criticism. "How skillfully Sir Greed can dress up to look like a pious man if that seems to be what the occasion requires, while he is actually a double scoundrel and a liar."[42] "God opposes usury and greed, yet no one realizes this because it is not simple murder and robbery. Rather, usury is a more diverse, insatiable murder and robbery... Thus everyone should see to his worldly and spiritual office as commanded to punish the wicked and protect the pious."[43]

Luther found the calculating entrepreneur extremely distasteful. He was convinced that the capitalist spirit divorced money from use for human needs and necessitated an economy of acquisition. From his *Sermon on Usury* (1519) to his *Admonition to the Clergy that they Preach Against Usury* (1540),

Luther consistently preached and wrote against the expanding money and credit economy as a great sin.[44]

> After the devil there is no greater human enemy on earth than a miser and usurer, for he desires to be above everyone. Turks, soldiers, and tyrants are also evil men, yet they allow the people to live ... But a usurer and miser-belly desires that the whole world be ruined in order that there be hunger, thirst, misery, and need so that he can have everything and so that everyone must depend upon him and be his slave as if he were God.[45]

Such usury, Luther argued, affects everyone. "The usury which occurs in Leipzig, Augsburg, Frankfurt, and other comparable cities is felt in our market and our kitchen. The usurers are eating our food and drinking our drink." By manipulating prices "usury lives off the bodies of the poor."[46] "The world is one big whorehouse, completely submerged in greed," where the "big thieves hang the little thieves" and the big fish eat the little fish.[47] Thus Luther exhorted pastors to condemn usury as stealing and murder, and to refuse absolution and the sacrament to usurers unless they repent.[48]

Luther's concern was not only about an individual's use of money, but also the structural social damage inherent in the idolatry of the "laws" of the market. Ideas of an "impersonal market" and "autonomous laws of economics" were abhorrent to Luther because he saw them as both idolatrous and socially destructive. He saw the community endangered by the rising financial power of a few great economic centers; their unregulated economic coercion would destroy the ethos of the community. Thus Luther considered early capitalism to constitute a *status confessionis* for the church.[49] To Luther early capitalism was doubly dangerous because it not only exploited people but also strove to conceal its voracious nature and to deceive people. Luther appealed for government regulation of interest rates and business practices. As a preacher and pastor, Luther understood that "the gospel's *primary* function is not – as assumed today ... – to change *obvious* injustice by introducing social legislation to establish *biblical* justice, but to unmask *hidden* injustice, thus saving the souls of duped Christians and opening the eyes of the secular authorities for their mandate to establish *civil* justice."[50]

Throughout his career Luther fought against what he saw as the two-sided coin of mammonism: the ascetic flight from money and the acquisitive drive for it. His foundation for this battle was the great reversal of the gospel that a person's worth is not determined by what he or she does or does not possess, but rather by God's promise in Christ. Thus money is not the lord of life, but the gift of God for serving the neighbor and building up the community. Luther believed that the church was called publicly and unequivocally to reject exploitative economic developments, and to develop a constructive social ethic in response to them. This social ethic contributed directly to the enactment of social welfare legislation in areas that accepted the Reformation, and called for public accountability of large business through government regulation. For Luther, the government

> is to help the poor, the orphans, and the widows to justice, and to further their cause... [T]his virtue includes all the works of righteousness: as when a prince or lord or city has good laws and customs; when everything is regulated in an orderly way; and when order is kept by people in all ranks, occupations, trades, businesses, services, and works, so that it is not said: "The people are without laws." For where there are no laws, the poor, the widows, and the orphans are oppressed... And this is equally true of buying, selling, inheriting, lending, paying, borrowing, and the like. It is only a matter of one getting the better of another, robbing him, stealing from him, and cheating him. This happens most of all to the poor, the widows, and the orphans.[51]

CONCLUDING PERSPECTIVES

Luther's struggle with the social-ethical issues of his time was "invariably rooted in his theology and his ethics... his positions have had a far-reaching and path-breaking effect. They have definitely contributed to the transforming of society."[52] Luther understood his task as theologian and preacher as to provide a clear critique of existing social structures, and to call the community to work in the different "estates" for the well-being of the neighbor and the common good. This preaching included freeing people from their ideologies and for service.[53] Justification by grace alone unmasked all claims for the redemptive power of human works, including all economic and political systems. Neither renunciation nor acquisition is redemptive or identifiable with the Kingdom of God. Because salvation is the foundation of life rather than its goal, the energy and resources previously devoted to acquiring both this-worldly and other-worldly capital can be redirected to this-worldly service to the neighbor. For Luther and his colleagues this meant that faith active in love to the neighbor is incarnated not only through the web of social relationships rooted in marriage and family, but also through government legislation for the common good.

Notes

1. See Yoshiro Ishida, "Luther the Pastor," in C. Lindberg, ed., *Piety, Politics, and Ethics: Reformation Studies in Honor of George Wolfgang Forell* (Kirksville: The Sixteenth Century Journal Publishers, 1984), 27–37; Oswald Bayer, "Luther's Ethics as Pastoral Care," *Lutheran Quarterly* 4/2 (Summer 1990), 125–42; and Johann Anselm Steiger, "The *communicatio idiomatum* as the Axle and Motor of Luther's Theology," *Lutheran Quarterly* 14/2 (Summer 2000), 125–58, especially 133ff.: "The *communicatio idomatum* in Luther's Ethics and Pastoral Theology."

2. *The Smalkald Articles* in Robert Kolb and Timothy J. Wengert, eds., *The Book of Concord: The Confessions of the Evangelical Lutheran Church* (Minneapolis: Fortress Press, 2000), 301.

3. For discussions of such ladder imagery, see Margaret Miles, *The Image and Practice of Holiness* (London: SCM, 1988), chapter 4: "Staying is Nowhere: Ascent," and Christian Heck, *L'Échelle céleste dans l'art du Moyen Âge: une histoire de la quête du Ciel* (Paris: Flammarion, 1997).

4. LW 22, 334. As few theologians before him, Luther emphasized the humanity of Christ. The saving presence of God for humankind is only there where God is bound to the humanity of Jesus Christ. See Bernhard Lohse, *Luthers Theologie in ihrer historischen Entwicklung und in ihrem systematischen Zusammenhang* (Göttingen: Vandenhoeck & Ruprecht, 1995), 241, 248.

5. LW 22, 520.

6. LW 12, 311–12.

7. See my "Do Lutherans Shout Justification But Whisper Sanctification?" *Lutheran Quarterly* 13/1 (Spring 1999), 1–20. Gerhard Ebeling argues that Luther's fight against the moralization of Christian faith led him to displace the medieval doctrine of virtues by a doctrine of good works informed by the commandments. "The concentration of Luther's exegesis of the Decalogue upon the First Commandment and upon faith as its fulfillment and therefore as the source of all good works is new in the history of theology." Gerhard Ebeling, "Luthers Kampf gegen die Moralisierung des Christlichen," in his *Lutherstudien* (Tübingen: J. C. B. Mohr, 1985), III:44–73, here 70 and 57, n. 34. See Luther's *Treatise on Good Works*, LW 44, 15–114. See also Ivar Asheim, "Lutherische Tugendethik?," *Neue Zeitschrift für systematische Theologie* 40 (1998), 239–60.

8. LW 31, 12. Luther continues: "Virtually the entire *Ethics* of Aristotle is the worst enemy of grace."

9. LW 21, 237.

10. LW 45, 172. See my "Luther's Concept of Offering," *Dialog* 35/4 (Fall 1996), 251–57; and Gerhard Müller, "Biblische Theologie und Sozialethik. Zum Denken Martin Luthers," *Evangelische Theologie* 59/1 (1999), 25–31, here 27.

11. WA 36, 340,12–16. By emphasizing that service to God occurred concretely in the world, Luther overcame the traditional separation between sacred and profane activity. See Hans-Jürgen Prien, *Luthers Wirtschaftsethik* (Göttingen: Vandenhoeck & Ruprecht, 1992), 179.

12. LW 33, 52.

13. A useful compendium of Luther's responses to personal pleas for advice and counsel is Theodore G. Tappert, ed. and trans., *Luther: Letters of Spiritual Counsel* (Philadelphia: Westminster, 1955).

14. Estate (*Stand*) basically indicates the web of relationships in which we exist or "stand," and which we have to protect if we are to perceive the various dimensions of historical existence in relation to the will of God. See Oswald Bayer, "Nature and Institution: Luther's Doctrines of the Three Orders," *Lutheran Quarterly* 12/2 (Summer 1998), 125–59; Peter Manns, "Luthers Zwei-Reiche- und Drei-Stände-Lehre, " in Erwin Iserloh and Gerhard Müller, eds., *Luther und die politische Welt* (Stuttgart: Steiner Verlag, 1984), 3–26; Reinhard Schwarz, "Luthers Lehre von den drei Ständen und die drei Dimensionen der Ethik," *Lutherjahrbuch* 45 (1978), 15–34; and Bernhard Lohse, *Luthers Theologie*, 259–64, 340–44.

15. See Oswald Bayer, "Martin Luther (1483–1546)," in C. Lindberg, ed., *The Reformation Theologians* (Oxford: Blackwell, 2001), 51–66.

16. LW 37, 365.

17. This felicitous phrase captures Luther's contribution to worldly spirituality as developed by Hans J. Hillerbrand in "The Road Less Traveled? Reflections on the Enigma of Lutheran Spirituality," in Daniel N. Harmelink, ed., *Let Christ Be Christ: Theology, Ethics & World Religions in the Two Kingdoms. Essays in Honor of the Sixty-Fifth Birthday of Charles L. Manske* (Huntington Beach, CA: Tentatio Press, 1999), 129–40, here 140.

18. Bernd Moeller, "Wenzel Links Hochzeit: Über Sexualität, Keuscheit, und Ehe in der frühen Reformation," ZThK 97 (2000), 317–42.

19. LW 44, 178–9.

20. LW 44, 176.

21. Steven Ozment, *The Age of Reform 1250–1550* (New Haven: Yale University Press, 1980), 381. See also his *Protestantism: The Birth of a Revolution* (New York: Doubleday, 1992), 151–68. Volker Press, "Martin Luther und die sozialen Kräfte seine Zeit," in Iserloh and Müller, eds., *Luther und die politische Welt*, 189–217, 200, refers to Luther's shattering of mandatory clerical celibacy as "the most significant social-historical consequence of the Reformation." Moeller, "Wenzel Links Hochzeit," 341–42, refers to clerical marriage as a "paradigm shift" away from a "piety of achievement" that served as something of a "demystification" of the church, creation, and human sexuality.

22. For the legal ramifications concerning impediments, divorce, and remarriage see John Witte, Jr., *From Sacrament to Contract: Marriage, Religion, and Law in the Western Tradition* (Louisville: Westminster John Knox Press, 1997) and his *Law and Protestantism: The Legal Teachings of the Lutheran Reformation* (Cambridge: Cambridge University Press, 2002), especially chapter 6: "The Domestic Church: Reformation of Marriage Law." For Luther's revalorization of marriage and family see Gerta Scharffenorth, *Becoming Friends in Christ: The Relationship between Man and Woman as Seen by Luther* (Geneva: The Lutheran World Federation, 1983); William Lazareth, *Luther on the Christian Home* (Philadelphia: Muhlenberg Press, 1960); Scott Hendrix, "Luther on Marriage," *Lutheran Quarterly* 14/3 (Autumn 2000), 335–50; and my "The Future of a Tradition: Luther and the Family," in Dean O. Wenthe, et al., eds., *All Theology is Christology: Essays in Honor of David P. Scaer* (Fort Wayne, IN: Concordia Theological Seminary Press, 2000), 133–51.

23. LW 33, 84.

24. Ozment, *Protestantism*, 153.

25. These mutual responsibilities included the education and training of the youth, including girls. "I hold that it is the duty of the temporal authority to compel its subjects to keep their children in school... so that there will always be preachers, jurists, pastors, writers, physicians, schoolmasters, and the like, for we cannot do without them." LW 46, 256. There is not space here to pursue this important contribution of Luther's social ethics. See Marilyn J. Harran, *Martin Luther: Learning for Life* (St. Louis: Concordia Publishing House, 1997).

26. LW 54, 441.

27. LW 54, 161.

28. Jacques Rossiaud, *Medieval Prostitution* (Oxford: Blackwell, 1995), 80–4, and *passim*.

29. See LW 44, 214–15; LW 3, 259.

30. LW 46, 267.

31. See Eberhard Winkler, " 'Weltlich Ding' oder 'Göttlicher Stand'? Die Ehe als Bewährungsfeld evangelischer Frömmigkeit," *Luther* 62 (1991): 126–40, here 128–29, 137.

32. LW 45, 39.

33. LW 44, 130. Theodor Strohm, "Martin Luthers Sozialethik und ihre Bedeutung für die Gegenwart," in Hans Süssmuth, et al., eds., *Das Luther-Erbe in Deutschland* (Düsseldorf: Droste Verlag, 1985), 68–91; 74, 83.

34. LW 45, 40.

35. Vilmos Vajta, *Die Theologie des Gottesdienstes bei Luther* (Stockholm: Svenska Kyrkans Diakonistyrelses Bokförlag, 1952), 314.

36. Michel Mollat, *The Poor in the Middle Ages: An Essay in Social History* (New Haven: Yale University Press, 1986), 44.

37. According to Luther, this theory of almsgiving combined with early capitalism to create a perverse "trickle-down theory" of charity when the rich claimed they needed higher interest rates and prices in order to earn more money to give in alms. The rich think they can gain a double profit – here and hereafter. WA 51, 417, 6ff. See Prien, *Luthers Wirtschaftsethik*, 81.

38. LW 9, 147–8.

39. See Matthieu Arnold, "La Notion d'*Epieikea* chez Martin Luther," *Revue d'Histoire et Philosophie Religieuses* 79/2–3 (1999), 187–208, 315–25.

40. For a detailed study of the Wittenberg common chest program see Stefan Oehmig, "Der Wittenberger Gemeine Kasten in den ersten zweieinhalb Jahrzehnten seines Bestehens (1522/23 bis 1547)," *Jahrbuch für Geschichte des Feudalismus* 12 (1988), 229–69; 13 (1989), 133–79.

41. The major collection of these church orders is in E. Sehling, ed., *Die evangelischen Kirchenordnungen des XVI. Jahrhunderts*, 16 vols. (Leipzig/Tübingen, 1902–1913/1955– ). See also Gerta Scharffenorth, *Den Glauben ins Leben ziehen...* (Munich: Kaiser, 1982), 114–18, 182–83. For discussion of these government policies and their implementation see my *Beyond Charity: Reformation Initiatives for the Poor* (Minneapolis: Fortress Press, 1993).

42. LW 21, 183.

43. WA 51, 422, 15–423, 2.

44. Luther frequently expressed himself publicly – and always critically – on the issues of early capitalism. His *Sermon on Usury* (1519) appeared in three editions; *Trade and Usury* (1524) appeared in seven editions; *Exhortation to the*

*Clergy to Preach against Usury* (1540) had four editions together with one in Latin. His critique of unregulated capitalism also appears in other writings. See Eberhard Schendel, "Martin Luther und die Armen: Sein Beitrag zur sogenannten sozialen Frage," *Lutherischen Kirche in der Welt* 36 (1989), 112–24, here 114–15.

45. WA 51, 396, 12.
46. WA 51, 417, 11–17.
47. LW 21, 180, 221; WA 51, 362; LW 25, 172; LW 13, 60; LW 45, 270.
48. WA 51, 367, 10–368, 16.
49. See Prien, *Luthers Wirtschaftsethik*, 221–22, and Ulrich Duchrow, *Global Economy: A Confessional Issue for the Churches?* (Geneva: WCC Publications, 1987).
50. Heiko A. Oberman, *The Impact of the Reformation* (Grand Rapids: Eerdmans, 1994), 62.
51. LW 13, 53.
52. Press, "Martin Luther und die sozialen Kräfte seiner Zeit," 216.
53. Marc Lienhard, *Martin Luther. Un Temps, Une Vie, Un Message* (Paris: Le Centurion, 1983), 252–54.

# 11  Luther's political encounters

## DAVID M. WHITFORD

In 1517, Martin Luther did not intend to start a revolution, but start one he most certainly did. By the time of his death, the religious, social, and political map of Europe was unalterably changed. Luther erupted on to the scene at a decisive moment. The Holy Roman Empire in the early sixteenth century was a society in flux; old orders were giving way to a yet-to-be deter-mined new order. Economically, northern Europe was recovering from the decimation of the fourteenth and fifteenth centuries. Its recovery, however, was dramatically different from what had preceded it. It was now more urban than rural, more based in manufacturing than agriculture. Politically, the greater nobles and the Free Imperial cities tried to stave off attempts at centralization by the emperor, while lesser nobles and rural towns tried to maintain their status as the economic world changed around them and thus marginalized them. Socially, the urbanization brought both a new middle class and at the same time a more entrenched poverty. Meanwhile, peasants had been chafing under the bit of serfdom for more than a century and a half. They were in search of justice and desperate for hope. Religiously, peo-ple both resented and depended upon the church. They resented the church because it controlled so much of the land and took too much in tax. They, however, depended on the church as the only avenue to salvation. It is little wonder, then, why Luther's religious message struck chords on many levels. Many people heard the religious message, but could not miss its social and political import.

For the great lords and the imperial cities the reformation was linked, by virtue of its fight against the centralized religious authority of the pope, to the fight against centralization politically. At the same time, the peasants heard in Luther an exaltation of Christian freedom, a sharp criticism of the church, and a nationalism that fed their desires and became a political manifesto.

In 1996, Bernhard Lohse wondered (only half in jest) if the Luther pre-sented by some scholars would recognize the Luther described by others.[1] This would be especially difficult when trying to recognize the "political"

Luther. On the one hand, Thomas Brady notes: "In the history of political thought, Martin Luther's role is a small one."[2] On the other hand, Luther has been given responsibility for nearly five hundred years of tyranny, oppression, and war in Europe.[3] Part of the reason for much of the confusion over Luther's political thought has been a failure to understand properly its theological dimension. Contra Peter Blickle who argues that Luther was "naïve" for not approaching politics more philosophically,[4] we shall argue that Luther's political judgments and opinions cannot be separated from his theological positions and presuppositions and are in fact only truly understood when placed within his theological framework.

## LUTHER'S POLITICAL THEOLOGY

Given the wide diversity of opinion on the importance and impact of Luther's political judgments and the variety of ways in which his judgments were initially received, it is important to remember what Luther did and did not intend when he wrote on political events.

First, Luther's political reactions must be read against the backdrop of his theological commitments. He always understood himself to be a pastor and understood his main responsibility to be the care of souls. Second, Luther never advocated social or political freedom as it has been understood in the modern *liberté, egalité, fraternité* sense. Luther's understanding of freedom was religious and paradoxical (i.e., the Christian is perfectly free servant of none, the Christian is perfectly bound servant of all). Finally, for Luther the Bible remained normative. Within this framework, we can discern three theological motifs that had lasting implications for Luther's political thought; the distinction between the law and the gospel, the two-kingdoms doctrine, and his understanding of authority. All derive from his commitment to preach the gospel in the midst of an ongoing struggle between God and the devil (between order and chaos).

Luther's political reactions cannot be properly understood without appreciating the significance Luther accords the battle against sin and chaos. When chaos (religious, social, or political) rules the day, people always suffer. To fight against this, God has ordered creation for the preservation and protection of humanity. The most fundamental aspect of this order is the gift of law and gospel. The law and gospel are a central dialectic in Luther's thought. Luther notes two proper uses of the law: the natural/civil/or political use and the theological. The law in its political sense is a good gift of God in that it limits human sin and avarice and thus promotes the common good. Theologically, the law reveals the utter uselessness and futility of salvation by works. Thus ethical and moral approaches to God (and their attendant social/political structures) are rejected. In their place Luther offers grace, paradox, and the doctrine of the Two Realms.

Echoing but also expanding and revising Augustine, Luther argues that God has established two realms for the regulation of creation: the spiritual realm (*das geistliche Reich*) and the temporal realm (*das weltliche Reich*). The spiritual realm is eternal and everlasting; it is the realm of revelation and faith. Two motifs run through Luther's thought about the spiritual realm: freedom and equality. Freedom allows one to act on behalf of others. Equality asserts that the spiritual realm is not governed hierarchically. In this realm all Christians are equal. The secular realm is the spiritual realm's dialectical partner; it is the realm of reason and unbelief. Whereas the spiritual realm is eternal and proleptic, the secular is finite and fleeting. Here the sword instead of service is definitive. The secular realm limits sin and malfeasance and thus insures that the unjust will not run rampant over the weak and downtrodden.[5] Thus, Luther attempts to set a new course in the relationship between the church and the state. Instead of one being the subject of the other, they shall each have clearly defined roles and spheres of influence that must be kept separate and distinct.

The final aspect is his understanding of authority. For Luther, the family is the primary form of authority. In his exegesis of the Fourth Commandment in his *Larger Catechism* he wrote, "All other authority is derived and developed out of the authority of parents."[6] The authority of parents flows directly from God. Thus, other authorities receive their sanction from God as well. Fathers, Burghermeisters, and princes are ordained by God for the maintenance of good and are thus due obedience (Rom. 13:1–7). While the argument that secular authority derived its authority separate from the pope was fairly longstanding, Luther's vehement rejection of this medieval legacy ushered the argument from the margins of legal debate to its very center; where before the issue had had little practical influence, it now gained traction. His emphasis on the obedience was far less out of the ordinary (almost no one in the Christian tradition rejected Paul's admonition in Romans), but has become very controversial. Luther advocated obedience because he feared the chaos of anarchy more than the tyranny of authority. However, as we will note below, he did not advocate a blind, totalizing, quietist approach to authority that has become the cliché.[7]

## LUTHER'S POLITICAL ENCOUNTERS

### To Worms and back

While Luther's *Ninety-five Theses* burst on to the European scene like wildfire, they were, frankly, not all that original or inflammatory. In fact,

Leo X (so the story goes) dismissed Luther's theses as the ranting of another "drunk monk." Where Leo saw a drunken monk, pamphleteers saw gold. They recognized early that Luther's *Theses* touched a raw nerve. The extent to which Luther gave voice to popular discontent surprised (even scared) Luther. Pamphlet publishers, meanwhile, turned out copies of the *Theses* at an extraordinary rate. This popular reaction brought Luther fame and influence, both of which would help and hurt him in the future.

The volatility and popularity of the *Ninety-five Theses* eventually made ignoring them impossible. In October 1518, Luther was called to meet with Thomas Cardinal Cajetan (the papal legate to the imperial diet). Cajetan examined Luther three times over the course of about a week. Cajetan was under explicit orders to get Luther to recant or to bring him to Rome for trial. Neither happened because the emperor's death in early 1519 put many things (least of all Luther) on hold. It would take until 1520 for things to begin to heat up again. Throughout this time, Luther continued to lecture and write in Wittenberg. In June and July 1519, he participated in a debate on indulgences and the papacy in Leipzig. Finally, in 1520, the pope had had enough. On June 15 the pope issued a bull (*Exsurge Domini* – Arise O Lord) officially charging Luther with heresy and giving him sixty days to recant or risk excommunication. Luther received the bull on October 10. He publicly burned it on December 10. On January 3, 1521, Luther was officially excommunicated.

Luther's excommunication was no longer simply a church matter; it now had legal and political implications. It placed his prince (Frederick) in the rather awkward position of harboring and supporting a declared heretic. The new emperor (Charles V) was urged to act. Luther could not simply be handed over to Rome, however. He had the right to a hearing in Germany, a right to which he clung. In the spring of 1521, Charles decided that Luther would get his hearing at the impending Diet of Worms. Instead of the hearing he was expecting, Luther was confronted with his works and told to recant. Again, Luther ignored the better part of valor and declared that "unless I am convinced by the testimony of the Scriptures or by clear reason... I am bound by the Scriptures I have quoted and my conscience is captive to the Word of God. I cannot and will not recant anything, since it is neither safe nor right to go against conscience. I cannot do otherwise, here I stand, may God help me. Amen."[8]

Despite the cliché that Luther demanded absolute obedience to the state, at Worms Luther gave personal testimony to its limits. From this point forward, Luther would remain consistent on the point that temporal authority cannot coerce the conscience. When the secular attempts to rule the realm of the sacred, salvation is jeopardized. They replace God's Word with human words and thereby drive "souls to eternal death."[9] To make matters worse, this program is all in vain. Salvation and the things of God's Kingdom are gifts to be freely received. The state may demand outward conformity, but it can never subvert the will or the heart. God has given the secular prince the power of the sword for the maintenance of order and justice. The emperor ought to devote himself to that, and leave the proclamation of the Word and the disposition of souls to God. Luther's next political encounter would engage him in a different, yet philosophically related, problem, church authorities attempting to coerce conformity.

### The Wittenberg disturbances

On May 25, 1521, Emperor Charles V officially banned Luther. Luther became, overnight, a hunted man. To insure his safety, Frederick the Wise had him "kidnapped" and sent him into hiding at the Wartburg fortress. This move assured his safety, but it also contributed to rumors of his abduction and death. Meanwhile in Wittenberg, Phillip Melanchthon tried to keep things going as they had before. At this point in his career, however (he was only twenty-four), he was unequal to the task. Into Luther's place stepped Andreas Karlstadt.

Karlstadt was already teaching in Wittenberg when Luther posted his Ninety-five Theses and had already made a name for himself as a Thomist scholar. Nevertheless, in 1517–18, he abandoned his Thomism and began to support and defend Luther. His new theological perspective did differ from Luther's in one major sense, however. While Luther's Christian anthropology is best defined by the phrase *simul iustus et peccator*, Karlstadt's anthropology was one of regeneration. In other words, the sinner (through the power of God's grace) is regenerated. The transformation from sinner to saint is integral to understanding Karlstadt's actions in the winter/spring of 1521/22.

A helpful metaphor for understanding regeneration is adoption. If you are adopted into a new family you are expected to adopt their worldview as your own; so that if they pray at dinner you are expected to bow your head as well. Similarly, as sinners adopted into the family of Christ, humanity must adopt new ways of living. This takes on a sense of urgency when errors that jeopardize salvation have been exposed. Karlstadt believed the errors of Rome had been unmasked and therefore had to be abandoned. As a parent would rush to save from harm a child wielding a knife, so too must a pastor rush to save his flock from error.[10] Thus, Karlstadt set out to reform church practice and life in Wittenberg; his reforms included communion in both kinds, the removal of images from churches, and clerical marriage. His reforms, however well intentioned, led to riots that resulted in the university nearly being closed and required Luther's recall from the Wartburg.

Luther responded to the Wittenberg Disturbances, as they came to be called, with his famous *Invocavit Sermons*. In the sermons Luther argues that what is at stake is the distinction between the law and the gospel. When the gospel (or church reforms) is transformed from gifts to requirements, the essence of the gospel is sacrificed and abandoned. Regardless of how well intentioned the reform, if it is forced upon someone's conscience it is not a reform at all but a new law. Luther's disagreement with Karlstadt had little to do with the types of reform, or even really the speed of implementation. Where Luther found fault was in how the reforms were implemented and why. Luther himself had argued for communion to the laity in both kinds, he was really indifferent about images, and was open to clerical marriage. Karlstadt's reforms were not the problem. For Luther, all these reforms were opportunities for the congregation – not commands. Because of Karlstadt's understanding of Christian identity, these reforms were not optional but necessary. In many ways, this difference in theology between Luther and Karlstadt regarding the implementation of reform foreshadows the much more serious crisis of the Peasants' War.

### The Peasants' War

With the possible exception of Luther's view of Jews, nowhere is Luther more controversial and more condemned than in his reaction to the Peasants' War of 1525. It was a short-lived "war" with plenty of atrocities on both sides to satiate the most bloodthirsty. It changed the course of the Reformation and probably hurt its development in southern Germany and most certainly hurt its appeal among the peasants. Martin Luther's role in the affair has been controversial ever since that unfortunate spring. He was attacked by conservatives claiming that the revolt was a natural outgrowth of his reforms. Supporters of the peasants agreed with the conservatives, but added condemnation to their criticism because having once encouraged them, Luther abandoned them at their crucial hour and led them to the slaughter.

Though the Peasants' War had antecedents stretching back decades, for all intents and purposes the "Peasants' War" was a series of events in the spring of 1525. The first period of the war was largely non-violent. It reflected the dissatisfactions of peasants, the emerging middle class in the towns, and some disenfranchised nobles. Their demands were best expressed in the *Twelve Articles of Upper Swabia* issued in late March or early April 1525.[11] In the *Twelve Articles*, the peasants hoped to tie their insurgency to Luther's reforms. The peasants' demands encompass the nature of the Peasants' War as an economic, political, and religious event. They demand a right to call their own pastors. They reject the "lesser" tithe. They call for an end to serfdom, for the freedom to gather wood in the forests and fish from the streams, and for the restitution of communal land. Finally, their demand to be judged in all that they said and did by the Bible was a self-conscious allusion to Luther's stand at Worms.

The *Twelve Articles* provided the common people with a standard around which to rally. It presented demands in ways that made it easily understood and quickly popular (some 25,000 copies were published). As spring 1525 dawned, the movement encompassed most of Franconia and Thuringia and was beginning to spread into Hesse and Saxony. Luther came into contact with the Peasants' War in Thuringia while on a trip. He was initially sympathetic to their demands but was later shocked by what he saw in riot-torn areas.

Luther wrote six essays in connection with the Peasants' War. The first, *Admonition to Peace* (c. April 15, 1525), addressed the demands of the peasants and set the blame for the present situation at the feet of the princes who did not administer their lands with justice. In the *Twelve Articles*, the peasants had called for mediation and Luther sought in his *Admonition* some middle ground in the hope of reconciliation. To further his hopes of reconciliation, he republished the Weingarten Treaty.[12] The Weingarten Treaty was made on April 17 between the Swabian League (a union of lesser estates in southern Germany) and a peasant association. Luther thought the Treaty provided a model of reconciliation so he republished it with a preface and a postscript in which he eagerly encouraged people to read and learn from its example.

By late April, however, the situation in Thuringia had degenerated significantly. Luther felt the sacking of non-combatant dwellings unalterably changed the situation. With his customary verve he issued *Against the Robbing and Murdering Hordes of Peasants* in the first week of May.[13] It is a blistering attack. He still felt that the peasants had just grievances but the actions of the rioters undermined the case for reconciliation. In an attempt to differentiate between the just demands of the peasants and the riotous actions of others, Luther published his second attack under the title, "Against the Murdering Hordes of *the Other* Peasants."[14] The tide was running in the other direction, though. Events outpaced Luther. His tract against the other peasants was quickly bound together with the first essay and the key "the other" was dropped thus leaving the impression that Luther was speaking of the same people in both.[15]

While Luther encouraged the princes to put down the rioting, Thomas Müntzer (leader of the peasants) continued to prepare for a war against the princes. He believed that the peasants had a God-given mandate to free the people from the oppression of the princes and establish the Kingdom of God on earth. Throughout late April and early May, Müntzer and his peasant army met little resistance. By May 12, in Frankenhausen, Müntzer was prepared to confront the leader of the princes (Count Ernst of Mansfeld) directly. The battle of Frankenhausen was over before it started. By the end of the day nearly 6,000 peasants were killed, while only six of the princes' soldiers were wounded. In all, the Peasants' War was a disaster for peasants. Contemporary estimates put the total killed in the war at 100,000.

It is absurd to think that the slaughter of 100,000 people pleased Luther. Luther did advocate a strong hand, but was equally blistering in his condemnation of the slaughter.[16] In this event, perhaps more clearly than in any other, we are able to glimpse how Luther approached political events. First he approached them biblically. Guided by key texts in Romans (13:1) and First Peter (2:13–14), Luther understood authority to be a great benefit to humanity. Again, for Luther the primary political threat was never tyranny but chaos. Second, he approached them theologically. In the Peasants' War the issue was the inverse of the Wittenberg Disturbances. Then, Luther condemned turning the gospel into a new law. Now, partially in the *Twelve Articles* but much more so in Müntzer, his concern focused on making a law the gospel (i.e., the avenue of salvation). For the peasant authors of the *Twelve Articles* and for Müntzer, salvation was achieved by doing certain things (ending injustice) or putting into place certain new policies (the right to choose a pastor). Luther's rejection is total; salvation must remain a gift to be received. To place on the gospel a set of demands to be accomplished (no matter how just) undermined his fundamental concern – the ultimate destiny of souls. Müntzer sought religious legitimation for his revolution, and thereby confused the lines between the spiritual and secular realms. Luther did feel that the peasants' demands were just; he said so, but argued that they were human rights, not special "Christian" rights. The problem was in mixing one's justifiable claims in the political realm with the gospel; the idea of special "Christian" rights was foreign to Luther. Finally, Luther looked at political situations pastorally. While it may seem odd, given the ferocity of his polemic, his concern in *Against the Murdering Hoard* ought to be understood pastorally. Chaos, as we've noted, was the devil's handiwork. Luther believed that chaos, riot, and pillage always hurt the weak much more than the powerful, the innocent more than the guilty. For Luther there was never a justification (and on this point he never wavered) for riot and rebellion. Soon, however, he would be confronted by the question of whether or not there is a difference between rebellion and resistance.

## The Augsburg Recess and Interim

While Charles V officially banned Luther in 1521, he was unable to devote much time (due to border skirmishes and other imperial intrigue) to the "Luther Affair" until 1529. His first attempt to deal with Luther was the Diet of Speyer. It, however, collapsed without finding any common ground for reconciliation or even accommodation. Charles was unwilling to let the situation continue unresolved, so he called another diet in which he asked the Protestant princes to explain their religious innovations. To prepare for the Diet, Luther, Melanchthon and others drafted a series of short defences of their reforms (on issues like communion, the sacrifice of the mass, clergy marriage, etc.) Because Luther feared for his safety, he did not travel to Augsburg but sent Melanchthon to represent Wittenberg.

When Melanchthon arrived he discovered that Johannes Eck had published a tract (*Four Hundred and Four Propositions*) linking Wittenberg to nearly every known heresy. Melanchthon was forced to scramble and present not just a defense of reforms (i.e., an apology) but also a positive declaration of what the Wittenbergers believed (a confession). The *Augsburg Confession* was presented to the Diet on June 25, 1530. Roman Catholic theologians quickly drafted a rebuttal or *Confutation*. The emperor accepted the latter and ordered that all reforms be abandoned and that the Protestants return to Rome. To add teeth to his command, he put into place a *Recess* that made provisions for the Imperial Supreme Court to try any who did not abandon the Reformation. This was a very real threat.

An indication of just how seriously the Protestant princes took the emperor's threat was Elector John of Saxony's proposal for a defensive league put forth the day after the draft of the recess was read. The princes decided that they would resist the emperor's attempt to coerce a return to Rome and looked to the theologians for support. To that end, leading theologians were summoned to Torgau (in October) to discuss the matter of the right to resist the emperor with the princes' legal scholars. Following the Torgau meeting, where the lawyers made a strong case for the legality of resistance, the theologians issued a memorandum (*Torgau Declaration*) in support of the right to resist.[17]

Following this meeting, the Landgrave Philip of Hesse asked Luther to publish a treatise for popular consumption expanding on the *Torgau Declaration*. Luther accepted and published *Warning to His Dear German People*.[18] The *Warning* is broken into three sections. First is a survey of the current religious and political situation, second is an apology for resistance, and finally a warning to those that would use force to suppress the Reformation.

In the apology for resistance, Luther lays the groundwork for the first two aspects of later resistance theory. First he asserts that within imperial law a right of resistance is acknowledged. Second, that natural law provides for a right to self-defense. Luther rejects the assumption that the contemplated resistance is rebellion. It is, instead, self-defense. Luther writes that, "if war breaks out – which God forbid – I will not reprove those who defend themselves against the murderous and bloodthirsty papists, nor let anyone else rebuke them as being seditious."[19] Resistance to the *Augsburg Recess* is not rebellion because (1) the Protestants had continually sought peace, (2) it was the emperor who would march against the Protestants and thus he was the peace-breaker, and (3) the Protestant position cannot be condemned without a fair hearing.

Many have condemned Luther for seeming to change his long-held position that one must be subject to authority in the *Warning*. They charge that while it suited his needs (e.g., in the Peasants' War) he advocated obedience; but when threatened himself he quickly abandoned that belief and rushed to defend a right to resist authority. This charge, however, misses the internal theological consistency to Luther's thought. First, Luther remained convinced that authority ought to be obeyed. However, this obedience is never blind.[20] It has limits because, echoing Matthew 22:21 (render unto Caesar) and Acts 4:29, God must be obeyed before men.[21] Thus, Luther writes, "The temporal government has laws which extend no further than to life and property and external affairs on earth, for God cannot and will not permit anyone but himself to rule over the soul."[22] Second, Luther was convinced that the realms of God's creation (the secular and spiritual) must not be confused. One of the more serious implications of this doctrine was to free each kingdom from undue influence on the other. Freeing the secular realm from ideological servitude to the spiritual realm (or vice versa) is an important and consistent position in Luther's thought. Third, the opinion here is actually in keeping with his concerns in the Wittenberg Disturbances and in the Peasants' War – the rejection of coercion as theological method.

### Temporal authority

Luther's strong polemics against the misuse of political authority and the perception that he vacillated in his understanding of the "power of the sword" raise the important question of how Luther understood civil government and what he believed was its proper role and authority. In 1526, Luther boasted that "not since the time of the apostles have the temporal sword and authority been so clearly described or so highly praised as by me."[23] Luther's choice of "sword" and "authority" is important because it reflects his fundamental understanding of government. Luther's primary word of choice when speaking of what we now call government was *Obrigkeit* (or authority). The idea of a "government" as a thing was foreign to Luther and largely foreign to the early modern era. For Luther and his contemporaries, government was not a "thing" but a "whom." Authority was vested in people not in "states."

The structure of authority was much less of a concern for Luther than the use (or abuse) of the authority; witness that Luther's response to the atrocities at Frankenhausen was not to question the structure of feudal society, but to question the abusive inhumanity of the princes. Authority, for Luther, ought to be guided by fairness (not equality – that was foreign to the sixteenth century), justice, and reason. Reasonable authority creates a protective space in which people can live, work, and raise their families. It is a gift of God that insures law, order, and peace. Luther did not believe that a ruler had to be a saint in order to accomplish this task, only wise.[24] Wisdom thus was the measure of a leader. A wise leader need not even be Christian. Because the temporal realm is a gift of God to all creation, even "heathen" magistrates could, Luther believed, lead effectively. This belief engendered Luther's rejection of religiously motivated war against non-Christians.

### Luther and war

For Luther war, like chaos, always brings destruction and was therefore evil. Luther kept with the Augustinian tradition's rejection of offensive war and added his own rejection of crusade. Luther did not reject all political violence, however. At times, war might be a necessary evil. The power of the sword is given to magistrates to limit chaos, crush evil, and promote justice on behalf of the innocent. Most often this sword is directed at the brigand in one's midst; but at times the brigand is an external force that must be repelled. Just as a father must discipline his children and protect them from harm, so too a magistrate must both discipline and protect. Thus, in his treatise *Whether Soldiers, Too, Can Be Saved* he notes that yes they most certainly can, but only if they fight for the right reasons.

> Let this be, then, the first thing to be said in this matter: No war is
> just...unless one has such good reason for fighting and such a good
> conscience that he can say, "My neighbor compels and forces me to
> fight, though I would rather avoid it." In that case, it can be called not
> only war, but lawful self-defence.[25]

Luther's era, like most, knew its share of war and Luther, ever the pastor, sought to limit its scope and define its parameters.

## CONCLUSION

Martin Luther is not the ogre of unlimited government and tyranny, nor is he the liberal-minded Enlightenment democrat. Luther was an early modern, living on the cusp of the medieval era and the not yet born modern world. His views are, from today's perspective, largely conservative; but that makes them no less revolutionary in their own time. Luther's understanding of freedom, his distinction between the Two Kingdoms, his rejection of coercion, his definition of authority, and his limited acceptance of resistance to tyranny became the font from which Protestant thinking drew throughout the sixteenth century. While others would go farther than he would have, they all acknowledged their debt to Luther.[26] That he did not always live up to his own standards is well known (e.g., he believed that blasphemy ought to be suppressed by the magistrate), but this points not to the fallacy of his convictions but to the frailty of the human condition.

### Further reading

*Primary bibliography (selected key works with political implications)*
*Heidelberg Disputation* (1518), LW 31
*Two Kinds of Righteousness* (1519), LW 31
*The Babylonian Captivity of the Church* (1520), LW 36
*To the Christian Nobility* (1520), LW 44
*The Freedom of a Christian* (1520), LW 31
*Concerning the Letter and the Spirit* (1521), LW 39
*A Sincere Admonition by Martin Luther to All Christians to Guard Against Insurrection and Rebellion* (1522), LW 45
*Invocavit (Eight Wittenberg) Sermons* (1522), LW 51
*Temporal Authority* (1523), LW 45
*Admonition to Peace* (1525), LW 46
*Against the Robbing and Murdering Hordes of Peasants* (1525), LW 46
*An Open Letter on the Harsh Book Against the Peasants* (1525), LW 46
*Whether Soldiers, Too, Can Be Saved* (1526), LW 46
*On War Against the Turk* (1529), LW 46
*The Augsburg Confession* (1530) [while not by Luther, it certainly represents his thought], *Book of Concord*
*Warning to His Dear German People* (1531), LW 47
*Smalcald Articles* (1537), *Book of Concord*

### Notes

1. Bernhard Lohse, *Martin Luther's Theology: Its Historical and Systematic Development*, trans. and ed. by Roy A. Harrisville, (Edinburgh: T&T Clark, 1999), 3–6.
2. Thomas Brady, "Luther and the State: The Reformer's Teaching in its Social Setting," in James D. Tracy, ed., *The Modern State in Germany* (Kirksville, MO: Sixteenth Century Journal Publishers, 1986): 31.

3. See Richard Marius, *Martin Luther: The Christian between God and Death* (Cambridge, MA: Belknap Press of Harvard University, 1999).
4. Peter Blickle, *Obedient Germans?: A Rebuttal, A New View of German History*, trans. by Thomas A. Brady, Jr. (Charlottesville: University Press of Virginia, 1997), 89f.
5. *On Temporal Authority*, LW 45, 91.
6. Robert Kolb and Timothy J. Wengert, eds., *The Book of Concord* (Minneapolis: Fortress Press, 2000), 405.
7. See Uwe Siemon-Netto, *The Fabricated Luther: the Rise and Fall of the Shirer Myth* (St. Louis: Concordia, 1995).
8. LW 32, 112–13.
9. *On Temporal Authority*, LW 45, 105.
10. Andreas Bodenstein von Karlstadt, *Whether One Should Proceed Slowly*, in Ronald J. Sider, ed. and trans., *Karlstadt's Battle with Luther: Documents in a Liberal-Radical Debate* (Philadelphia: Fortress Press, 1978), 65.
11. See *The Twelve Articles of Upper Swabia*, in Günther Franz, ed., *Quellen zur Geschichte des Bauernkrieges* (Darmstadt: Wissenschaftl. Buchgesellschaft, 1963). Reprinted in Tom Scott and Robert W. Scribner, eds. and trans., *The German Peasants' War: A History in Documents* (Atlantic Highlands, NJ: Humanities Press, 1991), 252–57.
12. WA 18, 336–43.
13. LW 46, 45–56.
14. Emphasis added. See WA 18, 344–56 for a discussion of the editions and their titles.
15. Hubert Kirchner, *Luther and the Peasants' War*, trans. Darrel Jodock (Philadelphia: Fortress Press, 1972), 11.
16. LW 46, 84.
17. LW 47, 8.
18. LW 47, 5–55.
19. LW 47, 19.
20. "Letter to the Elector Frederick, 29 May 1523," LW 49, 40.
21. "Letter to the Elector Frederick 7 or 8 March 1522," LW 48, 395ff.
22. *On Temporal Authority*, LW 45, 105.
23. *Whether Soldiers, Too, Can Be Saved*, LW 46, 95 (translation altered, compare WA 19, 625).
24. WA 27, 417f.
25. *Whether Soldiers, Too, Can Be Saved*, 121.
26. See David Whitford, *Tyranny and Resistance: The Magdeburg Confession and the Lutheran Tradition* (St. Louis: Concordia, 2001) for a discussion of Lutherans continuing his thought and Robert Kingdon, *Church and Society in Reformation Europe* (London: Variorum, 1985) for discussions of the Calvinist dependence upon and development of Luther's thought.

# 12 Luther's polemical controversies

MARK U. EDWARDS, JR.

Martin Luther was a theologian of remarkable rhetorical gifts who developed and displayed his theology in the give-and-take of ferocious, published debate; he was one of Christianity's great *polemicists*. In this chapter, we explore the role of printing, the worldview that grounded Luther's polemical approach, the developments in the larger Reformation movement that shaped the approach and style of polemical contests, and the interpretive challenges posed by the polemics of the older Luther.

During Luther's lifetime the Reformation went through two phases that shaped the character of Luther's controversial writings and their audience. In the first phase Luther defined a movement. He addressed most of his polemics to an empire-wide audience of readers and auditors. He pointed out the failings within the papally controlled Catholic Church and advocated reforms based on his understanding of the gospel. He attacked, but he also sought to persuade, to educate, and to inform. His main authority was Scripture.

In the second phase Luther was engaged in building and defending an institution. He addressed most of his polemics to readers and auditors who were already Evangelicals or more narrowly Lutherans. He continued to explain and educate but spent proportionately more effort exhorting his co-religionists. He continued to appeal to Scripture but supplemented these appeals with claims to personal authority based on his unique role within an Augustinian view of history.

The Peasants' War and the controversy among Evangelicals over the proper understanding of the Lord's Supper (the "Sacramentarian Controversy") mark a transition from the first, proselytizing phase of the Reformation to the second, institution-building phase.

## PRINTING AND POLEMICS

The printing press was invented in the Holy Roman Empire in about 1450, seventy years before the outbreak of the Reformation. By 1520 there were some sixty-two presses in the Holy Roman Empire and the Swiss confederacy, and Cologne, Nuremberg, Strasbourg, Basel, Wittenberg, and Augsburg were the leading publishing centers. With the exception of Cologne, which remained Catholic, the presses of these towns led the Evangelical media campaign.

Hans-Joachim Köhler estimates that approximately 10,000 pamphlet editions, that is first editions and reprints, issued from the presses of the German-speaking lands between 1500 and 1530. Of these almost three-quarters appeared between 1520 and 1526, and most were due to the Reformation movement. Martin Luther alone was responsible for approximately 20 percent of the overall total.

### Literacy and language

Only a small fraction of the population in sixteenth-century Germany could read German – perhaps 30 percent in the cities and 5 percent overall. An even smaller fraction could read Latin. So when authors wanted to reach a larger audience they wrote in German. They crafted their writing for oral transmission using colorful expressions, rhyme, engaging stories, and the like. They explicitly urged their readers to share their reading with others.

The Reformation move toward a broader audience can be seen in the printing statistics. As Köhler shows, the number of pamphlets written in German rose sevenfold from 1519 to 1521, and the proportion of German to Latin pamphlets went from about one German for every three Latin pamphlets to three German pamphlets for every Latin one. In the following year the presses of the empire put out nine German pamphlets for every Latin one. In 1518 not quite half the printings of Luther's works were in German. In 1519 this figure rose to over six in ten, then in 1520 and 1521 around eight in ten, and for the rest of the decade around nine in ten. Luther and his colleagues were targeting as large an audience as possible.

### From movement to institution

The most massive printing and reprinting of Luther's works came in the pioneering years of the Reformation movement – half of all printings appeared by 1525 and three-quarters by 1530. Eighty-five percent of these publications were in German. Two of every five printings through 1525 and one in three through 1530 were sermons, not polemics or theological treatises. The market was seeking out edifying, accessible publications.

The period of maximum reprints coincided with the period of maximum geographic appeal, measured by where works were reprinted. In the pioneering years of the Reformation movement (1516 through 1525) over a third of the printings occurred in southern cities, especially Augsburg,

Strasbourg, and Basel. After 1525 Luther became increasingly a regional author, writing largely for central and northern Germany. The printings in southern cities dropped to between a half and a third of what they had been during the heyday of the Reformation movement.

### Luther's dominance

Luther was by far the most prolific author in the vernacular among Evangelical publicists. Alejandro Zorzin has collected statistics on the leading eighteen Evangelicals who published pamphlets in German during the early years of the Reformation movement (1518 to 1525). These statistics indicate that Luther was printed or reprinted over eleven times more often than his nearest "competitor," Andreas Bodenstein von Karlstadt. Even the combined production of the other seventeen Evangelical authors (807 editions) is exceeded by Luther almost two to one.

Luther also greatly outpublished his Catholic opponents. Over the period 1518 to 1544, the printings and reprintings of Luther's works in German, excluding Bible translations, numbered at least 2,551. For the same period the Catholic publicists produced 514 printings (or 542 if all undated printings are to be counted within this time span). In stark terms this translates into about five printings of Luther for every Catholic printing. If we consider only Luther's anti-Catholic publications, the ratio drops to about five to three (875 for Luther to 514 for the Catholics), a much lower but still striking difference in output.

## LUTHER'S APOCALYPTIC WORLDVIEW

In his writings Luther placed the Reformation struggle into a larger Augustinian view of the dynamics of history, which had been the common property of Western Christendom for a thousand years. Luther and many of his contemporaries believed that practically from the beginning of the world the "true" and "false" churches had been locked in combat. Luther saw this struggle as involving a recurrent contest between true and false prophets and apostles, and he could trace this struggle from the biblical histories into his own time. What happened to the prophets and apostles in their day could and would happen to the church of his day. Their experiences established a paradigm of the dynamics of all sacred history.

By 1520 Luther had decided on the basis of this paradigm that the papacy was the antichrist described in Scripture. As Luther encountered additional opponents through the years, he integrated them into the paradigm. Opponents within Evangelicalism were deemed contemporary false prophets and apostles, like those who had plagued the true prophets and apostles.

The Turks were identified with Gog and the little horn in the Book of Daniel. Contemporary Jewry was seen as the remnant of a rejected people suffering under God's wrath for their rejection of the true messiah. They were all members of the false church. Luther understood his disagreements with them in the context of this struggle between God and Satan. Behind them all loomed the figure of the devil, the father of lies. Often Luther directed his attacks not at his human opponents but at the devil whom he saw as their master, and, of course, no language was too harsh when attacking the devil.

Since Luther was always drawing comparisons and parallels between these opponents and the opponents of the prophets and apostles, it was only natural that he would see the true prophets and apostles as having provided a precedent for the way to treat such opponents. As a result he could explain and justify his polemics and his stubbornness on points of doctrine by pointing to the example set by these men of God.

Luther's many attacks cannot be fully understood apart from this context. The self-righteousness, the vulgarity, and the violence owe much to Luther's intense conviction that he was engaged in the climactic battle between the true and false church, that the real opponents were not men but devils, and the stakes were salvation and eternal life.

## DEFINING A MOVEMENT

The Reformation movement began in academic debate over the power of indulgences and was extended by Luther's opponents to a debate over the doctrinal power of the papacy and councils. From late 1517 to the summer of 1520, Luther wrote Latin treatises and addressed them to a small, largely professional, elite. These writings include polemical accounts of Luther's appearance before Cajetan in Augsburg and his debate with Eck in Leipzig, and exchanges with various Catholic authors on the power of the papacy. His German works during this same period were more pastoral and devotional, though still critical of various Catholic practices.

The Reformation moved into an actively proselytizing stage with the great vernacular publications of late summer and fall, 1520: *On the Papacy in Rome, Against the Highly Famous Romanist in Leipzig; To the Christian Nobility of the German Nation, On the Improvement of the Christian Estate;* the only mildly polemical *On the Freedom of a Christian,* and the incendiary *On the Babylonian Captivity of the Church,* which Luther issued in Latin but which his Catholic opponent Thomas Murner astonishingly translated into German. In these and a series of other pamphlets and treatises, Luther rejected the authority of the papacy, claimed that pope and curia had perpetrated a series of frauds on Christendom, and called for Christendom's liberation from a papal captivity that distorted the sacraments and subordinated the laity to a clerical tyranny. In making this argument Luther also devoted substantial energy to laying out a positive understanding of the gospel and its implications for ordinary Christians and for the institutional church. Relying on "Scripture alone" he expounded his understanding of justification, Christian freedom, monastic vows, the priesthood of all believers, the sacraments, obedience owed secular authority, and much else. Luther also issued during these years his German translation of the New Testament (1522), outfitted with prefaces, marginalia, illustrations, and other aids to an evangelical (and anti-papal) understanding of Scripture.

Luther's Catholic opponents contested Luther's arguments and defended traditional beliefs and practices. Above all, they sought to portray Luther as "the destroyer of the faith of Christ" and as "a seducer of simple Christians," who sought to overturn all authority in society by inappropriately involving the common people in a debate over traditional belief and practice. As statistics show, the Catholic controversialists were badly outpublished by Luther and other Evangelical writers. They also received little help or encouragement from clerical authorities in the empire or in Rome. The polemical contest was massively one-sided.

### THE TRANSITION

The Peasants' War of 1525 with its accompanying polemical exchanges significantly diminished the popular appeal of the Reformation movement and gave ammunition to Catholic critics who saw the whole movement as subversive of authority. Divisions within the Evangelical ranks over the Lord's Supper led to a more regional focus and gave Catholic critics the opportunity to question whether Evangelicals could possibly possess the Holy Spirit given such divisions.

The splintering began in earnest with the controversy between Luther and Karlstadt over "divine law," images, and the Supper and continued with the Sacramentarian controversy between Lutherans on the one hand and south Germans and Swiss Evangelicals on the other. Between 1524 and 1527 Luther and the great humanist Desiderius Erasmus exchanged polemical treatises on the freedom of the will. Luther's contribution, *On the Bondage of the Will*, appeared in 1525; Erasmus, for his part, produced three treatises – *Diatribe or Discourse on Free Will* (1524), and *A Defense of the Diatribe*, part 1 (1526) and part 2 (1527). This learned exchange – both men wrote in Latin – made plain some of the crucial differences between Erasmian reform and Lutheran reformation. As the German Empire divided along religious lines, political considerations gained increased weight in religious debate. These changes and others shaped Luther's polemics in the last twenty or so years of his life.

## Divisions in Wittenberg

In 1522 Luther was called home from the Wartburg to deal with a theologian colleague, Karlstadt, and a fellow Augustinian, Gabriel Zwilling, who were instituting reforms with such haste and disregard for political realities and the sensibilities of sincere Christians that Luther felt it necessary to intervene. Luther also had to deal with the so-called Zwickau prophets who claimed direct revelation for their teachings.

Luther charged that Satan had once again sent his false prophets to mislead the true church. Clear evidence for the satanic motivation of these men, he believed, was their insistence that people were guilty of a sin if certain Old Testament commandments and New Testament examples were not followed to the letter. Such insistence imposed the secular kingdom upon the spiritual and re-shackled consciences with laws and regulations, while Christ freed them.

By 1523 Karlstadt had quit Wittenberg for a country parish where he undertook reforms as he saw fit and continued to publish treatises. Luther and the Wittenberg faculty lodged protests, Luther clashed with Karlstadt on Karlstadt's home turf, and, finally, the Saxon rulers expelled Karlstadt from Saxony.

The conflict between Luther and Karlstadt became public knowledge beyond the borders of Electoral Saxony in the autumn of 1524, following Karlstadt's expulsion and the publication of several of his attacks on Luther. Especially noted were Karlstadt's attacks on Luther's belief in the real presence of Christ's body and blood in the bread and wine of the Lord's Supper. Luther soon published a two-part reply, *Against the Heavenly Prophets* (1525). Although much of the treatise dealt directly with Karlstadt, it was actually Karlstadt's *spirit* (which, Luther maintained, was a *satanic* spirit and the same spirit driving Thomas Müntzer, the Zwickau prophets, and the other "heavenly prophets") that bore the brunt of Luther's attack. Karlstadt was faulted not only for what he had allegedly done but also for what his spirit was allegedly capable of doing, given the opportunity.

## The Peasants' War

In the spring of 1525 peasant unrest spread from southern Germany northward, and Thomas Müntzer, a former Lutheran, emerged as its leader in Thuringia. In southern Germany there appeared the *Twelve Articles*, the most widely circulated peasant manifesto, which called for religious, social, and economic reform and which buttressed its demands with citations from Scripture. Spokesmen for the peasant bands appealed to Luther and to Luther's teachings regarding Christian freedom to bolster their demands.

Eager to correct what he saw as a misunderstanding of the gospel and to disclaim responsibility for the unrest, Luther penned his *Admonition to Peace*, in which he replied to the *Twelve Articles*. In the first section, he blamed the unrest on the rulers' persecution of the gospel and their mistreatment of their subjects. In the second, he told the peasants that their rebellion violated the gospel, and both Christian and natural law. They were blaspheming the name of Christ by quoting the gospel to justify secular demands; the gospel taught obedience to secular authorities and the suffering of injustice. In the third section, Luther admonished both the rulers and the peasants that there was nothing Christian on either side. If they came to blows, it was their responsibility, not his or the gospel's.

The treatise seems to have had little calming effect and subsequent events swung Luther over to the princes' side. In May he wrote out his uncompromising *Against the Robbing and Murdering Hordes of Peasants*. Since Luther had concluded that the peasants were doing the devil's work and particularly the work of that "arch-devil" Thomas Müntzer, he felt that it was his responsibility to show the peasants their error and to advise the rulers how to proceed. The peasants had violated their oaths of obedience to their rulers, oaths confirmed by Christ and St. Paul. They were in open rebellion. And they cloaked their service to the devil under the name of the gospel. To the rulers Luther offered sanguine advice. Justice was on the rulers' side. Everyone who could was to smite, slay, and stab, secretly or publicly, for nothing was more poisonous, harmful, or devilish than a rebel. The end of the world was imminent. No devil was left in hell; they had all gone into the peasants.

The uprising was brutally suppressed by the princes. Müntzer was captured, interrogated under torture, and executed. Although the revolt was over, the question of Luther's role in it remained controversial. Catholic polemicists claimed that the Peasants' War demonstrated that Luther's position subverted authority. For his part, Luther easily fitted the uprising into his apocalyptic worldview.

### The "Sacramentarians"

From the outset of the controversy with Ulrich Zwingli, reformer of Zurich, and John Oecolampadius, reformer of Basel, Luther believed that they were simply following Karlstadt when they denied that Christ's body and blood were physically present in the Lord's Supper. This belief shaped much of the controversy that followed, for it led Luther to attribute the same satanic spirit to these new opponents that he had previously attributed to Karlstadt, Müntzer, and the Zwickau prophets. His opponents, naturally enough, did not appreciate this, and they complained of it repeatedly in the exchanges that followed.

Although they advanced slightly different arguments to support their positions, Zwingli and Oecolampadius were in substantial agreement with Karlstadt. Specifically, they denied that Christ's body and blood were or even could be literally and physically present in the elements either through the transformation of the substance of bread and wine (the Catholic doctrine of transubstantiation), or by "coexistence" in and under the bread and wine (Luther's belief). They argued that the words spoken by Christ at the Last Supper ("Take, eat; this is my body which is given for you. Do this in memory of me") must be taken symbolically, the words "This is my body" meaning "This represents my body" or "This is the sign of my body." They did acknowledge a real *spiritual* presence: Christ was truly present through and in the faith of the participants in the Supper. Hence they could even speak of a spiritual eating by faith, which was faith in Christ's act of redemption. But this presence was not tied to the elements, and it depended upon and was mediated by the faith of the communicants.

In various replies, notably *That These Words of Christ "This Is My Body," Etc., Still Stand Firm Against the Fanatics* (1527) and *Confession Concerning Christ's Supper* (1528), Luther argued that the words of institution were to be understood literally, and he challenged his opponents to prove that they must be understood figuratively. As he interpreted the controversy, his opponents' two basic arguments were that Christ's ascension to heaven to sit at the right hand of God removed him physically from the world and that John 6:63 ("The flesh is of no avail") made his physical presence unnecessary. Luther attacked the first argument by arguing that God's right hand refers not to some physical location in heaven but to God's almighty power, which at one and the same time was nowhere and yet everywhere. Christ's presence was not a circumscribed or local presence, but an essential presence that creates and preserves all things. Moreover, there was a special presence in the Lord's Supper, he argued, for there God was present *for you* and bound his presence through the Word.

John 6:63, Luther insisted, could not apply to Christ's flesh without simultaneously negating the incarnation. His opponents, he contended, misconstrued the words spirit and flesh as presented by the Bible. There were spiritual and fleshly acts, but not spiritual and fleshly things. The sacrament was a visible embodiment of God's promise of salvation through Christ. To call Christ's words into question here was to deny God's promise of justification through faith in Christ's sacrifice.

Since Luther and his opponents both appealed to the authority of Scripture but reached different conclusions about its meaning, Luther found it expedient to supplement his theological arguments with appeals to personal authority as the one whom God had used to initiate the Reformation.

The dispute raged for several years. Eventually Martin Bucer and the South Germans were able to reach an agreement with Luther and return to the Lutheran fold. Zwingli and Oecolampadius, however, remained firm in their convictions.

### BUILDING A CHURCH

Most of Luther's polemics after 1527 or 1528 were addressed to his own supporters. The time for proselytizing had largely passed. Now the Reformation needed to be consolidated and defended in the face of threats from Catholics, Turks, Jews and Jewish exegesis, and Evangelical "fanatics." The task demanded exhortation rather than explanation. Emphasis was placed on the righteousness of the Evangelical cause and on the wickedness and eventual futility of the opponents' cause. While there was still need for education in the tenets of the Evangelical faith, stress now was placed on the deepening of beliefs already held. It was time to rally the troops, to whip up passions for the battles ahead. This stage in the movement's history was well served by Luther's apocalyptic vision of the climactic struggle between the true and false church, between the followers of Christ and the minions of Satan. His highly charged rhetoric and liberal abuse of opponents proved useful to the movement's leaders and reassuring to its followers. Such were the treatises circumstances called for. Such were the treatises that Luther delivered.

### Princes, politics, and polemics

The Reformation movement was from the beginning religious *and* political. But in these later years political considerations, often divorced from religious concerns, gained the upper hand. A significant milestone in this transition was the formation of the League of Schmalkalden in February 1531, despite Luther's misgivings, to defend its members against Catholic attack. Its leaders were Landgrave Philip, who fully realized Luther's value as a publicist in support of the League, and Elector John, who was much more cautious about encouraging Luther's polemical talents. Another milestone came in 1532, however, when Elector John was succeeded by his son

John Frederick. The new elector was far more aggressive than his father or his uncle, Frederick the Wise, in voicing his support for the Reformation. Moreover, he was willing to go on the offensive and to encourage Luther to attack the Reformation's opponents in print.

This political and institutional phase began with Luther's polemics on the legitimacy of resisting a forceful attempt by Catholic authorities to suppress the Reformation. It continued with his treatises questioning the legitimacy of a General Council called by the pope and controlled by Catholics. Of course, it did not take much to induce Luther to attack the opponents of the elector or the League, and many of his published attacks in his later years were unsolicited. Nevertheless, there can be no doubt that these treatises were a support to Elector John Frederick's political goals and to League policy.

Under intense pressure from politicians and jurists who were unwilling to accept the theologians' reservations concerning armed defense of the faith, Luther first "allowed" a positive-law justification of resistance. But finally, much assisted by his apocalyptic expectations, he developed the theological argument that if the emperor attacked the Evangelicals on account of their faith then he would not be acting in his capacity as a superior secular authority but rather as a servant of the papal antichrist. These developments can be traced through his *Warning to His Dear German People* of 1530 and subsequent exchanges with Duke George of Ducal Saxony. Similarly, his publication justifying Elector John Frederick's seizure of the bishopric of Naumburg represents an accommodation to the wishes of his prince despite Luther's own misgivings. His two treatises concerning Duke Henry of Braunschweig-Wolfenbüttel also involved him in what was largely a political affair. Even his "matter of conscience," his *Against the Bishop of Magdeburg Cardinal Albrecht* (1539), appears to have served his prince's political interests, whatever Luther's own intentions.

Similarly, the numerous attacks on a papal council that flowed from Luther's pen in the 1530s and especially in the months following the League meeting of 1537 and leading up to Luther's 1539 masterpiece, *On the Councils and the Church*, were honest expressions of Luther's critical view of a papal council. But by discrediting the papal council in his readers' eyes, he also gave tacit support to the politicians' policy of non-attendance. Incidentally but importantly, in these writings Luther perfected the use of history to attack his Catholic opponents. Of the eighteen publications dealing with the proposed papally called council that Luther issued from 1532 to 1539, nine reproduced and commented on historical documents, four more reproduced and commented on immediately contemporary documents, and three more used historical arguments extensively.

During this period, and with encouragement from his prince, Luther also issued several admonitions to his fellow Germans to oppose the Turks. The early treatises – notably *On War Against the Turk* (1528/29) and *Army Sermon Against the Turks* (1529) – were less overtly apocalyptic than the later ones – notably *Appeal for Prayer Against the Turks* (1541). In all of these anti-Turkish treatises, the primary target is not the Turks themselves but the "papal antichrist." Catholic controversialists repeatedly faulted Luther and the Evangelicals for not doing more to assist in the defense against the Turks.

## LUTHER'S POLEMICAL "LAST TESTAMENT"

As Luther entered the 1540s he was more than ever convinced that he was engaged in the climactic battle between the church of Christ and the "synagogue of Satan." Everywhere he read signs of the approaching End Time. Before his death he felt that he must make his final testament against the enemies of God: the "papal antichrist," the Jews, the Turks, and the "false brethren" within the Evangelical ranks. He had to defend the Word against the devil's frantic last attack, he had to repudiate the false brethren, and he had to condemn all those who misused his name to support their pernicious doctrines and behavior. Of these final polemical works the most notorious, and most in need of explanation, are Luther's attacks on the "papists" and on the "Jews."

### "Papists"

In 1541 Luther published *Against Hanswurst* as his scatological contribution to a gutter fight between the princely leaders of the League of Schmalkalden and the Catholic Duke Heinz of Wolfenbüttel. Luther outdid even the virulence of *Against Hanswurst* in his 1545 *Against the Papacy at Rome, Founded by the Devil*. On the heels of these treatises he published a series of scatological and violent woodcuts that, in most graphic terms, suggested how good Christians should treat the papacy. In these and other treatises Luther bestialized his opponents, most frequently likening them to pigs or asses, or called them liars, murderers, and hypocrites. They were all minions of the devil. He directed the devil to his ass, he renamed the papal decretals "decraptals" (*Drecketalen*), and the Farnese pope "Fart-ass" (*fartz Esel*) and "Her Sodomitical Hellishness Paula III," and he threw around words for excrement with great abandon. In the woodcuts by Lucas Cranach commissioned by Luther near the end of his life, he had the papal church depicted as being expelled from the anus of an enormous she-devil, had peasants shown defecating in the papal crown, and suggested, once again in picture, that the pope, cardinals, and bishops should be hung from gallows with their tongues nailed alongside. While extraordinarily nasty even for Luther, *Against Hanswurst* and *Against the Papacy at Rome* also contained reasoned exposition of Scripture, history, and doctrine. Luther could never just attack. He always had to confess and profess as well.

### The Jews

One of the most shameful chapters in Christian history is the Christian treatment of Jews. For all his originality in so many areas, Luther was tragically unoriginal in this regard. He inherited a notorious tradition and passed it on with, if anything, increased vitriol. Ironically, Luther's first treatise on the Jews, his 1523 *That Jesus Christ Was Born a Jew*, advocated that Jews be treated in a friendly manner and denounced the treatment to which they were currently subjected. Perhaps if the Jews were dealt with in a friendly fashion and were instructed carefully from the Holy Scripture, "many of them would become true Christians and would return to the faith of their fathers, the prophets and patriarchs." To reject their beliefs so absolutely, allowing nothing to remain, and to treat them solely with arrogance and scorn, frightened them away from true Christianity.

In his last years, however, Luther ignored his own advice and in *On the Jews and Their Lies* and two other treatises, he rejected Jewish beliefs with all the scorn he could muster. The *primary* target of these attacks was the way in which Jewish rabbis understood the Hebrew Scripture. Luther interpreted the Old Testament or Hebrew Bible christologically and saw all promises by God in the Hebrew Bible as referring to Christ. Following medieval exegesis, he further believed that the Old Testament or Hebrew Bible testified not only to Christ but to the Trinity as well. Rabbinic exegesis, naturally, challenged both views. So the bulk of Luther's anti-Jewish treatises consist of an elaborate attempt to dissuade fellow Evangelicals from employing rabbinic exegesis. He attacked the exegesis itself, using historical, scriptural, and theological arguments. But he also recounted, without unequivocally accepting as true, some of the crudest charges traditionally lodged against the Jews and urged the rulers to deal exceedingly harshly with the Jews themselves and with their religion. While many of Luther's own contemporaries were shocked by these attacks and the treatises themselves saw little circulation, the harsh recommendations have been revived by some modern anti-Semites.

## ANGER, ILLNESS, AND DEPRESSION

Some scholars attribute the polemical excesses of the older Luther to ill health and aging. Others see the Reformation from its beginning as the product of a psychologically as well as physically sick man. What is the evidence for either position?

By his own admission, Luther was an angry man. Anger was his special sin. But anger could also be necessary and proper – and useful. It helped him, he said, to write well, to pray, and to preach: "Anger refreshes all my blood, sharpens my mind, and drives away temptations," he once commented.

A reading of Luther's polemical corpus does leave the distinct impression, however, that in his later years his anger became more shrill, and less leavened by compassion, humor, or even theological reflection. Moreover, his always pungent language became more coarse and scatological. The targets of his ire become under his pen the vilest of hypocrites, totally wicked and insincere, willing minions of the devil, deserving the most horrible fate.

What role did health or mental state play in this development?

### Luther's physical health

Throughout his career as a reformer Luther was often not well. He was sick during his appearance before the Diet of Worms in 1521, and he complained of severe constipation during his stay at the Wartburg. In subsequent years he suffered from frequent headaches and dizziness, roaring in the ears, an ulcer on his leg, uric acid stones, arthritis, ear infections, and angina which ultimately killed him. A confident diagnosis is difficult over so many centuries. Luther does seem to have suffered from an abnormally high concentration of uric acid in his system which would account for his uric acid stones and probably exacerbated his arthritis. His frequent spells of dizziness, fainting, and roaring in the ears suggest Ménière's syndrome, which is often caused by a severe middle ear infection that impairs the sense of balance.

Spasms caused by stone attacks are among the most painful experiences one can have. It seems likely that this intense pain together with headaches, dizziness, and probable arthritis aggravated his tendency to give way to anger. His generally poor health, and especially probable arteriosclerosis, with its usual circulation impairment, raises the question of possible senility or at least of reduced intellectual acuity in his later years. While Luther remained extraordinarily productive throughout his career, he does slow down in his later years and illness may be partly responsible for the gradual decline in productivity after 1530.

## Luther's mental health

The adult Luther's psychological health is even harder to diagnose than his physical health, although some investigators have confidently concluded that Luther suffered from a manic-depressive psychosis. Among the symptoms of this illness in his later years they list his frequent bouts of depression and spiritual temptation, his occasional expression of a death-wish, his vulgar and scatological language, his outbursts of rage and vilification, and his visions of and contests with the devil.

Most scholars freely concede the unusual and perhaps even abnormal aspects of Luther's personality, without accepting the diagnosis that attributes these traits to an underlying psychosis. By most standards, Luther *was* a neurotic man who, later in life, suffered from bouts of depression. Given all the evidence of productivity, clarity of thought, and ability to work with others, however, it is highly doubtful that he can be properly diagnosed as psychotic.

His biblically based view of the world, conjoined with apocalyptic hopes and fears, was common among both Catholics and Evangelicals. Luther's view of his own special role within the struggle between the true and false church was shared by many Evangelicals. As strange as this worldview may seem to us, Luther's beliefs did not separate him from ordinary folks in his time but rather gave him an extraordinary role to play in responding to their hopes and fears.

Finally, even the old Luther was never consistently violent or vulgar in his polemics. Throughout his later years he produced both violent and temperate polemics, as the situation warranted. It seems most likely that the vulgarity and violence was by choice. Luther could turn it on and off as it suited his purposes. His illnesses may have made him more irritable and less inhibited, but he had not lost complete control.

When all is said and done, the common description, and explanation, for Luther's polemics, and especially the polemics of the older Luther – that they are the product of an ill, aged, and psychologically unbalanced man – is not particularly illuminating historically. This explanation fails particularly to explain the wide range among the polemics of the older Luther, the theological depth of many of the polemics, and, finally, the educational and political functions the polemics performed within the larger Reformation movement.

# Part III

*After Luther*

## 13 Luther's function in an age of confessionalization

ROBERT KOLB

Like a storm wind, the words and images of Martin Luther swept across early sixteenth-century central Europe, decisively altering public life in German, Scandinavian, and Baltic lands, and even among peoples in Slovakia, Hungary, and Poland, where the Counter-Reformation later diminished his influence considerably. Luther's enemies viewed the currents aroused by his writings and his popularity among common folk and intellectuals as demonically destructive; his supporters experienced them as divine intervention for a beleaguered society and a tyrannized church.

### THE ANGEL OF THE APOCALYPSE, THE GERMAN HERCULES – TEACHER AND PASTOR

Historical personages always take on a new life in the traditions that convey their personalities and thought to succeeding generations. Twentieth-century scholars sometimes complained that the images of Luther and the summaries of his theology which have helped shape Western culture and Christian thinking do not accurately reflect the "real" reformer, but such is always true. Intensifying this commonplace in Luther's case is the fact that already during his lifetime his contemporaries experienced him as "larger than life."

None of his German contemporaries could remain neutral in regard to Luther. Few individuals have aroused so much and such many-faceted and strongly held passion and antagonism so quickly as did the monk-professor from Wittenberg when he penned and posted an invitation to debate the nature and impact of the practice of indulgences in late October 1517. His "Ninety-five Theses" that propelled him rapidly to center stage in German public life slowly came to command the attention of the papal court and launched yet another movement for ecclesiastical reform which, unlike earlier calls for change in the church, created a public persona through the use of the new public medium of the printing press. The cultural, social, political – to say nothing of religious, theological, and ecclesiastical – ripples from this academic exercise have made him the object of glorification and vilification for nearly a half millennium.

Those who dismiss or diminish Luther's influence have been rightly criticized for reading sources selectively or uncritically. Indeed, Luther yearned for a different church and society than the one he left in his wake. But his own theological appraisal of the mystery of continuing sin in believers' lives indicated that no reform could create a utopia. A century after his advent Germans may have behaved in much the same old ways, but the ways in which public leaders and peasants alike thought about God and themselves had changed.

Since about 1980 scholars have used the rubric "confessionalization" to analyze the effects of the disordering and reordering of public life that Luther initiated. Luther's concept of the Word of God gave "confessionalization" its name, his person and image helped shape the phenomenon, his ideas altered the paradigm for discussion and proclamation of the biblical message at the ideological heart of this "fundamental process in society, which ploughed up the public and private life of Europe in thoroughgoing fashion." It redefined society not only theologically and ecclesiastically but also in terms of political, social, economic, and cultural attitudes and structures.[1]

The definition of the church as an institution governed by its doctrinal pronouncements grew out of Luther's concept that God's Word should be proclaimed (confessed) boldly in order to define and govern the church. German society began to define itself in terms of the institution labeled a "confession" – a church defined by doctrinal statements – because Luther's followers had attained political legality as adherents of the "Augsburg Confession," a statement of faith composed for presentation to Emperor Charles V by Luther's colleague Philip Melanchthon at the imperial diet in Augsburg in 1530. As those pledged to the theological and ecclesiastical program summarized in that document, princes and cities of the German empire won an inferior but tolerated position in the empire in 1555. This program was labeled a "confession" because its author, Melanchthon, Luther's colleague in Wittenberg, shared his belief that God gave his people his Word in order that they might confess it publicly for the salvation of sinners. They believed that God's Word not only describes God's actions but actually serves as his instrument for accomplishing his will. One consequence of identifying Luther's call for reform as a "confession" is the label historians now employ for the broad spectrum of aspects embraced by "the ploughing up of European public life" between 1520 and 1650. Without Luther there would have been no confessionalization; without his concept of God's Word the phenomenon would have borne a different label.

## LUTHER IN THE JUDGMENT OF HIS CONTEMPORARIES

Luther's presence haunted the process of confessionalization from its dawning to its passing into the Enlightenment. Robert Scribner has identified three motifs employed by Luther's earliest publicists in print and portrait as his Reformation commenced: monk, teacher of the church, and man of the Bible or Word of God.

Ulrich Zwingli (1484–1531) is known as one of the Wittenberg professor's fiercest critics, but five years before the two fell into conflict over the Lord's Supper Zwingli had labeled Luther a contemporary Elijah, the eschatological prophet who was to proclaim the Word of the Lord in the last times. In 1520, three years after the Wittenberg monk and professor burst upon the larger stage of the European public discussion of critical ecclesiastical and social issues with his "Ninety-five Theses," not only Zwingli was lionizing Luther. Artists were depicting him as a saint, with nimbus and dove above his head, and as the humanists' symbolic exemplar, the ancient Greek demigod Hercules. His students heralded him in hymns and sermons as the angel of Revelation 14:6 who was to bring the eternal gospel to earth. His Roman Catholic opponents vilified and demonized him as an offspring of Satan himself. By accident, through the publication of his Ninety-five Theses, the first modern media event, Luther had helped shape a new world of public discourse in print, for his protest against the abuses of pastoral care in the indulgence trade struck responsive chords among intellectuals and common folk alike.

Intellectuals, particularly those involved in the movement for educational reform dubbed "humanism" by nineteenth-century scholars, were longing for a new order in learning, public communication and discourse, and society itself. Luther's critique of the old order, his focus on the study of the biblical texts in original languages, and his use of the ancient church fathers fired their imaginations. Humanists of his own generation finally distanced themselves from him, but the younger generation provided the shock troops for his Reformation. The common people were yearning with apocalyptic fervor for a prophet who could usher in the Kingdom of God in some form or other; whether they understood more or less of Luther's insights, their hearts were fired by his bold stance against the old order and selected elements of his call for dependence on God's grace and responsible service to God and neighbor. The painter Hans Holbein hailed him as Hercules, in battle with theologians of the old faith; Albrecht Dürer placed great hopes in this "man gifted with the Holy Spirit." Luther's fellow Augustinian monk Michael Stiefel composed a thirty-two-stanza hymn summarizing his teaching and associating him with the eschatological deliverance promised through the prophet Daniel's visions and John's angel with the gospel (Rev. 14:6). Other hymn-writers of the 1520s and 1530s associated him with the prophets and evangelists as well, echoing Zwingli's initial appraisal and enthusiasm.

Practically, these apocalyptic expectations translated themselves not only into popularity with the masses and widespread proclamation of his ideas from thousands of pulpits but also into policy decisions by ecclesiastical and societal leaders. Through a variety of publications Luther's proposals for reform of theology and of everyday life in church and society won adherence among preachers and political authorities. The printing press enabled this single intellectual to command the attention of peasants, prelates, and princes. Pastors repeated interpretations of texts they had read in his postils, the model sermons that constituted a continuing education program for the clergy of his day. They introduced his liturgy and had their people learning his hymns. They devoured his polemic against the old faith; they learned to preach and pray anew from his biblical comment in homiletical or academic form. They absorbed fundamental elements of his new paradigm for considering the biblical message even as they fit his way of thinking into their own, in their specific parish situations. They advised municipal leaders and counselors of princes to follow Luther's concepts of reform.

As governments actualized those concepts, Luther and his colleagues at the University of Wittenberg – particularly Melanchthon, but also Johannes Bugenhagen, Justus Jonas, and others – became a living adjudicatory body, providing a substitute for the authority of bishops and councils in answering questions regarding the proper interpretation of the biblical message or on the best way to solve the problems raised by the implementation of reform. Under the primary authority of Scripture, Luther's thought and judgment often served as a secondary authority for resolving questions of theology and church life. It was not always decisive to cite Luther, but a tract from his pen, or even better a memorandum or letter fresh from Wittenberg, carried an authority seldom if ever before accorded to a living theologian. Some of his contemporaries truly believed he was the Elijah of their times.

## LUTHER IN THE JUDGMENT OF HIS STUDENTS

In subsequent years Lutherans only slowly abandoned the conviction that God had sent Luther for special eschatological tasks in the history of the church. The first longer presentations of his life made crystal clear the unique place in human history that his students believed he had filled. In both the choice of genre and their content these initial Lutheran "biographies" reflect the religious convictions at the base of their authors' appraisal of their mentor, their prophet. The earliest Lutheran attempt at an extensive overview of Luther's life appeared in the martyrology of Ludwig Rabus (1556), a Wittenberg student in the early 1540s. He could define Luther as a martyr because of the consistent and fearless witness from his lips and pen that Rabus chronicled with extensive citations from a large variety of his works. Rabus called Luther not only the chief witness to the gospel of Christ but also "our dear father and the prophet of the German nation."

A decade later the biographical sermons of another Wittenberg student who had first arrived at the university in 1529, Johannes Mathesius, provided the outline of events of Luther's life that would inform subsequent biographers for several centuries. Mathesius' homilies rehearsed the episodes of Luther's public life with relatively little attention to his thought. Elements of the humanist art of life-writing mark these sermons, complete with citations of earlier sketches by Melanchthon, Johann Sleidan, and others. Yet they also reveal a Lutheran version of medieval hagiographical principles. Focusing on Luther's pastoral image and concerns, Mathesius depicted the reformer consistently as teacher of the church and "the worthy German prophet."

These titles and many more were ascribed to their common mentor by Cyriakus Spangenberg, another former Wittenberg student, among the youngest whose personal experience with Luther had fed upon and fostered eschatological perceptions of Luther's role as God's special prophet for the end times. His appreciation for his professor had been cultivated in his childhood by his father, Johann, Luther's devoted disciple and reformer in Nordhausen and Mansfeld. Between 1562 and 1573 the younger Spangenberg preached two sermons each year, on Luther's birthday and death-day, which examined his mentor in the roles of prophet, apostle, evangelist, pilgrim, priest, martyr – and many more. Published individually over the years and finally gathered into one volume, *Luther, Man of God* (1589), these sermons contained much less biographical description than Mathesius', but more theological analysis of the reformer's deeds and writings. Spangenberg had heard from Luther what he found to be the truth of God, the purest consolation of Christ; therefore he could deem Luther's proclamation of the gospel "David's slingshot, Paul's mouth, John's finger, Peter's key, and the Holy Spirit's sword ... he so powerfully internalized the dear apostle Paul ... that Paul is heard in Luther's words."[2]

Rabus, Mathesius, and Spangenberg found many imitators in Lutheran circles over the following century and a half. These works, undistinguished as new contributions but sometimes effectively wrought polemical or pedagogical instruments, presented themselves as biography for the poor preacher or as refutations of specific Roman Catholic or Calvinist attacks on the person or thought of the reformer. By the 1590s such biographical efforts also found form in dramas written for schools. These plays conveyed little more than the simplest fundamentals of Luther's theology in their often rather heavy-handed presentation of certain elements of his career, aimed at fostering faithfulness to the Lutheran church and animosity toward its opponents.

By the time the anniversary of the Ninety-five Theses occasioned grand celebrations in 1617, the expectation that Luther's appearance would herald Christ's return had disappeared. Calvinist governments took the lead in planning these celebrations, to arouse opposition to papal-imperial maneuvers against the Protestant estates of the empire. Lutherans joined in, however, also with biographical polemics. Luther's seventeenth-century biographers emphasized certain standard elements of his life and thought, largely in the service of German freedom and Lutheran truth. By the time Veit Ludwig von Seckendorff turned to archival research to refine the focus on Luther's life, in reply to the biographical assaults of the Jesuit Louis Maimbourg, *History of Lutheranism* (1682) and Jacques Bénigne Bossuet, *History of the Variations of the Protestant Churches* (1688), with his 1150-page *Historical and Apologetic Commentary on Lutheranism* (1692), a definite domestication of Luther's biography had set in. He remained the great hero of the struggle against papal tyranny and a theological genius, but earlier efforts to glorify him as God's special chosen instrument for the last times turned into more sober historical recitation. The panegyric formulas remained, but the excitement was missing.

## LUTHER IN THE JUDGMENT OF HIS OPPONENTS

### Roman Catholicism

From the beginning Luther's Roman Catholic foes had been convinced that he embodied demonic attack upon the truth and the church. His first biographer was the Roman Catholic theologian Johannes Cochlaeus, whose *Seven-Headed Luther* (1529) assessed selected treatises of Luther on eight doctrinal topics and concluded that "not the Holy Spirit, but Satan, an evil spirit, indeed, a whole legion of evil spirits, have spoken and written from this monk the last ten years." Twenty years later Cochlaeus' *Commentary on the Acts and Writings of Martin Luther* (1549) expanded that judgment. This work set the tone and model for a host of Roman Catholic biographical studies which attacked Luther's person; to them were joined countless critiques of his theology published to counteract his influence and win intellectuals and common people for the papacy. The Jesuit Ingolstadt professor Sebastian Flasch explained why he converted from Lutheranism to Roman Catholicism in a series of biographical-theological studies (1577–85), in which he cited Luther against himself in his demonstration that the reformer "was no holy prophet of Germany but pure filth." In 1582 Flasch's colleague Albert Hunger demonstrated that Luther's behavior and theology were thoroughly Epicurean, eliciting a storm of protest from Lutheran counter-biographers. The Council of Trent (1545–63) carefully addressed salient points of Luther's thought (among other reformers) with discriminating scrutiny and sensitive theological analysis, rejecting the fundamental principles of the Wittenberg paradigm. In this way Luther determined the confessionalized shape of Roman Catholicism to a significant extent.

### Reformed

Calvinist treatments of Luther were much more ambivalent. John Calvin himself did not share Zwingli's later reluctance to express a profound debt to the Wittenberg reformer. However, his disciples, particularly in Germany, were forced to define themselves in part in opposition to Luther's doctrine of the sacraments and predestination. Heinrich Bullinger, Zwingli's successor in Zurich, also influenced the German Reformed theologians in their understanding of biblical doctrine and their attitudes toward Luther. Therefore, their treatments of his work were reserved and in part sharply critical; they dedicated no little energy to disputing his authority as a teacher of the church. Heidelberg professor and former Wittenberg student Zacharias Ursinus rejected the special authority accorded Luther by Lutheran contemporaries, noting his errors and weaknesses in teaching and behavior, and warning against "papalist remnants" in his writings, especially on the Lord's Supper. The Palatine court preacher Daniel Tossanus argued that Luther himself had urged viewing his writings with a critical eye. The Nuremberg attorney Christoph Herdesian, also a former Wittenberg student and propagandist for the Calvinist Palatinate prince Johann Kasimir, tried rather to reinterpret Luther's positions on the Lord's Supper by arguing that the reformer's concerns differed significantly from the later Lutheran interpretation of his sacramental teaching. Luther's contributions had to be taken further and expanded into a "second Reformation," argued many in Herdesian's generation. Thus, in certain ways Luther also played a role in the self-conception of Calvinism.

## LUTHER'S THOUGHT IN THE THINKING OF HIS STUDENTS

To a far greater extent, the Wittenberg professor remained alive in the consciousness of his Lutheran followers long after his death in 1546. The plaintive cries of loss and grief heard in funeral sermons and orations held by colleagues and in tributes spoken and written across central Europe provide a good measure of the decisive, crucial role those who had experienced him believed he had played in their own lives and in human history. As is true of all historical figures, Luther left a legacy that had to be interpreted, adapted, and integrated into an ever-changing world. That interpretation formed a significant part of Lutheran confessionalization. By the time of his death his own career, with many other factors, had considerably transformed the world in which he had begun to proclaim the biblical message. The course of his heirs' discussion of how to employ his insights in their generation took place in circumstances of sharp disappointment forged by feelings of betrayal at the hands of comrades and friends.

The forecasts of judgment upon the German nation for not heeding Luther's call to return to God's Word more completely – issued often at his death in February 1546 – seemed justified to many of his disciples when, four months later, Emperor Charles V initiated the Smalcald War in order to eradicate the Lutheran faith. Imperial armies defeated the troops of two leading Lutheran princes, Elector John Frederick of Saxony and Landgrave Philip of Hesse, and their allies. Charles seemed triumphant, imprisoning these leaders, driving hundreds of Lutheran pastors into exile, and imposing a new, Romanizing reform program labeled the "Augsburg Interim" by its critics wherever his military power reached. Melanchthon led the Wittenberg faculty – which was placed under the new management of John Frederick's cousin Moritz, who had sided with Charles against his cousin and Philip (his father-in-law) – into a compromising situation, in which the Wittenberg colleagues attempted to stave off the imperial destruction of Saxon Lutheranism with a policy of concession labeled "the Leipzig Interim" by Lutheran critics. Their charges that Melanchthon and company were betraying Luther by supporting the political turncoat Moritz introduced a quarter-century of strife among Luther's heirs. Melanchthon reacted against the attacks by former colleagues and students, above all Nikolaus von Amsdorff, Matthias Flacius Illyricus, Nikolaus Gallus, and Joachim Westphal, with increasing bitterness because of their rejection of what he understood as a good-faith effort to save the Lutheran confession of the faith from suppression by imperial soldiers through adjustments in neutral matters of church practice (*adiaphora*) and minimal reformulating of public teaching.

The disputes that erupted from the crisis of the Smalcald War and the "Interims" had been foreshadowed in tensions within the Wittenberg circle since the 1520s, when Johann Agricola, among the brightest of Luther's earliest students, failed to capture Luther's distinction of law and gospel in a way that met his teacher's expectations. Particularly in dispute with Melanchthon, Agricola argued that the law played no role in the Christian life. First Melanchthon and then Luther fell into sharp controversy with Agricola (1527–28, 1537–40), rejecting his way of thinking because it destroyed effective repentance and used the gospel to perform the functions of the law. Other disagreements between Melanchthon and his and Luther's close friend Amsdorff also signaled questions that demanded further refinement and remained unresolved when disputes broke out over questions regarding the relationship of God's grace and believers' activities in the wake of the Leipzig Interim.

Parallel to those disputes came serious disagreement with the Lutheran reformer of Nuremberg Andreas Osiander, who from imperially imposed exile in Königsberg defended his view of the justification of the sinner by the indwelling of Christ's divine righteousness. Alongside all these controversies, challenges to the Lutheran understanding of how God's Word functions in the church, particularly in its sacramental form in the Lord's Supper, placed sacramental theology on the controversial agenda that required resolution. These challenges emanated both from outside the Lutheran churches – above all, from Calvinist and Bullingerian critiques – and from inside – above all, as some disciples of Melanchthon took his sacramental theology and Christology in a spiritualizing direction.

Among the first topics of controversy over the precise definition of Luther's theological legacy was the "necessity of good works for salvation," a proposal defended by Georg Major, formerly Luther's and Melanchthon's student and then their colleague in Wittenberg, in his attempts to justify the Leipzig Interim in the early 1550s. As arguments were exchanged in 1552 and 1553, it became clear from Major's opponents, later dubbed "Gnesio-Lutherans" by scholars, that this "Philippist" position was wrong not only because it undermined the biblical doctrine of justification by faith but also because Luther had condemned it. Seven years after his death Luther was being cited as a secondary authority for public teaching, an adjudicatory source of the truth. Magdeburg pastor Albert Christian used the reformer's *Disputation on the Works of the Law and Grace* (1537) as a text that authenticated Christian's critique of Major's proposition. In words reminiscent of 2 Peter 1:19–21, he confessed his conviction that "the holy man of God Luther was moved by the Holy Spirit as he spoke, and that his writings set forth the word of the prophets and apostles made more sure, as he laid waste the empire of the Roman Antichrist."[3] Cyriakus Spangenberg and other Wittenberg graduates of his generation shared Christian's opinion of Luther's authority and in fact used Luther's writings as Christian had, to validate their interpretation of biblical teaching. Johannes Wigand, at the time professor in Jena, placed Luther's writings among the confessional documents which were to govern public doctrine: the ancient Creeds, the *Augsburg Confession* and its *Apology*, the *Smalcald Articles* "and the writings of Luther," as well as a local confession of faith.[4] Official confessions of faith in several Lutheran lands also accorded the corpus of Luther's printed works as a whole this status as a substitute for popes, bishops, and councils, a standard of secondary authority for ecclesiastical teaching and practice. Luther's words could function in this way in part because of the humanist appreciation for the authority of rhetorically effective discourse and also because of his own concept of the power of God's Word to accomplish what God promises as the "living voice of the gospel" – and because he was considered a special prophet in God's plan for the church.

Yet not all of Luther's followers accepted his "complete works" as an authoritative interpretation of Scripture and adjudicator of ecclesiastical questions. It soon proved impossible to maintain the corpus of his writings as a secondary authority for the church. His *oeuvre* was too extensive, and his printed opinions had shifted between his earliest tracts and the publications of his mature years. Luther had always directed his thought to specific situations, and he could be cited against himself. In the disputes over *adiaphora*, original sin, and freedom of the will theologians from opposite sides of the debate assembled Luther citations against their foes – and their foes' Luther citations and interpretations. Finally, in the somewhat successful effort that produced the *Formula of Concord* and the *Book of Concord*, those who had used Luther as a weapon against those who favored certain elements of Melanchthon's thought had to give way on the public use of Luther's authority in order to win the day on doctrinal issues. It became politically incorrect to place too much authority in Luther's hand when some thought (not altogether correctly) that the *Formula* diminished Melanchthon's theological influence. The *Formula* recognized Luther's catechisms and the *Smalcald Articles*, along with Melanchthon's *Augsburg Confession*, accorded highest rank among the Lutherans' secondary authorities, and his *Apology* as the standards for public teaching of the biblical message. The *Formula* acknowledged Luther as God's instrument for bringing God's Word to light after the darkness wrought by the papacy, but it granted him no general authority for the church's continued exposition of that Word.

In the dogmatic tradition that grew out of the *Formula of Concord* and the development of Melanchthon's genre of organizing biblical material for preaching and teaching into theological topics by Martin Chemnitz (*Loci the-ologici*, 1591/92), Luther was much honored but not much cited. The great Lutheran teachers, such as Johann Gerhard in his *Loci theologici* (1610–22), and Johann Andreas Quenstedt in his *Theologia didactico-polemica, sive Systema Theologicum* (1685), defended the reformer against Roman Catholic attacks by placing a discussion of his vocation to reform the church within their treatment of the public ministry. They argued that he led the Reforma-tion as a regularly called priest and theological professor but that the Holy Spirit had given him the extraordinary assignment of reforming the church and revealing the antichrist. Gerhard and Quenstedt relied, however, more on Scripture and a score of other, largely more recent, theologians than on Luther for supporting their arguments. The general framework of Luther's thinking had set the Lutherans' agenda, but others, such as Chemnitz, pro-vided more quotable arguments for seventeenth-century dogmaticians.

Nonetheless, Luther's writings exercised widespread influence in the preaching and teaching of parish pastors, in the lectures and publications of university theologians, and in the conceptions and conversations of com-mon people who sang Luther's hymns, learned his catechism, and read or heard read his postils and other works. However his successors may have channeled and packaged his ideas, he continued to inspire and impel theo-logical formulation and expression in churches of the Lutheran confession.

## WITTENBERG'S DOCTOR *IN BIBLIA* AS TEACHER OF THE CHURCH

Luther's image of himself centered on his call as teacher of Scripture. His doctoral oath to teach the Bible faithfully and keep false teaching from bringing offense to the church was determinative in his own mind for the course of his career. His instruction quickly extended beyond his own lecture hall, for the invention of moveable type enabled him to send his ideas across Germany and beyond. By 1520 his thirty printed tracts or books had sold perhaps as many as 600,000 copies. Nothing like that had happened in the first decades of Gutenberg's revolution in public discourse. Luther's use of the printing press established a new cultural matrix for the dissemination of ideas and the persuasion of a populace. His message spread and made its impact largely through the oral proclamation of preachers and laity who read his tracts in public places, but this oral proclamation was made possible and empowered by the diffusion of his message in print.

Luther's use of Gutenberg's invention not only changed the ways in-tellectuals exchanged ideas and attracted followers. It also transformed the way common people worshiped and learned the Christian faith. Mark U.

Edwards Jr. has shown that in any given area, decisions of local printers highlighted different sides of Luther. But the general re-formation of pious practice and perception developed under the Wittenberg model no matter what initial accents had been prominent in local readings of his works. The publication of Luther's handbook (*enchiridion*) for Christian instruction converted the word for that instruction – catechism – into a word for the book itself, and the memorization of Luther's *Small Catechism* began its 500-year-long history of shaping basic Christian knowledge for countless boys and girls. Luther's hymns edged their way into the pious practice and consciousness of parishioners; worship in Western Christendom was altered forever by his combination of music and lyrics. Devotional material for the families of literate artisans and peasants, postils and commentaries for their pastors, treatments of social questions for city councilmen and princely counselors reconstructed significant parts of popular piety and public policy, because Luther's ideas penetrated parsonages and princes' courts alike through his publications.

Luther's writings continued to play such a role, even if in a more limited way, after his death. The reprinting of his works found ready markets deep into the seventeenth century, and even thereafter. Without the printing press there would have been no confessionalization, and without Luther's continued presence on the booksellers' lists its shape would have been quite different. Those who could afford it could obtain Luther's "complete" works and have ready reference to the reformer's thought always at hand. No living personality had made it worthwhile for a printer to produce an *opera omnia* before 1518, the year in which the Basel printer Johannes Froben commissioned the local cathedral preacher Wolfgang Capito to edit the first *Luther's Latin Works*, in one volume of five hundred pages. Erasmus protested, and he was the exceptional author whose voice publishers heed. In addition, papal excommunication and imperial outlawry made it dangerous for printers in Basel and Strasbourg to continue to issue subsequent editions.

Twenty years later, however, Luther's own colleagues – against his protest – began a massive project of producing his "Works." When completed twenty years later (1539–59), the Wittenberg Edition embraced twelve German and seven Latin – massive folio – volumes. It had also provoked a rival undertaking, the Jena Edition, because the latter's Gnesio-Lutheran creators suspected that the Philippist editors of the former had altered certain passages too freely (an exaggerated verdict). Its volumes appeared rapidly: eight German between 1555 and 1558 and four Latin between 1556 and 1558. Individual volumes of both editions were reprinted into the seventeenth century.

One of those who planned the Jena Edition, Luther's former amanuensis Johannes Aurifaber, sought to fill in the very few gaps that remained in these two "complete" works. He obtained some support from the ducal Saxon government to publish two supplementary volumes (1564/65) plus two of Luther's correspondence (1556, 1565), but lack of commercial success ended his projects. Much more successful was Aurifaber's publication of student reports from Luther's dinner table, his *Table Talk*, organized by topics. At least twenty-three editions, some modified by other editors, appeared in print between 1566 and 1621.

By the later seventeenth century the government of Saxony-Altenburg deemed it necessary to issue a ten-volume revision of the German Jena edition, the Altenburg Edition (1661–64); in 1729–40 the Leipzig publisher Johann Heinrich Zedler (1706–1763) brought out twenty-two volumes in German, the Leipzig Edition. The Jena professor Johann Georg Walch was already at work at a twenty-four-volume "Luther's Works" in modernized German (1740–53); it was extensively revised and republished by A. H. Hoppe and others in St. Louis for German-American pastors (1880–1910). By that time critical editorial standards were being developed, and these standards guided the production of the Erlangen Edition (67 German volumes, 1826–57; 26 Latin, 1829–86) and the Weimar Edition (101 volumes, 1883–1993).

In the sixteenth and seventeenth centuries editors and publishers recognized that many pastors could not afford the whole of Luther's works, so they prepared single works or florilegia of Luther citations on specific subjects, ranging over many topics Luther had addressed. His postils remained popular; his *Church Postil* appeared at least a dozen times during the fifty years after his death; his *House Postil*, designed for family use, in at least thirty-five editions. Other pieces or collections of his prayers and biblical comments for such devotional use were frequently printed well into the seventeenth century; at least four editors assembled selected prayers from his pen to aid pious meditation. Luther's hymns remained on people's lips and in their hymnbooks. Even when a hymnal contained few of his hymn texts, his name frequently appeared on the title page. Luther's heirs associated his name inseparably with song and praise.

Although the course of polemic with Roman Catholics and Calvinists developed in ways that demanded new expressions of Lutheran theology, Luther was occasionally republished in order to defend his teaching against those who were attacking it. For those who wanted to study his thought within the framework of systematic theology as Melanchthon had organized it, into topics from "God" to "the resurrection of the dead," a new genre, the *loci communes Lutheri*, was conceived in the 1560s. By 1600 five such collections had appeared to provide readers with a pre-digested synopsis of his thought. For the most part they actually offered sufficiently extensive citations to furnish users with substantial material for thought and for preaching and teaching. In 1584 the first of many collections of short citations – aphorisms and maxims suitable for embellishing sermons – came from Michael Neander's pen. This genre still finds users in the twenty-first century among Lutheran preachers.

## LUTHER'S INFLUENCE ON LUTHERAN THEOLOGY IN THE AGE OF CONFESSIONALIZATION

Luther presumed that the entire life of the church proceeded from the Word of God, and he spent his life interpreting and proclaiming it. Convinced of his understanding of the biblical message, he wanted to pass on to his followers what he had learned. Yet every generation reformulates its own expression of its theology, even when paradigm shifts of the magnitude introduced by Luther and Melanchthon cannot be part of each age's task. Students of these two Wittenberg professors are often "accused" of not being their equals in originality – an impossible demand – or of changing and shading their message – a necessary historical development. Indeed, it did not fall to sixteenth- and seventeenth-century Lutheran "epigones" to be Luther and Melanchthon. But they did take seriously what these two had bequeathed them as they addressed the changing world of early modern Europe. Their times, other elements in their framework of thinking from medieval and humanistic as well as patristic sources, and their epistemological equipment did affect the way they used what Luther had left them.

Luther was a "conservative" reformer, as all reformers are, in certain ways. He preserved much of the medieval heritage, and his followers hauled more or other aspects of their medieval inheritance back into church. But at the heart of theological enterprise – and at the heart of piety – Luther proposed profound shifts in the way Christian people thought of God and his way of working in a fallen world, of themselves, and their relationship to their neighbors. The most important elements in this paradigm shift proceeded from his reprocessing his nominalistic heritage as he wrestled with what might be called the paradox of two sets of responsibility. His professors had helped Luther recognize that the biblical concept of the sovereign Creator posited a God who holds all things under his control; from this presupposition he fashioned his doctrine of providence and his concept of grace and of free forgiveness of sin and life in Christ. This teaching he labeled "gospel." At the same time he assumed that God had so designed human creatures that they are also totally responsible for that which God has given them to do. Divine expectations for human creatures are what Luther called "law."

Out of this paradox of divine and human responsibilities (a term Luther did not himself employ) arose his hermeneutical principle of the proper distinction of law and gospel. The gospel is God's means of re-creating his elect children out of sinners as he gives them this new identity through Christ's death and resurrection; the law unfolds God's expectations for the performance or behavior of God's human creatures. The law crushes and accuses sinners; the gospel gives them the forgiveness of sins, restoring them to people whose lives center in trust in God as he has revealed himself in Christ. The anthropological corollary of this paradox is Luther's distinction of two kinds of righteousness. He taught that human creatures are righteous in God's sight "passively," as children, only because God looks on them with favor, mercy, and love. They are right or righteous in relationship to God's creation by carrying out his commands in deeds of love. The societal and ethical implications of the paradox are expressed in Luther's distinction of two realms in which God operates. The vertical or "heavenly" realm of faith embraces the gospel's forgiveness and the believer's responding trust in Christ. The horizontal or "earthly" realm of love embraces the good works of care for the neighbor and all of God's creation. Alongside this paradox of divine and human responsibility Luther took seriously the mystery of the continuation of evil in believers' lives. Therefore, he emphasized the necessity of lifelong daily repentance.

Luther's second fundamental presupposition that guided several elements of his theological system lay in his understanding of God's Word. God reveals himself in such a way that human creatures are totally dependent on his Word, which Luther contended can be found alone in Scripture (and human conveying of its message). Therefore, in what he called the "theology of the cross," he not only affirmed the atonement wrought through Christ's death and resurrection but also the distinction between the Hidden God, inaccessible to human reason, and the Revealed God, whom faith grasps as it is created by God's revelation of himself in Christ and in Scripture.

God's Word not only reveals information about God. It is performative speech, God's instrument of creative and re-creative power. It does what God says: law condemns sinners, gospel forgives and bestows new life upon the elect whom the Holy Spirit brings to faith through its proclamation. Luther believed that reality proceeds from God's speaking; he held an ontology of the Word, and the reality of human life in God's sight is determined by the faith God's promise of life creates.

According to Luther, God's Word, in the form of human language – in oral, written, and sacramental forms – is not bound by presuppositions imposed by spiritualizing philosophies, such as the then ever more popular forms of Platonic thought which asserted that spiritual blessings could not be conveyed by material elements. Luther maintained that God has chosen certain material elements, including the human language of the gospel and sacramental elements, including water, bread and Christ's body, wine and Christ's blood, to deliver forgiveness of sins, life, and salvation.

These larger conceptual frameworks for interpreting and applying biblical thought did not fit neatly into the epistemological structures of the time. Luther clearly formulated the distinctions between law and gospel and between two kinds of righteousness as well as his "theology of the cross." But without a clear epistemological framework he did not unambiguously pass his method of thinking on to his students. They indeed struggled with the application of his method, but did so with the tools given them by Melanchthon, chiefly the method of organizing material by specific topics (*loci communes*). These discrete units of ideas, packaged for effective delivery to listeners or readers, permitted no larger view of a framework for thinking. Thus, Luther's disciples reduced the dynamic of his insights into forms manageable as *loci communes*.

Most of their controversies arose from their different perceptions of the paradox of two responsibilities and of the nature of God's Word as his active instrument for effecting salvation. In contending over the role of good works in the Christian life, Philippist followers of Luther and Melanchthon paid special attention to the human responsibility of obedience to God's commands, an accent the two Wittenberg professors had stressed since their encounter with dissolute peasant life in the visitation of 1527/28. Thus, under Major's leadership they argued that good works are necessary for salvation. Gnesio-Lutheran opponents emphasized God's grace. Few went so far as Amsdorff, who revived Luther's statement regarding the use of good works as meritorious, for self-justification, "good works are detrimental for salvation." But all affirmed that good works play no role in salvation even though many used the expression, "good works are necessary in the Christian life." Others in this group opposed any association of "necessity" with the performance of God's Word, fearing that such language would lead the pious to believe that they could win God's favor through their own behavior. These Gnesio-Lutherans urged that Christians do good works "spontaneously," "from a free, merry spirit," in their effort to preserve Luther's distinction between two kinds of righteousness.

The Wittenbergers' students also disagreed on the bondage or freedom of the will. Gnesio-Lutherans tended to accent the will's bondage in sin until freed by the Holy Spirit through the use of God's Word. They preserved Luther's "broken" doctrine of predestination, teaching within the framework of distinguishing law and gospel that God's unconditioned choice of believers is the sole cause of their salvation while denying that God is responsible for the damnation of unbelievers, who under the law must take responsibility for their rejection of God. Philippists, on the other hand, focused on human responsibility. They confessed God's total responsibility for the salvation of his people, but they also took seriously the concerns that caused Melanchthon to explore what the will does in coming to faith and continuing repentance. As they defended themselves against Roman Catholic charges of "stoic determinism," probed ways to communicate the gospel with effective rhetoric, and investigated the psychological dynamics of cultivating repentance and public discipline, they focused on the actions of the will. The Gnesio-Lutherans affirmed that the will acts, but turns to Christ, they asserted, only under the power of the Holy Spirit. Although the *Formula of Concord* confessed the latter position, seventeenth-century theologians continued to search for ways to clarify the will's role that sometimes abandoned the paradox of divine and human responsibility and gave more credit to the will's actions than Luther had done.

Andreas Osiander challenged Luther's concept of the Word of God in the doctrine of justification. Influenced by the Platonic principles of his training in cabalistic thinking, he taught that sinners are saved by grace alone through faith in Christ. But he did not capture Luther's concept of the re-creative power of God's Word of forgiveness. He could not understand Luther's ontology of the Word, that God's speaking creates reality. Osiander therefore concluded that justification takes place because the righteousness of Christ's divine nature comes to dwell in believers through faith. With one accord Luther's and Melanchthon's students, Gnesio-Lutherans and Philippists alike, recognized that Osiander failed to understand Luther's fundamental approach to salvation through Christ's obedience to the Father in his death and resurrection. Osiander's thought remained a symbol for error but exercised no effective role in Lutheran thinking.

A much deeper influence on the confessional sense of Lutherans was the controversy over spiritualizing views of the Lord's Supper and Christology that some Melanchthon students introduced at the University of Wittenberg in the 1560s. Accused of "crypto-Calvinism," this new generation of Wittenberg theologians – Casper Peucer, Christoph Pezel, and others – actually were working out insights of Melanchthon in directions opposed to the way in which other Melanchthon students (Martin Chemnitz, Nikolaus Selnecker, David Chytraeus, and others) were taking his ideas. Chemnitz, for example, repeated Luther's insistence upon reading Christ's words, "This is my body," literally since God's almighty power was able to design means of conveying salvation in any way he pleased. Chemnitz also used Luther's explanation that Christ's body and blood could truly be present in the Supper because of the ancient doctrine of the communication of attributes (Lat. *communicatio idiomata*) between Christ's divine and human natures. Others, such as Johann Brenz and Jakob Andreae, emphasized the christological argument even more strongly. The *Formula of Concord* confirmed Chemnitz's approach, which seventeenth-century Lutheran theologians followed, even though its christological aspects were the subject of dispute between theologians at Tübingen and Giessen in 1616–27.

In the year 2000 North American and European lists of the most significant personalities of the second Christian millennium consistently placed Luther near the top, probably for different reasons than central Europeans regarded him as important in 1650. They would have recognized his political and cultural significance but emphasized his theological influence on public thinking. Strained as it was through alien forms of communication, in the Aristotelian-Melanchthonian dialectic of dogmatic theology, Luther's proclamation of the gospel of Jesus Christ remained alive in his literary legacy and in forms of thinking which his paradigm shift in theology had effected.

### Notes

1. Heinz Schilling, "Confessionalization in the Empire: Religious and Societal Change in Germany between 1555 and 1620," in *Religion, Political Culture and the Emergence of Early Modern Society* (Leiden: Brill, 1992), 205–45.
2. *Warhafftiger Bericht von den wolthaten/die Gott durch Martin Luther...erzeigt...* (Jena: Rhebart, 1561), A4a-B1b.
3. *Disputatio Reverendi patris D. Martini Luther de operibus legis & gratiae...* (Magdeburg: Lotther, 1553), A3b.
4. *De confessione in doctrine divina...* (Jena: Rödinger, 1569), c5b–c6a.

# 14 The legacy of Martin Luther

HANS J. HILLERBRAND

Martin Luther had a fairly low opinion of himself, though one must leave open the question if this was because he was profoundly convinced that such was the case, or because he thought it to be good politics to say so, or because he saw himself as analogous to the Old Testament prophets who similarly had a way of denouncing their own importance. "I am but a stinking bag of worms," he observed on one occasion.[1] And even though he had also insisted that at his death all his books and writings should be burned and "the children of God not be called by my name," neither, in fact, proved to be the case.[2] Luther's long shadow fell over the subsequent centuries. With the passing of time, posterity chose not to take Luther at his word, and the importance he had attained during his own lifetime was dwarfed by an ever-increasing importance afterwards. Arguably, Luther's legacy has been one of the most striking phenomena in Western intellectual history.[3] The fundamental observation, all the same, is that such dramatic eminence notwithstanding, Martin Luther has also been one of the most controversial figures in Western life and thought. Indeed, there has been controversy not only about his theology, but also about his impact on German history. For a long time, mentioning the name of Luther meant to step on to the barricades.

Three facets have intermingled to mold Martin Luther's legacy – judgments made about his person; evaluations of his theology; and assessments of his ecclesiastical influence. Obviously, these three facets interweave. Those who admire his theological prowess were also most likely to admire him as a person as well. However, conceptually these three facets can be kept separate.

## THE LUTHER OF HISTORY

Luther's legacy began already during the reformer's own lifetime, and sentiment about him, expressed by friend or foe, had a way of setting the course for the centuries that followed. As early as 1521, Albrecht Dürer wrote in his diary, upon learning that Luther might have been killed by Charles V:

"Oh, if Luther is dead, who will henceforth expound to us the true gospel."[4] Luther's colleague and co-worker Philip Melanchthon's funeral oration for Luther movingly expressed deep filial appreciation:

Thus he must be counted among the number and order of those mighty and special people, whom God sent to gather his church on earth... Luther brought the true and pure Christian teaching to the light of day... I will not quarrel with those good-hearted men who tell us that Dr. Luther was a bit too rough, but will use Erasmus's answer often given by him, namely that God prescribed a harsh and bitter physician for these last days, when a grave illness had begun to take over.[5]

Melanchthon also confessed later that he had found Luther's dominating personality oppressive: "In earlier days I had to submit myself to Luther like a servant, since he frequently persisted in his disturbing stubbornness, which was not a minor characteristic, rather than in a concern for his own person and the common good."[6]

Soon after the reformer's death his disciple Matthias Flacius Illyricus began to publish his *Ecclesiastica Historia integram ecclesiae Christi ideam complectens*, the so-called "Magdeburg Centuries," a history of the church from apostolic times to the present. Tellingly, as Flacius put it on the very first page, the story of the church is described as "the beginning, progression, and ruthless efforts of the Antichrist," surely a rather gloomy perspective which allowed Flacius, all the same, to put Luther into an even more striking light.[7] What in Philip Melanchthon and in other contemporaries of Martin Luther had been a deep appreciation of Luther's theological and biblical insight, was made by Flacius part and parcel of universal salvation history. The assertion was that Luther had been the sole authentic interpreter of the gospel since the days of the apostles. This was a different tone than that expressed by Luther's own contemporaries. The Lutheran veneration of the reformer had its beginning right then and there. Melanchthon's had been the voice of Luther's contemporaries.[8] Flacius spoke as a filial worshiper.

Luther's foes, in turn, were in the reformers' camp as well as in the Catholic phalanx. Luther's erstwhile supporters Thomas Müntzer and Andreas Bodenstein Karlstadt were illustrative of former supporters, while Johannes Cochlaeus and John Eck were representative of the phalanx of Catholic protagonists. All four offered vehement and vitriolic criticism of Luther. The two fellow reformers, Karlstadt and Müntzer, offered the same strident criticism, but made subtle distinctions. For both, Luther was not "radical" enough. But while Karlstadt argued that Luther had failed to see the full ramifications of his own theological premises, Müntzer concluded that Luther had surrendered his biblical insights to an easy accommodation with the rulers and political authorities. Müntzer called Luther the "soft-living body in Wittenberg," while an Anabaptist writer observed that Luther had "broken the pope's pitcher, but had kept the pieces in his hand."[9] This notion, stated in varying degrees of judgmental theological appraisal, may be seen as the common denominator for all Protestant, non-Lutheran views of Luther. This is understandable, of course, in that the existence of separate Protestant traditions apart from Lutheranism meant that in one way or another one had to find fault with Luther.

The Catholic polemicists, in turn, found in Luther a plain old-fashioned heretic. Johannes Cochlaeus, while by no means Luther's foremost theological opponent (that credit must go to Johann Eck), was the major Catholic polemicist when it came to Luther, pursuing him from 1520 onward with a steady stream of polemics. After Luther's appearance before the diet at Worms in 1521, Cochlaeus published an account of his discussion with Luther, and from then on he regularly added his vitriolic commentary on specific writings of Luther's as they appeared. In 1529 he published *Septiceps Lutherus, ubique sibi, suis scriptis, contrarius in Visitationem Saxonicam* in which he found Luther to be "seven-headed," a hardly complimentary reference to the biblical dragon with the seven heads, the symbol for evil identical with the devil or representative of him. Cochlaeus meant inconsistency among the seven Luthers – the "doctor," "Martinus," "Lutherus," "ecclesiastes" (preacher), "Suermerus" (radical), and "Barrabas" (spiritualist). In 1549 Cochlaeus published his lengthy *Commentaria de actis et scriptis Martini Lutheri* on Luther's life and thought. Even though Cochlaeus got a crony of his to write a preface on the "proper way to write history" (*de ratione scribendi historias*), his book is a passionate compilation of all the negatives about Luther's life and the congruence of Luther's teachings with ancient heresies. Not surprisingly, Cochlaeus' book became the standard arsenal for virtually all Catholic anti-Lutheran assessments and polemics until the twentieth century.[10]

The Catholic polemics were clear in their rejection of Luther, though strikingly they seemed to be most concerned to garner adverse details about his life. The notion, of course, was that by demonstrating a despicable life, Luther's theology would be also discredited.[11] In the generation after Luther's death (in fact, already anticipated in Luther's later years) something else of importance for Luther's legacy came to the fore – stark disagreement among Martin Luther's own followers as to what was, in fact, the reformer's authentic teaching. In a way, this was surprising, for no such disagreement characterized the followers of John Calvin.

This had, at least on the face of things, a good reason. Luther was not a systematic theologian in the sense of having written a systematic exposition of theology. He was what might be called a "polemical" theologian – Karl Barth used the term "irregular" theologian to characterize the likes of Luther.[12] His theology was not expressed in works of a systematic nature and character, but in polemical works, books and treatises written with specific controversial issues in mind (much like those characteristic of St. Augustine), and in biblical commentaries, where specific scriptural passages determined topic and compass of exegesis. This fact makes it understandable why there was among Martin Luther's followers far more disagreement about his teaching than, say, among the followers of John Calvin. Other than in his two catechisms and the *Schmalkald Articles*, Luther did not offer a coherent exposition of the faith. He wrote on specific topics, usually in the context of a fierce controversy – against the Anabaptists, against John Eck, or Huldrych Zwingli. To be sure, it is possible to systematize Luther's utterances from various settings – Martin Luther *did* have a coherent theology – but it is not easy. That some of his followers were able to read one kind of notions into his writings, and others quite different theological notions, becomes understandable.

In the sixteenth century this disagreement among Luther's disciples found expression, beginning already during Luther's own lifetime, in several theological controversies and disagreements among his followers. No less than six theological controversies beset German Lutheranism in the sixteenth century. The points of contention of these controversies strike us today as quite foreign as will the intensity with which these fraternal battles were fought. Intriguingly, protagonists on both sides of the various issues saw themselves as authentic advocates of Luther's understanding, and thereby also of the gospel.

The Antinomian controversy had to do with the contention of Johann Agricola that the Decalogue, thus the law, had no place in the Christian proclamation. The Adiaphoristic controversy was triggered by Philip Melanchthon's notion that certain matters, such as details of the liturgy, were *adiaphora*, "matters of indifference," and could be changed or modified without affecting the fundamental fidelity to the gospel. The Majoristic controversy pertained to Georg Major's argument that good works were necessary for salvation, an argument that led to the Gnesio-Lutheran retort, propounded by Nikolaus Amsdorf, that reliance on good works was in fact detrimental to salvation. The Synergistic controversy focused on the question of human co-operation – through human will or human effort – with divine grace in salvation. The Osiandrian controversy took its name from the

Nuremberg reformer Andreas Osiander, who held that the believer will overcome the lack of righteousness because the indwelling Christ in the believer
will bring about all sorts of good works. The Crypto-Calvinist (or "hidden
Calvinist") controversy, finally, had to do with the manner of Christ's
presence in the bread and wine of the Lord's Supper, seen by Calvinists
as a symbolic or spiritual presence, the charge being that some alleged
Lutherans were in fact holding to the Calvinist point of view and were thus
"crypto" Calvinists.

In one way, these controversies were hardly noteworthy in that through
the centuries before as well as after the Reformation, disagreements among
theologians have neither been confined either to the sixteenth century or
to theologians of Lutheran persuasion. It was an important characteristic
of these controversies, however, that all protagonists, especially the Gnesio-
Lutherans, claimed fealty to Martin Luther. That they were able to do so,
at least with a modicum of justification, was the outgrowth of the nature
of Luther's theologizing, to which should be added Luther's rather broad-
minded attitude when it came to ensuing disagreements among his followers during his lifetime. The fierceness of these controversies about Luther's
theological legacy was no less fierce than that between Catholics and Protestants in that age.

After the Peace of Augsburg, of 1555, this internal Lutheran discord
in Germany had woeful consequences. The Gnesio-Lutherans rejected the
Philippists' claim of the *Augsburg Confession* as their confessional statement, thus arguing that the theological disagreement between the two factions was not over peripheral matters but pertained to the very heart of the
Lutheran understanding of the Christian faith. Even more importantly, the
internal controversies sapped the external vitality of German Lutheranism.
Energies were consumed by these controversies, and little attention was
paid to the dissemination of the Lutheran faith beyond the territories and
cities in which Lutheranism had been established. Calvinism, on the other
hand, was free from such internal dissension and was able to devote its
energies to a dramatic expansion of the Calvinist faith throughout Europe.

The resolution of these intra-Lutheran controversies in 1577 through the
*Formula of Concord* and, in 1580, through the *Book of Concord*, was more
than the end of this incessant internal feuding. It also marked the promulgation of the definitive statement of the meaning of Luther's theological legacy.
The *Book of Concord* expressed what was understood to be Luther's interpretation of the gospel. It included several creeds and confessions which
had remained unchallenged in the various controversies: the Apostles'
Creed; the Nicene Creed; the Athanasian Creed; the *Augsburg Confession*,

together with the *Apology of the Augsburg Confession*; Luther's two catechisms; the *Schmalkald Articles*, and the *Formula of Concord.* Luther's theology was made – through the inclusion of his catechisms and the *Schmalkald
Articles* – the incisive standard for the Lutheran churches as to how to interpret the ancient creeds. Prior to 1580, any number of Lutheran churches in
the various German territories and free cities had adopted their own bodies of normative doctrinal writings, the so-called *corpus doctrinae*, as their
respective rules of faith. A Lutheran pluralism existed. After 1580, such pluralism was replaced by the affirmation of a single book, the *Book of Concord.*
Formal Lutheran theology had been definitively delineated. The controversies ceased. Lutheran pastors pledged allegiance, in their ordination vows,
to the *Book of Concord.*

A further point is worth noting. The theological controversies were resolved not by the instigation of theologians, but by the active intervention of
the political authorities. Though the initial efforts of the Lutheran rulers at
so-called "peace synods" had failed to produce theological agreement, it was
their persistence that in the end carried the day. Without the intervention
of the rulers, the theological controversies would have lasted longer and
been more tediously resolved. As a result of such governmental intervention, however, the power and authority of the rulers, particularly the more
important ones, such as the Saxon elector or the Hessian landgrave, over
ecclesiastical affairs were enhanced. This was a fateful development which –
while by no means confined to Germany and the Lutheran churches – gave
Lutheran rulers in Germany a particularly powerful role in church matters.
This was the beginning of the fateful alliance of "throne and altar," which
tied the Lutheran churches to inordinate subservience to the ruling authorities. In the eighteenth century, to cite just one example, the Prussian King
Frederick William I issued royal directives dealing with liturgical details of
the Lutheran worship service, while early in the nineteenth century King
Frederick William III forced the Lutheran and Reformed churches in Prussia
into a merger, the so-called Church of the Prussian Union.

Martin Luther's increasing importance in the religious tradition he
brought about found expression in the fact that the "churches of the
Augsburg Confession" (as the "Lutheran" churches circumspectly referred
to themselves) adopted the name "Lutheran" in the second half of the sixteenth century, and quite proudly so. Until that time, the term "Lutheran"
had only been used disparagingly by Catholics, while Lutherans themselves
used various circumlocutions, if for no other reason than they wanted to
record their public abhorrence of partisan labels. They called themselves
"evangelicals," "protesting churches" (referring to the "protest" lodged at
the Diet at Speyer in 1529 by the "adherents of the Augsburg Confession").

Aided by such anniversaries as 1583 (the centenary of Luther's birth) and 1617 (the centenary of the Ninety-five Theses), Luther increasingly became the theological canon for the ecclesiastical tradition that bore his name. Moreover, by the end of the sixteenth century Luther himself had become an object of increasingly exuberant veneration.

During the period of the Orthodoxy, which dominated the better part of the seventeenth century, it was, understandably, a theological Luther who was esteemed and lauded. Luther had recovered the pure teaching of the gospel and he was valued because of his teaching.[13] Luther's writings were "a treasure above all treasures." Indeed, Luther was increasingly identified as the apocalyptic angel of the Book of Revelation (14:6), always with the notation that his contribution lay in his recovery of the true biblical teaching.[14] By the middle of the seventeenth century Martin Luther had become, for the Lutheran tradition, the personification of the gospel, which, as professor of theology, he had a bounden duty to interpret properly. At the same time, Orthodox theologians showed little interest in the person of Martin Luther. The divine authorization of his teaching was all-important. At the same time, however, there were also different voices to be heard, that of Johann Saubert, for example, who in his *Lutherus Propheta Germaniae*, of 1632, related Luther's dire warnings of a decline of spirituality in the church to the state of church affairs in the middle of the seventeenth century.

When the Lutheran clergyman Philip Jakob Spener published his *Pia Desideria* in 1675, as a call for enhanced spirituality and piety in the Lutheran churches, and in so doing launched the Pietist movement, he insisted emphatically that he was only seeking to implement what Martin Luther had himself always wanted. Spener acknowledged that Luther's theology was authentically biblical. Quite appropriately Spener wrote that "we praise Luther most highly and almost make an idol of him."[15] But criticism of Luther's personal demeanor – that he was too impulsive, too intense, too uncouth – is also voiced.

At the same time, Spener and the other Pietists expressed grave misgivings about the state of piety in the Lutheran churches, thus echoing the sentiment already found in Saubert's book. Thus, they criticized the tradition that bore Luther's name. Not surprisingly, therefore, the Lutheran establishment felt that the memory of Luther was severely assailed by the Pietists. The Pietists in turn sought to justify their own theological emphases by appealing to the "young" Luther, that is, to the Luther before the year 1525, as over against the "old" Luther. This dichotomy found a first, but classic, expression in Gottfried Arnold's *Unpartheyische Kirchen- und Ketzerhistorie*, of 1699.

The Enlightenment continued to express enthusiasm for Martin Luther, except that it now was a blatantly non-theological Luther who was hailed and praised. The eighteenth century cared little about Luther's theological sentiment, such as his notion of the "hidden God," the *deus absconditus*, but saw him as a gifted and virtuous individual, one who composed Christmas carols which he sang with family and friends around the Christmas tree, one who proved to be a warrior against medieval superstition, an advocate of religious freedom and conscience. Luther's pointed theological opinions about the theology of the cross or about justification were characterized as the "unprofitable, dogmatic extravaganzas of a profound and courageous, though occasionally one-sided spirit."[16] He was the liberator from servile, foreign collectivism, supra-naturalism, superstition, in short, the herald and hero of a new age and the creator of the modern spirit. Luther's historical significance is seen in his courageous defiance of medieval superstition and intolerance, against which he set out his own convictions derived freely from the Bible. Luther was, according to one eighteenth-century author, "a veritable guardian angel for the rights of reason, humanity, and Christian liberty of conscience."[17]

The Luther image of the nineteenth century largely continued the eighteenth-century understanding of the reformer. This image, however, must be seen against the backdrop not only of the theological climate of the nineteenth century, but also of the German intellectual and political history. Most of the anniversaries of the Reformation celebrated in the nineteenth century – the anniversaries of 1517, 1521, 1530, to cite just a few – fell into a time of an emerging German national self-consciousness and nationalism. Not much that was new was said about the theological Luther; the standard Orthodox, Pietist, and Enlightenment perspectives were simply reiterated. What was new, however, was the appropriation of Luther as the quintessential German, the hero of German history. These elements significantly shaped a new Luther picture. Luther was interpreted according to the categories of German Idealistic philosophy. Alongside the reiteration of notions that had been bandied about in the eighteenth century, there now was added a nationalistic sentiment. This distinctly German nineteenth-century appropriation of Luther surely served the need for a common legacy that would serve to give the diverse German states a unified German past. Given the ever-increasing Prussian hegemony in setting a German agenda, Martin Luther suggested himself as an appropriate figure.

This theme was picked up by the German historians of the time, by Leopold von Ranke, Heinrich von Treitschke, and others. Thus, Heinrich von Treitschke wrote in his memorial address on the occasion of the quadricentennial of Luther's birth in 1883:

A foreigner may well ask with consternation how such wonderful contradictions can be together in a single soul – this power of overwhelming anger and this intensity of pious faith, this sublime wisdom and this childish simplicity, this profound mysticism and this *joi de vivre*, this uncouth roughness and this tenderheartedness... We Germans do not find any of this an enigma, we simply state: This is blood of our blood. Out of the deep eyes of the unspoiled German peasant son flashed the ancient "Teutonic heroism which does not seek to escape from the world but seeks to dominate it through the power of the moral will."[18]

Nineteenth-century Protestant theologians from Schleiermacher to Harnack reiterated traditional notions about Luther. Interestingly enough, the most penetrating theological assessment of Luther in the nineteenth century, Theodosius von Harnack's *Luther's Theology* (1862–86), hardly influenced either the theological or the public appropriation of Luther. For non-theological readers it was too theological a work, while theologically interested readers concluded that it was too far removed from concerns of the time. It was too theological, while the perception of Albrecht von Ritschl, who was in fact far less thoroughly acquainted with the reformer's writings, did make an impact in that it succeeded in presenting a picture of Luther that corresponded to the *Zeitgeist*.

Early twentieth-century perceptions of Luther are foremostly associated with the work of Ernst Troeltsch who started out as a systematic theologian but switched to a professorship in philosophy because of his uneasiness with normative, confessional scholarship. Troeltsch doggedly attacked the prevailing picture of Luther that had made him into a champion of modernity and an ur-German. According to Troeltsch, Luther was anything but the progenitor of the modern world. His worldview was medieval, as were his theological concepts. In regard to German political history, Luther was nothing short of a catastrophe, because his conservative-patriarchic worldview made for an undue authoritarian emphasis in German political life, a political passivity of the German people. Moreover, the complete absence of an ethos of a Christian society in Germany must be laid at Martin Luther's doorstep.

Troeltsch was vehemently contested, but his jaundiced view of Luther informed a great deal of the non-confessional perceptions of Luther in the twentieth century. Troeltsch's great opponent was Karl Holl, who more than any other single scholar was responsible for what has been the "Luther Renaissance" of the twentieth century. That is, Holl laid the groundwork for theological appraisals of Luther in the twentieth century. Thus, Holl's themes were Luther's understanding of justification, the wrath of God, and predestination.

Holl inveighed against Troeltsch not only with his insistence that Martin Luther was the pivotal theological figure in the sixteenth century, with all other theologians of the time dependent on him, but also with his argument that Luther was also the pivotal figure for the emergence of modernity in all areas of culture.

The Luther picture of Neo-Orthodoxy essentially echoed the themes of Holl. It is surely telling that many of the scholars who contributed to Luther research in the course of the twentieth century were in fact not historians but systematic theologians, suggesting that the theological appropriation of Luther was as important as the historical one. The names of Paul Althaus, Philip Watson, and Gordon Rupp come to mind.

This close connection between systematic theology and Luther scholarship at once offers an explanation as to why Luther scholarship has been dominated by scholars of Lutheran orientation or sympathies: Germany and the (Lutheran) Scandinavian countries were the centers of scholarship throughout the twentieth century and continue to be highly influential in the present. The English-speaking world of scholarship has tended to be dependent on European continental scholarship.

Not surprisingly, the current phase of Luther scholarship was the result of a convergence of the impact of the Nazi totalitarianism in Germany between 1933 and 1945 and the role the Lutheran churches and theology played during that time, the general increasing focus of historical scholarship on social issues in the past, and also the Luther anniversary.

In short, the Luther of history is a complicated figure, no less ambiguous than sixteenth-century contemporaries found the historical figure. This amazing malleability may convey bewilderment, yet it also denotes a richness of appropriation and helps explain the enduring significance of the reformer. Martin Luther proved a worthwhile paradigm not only for theologians and churchmen, but for statesmen and politicians as well. However guardedly, even Hitler and the Nazis found strikingly positive words to say about the reformer.

## THE GEOGRAPHIC DIMENSION

Martin Luther's influence triggered the establishment of churches eventually bearing his name in many parts of Europe. The Lutheran tradition had its beginnings in Central Germany, from where it spread essentially into a northerly direction. By the time the ecclesiastical ways of Europe had stabilized by the early seventeenth century, two major locales of Lutheran influence had been established – Central and Northern Germany and Scandinavia. In addition, a number of South German cities, such as Nuremberg, had embraced Lutheranism, even as there were pockets of Lutheran congregations in southeastern Europe. Moreover, Lutheran churches were official in central and northern Germany. They had been granted official recognition through the Peace promulgated by the diet at Augsburg in 1555. This Peace stipulated that the ruler should determine the religion of his subjects, a policy which subsequently was expressed by the phrase *"cuius regio, eius religio."* Consequently, Lutheranism in Germany developed along territorial lines.

In Scandinavia, King Gustava Vasa had severed the ties of the Swedish Church with Rome in 1527. As was to be the case in England less than a decade later, this rupture did not entail immediate theological significance, even though the standard Reformation slogans, such as the centrality of the Word of God or the rejection of human tradition, were variably voiced by those advocating reform. In Sweden, even as subsequently in England, the introduction of the Protestant faith was an act of state. Vasa was little interested in theological issues but discerned astutely that the religious turbulence allowed him to confiscate the property of the church and to curtail its political power, both important objectives. Changes in church life, liturgy, and theology were slow in coming. The same held true for Finland which, in the sixteenth century, was part of Sweden.[19] Importantly, the only confessional adapted by the Swedish Church in the sixteenth century was the *Augsburg Confession*, the most ecumenical of Lutheran confessional statements. Moreover, the historic episcopate was retained in Sweden, when in 1531 the Lutheran Laurentius Petri was consecrated by Petrus Magni, bishop of Västeras, and other Swedish bishops, as Archbishop of Uppsala. The bishops undoubtedly saw Laurentius Petri as an Erasmian reformer, albeit fundamentally Roman Catholic. They were mistaken. Laurentius proved to be a determined Lutheran, who capped his many years as archbishop with the promulgation of a church ordinance in 1571 that still lacked Lutheran specifics. Toward the end of the century, under King John III, Sweden almost returned to the Catholic fold. Indeed, had Pope Gregory XIII been willing to accept a married clergy, the vernacular mass, and communion under both kinds, John would have taken the country back to Catholicism. A similar situation occurred under Sigismund III, himself a Catholic. By that time, however, both clergy and people had become so solidly swayed by Lutheranism that Sigismund's efforts failed. Laurentius Petri's church order, which Sigismund had abolished, was reinstated and subscription to the *Augsburg Confession* was required by the Swedish kings.

Perhaps the most notable Luther disciple and critic in the nineteenth century was the Dane Sören Kierkegaard whose own legacy, however, lay not so much in his own time as in posterity, especially in twentieth-century Neo-Orthodoxy.[20] Kierkegaard combined a deep appreciation for Luther, expressed, for example, in his statement "Oh, Luther is, after all, the master of all masters" with increasing criticism of the reformer that matched, in its intensity, the most strident comments levied in the sixteenth century.

When Europeans emigrated to North America in the course of the eighteenth and nineteenth centuries, a notable portion were Lutherans from Scandinavia and Germany. They brought their Lutheran faith with them and the churches they established not only used the Swedish, Finnish, Norwegian, or German vernacular, but were also organized in ethnic synods. Not until the twentieth century did a series of mergers bring about Lutheran ecclesiastical bodies in the United States that transcended the various European ethnic backgrounds.

## Notes

1. WA 188/x, viii, 685.
2. WA 50, 657.
3. The literature on the historical legacy of Martin Luther is extensive. I cite the most important publications: Horst Stephan, *Luther in den Wandlungen seiner Kirche*. 2nd edn. (Berlin: Töpelmann, 1951); Ernst Walter Zeeden, *Martin Luther und die Reformation im Urteil des deutschen Luthertums. Studien zum Selbstverständnis des lutherischen Protestantismus von Luthers Tode bis zum Beginn der Goethezeit*. 2 vols. (Freiburg: Herder, 1950–52); Heinrich Bornkamm, *Luther im Spiegel der deutschen Geistesgeschichte*. 2nd edn. (Göttingen: Vandenhoeck & Ruprecht, 1970); Jaroslav J. Pelikan, ed., *Interpreters of Luther* (Philadelphia: Fortress Press, 1968); A. G. Dickens and John Tonkin, *The Reformation in Historical Thought* (Cambridge, MA: Harvard University Press, 1985).
4. Ernst Heidrich, *Albrecht Dürers schriftlicher Nachlass* (Berlin: J. Bard, 1920), 95f.
5. Zeeden, *Martin Luther*, 1:4ff. Cf. Martin Brecht, *Martin Luther: The Preservation of the Church 1532–1546*, trans. James L. Schaaf (Minneapolis: Fortress Press, 1993), 378–82 and Robert Kolb, *Martin Luther as Prophet, Teacher, and Hero: Images of the Reformer, 1520–1620*. Texts and Studies in Reformation and Post-Reformation Thought (Grand Rapids: Baker, 1999), 34–37.
6. Ibid., 11.
7. On Matthias Flacius Illyricus see Oliver K. Olson, *Matthias Flacius and the Survival of Luther's Reform* (Wiesbaden: Harrassowitz, 2000) and Olson, "Flacius Illyricus, Matthias" in Hans J. Hillerbrand, ed., *The Oxford Encyclopedia of the Reformation*. 4. vols. (New York: Oxford University Press, 1996), ii:110–11.
8. Robert Kolb, *Luther's Heirs Define His Legacy: Studies on Lutheran Confessionalization* (Brookfield, VT: Variorum, 1996).
9. A. J. F. Zieglschmid, ed., *Die älteste Chronik der Hutterischen Brüder* (Ithaca, NY: The Cayuga Press, 1943), 43.

10. Adolf Herte, *Die Lutherkommentare des Johann Cochlaeus* (Münster and Westfalen: Aschendorff, 1935).

11. The most extensive survey of Roman Catholic appraisals of Martin Luther is Adolf Herte, *Das katholische Lutherbild im Bann der Lutherkommentare des Cochlaeus*. 3 vols. (Münster and Westfalen: Aschendorff, 1943).

12. Karl Barth, *Church Dogmatics*. Vol. I/2. (Edinburgh: T&T Clark, 1975), 7.2. The German original is the *Kirchliche Dogmatik* I/I, 292ff.

13. Zeeden, *Martin Luther*, II/101.

14. Ibid., II/105.

15. Ibid., II/195.

16. Christoph Friedrich von Ammon, *Handbuch der christlichen Sittenlehre* (Leipzig, 1823), 77, as quoted by Bornkamm, *Luther*, 17.

17. Friedrich Germanus Lüdke, *Über Toleranz und Geistesfreiheit, insofern der rechtmäßige Religionseifer sie befördert und der unrechtmäßige sie verhindert* (Berlin, 1774), 204.

18. Bornkamm, *Luther*, 45.

19. Simo Heininen, "Finland" in *The Oxford Encyclopedia of the Reformation* (New York: Oxford University Press, 1996), II:106–08 (with bibliography).

20. Probably still the best study placing Kierkegaard into a broader theological context is Jaroslav J. Pelikan, *From Luther to Kierkegaard* (St. Louis: Concordia Publishing House, 1950).

# 15 Approaching Luther

JAMES ARNE NESTINGEN

## THE PERSON AND THE SYMBOL

Martin Luther the historical figure assigned to teach biblical studies at an obscure university in the eastern part of what is now Germany and Martin Luther, cultural symbol, parted company on or about October 31, 1517, and have had an unpredictable relationship ever since. Assessing the differences is the critical task in approaching this compellingly attractive and equally repugnant man.

The historical dimensions of Luther's life follow a familiar pattern. The son of an upwardly mobile miner, Hans Luder or Ludder, and of the daughter of a fairly prominent family, Margarethe Lindemann,[1] he was set aside for a career in law. In the course of his studies, Luther believed himself to have been redirected toward a religious vocation – a crossover well known to law and theological faculties. When he took orders as an Augustinian monk, Luther attracted a mentor, Johan von Staupitz, who promoted his career, moving him forward in the order.[2]

Luther's academic career was also fairly routine, at least in its outline. Upon completion of the doctorate, while taking his share of pastoral duties, the young monk was assigned to teach courses in Old and New Testament at the University of Wittenberg, a town of 2,000 that was the capital of Electoral Saxony. As a teacher, he was caught up in an occupational hazard of academic life: academic, churchly, and political polemics. Though his personal circumstances changed – most dramatically in being excommunicated, outlawed, and for all of this, marrying[3] – Luther continued his vocation until his death, in February of 1546. If events had not combined to put him in a symbolic spotlight, the story would have ended right there.

The beginnings of Luther's career as a symbol, in which he was taken as a representative of something larger, beyond himself, are also touched with the common. Like many a young theologian, as he worked with the assigned sources, he came to the conviction that the Catholic tradition had missed the heart of the biblical witness. Living in a daily monastic rhythm of the Psalms,

240

working particularly closely with Paul's Letter to the Romans, Luther came to believe that God's grace is not an addition to creation but a sovereign act of new creation in Christ, freeing his own to live in a naked trust of the goodness of God.[4] At some point in this process of reinterpretation, following an intellectual fad, he changed his name, shifting the spelling of the family name to give it a more ancient but radical ring – Lu*th*er is a pun on the Greek word for freedom, *eleutherius*.

Luther's "evangelical breakthrough," as it has often been called, might have been enough by itself to give him some symbolic status. Historically, the church has had difficulty with words like grace, especially as correlated with faith and freedom.[5] But even if unaware, Luther himself provided occasion for the escalation that followed. Seeing a stark contrast between his newly refined biblical understanding and the medieval practice of penance, particularly the sale of indulgences as entitlements to absolution, he went looking for a public debate. For this purpose, he posted a series of Ninety-five Theses on the town bulletin board, the church door. In the remarkable chain of events that followed, acting but even more acted upon, Luther was swept up by the symbol-making forces of late medieval culture and has remained a primarily symbolic figure ever since.[6]

To the extent that Luther contributed to this process, a critical factor was undoubtedly his power with language. His mother tongue was Middle High German, the dialect spoken in his native Saxony. He was equally at home in medieval Latin, the international language of the time, and had mastered both Hebrew and Greek. Though he had a strong preference for oral forms like preaching and lecturing, Luther quickly learned to exploit the comparatively recent medium of print. Concrete, colorful, tender, humorous, extravagant, laced with both irony and outrage, often gross and occasionally obscene, generally precise yet also apparently hyperbolic if not inflammatory, Luther's language drew him a large audience.[7]

Luther wrote voluminously the rest of his life, multiplying treatises with popular tracts, educational works, and letters. What he didn't put to paper himself, his students transcribed, lectures and sermons as well as table conversations. The Weimar Ausgabe, the critical edition of his collected works, runs to over 125 folio size volumes.

Recognizing a ready market, unrestrained by copyright laws, printers picked up what was published in Wittenberg to sell their own editions. At a point in the 1520s, three-quarters of the work in print in German came from Luther's pen.[8] His translations of Christian Scripture – he did the Old Testament in its entirety twice and the New Testament three times – had a more lasting impact than all the polemics. Luther is considered to hold the same position in the German language that Shakespeare and the King James Bible have in English.

But if Luther had a singular power with language, there were bigger forces at work in sixteenth-century life inflating his work with significance far beyond his own intentions.

One such force was Northern European Renaissance humanism. A loosely affiliated movement of academics, churchmen and politicians with a working loyalty to Erasmus of Rotterdam, the great intellect of the period, they shared a historically romantic vision of personal and public reform. The humanists quickly saw Luther's potential for their program and began to spread his Theses. In the process, they made Luther into something he hadn't wanted to be and in fact, resisted. They made him a reformer.[9]

The Roman Catholic curia, the papal court, was just about as fast, if not faster, at making Luther a symbol. Sensing a threat to papal preeminence before he even thought of the possibility, they took hasty steps to limit damages, moving against Luther through the Augustinians and then in other quasi-official ways. In the process, the "papists," as they were called, not only pushed Luther to draw out more radical implications of his breakthrough but also made him symbolize something he didn't want, rebellion against the Catholic tradition.[10]

German politicians, long frustrated with Mediterranean political and economic dominance, weren't far behind the humanists and church officials, sensing the symbolism of Luther's protests. They saw in him the possibility of rejoinder against the cultural hegemony of southern Europe, moving to greater independence. Here Luther was more amenable. As the controversy occasioned by the Ninety-five Theses escalated, he wrote one of his classic treatises of 1520, *To the Christian Nobility of the German Nation*, calling them to take a hand in reshaping the German Church.

Another lesser known but in the end even more important group also began to sense a symbol in Luther's protest. Economic factors, among them inflation induced by returns from the great voyages of European discovery in Africa, Asia, and the Americas, were forcing Europe as a whole and Germany in particular out of the feudal system into a cash economy. This along with dramatic population growth produced deep discontent on the farms and with it an exodus to the newly developing German cities. Farmers and city migrants seeking a new way of life saw in Luther a symbol of new possibilities. Though the Peasants' War of 1525 strained Luther's relationship with farm protest, here, too, he was much more amenable to his symbolic employment, speaking and writing for the popular audience. His reinterpretation of the tradition was especially important in the emerging cities.[11]

Still another symbolic interpretation grew out of the tenor of late medieval life. As Heiko Oberman pointed out in his definitive work on the context of the Reformation, it was an apocalyptic age, conditions of the time combining to support a widespread conviction that the end of the created world was imminent, that Christ would be returning momentarily to bring all things under his judgment.[12] In fact, when Jean Hus, the Czech reformer of a century earlier, was burned at the stake, he allegedly punned on his own name, saying, "Now they roast a goose, but in a hundred years they will hear a swan singing, which they will not be able to do away with…"[13] It was widely believed that Luther was the swan Hus had prophesied, the swan becoming a common sign for Luther's work and he himself being regarded as a prophet of biblical proportions, a new Elijah sent in preparation for the impinging end. In fact, later on in the reform, Luther accepted this interpretation of his work.[14]

The dramatic events of the early 1520s gave credence to Luther's prophetic standing. From the obscurity of his monastic, pastoral, and academic work in Wittenberg, he was catapulted to the center of German and even European public life, drawing support and attacks from as far away as England. Late in 1520, he responded to a final papal attempt at subordination by gathering faculty and students by the River Elbe to burn the canon law. This occasion, in which the traditional regulations of the law of the church were set aside on the basis of Scripture and the claims of conscience, has been interpreted as the end of the Middle Ages and the beginning of the modern period, a prophetic turn.[15]

Luther quickly began to collect a prophet's reward. Excommunicated in January of 1521, he was soon summoned to appear before the Holy Roman Emperor, by connections if not by office the most powerful political figure in Europe. Standing alone before the crowned heads of the German people, he spoke in phrases that quickly became legendary, even if not fully attested: "Unless I am convinced by the testimony of Scriptures, or by evident reason… I am bound by the scriptural evidence adduced by me, and my conscience is captive to the Word of God… Here I stand! I can do no other!"[16] Condemned as an outlaw, Luther was spirited away to the Wartburg castle, eventually returning to Wittenberg. In the minds of theologians like his closest associate, Philip Melanchthon, and John Calvin, who regarded himself as Luther's successor, as well as in the popular imagination, Luther had been confirmed as a "different order of man," God's prophet.[17]

Luther has retained his symbolic standing since the sixteenth century, even if more recently it has become primarily negative.

Lutherans themselves divided over his legacy not long after his death. In the later 1530s and early 1540s, Melanchthon – Luther's first interpreter – had given Luther's dialectics his own turn. Even as they divided amongst themselves over his revisions, Melanchthon and his students made Luther into the restorer of *reine Lehre*, pure doctrine, setting the foundations for Lutheran orthodoxy.[18]

Pietism and Rationalism, later schools of Lutheranism, claimed Luther's symbolic authority for their own idiosyncrasies. To the Pietists, Luther's religious experience – his despairing quest for assurance and his conversion – became normative. The Rationalists focused on Luther's critical assessment of Scripture and the church's tradition, presenting him as a pioneer in the liberation of the individual conscience.[19]

Just this is enough to indicate the peril in approaching Luther on the basis of Lutheranism. The historical connection between the man and the church that still bears his name is so qualified by other influences, causes, and conditions, that correspondence cannot be assumed. Rather, it has to be established according to the canons of historical argument.

Other Christians in the sixteenth century had their own interpretations of Luther. The polemics against him generated early in the Reformation continued unabated among Roman Catholic theologians. His father was an incubus, a minor devil in human form, his mother a bath house attendant; together they produced the heresiarch who divided the church to seduce a nun into his clutches. In fact, such treatments survived well into the twentieth century.[20] The Protestant tradition, developing out of the southwest German and Swiss reform to take hold, under dispute, in France, the British Isles, and the Netherlands, treated Luther in a more positive, measured way. He provided a starting point to be adjusted and corrected on the basis of the standard being proffered as the more appropriate alternative.

With the establishment of the Enlightenment in Western Europe and North America, Luther's symbolic fortunes have varied. Treated by some as a romantic hero standing in the face of established authority for the sake of individual rights, he has also been suspected of dogmatic authoritarianism. Either way, for German theologians in particular, he remained a shibboleth. Neo-Orthodoxy – the theological movement that developed out of the ashes of World War I – again made Luther a principal partner in theological conversation.[21]

Since World War II, Luther's symbolic standing has lost much of its luster, two indictments detaching themselves from historical inquiry to gain a life of their own in the culture. One is a charge of political passivity, originally set out forcefully in the American theological discussion by Reinhold Niebuhr and his students.[22] Popularized by William I. Shirer in his *Rise and Fall of the Third Reich*, this criticism is commonly invoked as axiomatic.[23] More recently, a particularly vituperous treatise Luther wrote in the 1540s has generated a standing charge of anti-Semitism. The issue has produced some extensive scholarship, indicating its historical complexity.[24] Again Luther's linguistic power, magnificent and horrible, has provided a basis for detaching the indictment from its historical origins to make it a standing assumption about his work, as is evident in the treatment of Luther in the Holocaust Museum in Washington, D.C. In a popular culture that treasures openness as a supreme virtue, this by itself is commonly considered grounds for dismissal.

Luther's symbolic standing made him one of the prime candidates for study in the advent of historical criticism in the nineteenth century, an examination that has continued ever since, ranking him with the apostle Paul and St. Augustine as the most scrutinized. Such an old, rich, and variegated tradition of studies has made it possible to break in underneath the symbolic discussion to analyze the historical proportions of the person and his work. Cultural symbols have their own value and purpose, to be sure, and will continue to exercise influence regardless of the findings of scholarship. But just such standing demands continuing historical review if the symbolic is not going to empty itself into meaninglessness. Luther studies make such historical examination possible.

## THE TEXTS

The first task in a historical approach to Luther is to establish just what he said and didn't say, a task rendered difficult by Luther's preeminence and the chaotic flow of print in the Reformation. In fact, some important works, such as Luther's early commentaries on the Epistle to the Romans and the Book of Hebrews, weren't even located until early in the twentieth century. But while there are still occasional discoveries of, for instance, a sermon or a letter, after more than a century and a half of critical research, the texts have been established and are widely available.

The Walch or St. Louis and the Erlangen editions are among the most important early attempts to set out critically attested texts. Both were significant advances in their times, the eighteenth and nineteenth centuries. They were superseded by the Weimar Edition, which began publication in the 1880s. There may be some rare instances where the Weimar requires slight correction, but it is the definitive text of Luther's German and Latin, the standard for critical work.[25]

Early on, English translations of some of Luther's work began to appear. The best known is the Middleton Edition of the Galatians Commentary.[26] Luther's text was produced from notes by one of his most reliable editors, George Rörer, in 1531 and revised by Luther for publication in 1535. It was translated by Erasmus Middleton later in the sixteenth century and reissued in a modern edition in the 1950s.

One of the best twentieth-century collections of Luther's works in English was edited by Henry Eyster Jacobs and published in 1915. Translated by a group of faculty and parish pastors that included Jacobs himself, his brother Charles M. Jacobs, and several others, the six volumes came to be known as the Holman or, more commonly, the Philadelphia edition.[27] It went through several printings and, into the 1950s, set the standard for English language texts of Luther's treatises. Though long out of print, it is still treasured by those who know it and can sometimes be found for sale.

Another English selection of Luther's writings, once again widely available but of limited value, contains some of his examinations of the texts assigned to various Sundays of the church year. Though published under the title *Sermons of Martin Luther*,[28] they are more sermon helps written to assist preachers in their own preparations. Such work was called a *Postil* – Luther began work on it when he was at the Wartburg castle. Picking up the project again in the mid-1520s, he completed about half of the church year. A later editor threw together notes from the preaching of Luther and others to complete the cycle, publishing the collection over Luther's objections in the 1540s. J. N. Lenker edited an English translation in 1905 that has been reissued. Some of the earlier helps turn into classic sermons but the later editorial work and inadequate translation make the collection unreliable for scholarly purposes.

In the 1950s, the American Edition of Luther's Works (LW) began publication under the editorship of Helmut Lehman and Jaroslav Pelikan. Fifty-five volumes in contrast to the Weimar, more than twice its size, the American Edition still contains almost all of Luther's most important work. The first thirty volumes are devoted to Luther's exegetical lectures. The remaining twenty-five volumes translate Luther's occasional writings. They are organized by topics, beginning with Career of the Reformer (31–34), then Word and Sacrament (35–38), Church and Ministry (39–41), Devotional Writings (42–43), The Christian and Society (44–47), Letters (48–50), and Sermons (51–52), followed by single volumes of Liturgy and Hymns, the Table Talk and an index.

The work of a number of scholars, some of them more at home in the language than in Luther scholarship, the American edition is not entirely even in quality. The volumes of letters, edited by Gottfried Krodel of Valparaiso University, set the highest standard. For scholarly purposes, all the translations have to be checked against the original texts in the Weimar, a problem given the American Edition's failure to provide corresponding

pagination in the Weimar text.[29] But that said the American Edition provides the current standard for English translations.

Two other single volumes should be noted. One is the translation of
*The Bondage of the Will* by Packer and Johnston, which captures some more
of the spirit of Luther's great polemic against Erasmus.[30] Another, originally published in the Library of Christian Classics, is *Luther's Letters of
Spiritual Counsel*, edited by Theodore G. Tappert. It provides an invaluable
introduction to the pastoral dimension of Luther's work.[31]

Timothy F. Lull has edited the best one-volume selection, *Martin Luther's
Basic Theological Writings*, using the American Edition texts.[32] For preliminary acquaintance, Lull's collection is the place to begin.

Such a one-volume work illustrates a compelling problem in Luther's
studies, wading through the sheer mass to get to what is most important.
It often appears that if Luther did not write down everything that came
into his head, one of his students or another admirer was ready at hand to
transcribe it. Though he had firsthand experience with the power of print,
he had little or no concept of the use that would be made of his work. When
he did think about such a problem, he spoke of himself in self-deprecating
terms, expressing the hope that most all of his writings would disappear.[33]

With this, however, Luther singled out a few works that he considered
worth survival: the Catechism, a term assumed to apply to his *Small* and
*German* or *Large* Catechisms, written late in the 1520s, and *The Bondage of
the Will*. Upon further reflection, he certainly could have added the 1520
treatise, *On the Freedom of the Christian*, and his Galatians Commentary of
1535. There are some other works, all of them included in Lull, that Luther
scholars might want to add to such a short list, the sermon on *Two Kinds of
Righteousness*, for example, but these clearly hold the center. Any historical
interpretation of Luther has to be tested by such works.

READING LUTHER

Best known as a reformer and theologian, Luther was at the same time
a pastor, teacher, confessor, outlaw, prophet, political advisor, husband, and
father. Juggling these vocations, he had a prodigious capacity for work,
regularly disappearing into his study for days at a time. But the relentless
demands still required him to write catch-as-catch-can, spinning off pamphlets, picking up a treatise for some work, dropping it and returning to it
later.

While it isn't the only factor involved, the helter-skelter points to a basic
characteristic of Luther's writing: it is occasional. While working out distinctions he thought required by his leading assumption, God's justifying

act in Christ Jesus, he at the same time closely considered the particular situation that drew his attention and addressed it specifically without apparent regard for what might be required in another circumstance. For this reason, approaching individual comments or works of Luther, whether on their own terms or in comparison with other works, the occasion always has to be registered.

Luther's attitudes on political resistance provide a classic example. In the 1520s, the threat of the emperor declared in the Edict of Worms, which proscribed the Wittenberg reform, was compounded by rising insurgency in the farming communities. At this time, Luther was convinced that armed resistance would just exacerbate injustice and wrote some treatises, such as *Temporal Authority: To What Extent It Should Be Obeyed*,[34] in which he urged what is now called passive resistance. In the later 1530s and 40s, as Charles V was claiming the religious authority to enforce an end to the Lutheran movement, Luther saw a parallel to the biblical books of Daniel and Revelation and opened up the possibility of violent resistance.[35] If the writings of either the 1520s or the 1540s are abstracted from their situation to be treated in isolation, the picture is incomplete.

Similarly, Luther's attitude toward Judaism changed over the years. Through the earlier part of the Reformation, he made numerous statements that in light of the prevailing anti-Semitism of medieval Europe have been considered positive. As reprehensible as it is, Luther wrote *On the Jews and Their Lies* in a specific personal and relational situation. While these occasional characteristics do not justify such writing, they do qualify historical claims to anti-Semitism.[36] Either way, treated in isolation, neither the earlier comments nor the later writing are sufficient to establish a reliable academic argument.

A second characteristic feature to be noted when reading Luther is the shape of his dialectic. Post-Enlightenment theological work reflects the Hegelian thesis-antithesis-synthesis scheme, the synthesis interpreted as gathering up and embracing or "dirempting" (Hegel's term: *aufheben)* the prior thesis and antithesis in order to form yet a new statement or thesis. At the University of Erfurt, Luther studied with one of the two greatest logicians in late medieval Europe, Jacobus Trutvetter, a Nominalist who by his philosophical training was hesitant about the possibility of establishing a synthesis, specifically in relationship to God.[37] Luther's dialectical reasoning is pre-Enlightenment in this sense. Instead of attempting to resolve them into a synthesis, Luther sets out thesis and antithesis and lets them stand. In fact, he delights in the opposition, pushing out the poles of the dialectic so that while they appear to be mutually exclusive, they in fact are both true and so qualify one another.

A definitive example can be seen in Luther's statements about the law. One of the immediate consequences of Luther's conviction of God's sovereign act of grace in Christ Jesus is a particular appreciation for the Pauline critique of the law. In Luther's reading, the logic is irrefutably simple: if Christ justifies, the law not only cannot but was never meant to do so.[38] At this pole of the dialectic, he regularly argued the termination of the law – its futility, emptiness, and suspension in the faithful's sense of self in relation to God, the neighbor, and the earth itself (the conscience). Just so, however, having been reduced to terms, at the other pole of the dialectic, the law shows its real value in regulating creaturely life and, under the power of the Holy Spirit, driving the sinner to Christ. Thus working the dialectic, Luther can declare that Moses, personifying the law, is dead, "his rule ended when Christ came," but can also call Moses the first Christian, "the fountainhead out of which all good works must flow."[39]

Given this way of thinking, approaching Luther historically requires recognition of both sides of the dialectic and leaving them where Luther did, at loose ends. If one pole is taken in isolation from the other, a temptation given the characteristic color and apparent extravagance of the statements, the essential qualification of the other pole gets lost. By the same token, resolving the dialectic may serve the purposes of a post-Enlightenment way of thinking more confident of its ability to make ultimate sense of the world, but requires a historical disconnection from the sources.

## SECONDARY SOURCES

### Biographies

Luther's strategic importance in the Reformation, his symbolic standing in Western culture, and his self-disclosiveness have combined to draw the attention of a whole series of biographers, some more popular, some more psychological, and others more scholarly.

Roland Bainton, who had a wonderful sense of Luther's color and humor, produced what has long been a standard for English readers, *Here I Stand*. James Kittelson's *Luther the Reformer* catches the same spirit as Bainton's romanticism. Two other volumes, also written for a wider audience on the basis of careful scholarly work, are Eric Gritsch's *Martin – God's Court Jester* and Peter Manns' originally coffee-table-size illustrated work, *Martin Luther*. Manns, a German Roman Catholic, had a particularly well-developed sense of the Catholic elements of Luther's work. Any one of these works makes a good starting point.[40]

Though it has been critically faulted historically, Erik Erikson's *Young Man Luther* has long drawn interest for its psychological treatment. John

M. Todd, who represents a recent Roman Catholic interest in Luther, also offers a more psychologically oriented portrait in his *Luther: A Life*.[41]

The standard for scholarly biography was set in the twentieth century by Heinrich Boehmer's *Road to Reformation*, which ends with the Diet of Worms. Heinrich Bornkamm, a great German scholar, wrote a sequel entitled *Luther in Mid-Career*, finishing his work with the Diet of Augsburg in 1530. Both volumes are now somewhat dated, but they are classics. Martin Brecht has claimed the new standard in his three-volume *Martin Luther*. The third volume covers Luther's later years, which were also the subject of H. G. Haile in *Luther: An Experiment in Biography*. Haile is less methodical than Brecht but has something of Bainton's flare. An important one-volume scholarly biography that should be noted is Heiko Oberman's *Luther: God Between Man and the Devil*.[42]

### Theology

A massive library confronts those who wish to study Luther's theology, whether as a whole or in any of its various parts. Here, too, there are some classical studies written for a wider audience that provide starting points, along with full-dress scholarly treatments which have been orienting.

Lennart Pinomaa, long-time professor at the University of Helsinki who came to his studies of Luther out of a broadly Evangelical tradition, wrote one of the very best introductions to Luther's theology for a wider audience in *Faith Victorious*. Though long out of print, it is well worth the search. Gerhard Forde's *Where God Meets Man: Luther's Down to Earth Approach to the Gospel* uses a different method but to even greater effect, focusing on the turnabout at the center of Luther's theological work and its consequences for his thought.[43]

Though he was personally compromised in the rise of Nazism, Paul Althaus' single-volume scholarly survey of Luther's theology served a generation. Its place has recently been taken by two volumes from Bernhard Lohse, a leading German Luther scholar of a later generation. The first, *Martin Luther: An Introduction to his Life and Work*, summarizes the main features and problems in Luther biography and then gives an invaluable overview of Luther scholarship, going back to the beginnings of what has been called the Luther renaissance. The second, *Martin Luther's Theology: Its Historical and Systematic Development*, exposes the anchors of Luther's theological reflection in his historical conditions before expositing some of the main themes. The discussion of the conflict between Luther and Erasmus and Lohse's treatment of Luther's understanding of predestination are not up to the same standard, but the two volumes together set a benchmark for Luther studies.[44]

Making a list of definitive scholarly studies of individual themes in Luther's theology always invites correction – inevitably, there is just one more that should be added. But there are some works that have so distinguished themselves that no approach to Luther would be complete without their mention. Some of the most important follow.

Though they come from early in the twentieth century and are controlled by an idealistic understanding of conscience no longer widely accepted, Karl Holl's studies in Luther are foundational. A basic selection is available in *The Cultural Significance of the Reformation* and *The Reconstruction of Morality*. One of Holl's students, Wilhelm Pauck, taught at Union Seminary in New York, shaping a generation of American Luther scholars, and left his own legacy in *The Heritage of the Reformation*.[45]

Since Holl, German Luther scholarship has laid claim to a prior authority in Luther studies. One classic is Walter von Loewenich's *Luther's Theology of the Cross*. Translated into English some fifty years after it was written, it is still an orienting work. Hans Joachim Iwand, regarded by some leading scholars themselves as the best Luther scholar of the twentieth century, has still not been translated. His studies of Luther's doctrine of justification, shaped out of a lifelong conversation with Karl Barth, are formative. A contemporary of Iwand's, like him an implacable critic of the Nazis, was more exclusively Lutheran – Hermann Sasse. He wrote the definitive treatment of Luther's sacramental theology, *This is My Body*. Gerhard Ebeling, best known for his theological work with existentialism, was also a meticulously careful expositor of Luther. Though it can test a reader's patience, his *Word and Faith* offers some definitive studies in Luther's two-kingdoms distinction and his understanding of law.[46]

The other main center of Luther scholarship in Europe has been in Scandinavia, which has had its own scholarly traditions, less indebted to German Idealism and more oriented toward Luther's understanding of creation and creatureliness. For several generations, the center of such work was the University of Lund, in southern Sweden. Though the English translation has often been criticized, Regin Prenter's *Spiritus Creator* is a classical study of Luther's doctrine of the Holy Spirit. Gustaf Wingren's *Luther on Vocation*, interpreting the concept of the callings of everyday life, has been definitive. More recently, Leif Grane, teaching at the University of Copenhagen, has carried on the tradition. Though it hasn't ever been translated, his study of Luther's early theological method is basic. Tuomo Mannermaa, Pinomaa's successor at Helsinki, has been particularly influential in ecumenical studies of Luther.[47]

Two other Europeans have to be mentioned. Gordon Rupp, an English Methodist, collected some classic essays in *The Righteousness of God*, which has been widely influential, especially for English speakers. Writing in French while teaching in Strasbourg, on the German border, Marc Lienhard published the definitive study of Luther's Christology in *Luther: Witness to Jesus Christ.*[48]

One of the most important developments in twentieth-century Luther scholarship was the emergence of a much more appreciative school of Roman Catholics. For generations, Catholic scholarly approaches to Luther were shaped by Heinrich Denifle, a late nineteenth-century Vatican librarian whose *Luther und Luthertum* was a virtual catalog of polemics. Joseph Lortz, a German Catholic of World War II vintage, turned the tide, arguing that Luther had reacted against a Catholicism insufficiently Catholic in that it had departed from its proper Thomistic origins. There is a rich catalog of work since Lortz, but two in particular should be mentioned. One is a massive comparison of Luther and Thomas by Otto Pesch, still not translated. The other, provocatively mistitled by its American publishers *Luther: Right or Wrong?*, provides an extended analysis of Luther's arguments on the bound will, written by Harry McSorley. Roman Catholic Luther scholarship has had a strong influence in the American ecumenical discussion.[49]

Since Bainton and Pauck, American Luther scholarship has been generated primarily out of two sources: Harvard University, particularly in the years of Heiko Oberman, who after some years back in Europe returned to teach at Arizona; and Stanford University under Lewis Spitz. Oberman's Harvard legacy has been in the hermeneutics of Luther; Spitz's in the relationship of the Renaissance and the Reformation. In the last decades of the twentieth century, the theological study of Luther lost its preeminence to social, political, and other forms of historical study. Duke University in particular but also Princeton and some of the Lutheran seminaries have carried on the tradition.

In addition to book-length studies, there are some periodical sources that are essential. The *Luther Jahrbuch*, which has been published in Germany since 1919, provides a yearly review of critical scholarship. The *Archiv für Reformationsgeschichte* is the important German journal. In English, the *Luther Digest*, published by the Luther Academy in Crestwood, Missouri, offers "An Annual Abridgement of Luther Studies," using both English-language and European sources. The *Sixteenth Century Journal*, the *Lutheran Quarterly* and *Dialog* also publish articles of interest.

### Notes

1. Ian Siggins, *Luther and His Mother* (Philadelphia: Fortress Press, 1981), 20–29.
2. David C. Steinmetz, *Luther and Staupitz: An Essay in the Intellectual Origins of the Protestant Reformation* (Durham: Duke University Press, 1980).

3. The best introduction to Katharina von Bora, who gained a status in the Wittenberg reform beyond her marital vocation as Mrs. Martin Luther, is in Roland Bainton, *Women of the Reformation in Germany and Italy* (Minneapolis: Augsburg Publishing House, 1970), 23–44.

4. For one of Luther's accounts, see LW 34, 336–37. The dating and nature of Luther's "tower experience," his evangelical breakthrough, have been the subjects of extensive scholarly debate. For a classic statement, see Gordon Rupp, "The Righteousness of God," in *The Righteousness of God: Luther Studies* (London: Hodder and Stoughton, 1953), 121–37.

5. For a historical perspective on the issue, see Walter Bauer, *Orthodoxy and Heresy in Earliest Christianity*, ed. Robert Kraft and Gerhard Krodel (Philadelphia: Fortress Press, 1971). For a larger perspective, see Fyodor Dostoyevsky, "The Grand Inquisitor," in *The Brothers Karamazov*.

6. Robert Kolb, *Martin Luther as Prophet, Teacher, and Hero: Images of the Reformer, 1520–1620* (Grand Rapids: Baker, 1999), 9.

7. Luther's concept of language, particularly of the power of words to break beyond signification to affect what they declare, is critical to understanding his way of thinking. As he wrote in a programmatic set of theses early in his career, the *Heidelberg Disputations*, "The law says, 'Do this,' and it is never done. Grace says, 'Believe in this,' and everything is already done" (LW 31, 41) – the law is significative, depending on the will of its hearer for its implementation; in grace, God's word creates the new reality. See Gerhard Ebeling, "The Word of God and Tradition," in *The Word of God and Tradition*, trans. S. H. Hooke (Philadelphia: Fortress Press, 1964), 102–47.

8. Elizabeth L. Eisenstein, "The Advent of Printing and the Protestant Revolt: A New Approach to the Disruption of Western Christendom," in Robert M. Kingdon, ed., *Transition and Revolution: Problems and Issues of European Renaissance and Reformation History* (Minneapolis: Burgess Publishing Company, 1974), 235.

9. Even though known by the title, Luther did not think of himself as a reformer. He had a more proximate goal, in keeping with his vocation – to improve the preaching. See Bernhard Lohse, *Luther: An Introduction to his Life and Work*, trans. Robert C. Schultz (Minneapolis: Fortress Press, 1980), 92.

10. Luther's relationship to the Catholic tradition has been heavily debated. An argument for his identification with Catholicism is Jaroslav Pelikan, *Obedient Rebels: Catholic Substance and Protestant Principle in Luther's Reformation* (New York: Harper and Row, 1964).

11. The foundations for this argument were laid by Brend Moeller in *Imperial Cities and the Reformation: Three Essays* (Philadelphia: Fortress Press, 1972), and built upon by Steven Ozment, *The Reformation in the Cities* (New Haven and London: Yale University Press, 1975).

12. Heiko Augustinus Oberman, *Forerunners of the Reformation: The Shape of Late Medieval Thought* (New York: Holt, Rinehardt and Winston, 1966), 9ff. See also his *The Harvest of Medieval Theology: Gabriel Biel and Late Medieval Nominalism* (Grand Rapids: William B. Eerdmans Publishing Company, 1967).

13. Oberman, *Forerunners*, 18.

14. Ibid. See also Karl Holl, "Martin Luther on Luther," in Jaroslav Pelikan, ed., *Interpreters of Luther: Essays in Honor of Wilhelm Pauck* (Philadelphia: Fortress Press, 1968), 9–34.

15. Gordon Rupp, quoted by James Atkinson in *The Trial of Luther* (New York: Stein and Day, 1971), 95.
16. Ibid., 161f.
17. LCC 22, 185.
18. The relationship between Luther and Melanchthon is a perennial issue in Reformation studies: it has been the topic of two International Luther Congresses. For a range of views see Franz Hildebrandt, *Melanchthon: Alien or Ally?* (Cambridge: Cambridge University Press, 1946); Vilmos Vajta, ed., *Luther and Melanchthon* (Philadelphia: Fortress Press, 1962) and Timothy J. Wengert, "Beyond Stereotypes: The Real Philip Melanchthon," in Scott Hendrix and Timothy J. Wengert, eds., *Philip Melanchthon Then and Now (1497–1997)* (Columbia, SC: Lutheran Southern Theological Seminary, 1997), 9–32. On later sixteenth-century interpretations of Luther see Kolb, *Martin Luther*, 17–126.
19. Theodore G. Tappert, "Orthodoxism, Pietism and Rationalism (1580–1830)," in Harold C. Letts, ed., *Christian Social Responsibility*, II, *The Lutheran Heritage* (Philadelphia: Muhlenberg Press, 1957), 36–88.
20. Siggins, *Luther and His Mother*, 32–44. The most influential popular Roman Catholic treatment of Luther from an earlier day is an adaptation of a three-volume German work by Hartmann Grisar, S.J., *Martin Luther: His Life and Work*, adapted by Frank J. Eble, ed. Arthur Preuss (Westminster, MD: The Newman Press, 1954).
21. For a study of this period see James M. Stayer, *Martin Luther: German Saviour: German Evangelical Theological Factions and the Interpretation of Luther, 1917–1933* (Montreal and Kingston: McGill-Queen's University Press, 2000).
22. For a discussion of Niebuhr's critique, see Wilhelm Pauck, "Luther and the Reformation," in *The Heritage of the Reformation* (Oxford: Oxford University Press, 1961), 12–16. See also Douglas John Hall, *Lighten our Darkness: Towards an Indigenous Theology of the Cross* (Philadelphia: Westminster Press, 1976), 146ff.
23. For a critical review of the arguments, see Uwe Siemon-Netto, *The Fabricated Luther: The Rise and Fall of the Shirer Myth* (St. Louis: Concordia Publishing House, 1995).
24. Heiko A. Oberman, *The Roots of Anti-Semitism in the Age of Renaissance and Reformation*, trans. James I. Porter (Philadelphia: Fortress Press, 1984).
25. The challenge of cross-referencing texts in the various editions can be met by using Kurt Aland, Ernst Otto Reichert and Gerhard Jordan, *Hilfsbuch zum Lutherstudium*, 3rd edn. (Witten/Ruhr: Luther-Verlag, 1970).
26. Philip Watson, ed., *A Commentary on St. Paul's Epistle to the Galatians*, rev. and completed edn. (Cambridge and London: James Clark & Co., Ltd., 1953).
27. Henry Eyster Jacobs, ed., *Works of Martin Luther* (Philadelphia: A.J. Holman Co., 1915).
28. J. N. Lenker, ed., *Sermons of Martin Luther*, trans. John Nicholas Lenker and others (Grand Rapids: Baker, 1983).
29. Heinrich J. Vogel has corrected this problem in a separate volume, *Vogel's Cross Reference and Index to the Contents of Luther's Works* (Milwaukee: Northwestern Publishing House, 1983). Vogel uses the Aland-Reichert-Jordan numbers, correlating LW with WA, the Erlangen edition and the Walch.

30. J. I. Packer and O. R. Johnston, eds. and trans., *Martin Luther on the Bondage of the Will* (Westwood, NJ: Fleming H. Revell Co., 1937).
31. Philadelphia: Westminster Press, Library of Christian Classics, 28.
32. Minneapolis: Fortress Press, 1989.
33. LW 34, 283, 328.
34. LW 45, 75–130.
35. W. D. J. Cargill-Thompson traces Luther's development on this issue in "Luther and the Right of Resistance to the Emperor," in C. W. Dugmore, ed., *Studies in the Reformation: Luther to Hooker* (London: The Athlone Press, 1980), 3–41.
36. Mark U. Edwards Jr., *Luther's Last Battles: Politics and Polemics, 1531–46* (Ithaca and London: Cornell University Press, 1983), 115–42.
37. Nominalism and Luther's relationship to it have been closely studied over the past several decades, following the publication of Oberman's *Harvest of Medieval Theology* – see note 12.
38. WA 39.1, 347.
39. LW 35, 165; BoC parag. 311 (p. 428).
40. Roland H. Bainton, *Here I Stand* (Nashville: Abingdon-Cokesbury, 1950); James M. Kittelson, *Luther the Reformer: The Story of the Man and his Career* (Minneapolis: Augsburg Publishing House, 1986); Eric W. Gritsch, *Martin – God's Court Jester: Luther in Retrospect* (Philadelphia: Fortress Press, 1983); Peter Manns, *Martin Luther: An Illustrated Biography* (New York: Crossroad, 1982).
41. Erik H. Erikson, *Young Man Luther: A Study in Psychoanalysis and History* (New York: W.W. Norton and Co., 1962); John M. Todd, *Luther: A Life* (New York: Crossroad, 1982).
42. Heinrich Boehmer, *Road to Reformation: Martin Luther to the Year 1521*, trans. John W. Doberstein and Theodore G. Tappert (Philadelphia: Muhlenberg Press, 1946); Heinrich Bornkamm, *Luther in Mid-Career, 1521–1530*, ed. Karin Bornkamm, trans. Theodore Bachman (Philadelphia: Fortress Press, 1983); Martin Brecht, *Martin Luther: His Road to Reformation, Shaping and Defining the Reformation, The Preservation of the Church*, trans. James L. Schaaf (Philadelphia: Fortress Press, 1985); H. G. Haile, *Luther: An Experiment in Biography* (Garden City: Doubleday, 1980); Heiko A. Oberman, *Luther: God between Man and the Devil*, trans. Eileen Walliser-Schwarzbart (New Haven: Yale University Press, 1989).
43. Lennart Pinomaa, *Faith Victorious: An Introduction to Luther's Theology* (Philadelphia: Fortress Press, 1963); Gerhard O. Forde, *Where God Meets Man: Luther's Down to Earth Approach to the Gospel* (Minneapolis: Augsburg Publishing House, 1972).
44. Paul Althaus, *The Theology of Martin Luther*, trans. Robert C. Schultz (Philadelphia: Fortress Press, 1966); Bernhard Lohse, *Introduction*, see note 9; *Martin Luther's Theology: Its Historical and Systematic Development*, ed. and trans. Roy A. Harrisville (Minneapolis: Fortress Press, 2000).
45. Karl Holl, *The Cultural Significance of the Reformation*, trans. Karl and Barbara Hertz, John H. Lichtblau (Cleveland: The World Publishing Co., 1959); *The Reconstruction of Morality*, ed. James Luther Adams and Walter F. Bense, trans. Fred W. Meuser and Walter R. Wietzke (Minneapolis: Augsburg, 1979); Pauck, see note 22.

46. Walther von Loewenich, *Luther's Theology of the Cross*, trans. Herbert J. A. Bouman (Minneapolis: Augsburg Publishing House, 1976); Hans Joachim Iwand, *Rechtfertigungslehre und Christusglaube: eine Untersuchung zur Systematic der Rechtfertigungslehre Luthers in ihren Anfängen* (Munich: Kaiser Verlag, 1961); Hermann Sasse, *This is My Body: Luther's Contention for the Real Presence in the Sacrament of the Altar*, rev. edn. (Adelaide, South Australia: Lutheran Publishing House, 1977); Gerhard Ebeling, *Word and Faith*, trans. James W. Leitch (London: SCM, 1963).

47. Regin Prenter, *Spiritus Creator*, trans. John M. Jensen (Philadelphia: Muhlenberg Press, 1953); Gustaf Wingren, *Luther on Vocation*, trans. Carl C. Rasmussen (Philadelphia: Muhlenberg Press, 1957); Leif Grane, *Modus Loquendi Theologicus: Luthers Kampf von die Erneuerung der Theologie (1515–1518)* (Leiden: E. J. Brill, 1975); Tuomo Mannermaa, *Der im Glauben gegenwartige Christus: Rechtfertigung und Vergottung zum Oekumienischen Dialog* (Hanover: Lutherisches Verlagshaus, 1989).

48. Rupp, see note 4; Marc Lienhard, *Luther: Witness to Jesus Christ: Stages and Themes of the Reformer's Christology*, trans. Edwin H. Robertson (Minneapolis: Augsburg Publishing House, 1982).

49. Heinrich Denifle, *Luther and Lutherdom*, trans. Raymund Volz (Somerset, O.: Torch Press, 1917); Joseph Lortz, *The Reformation in Germany*, trans. Ronald Walls (New York: Herder and Herder, 1968); Otto Hermann Pesch, *Theologie der Rechtfertigung bei Martin Luther und Thomas von Aquin* (Mainz: Matthis Gruenewald-Verlag, 1967); Harry J. McSorley, *Luther: Right or Wrong? An Ecumenical-Theological Study of Luther's Major Work*, The Bondage of the Will (New York: Newman Press and Minneapolis: Augsburg Publishing House, 1969). The best English-language study of the issues in the relationship of Luther and Thomas is Denis Janz, *Luther and Late Medieval Thomism: A Study in Theological Anthropology* (Waterloo, Ont.: Wilfrid Laurier University, 1983).

**Part IV**

*Luther today*

# 16  Luther and modern church history

JAMES M. KITTELSON

There are at least two respects in which this subject can easily conceal more than it elucidates. The more obvious of these is the all-too-tempting impetus to ascribe to Luther everything in contemporary Christianity of which the author approves. This tendency is most obvious in the pictures of Luther that derive from German Protestants and Lutherans in particular. Thus, Luther was depicted in his own time as the one who, by the grace of God, recovered the gospel from centuries of neglect and abuse. In the seventeenth century Lutheran Orthodox theologians valued him as the one who taught the true collection of doctrines with which they associated true Christianity. Later Pietists found in him the Christian man of great interior faith, the Rationalists of the eighteenth century hailed him for freeing the human intellect from medieval superstition, and more Romantic thinkers of the nineteenth century saw him as the stalwart German who freed Germany from papist, that is Italian, cultural tyranny. More recent times have celebrated Luther the existentialist, enlisted his support for the National Socialist regime of Adolf Hitler and its anti-Semitic atrocities, and even singled him out, along with Albert Einstein, as one of the great raw intellects in the history of the Western world. The other pattern, which goes almost without repeating, is that by contrast both former and latter-day opponents of Luther have found in him all the characteristics of whatever they have identified as most loathsome in their own time.

At present, there is also a subset of the first tendency mentioned above – that is, an urge to find praise or at least support in Luther for whatever the reader currently regards as most praiseworthy or desirable in his or her own time. From the perspective of those who seek the most precise and unvarnished truth about Luther possible, the currently most guilty party on this score is the ecumenical movement as it has been pursued in many quarters since Vatican II. Those among them who seek the formal reuniting of separated churches and at the same time carry the label "Lutheran" are particularly prone to seek in him elements that might be used in service to their agenda of contemporary institutional ecumenism. Thus, one group of Finnish scholars seeks *rapprochement* with the Orthodox at least in part on the barest shreds of material evidence regarding the presence of Christ in the justified, which they then weave together with a silk cord of highly sophisticated but largely irrelevant theological technicalities. All the while, they argue that the problem with disagreement on this matter is the fault of later Lutheran developments at the hands of his colleague, Philip Melanchthon, and of the Formula of Concord in particular.

Another group, North Americans all, pursue one version or another of the argument that in his heart of hearts Luther wanted to reform the Church of Rome and deeply regretted the division that nonetheless followed and remains characteristic of Western Christianity to this day. Roughly speaking, this party, which calls itself "evangelical catholics," divides into two groups. One seeks accommodations between evangelical and Roman Catholic teaching on the central subjects of justification, faith, grace, and the like, while the other gives up on the core of Luther's theology and turns directly to his (allegedly) undeveloped understanding of "the church" as both spiritual and this-worldly reality. Some of course take both avenues toward their goal, which is, quite simply, full reunion with the Church of Rome. In each case, the historical record blocks their path of seeking support from Luther for their fondest undertaking, unless they falsify, distort, or minimize it. It should be no surprise to those familiar with the history of Luther research that both approaches owe much to the pioneering work and methods of Josef Lortz and his followers from about the middle of the twentieth century, although North American ecumenists rarely, if ever, acknowledge it.

How, then, is a reasonably open-minded student of Luther to avoid falling into one of these errors or the other? The first step must be to identify and to name the problem. To assist in this effort, one violation of basic historical principle is characteristic of both the older and the more recent general approaches to assessing Luther's contemporary significance for Christians: they all indulge themselves in the follies of what Marc Bloch identified and named the fallacy of "the search for origins." Those who at base are seeking to find themselves in the past are usually successful in doing so, if only because almost anyone can rummage through Luther, his works, and his many writings to find at least some support for whatever she or he might be seeking. Thus, the real challenge to fruitful church historical scholarship is to avoid following suit. One way to do so (at least partially) is to seek to identify characteristics of modern Christianity that *cannot* trace their origins back to Luther in any persuasive way. Thereby, it becomes at least theoretically possible by means of indirection to identify those aspects of the "one, holy, catholic, and apostolic church," as the Nicene Creed puts it, to which Luther in fact may have made a difference with respect to ecclesiastical life today. These "leavings," as it were, will prove to be relatively simple to formulate and possibly revolutionary at the same time. Above all, it will become apparent that the care of souls (*cura animarum*), but not the church as such, was the driving force in Luther's personal development and in his career as friar, professor, theologian, and even reformer. Hence, this simple but neglected matter – the care of souls – will emerge also as the hermeneutic by which to understand both his life and his works and to assess their significance and/or utility for church life in the twenty-first century.

The first element of this exercise in indirection is therefore a negative one. Luther did not become or act as a "teacher of the church" with a mind to reconsidering the nature of "the church" (whatever might be intended by this deceptively simple term) or even, at least initially, to reform it and thereby however unintentionally contribute to its modern history. As he himself wrote in the preface to his *Latin Works* of 1545,

> Let [the reader] be mindful of the fact that I was once a monk and a most enthusiastic papist when I began that cause. I was so drunk, yes, submerged in the pope's teachings that I would have readily murdered all, if I could have, or cooperated willingly with the murders of all who would take but a syllable from obedience to the pope...
>
> Here, in my case, you may also see how hard it is to struggle out of and emerge from errors that have been confirmed by the example of the whole world and have by long habit become a part of nature, as it were. How true is the proverb, "It is hard to give up what is customary," and "Custom is second nature." How truly Augustine says, "If one does not resist custom, it becomes a necessity."
>
> So absorbed was I, as I have said, by the example and the title of the holy church, as well as my own habitual [way of thinking], that I conceded human right to the pope, which nevertheless, unless it be founded on divine authority, is a diabolical lie... For that reason I can bear with a less hateful spirit those who cling in too determined a fashion to the papacy, particularly those who have not read the sacred Scriptures, or even the profane, since I, who read the sacred Scriptures most diligently so many years, still clung to it so tenaciously.

By his own words, the nature, the proper structure, and the reform of the church were simply not on his mind as he began his journey. Given the Western Schism, the Conciliar Movement, and the writings of, for example, Pierre d'Ailly and Nicholas Cusanus, he, as did many others, might very well have devoted himself to a career of reconsidering the church as such.

But he did not. He never held ecclesiastical office, unless one wishes to dignify beyond all recognition his service as prior for the Saxon Augustinians. Earlier, he did travel to Rome, once, on business for the Observants, of which he was one and merely the traveling companion to an older, more experienced brother. No, Luther was first and foremost a pastor with the care of souls and a professor of the Bible, the chair he held in the faculty of theology in Germany's youngest and least distinguished university, or "little Wittenberg," as he called it. Indeed, it is at least arguable that, save for one early disputation, which he mentioned in his memoir but which has been lost, he did not even think about the church as such until he was forced to it in 1519 by the impending debate with Johannes Eck at Leipzig. Then he wrote a friend that he had been studying the history of the church and commented, "I whisper this in your ear. I cannot decide whether the pope is the Antichrist or merely one of his chief henchmen, so violently does he deny Christ in his decretals and canons." The words and the manner of their utterance suggest that this was a startling experience.

The first conclusion seems therefore both obvious and reasonable. Whatever might be alleged to be Luther's impact on the modern church, as conceived in any of its various institutional forms, did not develop as a direct result of intentional, long-term planning or thinking on his part. Unlike, for example, Einstein in mathematics and physics, he did not set out to solve a particular problem or to correct errors within the church as a distinct area for thought and action. He was indeed driven by other concerns that were related to the church, but tangentially and even contingently so.

As was asserted above, Luther was seized with the problem of the *cura animarum*, the care of souls. Indeed, he is probably best known for his early and intensely personal interest in this issue. His own zeal to come to terms with God drove him, as it did many others, into the monastery in the first instance. Additionally, the seriousness of his quest is evident not only in his pursuing it contrary to the wishes of his father, who thereby lost the family's insurance policy, but also in his choice of where to follow his religious vocation. Erfurt, the city in which he lived as a student, featured many pious foundations, and Luther chose the most rigorous of them all, the Black Cloister of the Observant Augustinians. He himself declared that "I lived as a monk without reproach," which was a scarcely typical understatement, as the list of his preferments indicates. He was ordained to the priesthood, selected to return to the world at least of the Erfurt theologians so he could become a teacher for his fellow friars, and had thrust upon him the responsibilities of district vicar to Johannes Staupitz. Most strikingly, the same superior, Staupitz, ordered him to become his successor as professor of the Bible at Wittenberg. Luther was a zealous friar for the sake of the care of his own soul, about which he nonetheless remarked, "When I became a doctor, I did not yet know that I could not expiate my own sins." In much the same vein, he declared that some time before the Leipzig Debate of mid-1519, "I had also acquired the beginning of the knowledge of Christ and faith in him, i.e. that we are made righteous and saved not by works but by faith in Christ." Thus, Luther's concern for the care of his own soul, as well as the necessity of telling his students the truth as he lectured to them on the Psalms (1513–15), Romans (1515/16), Galatians (1516/17), Hebrews (1517/18), and on the Psalms again (1518–21), drove both his teaching and his reading.

To read Luther's own account of his development, this rhythm of work at his calling was also personally productive. Indeed, as scholars have demonstrated in studies on one theme after another, there is reason to have pity on the students of a beginning professor whose teachings in his lectures throughout these early years gradually changed as he progressed some time in early 1519 to what he described as an intensely personal discovery. "Meanwhile," he wrote in 1545, "I had already during that year [late 1518] returned to interpret the Psalter again. I was confident in the fact that I was more accomplished" as an exegete by virtue of his earlier work. Now he was "captivated" by "a single word in [Romans 1:17]" where Paul wrote, "In it the righteousness of God is revealed." Because he was taught that righteousness was a quality of God by which God judged unrighteous sinners, he instinctively read the words "the righteous shall live by faith" as limiting the life of faith to those who were already righteous. But by early 1519 he had put his teachers' judgments on their head and concluded, "the righteousness of God is that by which the righteous live by a gift of God, namely by faith." He then added, "Forthwith, I ran through the Scriptures from memory. I also found analogies in other items, such as the work of God, that is, what God does in us, the power of God, with which he makes us strong, the wisdom of God, with which he makes us wise, the strength of God, the salvation of God, the glory of God."

By his own later account, Luther's religious thinking therefore underwent a revolution in which God and all his attributes became gifts to humanity through faith, which he also gave. The result was at least a personal solution to the problem of assurance, which was the cornerstone of the care of souls. Just how deeply personal this resolution was is evident by two separate remarks from the same text; "Here I felt that I was altogether born again and had entered paradise itself through open gates," and now "I highly praised my sweetest word with a love as great as the hatred with which I had earlier despised the word, 'righteousness of God.'" Luther was released at least from the personal vocational and theological side of his search for a God who was both righteous and gracious.

But there is a problem here, and all those who seek even a rudimentary understanding of Luther must confront it. The text from which these bits of evidence come was written in 1545, which is about a year before the author's death and twenty-seven or so years after the events it reports. Some suggest that it was composed too far from these early years when his mind was in motion to be reliable as an historical source. Others also allege that Luther's age and storied illnesses were other factors that might have rendered his memory of long-ago events less than perfect and his account of them therefore suspect. For most scholars, however, the internal consistencies that characterize the text itself tend to validate its somewhat rambling treatment of one occurrence after another. If this internal validation were not enough, the details of the whole also are verified in other accounts of events that were and remained both external to and contemporary with what Luther was describing but were *never* of the author's own creation. As memoirs or autobiographical comments, Luther's recollections certainly remain therefore at least as reliable as those that have been written in the recent past, if not more so.

On the other hand, it is a different matter to infer from these accounts the much broader assertion that the care of souls was Luther's central personal (and later public) concern. Evidence of a different sort is necessary, and it is to be found in two forms. First, the care of souls was a central, perhaps even neuralgic, emphasis of pastors and theologians in general during the late Middle Ages. Secondly, the centrality of the *cura animarum* continued throughout Luther's later and vastly more public career and had consequences for his thinking and action on many ecclesiastical issues that have become of late relatively independent specializations among systematic theologians in particular.

Treatments of the late medieval history of this subject are to be found in an unlikely place, namely in discussions of the sacrament of confession and penance, or what one scholar called "sacramental confession." The problem was simple. Granted that the penitent must confess his or her sins before receiving absolution for them, how thorough a confession was necessary? Obviously, no unconfessed sin could be forgiven, no matter how lengthy and onerous the penance that followed. To put it differently, in the strict sense a partial confession led to partial absolution. The unconfessed sin and its stain remained, as did the beckoning fires of purgatory or hell itself. Hence, as Luther once put it half in jest, "If you would confess all your sins in a timely manner, you had to carry a confessor around with you in your pocket!"

Herein lay the heart of the problem, *de cura animarum*, as it presented itself during the late Middle Ages. According to the Third Lateran Council, every Christian must make a plenary confession at least once a year, usually during Lent. But how should the confession be conducted? Should the priest simply ask the penitent to list her or his sins, declare them absolved, assign appropriate acts of penance, and let the matter go at that? If so, the priest ran the risk – and it was his own doing that now lay on his conscience – of allowing people to leave the confessional in almost precisely the state in which they came. The laws of the church would have been satisfied, but only according to their letter and not to their spirit.

Medieval theologians and priests were not fools when the matter concerned knowledge of their parishioners' behavior and inner urgings. They knew that these penitents, many of whom came because they were coerced into doing so, would either "forget" one or another of their sins, suppress them, or simply did not know that at least some of the things they had done, thought, or felt were in fact sins. Who, after all, would come unaided to the knowledge that enjoying sexual intercourse with one's spouse but without thought of any child that might follow as a consequence of the act was a sin, as were any variations on what came later to be called "the missionary position"?

Some sort of questioning of the penitent was therefore necessary. Hence, the only remaining issue concerned the degree of rigor that a confessor should employ. Naturally, opinions differed, with some recommending more and some less. From his behavior, it would appear that Luther was brought up in the more rigorist pattern, while his confessor, Staupitz, who once commanded him to go and commit a real sin before he returned, was rather more lax. In any event, obligatory confession of "secret" sins was one of the late medieval practices with which the mature Luther struggled the most mightily. It appears in both *To the Christian Nobility of the German Nation* (August 1520) and *On the Babylonian Captivity of the Church* (September 1520), where he denounced cases of "secret sins" that were reserved to higher prelates. He took two further steps in the second treatise. At the beginning he declared, "It is enough if we sorrow for those sins which are actually gnawing at our consciences and which can easily be recognized in the judge of our memory." In the body of his discussion, he commended confessing one's "secret sins," if they were troubling, to any brother or sister. But by its end he granted that "there are, strictly speaking, but two sacraments . . . baptism and the Lord's Supper, because we find in these alone a sign divinely instituted and here alone the promise of the forgiveness of sins. I added the sacrament of penance to these two, but it lacks a visible sign and was not divinely instituted. And, as I said, it is simply a means of reaffirming our baptism." At the very least, confession and penance were no longer means of appeasing a righteous God, but useful practices to relieve troubled consciences and strengthen faith.

The place that the care of souls occupied in the remainder of Luther's ever more public career is almost self-evident. It is especially so as circumstances forced him to address the remaining issues of what came to be called "the Reformation." Thus, this issue appeared in such dramatic moments as his hearing at Worms and in his daily life both personally and in working with others. In his concluding statement in 1521 he referred to the target of the care of souls twice with the words, "my conscience is captive to the Word of God" and "it is neither safe nor wise to act against conscience." There can also be no doubt that as early as the Indulgence Controversy the conscience and the care of souls were at stake. Thus, he wrote in the *Explanations of the Ninety-five Theses*, "Whoever sincerely contributes to the building of St. Peter's ... for God's sake acts much more securely and better than those who buy indulgences for it, because there is the danger that the person may make a contribution for the sake of the indulgence rather than for God's sake." Rather, "before all things (either the building of St. Peter's or the highly-regarded indulgence), you should give to your poor neighbor, if you want to give something." The mention of "safety" and "danger" refer to the old problem about sacramental confession and penance. Thus, passion for the care of souls was present in the very first act that brought the obscure professor at an equally obscure university to public attention.

It must be added that, with the possible exception of his occasional bouts with what may tentatively be identified as clinical depression, the care of his own soul and its assurance remained alive in a personal sense as well. He continued throughout his life to confess his own sins daily and, at least on one occasion, received much the same response from his colleague Johannes Bugenhagen that he earlier earned from his superior, Staupitz. After hearing Luther's litany of shortcomings and doubts, Bugenhagen turned from him, raised his hands to the heavens, and shouted, "You have blessed this man with so many gifts and through him let your gospel free, and now he doubts your graciousness! What am I to do with him?" Withal, Luther's personal and continuing correspondence is of even greater importance in recognizing the centrality of pastoral care, albeit one utterly void of social scientific underpinnings or objectives. He wrote hundreds of letters to people with, or in danger of acquiring, troubled consciences, and shared with them techniques for warding off Satan, whom he identified as the source of all these doubts and anxieties. "To raise one conscience up out of despair is worth more than a hundred kingdoms," he once declared.

To demonstrate the centrality of the *cura animarum* in Luther's life and work, if left by itself, nonetheless accomplishes precisely nothing by way of elucidating his importance to modern church history. On the one hand, as hinted earlier, contemporary pastoral care as it is taught in seminaries and elsewhere has virtually nothing to do with the care of souls as Luther understood it. By the same token, the many (growing) churches that tout Christianity's therapeutic value do no more than provide a religious patina to effective treatments that are available elsewhere. Instead, Luther's contribution, which is deeply rooted in the care of souls by means of proclaiming law and gospel, goes to the heart of the church's entire message and structure, although it is ignored in many places, including some that bear his name. A cursory tour through the following topics will serve at least to illustrate the point: (1) the evidence and origins of the church's earthly existence; (2) its patterns of worship; (3) its ministry and structures.

The Lutheran Confessions provide the obvious and most accessible sources for the evidence and origins of the church. Thus, the *Augsburg Confession* (1530) began by endorsing the decree with which Charles V called the Diet of Augsburg on the grounds (in part) that "Inasmuch as we are all enlisted under one Christ, we are all to live together in one communion and in one church." Further, at the beginning of the section on "disputed articles," it insisted, "Nothing contrary to Holy Scripture or to the universal, Christian church is taught in our churches concerning articles of faith." As it was put in the Nicean Creed, there was but "one holy, catholic, and apostolic church," which was founded by Christ himself.

Given the context, this much was in truth a trivial matter, for the simple reason that, as Luther had put it in *To the Christian Nobility of the German Nation*, the hierarchical structure of the church had no role to play either in its existence or evidence of its existence. In article eight, during the course of condemning the Donatists, the *Augustana* declared that "the church is, properly speaking, the assembly of saints and those who truly believe." Moreover, one article earlier Melanchthon described the church as "the assembly of saints in which the gospel is taught purely and the sacraments are administered rightly." As he put it later (1552) in a little book to help candidates for ordination prepare for their final examination, "In this life, the Christian Church is a visible assembly of all men who cleave to the pure teaching of the Gospel and have the right use of the Sacrament." By means of the preaching of the Word and the administration of the sacraments, the church was evident to all who had "eyes and ears." Or, as he concluded, "Where is it? Namely, where these signs are found."

For Luther, this last point was critically important, because assurance or the care of souls came solely from hearing the Word and receiving the sacraments in faith. In 1539 he was called to preach in Leipzig at Castle Pleissenburg as part of the festivities that surrounded the death of the fervently loyal Catholic, Duke George, and the succession of a prince favorable to the evangelicals. Taking John 14:23–30, which begins, "All those who love me will keep my word," he raised the question of what the ordinary Christian should do if anything except or in addition to the gospel was preached. After insisting that Christ himself "here describes and tells us what and where [the church] is, namely, where his word is purely preached," he added, "So, where you hear this, there you may know that this is the true church." By contrast, "St. Paul therefore warns us that we should flee and avoid those who lead us away from God's word, for if anyone defiles God's temple, which we are, God will destroy him." Therefore, the church had its origins in the gospel and was to be recognized wherever the gospel was preached. From it alone came the true care of souls: "here there is to be a little flock of Christ, who hear God's Word and keep it and rely upon it in every misfortune."

It goes almost without saying that this origin and evidence of the church's existence carried weight when Luther and his colleagues turned to the forms of worship that were to surround the preaching of the Word and the administration of the sacraments. Of late, in the so-called "liturgical revival" of the late twentieth century, much has been made of Luther's conservatism on such matters and an alleged desire to retain much of Roman practice for a variety (aesthetic? traditional? ecumenical?) of reasons. There can be no doubting his "conservatism," at least in comparative terms. But the reason to which many turn to explain it is badly off the mark. As Luther's reaction to Karlstadt's activities while he was in the Wartburg and not present in Wittenberg amply testifies, those who were weak in faith and might be shaken into unbelief by the demand, for example, that everyone receive both the wine and the bread at the Lord's Supper, were uppermost in his mind. Moreover, he continued in just this manner later in life and even revealed a potential preference for yet simpler liturgical forms in the *Preface to the German Mass* of 1526. There he described the ideal congregation in which believers gathered to be instructed in the Word, to pray together, to admonish one another, and to collect gifts for the poor. "But," he added, "I neither can nor desire to begin such a congregation or assembly or make a design for it. For I do not have the people or persons for it."

Finally, Luther and his colleagues completed the circle at whose center lay the *cura animarum*, when they turned their attention just before and after the Diet of Augsburg to the problem of providing for the ministry and structures of the church. Luther in fact began the process as early as 1520 in *To the Christian Nobility* with the assertion, "To call popes, bishops, priests, monks, and nuns the religious class, but princes, lords, artisans, and farm workers the secular class, is a specious trick invented by certain time-servers." By contrast, "baptism, gospel, and faith alone make men religious and create a Christian people." Thus, in his own words, the famous doctrine of the priesthood of all believers and the creation of the church knew no distinction, save of function, between clergy and laity. "All have spiritual status and all are truly priests, bishops, and popes, but not all Christians follow the same occupation."

This leveling of the clerical estate is almost never acknowledged in the writings of those who call themselves ecumenists. Somehow, some way, some sort of special quality needs to be found in those to whom the ministry of word and sacrament is entrusted if there is to be any reuniting of the various churches that have, in reality, become institutions. That ministry as such was the consequence of divine action was not in question. But so, too, as Melanchthon put it in the *Apology to the Augsburg Confession*, were the offices of prince, spouse, alms-giver, and so forth. The Word had to be proclaimed and the sacraments administered; hence there must be proclaimers and administers. Just as, if buildings were to be built, there must be masons and carpenters.

In this regard, the most revealing fact about Luther and his colleagues is that they personally did not rest content with blueprints and exhortations, but helped to bring it into being by what they did. This work is nowhere more evident than in the way they chose to "ordain" the new pastors without whom the Lutheran Reformation would have remained no more than a bundle of theological ideas. Traditional teaching had it that someone who was ordained had undergone a change in their very being that fitted them to preside at the sacrifice of the mass and brought them sufficiently closer to the divine that they were able both to handle the sacred elements and transubstantiate bread into the body and wine into the blood of Christ. Nothing could fight more basically with Luther's doctrine of the priesthood of all believers than entrusting the care of souls only to an ordained priesthood in this way.

Though Luther did not approve, he and his colleagues continued to use the word "ordination" in all its forms. But they intended something very different by it. The best evidence for the fundamental change they wrought is to be found in a series of recently rediscovered manuscripts that resides in Wittenberg and that marks the development of a distinctly evangelical form of ordination to the ministry of Word and sacrament. To summarize briefly, to be eligible for ordination the candidate must first have an authentic call from a congregation and secondly pass a theological examination held the day before the ceremony. The ritual itself was brief, perhaps five to seven minutes in length, and placed between the sermon and the concluding benediction. Members and elders of the calling congregation, clergy in that region, and the ordinand were the chief actors. An *ordinator*, who was frequently of lower rank than the one to which the ordinand was called, did little more than preside in the reading of Scripture, posing questions of the congregation and the ordinand (to which the obligatory answer was "Ja!"), and leading all in the Lord's Prayer. At the appropriate moment, sometimes he and sometimes the entire congregation laid their hands on the ordinand's head and joined in prayer for him. Some territories forbade any laying on of hands whatsoever, lest this old symbol suggest that some special status was thereby being conferred. Of perhaps greatest importance is that no one who represented the whole church, as in "The Church," was evident in any essential role at any point in the proceedings. This order was used throughout Germany through the eighteenth century and beyond. It also reached Denmark-Norway through the work of the Danish reformer, Petrus Palladius. With this order, Luther and his colleagues therefore did, as well as wrote and preached, their utmost to guarantee that Word and sacrament as preached and administered in the local congregation were and remained the only evidences of the true church.

Does what must be accepted by all as based on fact carry the inference that therefore Luther was a congregationalist or an exponent of the "free church?" By no means. The exact social structures, as well as the property relationships, of individual congregations were far too complex to allow such an anachronistic conclusion. In addition, and as article seven of the *Augsburg Confession* clearly stated, church order was an indifferent matter so long as it did not contradict, detract from, or add to Word and sacrament. With Word and sacrament came the *vera cura animarum*, which found its end in the gracious work of God through the cross of Christ. These brought the church into existence, informed it, and sustained it. And they alone did so.

Consequently, Luther's contribution to the modern church was a sustained and single-minded attention to a care of souls that came to fruition solely in the graciousness of God, just as Luther explained it with reference to the third article of the creed.

> I believe that I cannot by my own reason or strength believe in Jesus Christ my Lord or come to him, but instead the Holy Spirit has called me through the gospel, enlightened me with his gifts, made me holy, and kept me in the true faith, just as he calls, gathers, enlightens, and makes holy the whole Christian church on earth and keeps it with Jesus Christ in the one, common, true faith.

Finally, the notion of accomplishment or, in some sense, abiding victory, lurks beneath the surface of any treatment of a historical figure's relationship to modern times. It should be added, therefore, that this particular understanding of the church has never been particularly popular, even among

Lutherans. In place of Luther's straightforward reliance on the proclaimed gospel and it alone, those who call themselves Christians have been tempted repeatedly to put their trust in structures made both of building materials and of rules for the conduct of life, worship, and coming to feel better about themselves and their circumstances. As Luther put it in the explanation to the First Commandment as found in his *Large Catechism*, doing so amounted to nothing less than idolatry. Luther's contribution to modern church history amounts therefore to a stern caution.

# 17 Luther's contemporary theological significance

## ROBERT W. JENSON

This chapter cannot be written from a strictly analytical or historical point of view. An earlier theologian's contemporary theological importance can only be assessed from within the church's present theological enterprise, that is, from within her continuing reflection on her mission. Since the church's mission is to make and be faithful to the claim that the God of Israel has raised his servant Jesus from the dead, we may also think of theology as the intellectual labor internal to speaking this "gospel" intelligibly in the always new times and places which the mission reaches. Theology is thus a temporally extended debate – sometimes a calm discussion, sometimes a shouting match – about Christ and the church, which has now continued for nearly two millennia. As such a protracted conversation goes on, participants drop out, leaving their influence and writings behind them, and new ones enter, from new historical contexts.

Such considerations must give this chapter its method. Active participants in the continuing theological argument are inevitably and properly cannibals of their predecessors. They dismember predecessors' systems or structures of intuition, and use bits and pieces for their own purposes. To ask about Luther's contemporary theological significance is, therefore, to ask for suggestions that such and such aspects or parts of Luther's theology are likely to further the present enterprise.

Any such list is individual; others might cut along different lines. But the choices need not be arbitrary or idiosyncratic if the nominating theologian is both faithful to the church's tradition of teaching and taken up by the questions now being posed. Proof that these conditions are fulfilled must be, of course, circular: only the usefulness of the suggestions made can show that they were the right ones. In the view of the present writer, two mandates determine what we should now take from Luther.

First is the ecumenical imperative. Luther was indeed one of "the Reformers," whose proposals triggered lasting schism in the Western church. Whether he would have pressed his convictions in quite the same way had he been able to look farther into the future, we cannot know. In any case, the aspects of Luther's work over which the church divided – whatever they may in fact have been[1] – have long since had their effect for good and ill. The situation in which theology must now be done is one in which the Western church has – by whomever's fault – been divided but is no longer able to accept the division, one in which we can neither be in fellowship with one another nor yet any longer presume to unchurch one another.

We therefore must not now seek Luther's theological contribution – or that of Eck or Zwingli or any other of the time's important figures – in what made them divisive. Were Luther not a profound and creative thinker *within* the continuing tradition of Western catholic theology, independently of the positions and contingencies that divided the church around him, we ought not now to concern ourselves with him theologically. Fortunately for this chapter, he was just such a thinker.

The second circumstance that determines what is now valuable in Luther is the general upset of the structures of plausibility that a – however imperfectly – Christianized culture long provided to Western theology. This is not the place for a diagnosis of the West's desire for religious and intellectual self-destruction; the mandate for theology is anyway clear.

The Western church can no longer rely on the culture around her to do any vital part of her work for her; on the contrary, she must expect the culture to arrive at its convictions precisely by negating Christian teaching. In this situation, theology must be very suspicious when the culture seems to bring conceptual and religious gifts,[2] and this suspicion can well become retrospective.

We adduce an instance that also lets us cite Luther for a first time, and indeed introduce an aspect of his theology that hovers over all the following. The general tradition of theology has supposed that the Johannine Prologue's *ò Lógos*[3] must be the *Logos* of antecedent Mediterranean religious culture, that is, the concept God has of himself. Perhaps the culture's disengagement is now liberating us to attend to a self-evident point, that John is parodying Genesis 1, where God does not think the world into being but rather speaks it into being. As Luther said, consciously correcting received interpretation, "Moses uses the word *amar*, which straightforwardly denotes the spoken word...By a mere word that he speaks, God makes heaven and earth from nothing."[4] And therefore the Johannine *Logos* also, that is "in the divine being," is "an uttered word..."[5]

Luther has a remarkable ability to see other conceptual possibilities than those provided by cultural or churchly convention. His biblical interpretation can suddenly pierce through many layers of received exegesis; in Christology he follows primal Christian insight though it lead where few

϶ dared to go; he makes metaphysical moves that are, to say the least,
łacious. Often his forays are just what is now needed, as so much of
϶ology's conceptual structure is up for grabs.

Thus readers may be surprised not to see some famous Reformation
slogans among the headings below. There is no heading "justification by
faith;" nor do the various formulations with *sola* appear. We associate these
formulas so closely with Luther because of the unintended circumstances
that made them into shibboleths.[6] As items in this volume – which they
certainly must and will be – they belong in other entries.

## COMMUNICATIO IDIOMATUM, GENUS MAIESTATICUM

As Luther is often still taught, his radical Christology is put on the periphery of what we should learn from him, if indeed it is not regarded as an
embarrassment. The matter did not appear so to Luther's earliest theological
followers. The Lutheran theologians of the sixteenth and early seventeenth
centuries developed from his christological remarks an immense conceptual structure which dominated their systems.[7] And a school of Lutheran
philosophers was constructing an entire revisionary metaphysics to accommodate this Christology, until German scholarship was disrupted by the
Thirty Years War.[8]

It is an agreed foundation for all Christian theology: as "one and the
same" identifiable person, Christ is both "one of the Trinity" and one of
us. In the standard language of Christology after the Council of Chalcedon,
the incarnate Christ is "one hypostasis," of "two natures," one "divine" and
the other "human." There has, however, been no general agreement about
material consequences of this "hypostatic union."

Having laid down the language of hypostasis and natures, Chalcedon
failed to say what sort of ontological category "hypostasis" might be, and
nor therefore could it say what the hypostatic unity of two different natures might mean for them.[9] Indeed, given what Chalcedon does say about
the "natures," one can read the text to suggest that the "one hypostasis" is
nothing actual, and that the natures' union in one hypostasis has no material consequences for the state or activity of either nature. This vacuum
at the heart of Chalcedon's analyses left the field open for the subsequent
succession of christological controversies in the Eastern church, and for development in the Western church which has tended to honor Chalcedon by
faithfulness to a merely notional analysis of "one hypostasis."

Christological discussion in Luther's time was precipitated by controversy over the risen Christ's bodily presence in the Eucharist. What accounts

for the truth of "This is my body," when it is recited in the Eucharist? Indeed, in what way is the proposition true? One would have thought that Christology itself should provide answers to these questions, but standard Western Christology could not.

The usual Western Christology, faithful to Chalcedon precisely in what the council did not say, cannot regard the "one hypostasis" as an actual agent. Therefore the works of Christ, before or after his Resurrection, must according to this Christology be done either "according to" the human nature or "according to" the divine nature, each "doing what is proper to it, in fellowship with the other."[10]

Assuredly it is not "proper" to a human body to be in more than one place at a time, whereas to a divine entity spatial separation is no impediment. Therefore, if the risen Christ is present with his body at many Eucharists simultaneously, a *christological* account of this fact, remaining within the established conceptuality, would be that the embodied *humanity* is present in virtue of the *divinity's* transcendence of spatial division.

But to assert that Christ is bodily present by virtue of his divine ubiquity supposes that the hypostatic union involves Christ's active exercise in one nature of what is properly attributed to the other, which is precisely what Western Christology says does not happen. The "communion of attributes," that is, the truth of such christological sentences as "Jesus saves" or "The Son of God suffered," which attribute to a subject named according to one nature a character proper only to the other, is supposed to be notional and not material; e.g., that "Jesus saves" is a true sentence, but not because the person Jesus in his humanity has this divine ability, or because the subject-active verb sentence grammatically reflects the fact it evokes.[11]

Therefore medieval theology had to regard the eucharistic multi-presence of Christ's body as a strictly "supernatural" event, that is, one contrary to the normal metaphysics of embodiment, even of the incarnate Son's embodiment.[12] That "This is my body" is true is thus not enabled in any diachronically established fact, not even of the incarnation, and so must be established anew on each occasion of its true uttering. In decidedly ad hoc fashion, this was then said to be guaranteed by a character of ordained priesthood: the priest – within, of course, the mandated ecclesial and liturgical context – has God's authority to recite "This is my body" and have it be true because he has recited it.[13] As Reformation controversy called such qualifications of ordained ministry into question, the truth of "This is my body" itself was made problematic.

Some reformers so interpreted "This is my body" as to make its truth metaphysically unremarkable: for the more radical, "This is my body" really means "This reminds you of my body"; for Calvin and others it is not Christ's body as such that transcends spatial division but the believer's Spirit-worked faith. But from the first appearance of such interpretations, some of Luther's more particular supporters were offended by them, and set out to maintain the traditional affirmation of Christ's presence, without the medieval ad hoc explanation, by construing a Christology able in itself to account for Christ's bodily presence.

According to the proposal of a group of Luther's younger followers, the mystery of the incarnation is itself the mystery of eucharistic presence; no further systematic constructions are needed.[14] What we *analytically* refer to as Christ's deity and humanity are only *actual* as one sole agent, the hypostasis, so that where God the Son actually comes and works, there the bodily risen Jesus must be. And that God the Son is everywhere is not disputed. Thus Christ's bodily availability as the elements of Eucharist is but a specific mode of the universal presence of his embodied humanity: this man is present hiddenly to all creation, is present audibly in the preached Word, is present communally in baptism, and is present in the Eucharist to be seen and touched and taken.

It is of course Christ's divine nature only to which ubiquity is *proper*, but the one person, who is what actually exists, now possesses this property only as the person of the human nature also: divine ubiquity – with other attributes of "majesty" – is actually and not merely notionally communicated to the human nature.[15] "Jesus transcends spatial division" – or "Jesus saves" – are statements of fact as they stand, and properly reflect in their grammatical form the facts of which they speak.

Once the controversy had begun, Luther joined it, and then with surprising polemical vehemence. If we examine these writings for Luther's motive in joining the fray – which his previous writings would not necessarily have required him to do[16] – we see that it is not mere insistence on the literal truth of "This is my body,"[17] or any point of sacramental theology narrowly conceived. Luther's attention has been called to a looming evil, and an elemental theological passion pervades the writings.

"Beware! Beware, I tell you, of the '*alleosis*'![18] It is the devil's mask. In the end, it construes such a Christ, that were Christ indeed so, I would not want to be a Christian." Zwingli's Christ would be a "wretched savior."[19] As for the God who appears in his opponents' Christology, Luther can only cry, "Don't give me any of *that* God!"[20]

The object of Luther's horror is any presence of God that is not a presence of the human Jesus; and such a possibility is indeed posited if we say that Christ as God is ubiquitous but Christ as man is not. What appalls Luther is the thought of anywhere encountering a "sheer separated God and divine person, without humanity..."[21] To someone whose teaching proposes such a possibility, Luther can only say, "No, buddy! Anywhere you confront me with God, there you must just so confront me with his humanity."[22]

Luther therefore insists on a Christology which guarantees that "anywhere you can say 'Here is God,' you must also say 'Here is Christ the man.' "[23] In Luther's christological discussions, "person" – not "hypostasis" – is the central concept, and is used very much in a modern sense, for the protagonist of a history. Only the person of the God-man appears as an actual someone or something; the two natures appear only in the abstract, as "deity" and "humanity."[24] Thus the one agent of salvation is the person; if Christ's works could be assigned to one or the other nature, this in Luther's view would mean that he was not in fact one person at all and that there was no incarnation.[25]

So Luther teaches the communion of attributes without backing or filling. At a first step, "One must attribute to the whole person whatever happens with either of the natures..."[26] At the next step, "...because deity and humanity in Christ are one person, Scripture attributes...also to the deity everything that happens with the humanity, and vice versa." And if this suggests that suffering and death must be attributed to God the Son even *as* he is divine, seemingly contrary to the dictate of "reason" that deity cannot suffer or die, Luther is willing to say that while "deity" *as such* in the abstract cannot suffer, "nevertheless" the man's suffering is God the Son's suffering, also according to his divine nature.[27]

What profit might we now draw from all this? Much, both from Luther's horror and from his positive teaching.

On the one hand, nothing would be more beneficent for the contemporary church than to acquire some of Luther's fear of mere deity. The magisterial and mainline churches have forgotten an elemental fact, both of Scripture and of any but the most sheltered religious experience: that deity is not necessarily a beneficent predicate, that gods by and large are if not moot then monstrous. Consider only Moloch the baby-eater, or the Dialectic of History, or the Invisible Hand, or Sophia the cosmic sentimentalist. "Inclusive" adaptation to whatever religious experience the culture may be having is no mere tactical error, it is deadly dangerous; it leads either to spiritual coma or to horror.

More particularly, if there were a God who was otherwise like the one described in Scripture *except* for his incarnation, this God would be sheer death and destruction. No one can see the biblical God and live, except in the face of the Son. That Israel's and Jesus' face is the only one the real God actually has, is according to Luther the very fact of salvation.

We might in fact learn something about the fear of naked deity from our culture, as it abandons faith in Christ but has no picture of God not shaped by the Bible. Much late modern and postmodern atheism is mere numbness, but some is the apprehension of horror where God should be. Or perhaps we should say, of an omnipotence with emptiness where the face of Christ once was. Anyone who has sampled the atmosphere of the *Thingstätte* Hitler built in anticipation of his victory celebration, on the "Holy Mountain" over the Neckar, may have some intuition of what Luther feared.

On the other hand, the gospel for a world burnt by the fire of God unincarnate can only be one based on Luther's sort of Christology, on an utterly unmitigated affirmation of the incarnation, both in teaching and practice.[28] We need not adopt all Luther's formulas, which are open to critique from several justified viewpoints. But we must abide their impact, somewhat as follows.

"God the Son is Jesus" is an identity statement, and this syntactical observation must control all discourse in the church. "This is my body" is again an identity statement, and that it is must be a rule controlling all the church's liturgical practice. "Who hears you hears me" is not a trope; and the preacher who dares not believe it should now not preach at all. There is a way in which the history of modern theology is the history of a long attempt to evade these identities. Whatever may have been the good things found on this path also, we have reached its dead end. Our next heading is the signpost there.

## DEUS ABSCONDITUS

Despite the pretentious character of much "postmodernist" rhetoric, it evokes a real phenomenon of the past century, which moreover shows no sign of abating in the new one: the fracturing of discourse and particularly of discourse about God.[29] We are at a loss what to say for him or to him, and when we do nerve ourselves to affirmation, feel obscurely pressed to retract in the next sentence.

Certainly the horrors of the past century are much of our difficulty, intruding their memory between subject and predicate of our intended utterance: "God," we begin, and as we are about to continue "is just," we think of Auschwitz. But it is not just the Shoa and its imitations that interrupt our prayer and preaching; Nietzsche already knew what was coming, merely by plotting our civilization's general course. The proposal of this section is that Luther's theology of God's hiddenness might enable the church to face what is actually going on around her, and provide also some word of gospel in the catastrophe.

Luther knew three ways in which God hides himself. We will take them up in sequence. The first is the least often faced; scholarship has sometimes even tried to pretend it can be excised from his theology without other damage. God, insisted Luther, hides himself by the way he rules his creation. We will put the awesome dictum up front: if we consider what in fact happens under God's governance, whether materially or spiritually, and judge by any available standard, we must conclude "either that God is wicked or that he is not" (*aut malum aut nullum esse Deum*).[30] Supposing that the Bible is right, that God is good, he could hardly hide himself more decisively than he does behind events that urge such a verdict. Evoking the cry from the extermination camp, "Where is God?" may have become a cliché, but it is for good reason that it has. And precisely believers, who know that God is good, are the ones who must most often and deeply experience the contradiction.

Not every God need be thus hidden by his or her associated world, even were it this fallen world. Gods whose deity consists in metaphysical distance, across which we must project our metaphors if we are to speak of them, may be kept safely shielded from the actual course of worldly events; we need only choose vague metaphors. But the real God, the Creator, whose omnipotent agency is closer to every grain of sand than it is to itself, cannot so easily be excused. The torture of even one child, as in Ivan Karamazov's parable, furnishes more than sufficient reason to reject this God. Did God will the Shoa? No. Could he have prevented it? Obviously, if he is. What then are we to say?

It would be a great apologetic advance, were the church's address to the world simply to speak such truth. We cannot make God's providence morally comprehensible.[31] We cannot justify his ways. Our praise of God will always falter if hard pressed, not because he is not good but because we cannot say so without stuttering.[32] Atheism, or sheer anger, are in fact reasonable responses to God's governance of his creation. The church's theology should say all that, in public. That God is the good Creator can only be affirmed following an anguished "Nevertheless!"

Notoriously, Luther's mandate to those facing this first hiddenness of God was to flee from it, and cling instead to the Cross.[33] Protestantism now makes this call the invitation to a cozy sort of comfort: behold, after all, at least at this one place, the good, kind, and accepting God. That is not what Luther meant to provide. For him, the Cross was the place of a second hiding of God.

If we follow Luther's pointing finger to the Cross, we find God yet more deeply hidden than by his governance. Can the man hanging there help us in our weakness? He who does not even help himself? Can he convince us of God's goodness and justice and so lift the first hiddenness, as he cries "My God, why have you abandoned me?" Staring at him, will we see reason to halt less when speaking of God? Was his mother Mary inspired to praise, when she stood below?

The Cross undoes our speech about God a second time, since so much of it is idolatrous. For it is precisely in seeking to evade the suffering face of God, the face with nothing in its "appearance that we should desire him," that we make our idols.[34] We do not want God to be the Suffering Servant, neither as Servant Israel nor as the one Israelite. We would be rid both of the Jews and of the Jew Jesus, if God did not keep reappearing with them.

What we want from the gods we project is affirmation and empowerment. We demand deity that fulfills us, if only – à la Western versions of Eastern religion – by its comfortingly superior nothingness. But the real God appears with nails in his extremities and mockery over his head, so that if we want images of security and peace, we must make them up ourselves. These are the idols.

It is in every age the church's calling to free humanity from its idols. "No," the church is always to say, "God is not rightly represented by a potent bull-calf, but by the Crucified." "No, we cannot image God from what we affirm – or deny – about ourselves, whether we are male or female, oppressed or liberators, since God has himself drawn his image, on that tree."[35] "No, God's Son is not a Christ-principle, or Principle of incarnation, or whatever manipulable entity; he is that tormented Jew." But the present moment is perhaps special: it does indeed seem that at no time since the collapse of its first culture has the West been so prone to idolatry, indeed to primitive superstition, or more in need of the church's mission of liberation from idols.

The problem of course is that the church herself is in every age more tempted to idolatry than is the world around her; the world has at least the restraint of mere irreligion and skepticism. And in the late modern church, incomprehension of the Second Commandment is perhaps uniquely pervasive. Just so, if the church's theology does not now set out to enforce the Second Commandment with special rigor, the church's message and worship will shortly be of no interest whatever – which of course is the condition to which Western Protestantism is rapidly approximating. Repentance would be to obey Luther's direction to God hidden on the Cross.

Luther knew a third way in which God hides himself. Faith itself, he said, is God's hiding himself in the human soul. Faith according to Luther is a "paradoxical sort of cognition," less an illumination than a spreading darkness, which Christ wraps around his dwelling in us just as the Lord spread darkness around his dwelling on Sinai.[36]

"In faith simply as such, Christ is present."[37] The proposition will be the theme of our next section. In the present context, it is the hiddenness of that presence we are to acknowledge. What is faith? The question is variously answered. Faith is a theological virtue. It is knowledge of God in Christ. It is trust. All these specifications are surely true. But in them it is *I* who appear as the subject: I have this virtue; I know Christ; I trust in him. Just so, these true specifications do not finally distinguish faith from other subjective modes that are *not* faith. The faith of which I am the subject is but the dark cloud that Christ wraps round him, as he rules in me. What distinguishes faith from unfaith is what hides *behind* my virtue and knowledge and trust, the ruling presence in me of one who I am not.

That is why we cannot control faith. It is why the faith-rhetoric of late modern Protestantism is so destructive precisely of faith. I cannot "share" my faith. All I can share is my virtue and knowledge and trust; whether Christ comes to dwell in them is up to him. I cannot answer the question, "Do you really believe?" For all I can find in myself is, in the best case, my virtue and knowledge and trust, within which Christ hides – or does not. Nor is christological faith a species of faith as a generic religious possibility, since merely as virtue and knowledge and trust faith simply *is* the generic religious possibility, and as the presence of one embodied human at the heart of another it is *sui generis*.

It is an imperative specific to our time: the church must stop promoting faith, offering self-help courses in how to grow in faith, making faith easy or hard. We must learn to abide the deepest of God's ways of hiding, in the obscurity of our own souls. Luther can teach us.

## THEOSIS

We have been commending aspects of Luther's theology in part for their relevance to the late modern or postmodern West. Thereby of course we may have risked the very peril early warned against, of receiving fatal gifts from the culture. Under the present rubric, Luther's thought will be commended simply because it is true, and is now needed by theology for that purest of reasons.

"Everything [Christ] is and does is present in us and there works with power, so that we are utterly deified, so that we do not have some part or aspect of God, but his entire fullness."[38] That is Luther, but except for some turns of diction, it could be any of the Greek fathers. It has been a maxim of much Luther scholarship: the fathers' teaching of "deification," that "God became man so that we might become God," is one thing, and Luther's "new" understanding of the gospel is another and incompatible thing. This maxim is very nearly the opposite of the truth.[39]

In this context we have finally to adduce Luther's teaching that we are "justified by faith." The question here relevant is: *How* does faith justify?

The surely most loved of Luther's treatises, *The Freedom of a Christian*, sets itself to answer this question. Readers often finish the treatise filled with admiration but more confused than before. Perhaps the cause of our bewilderment is that the answer Luther gives is so different from the one we were antecedently certain must be there.

"Believe in Christ," Luther admonishes, "in whom are promised all grace, righteousness, peace, and freedom. If you believe, you have it; if you do not believe, you do not have it."[40] That is what we expected him to say – except perhaps for the bundling together of justification's "righteousness" with all manner of other divine good things.

But our initial question remains: *Why* does the one who believes the word of promise merely thereby "have" the "good things" that are its content? The connection, according to Luther, is an ontological mutuality of the soul and words: the moral content of the addresses to which someone attends determines the moral quality of his or her soul. The one who believes the gospel is righteous, etc., because the word of the gospel "has all good things for its content"; and because "the soul of the one who clings to the word in true faith is so entirely united with it that all the virtues of the word become virtues of the soul also."[41]

Luther is here exploiting a metaphysical innovation he made early in his theological development. Aristotle – and after him the medievals – had observed that there is nothing *to* the intellectual soul but on the one hand a sheer potentiality of apprehending something, and on the other hand whatever is apprehended.[42] We may make Aristotle's observation on our own: What indeed is there to my consciousness except that *of* which I am conscious and the fact that I am the one *whose* consciousness this is? If we say "Consciousness is . . . ," where the ellipse is the place for anything that can be *described*, consciousness just "is" what it contains, the soul is what it knows. In Luther's own formulation of the Aristotelian principle, "So the objects [of minds] are the being and act of minds, without which they would be nothing, just as matter without forms would be nothing."[43]

Luther adopts Aristotle's principle, but changes its import. For Aristotle, the paradigm mode of apperception was *seeing*, so that in Aristotle's doctrine we are what we stare at. The soul – if we may put it so – is a great eye. For Luther the paradigm mode of apperception is *hearing*, since we are both created and saved by God's speech to us.[44] The soul – we may say – is a great ear, rather than a great eye. We should note also, that in switching from seeing to hearing as the paradigm of apperception, Luther replaces a merely cognitive relation of the soul to its objects with a *moral* relation. To *hear* the world is to perceive it teleologically, in its adaptation to God's good purpose.[45]

Thus Luther's remarkable parody of Aristotle's metaphysics of apperception: morally and spiritually we *are* what we *hearken* to. "Do not be surprised when I say we become the Word. The philosophers too say that the intellect, through the act of knowing, *is* the known object, and that sensuality, through the act of sensual perception, is the sensed object. How much more must this hold of the spirit of the Word"?[46]

We *are* the "good things" we hear in the gospel, just in that we hear them; they enter us with the discourse on which we are intent. Luther's actual doctrine of justification by faith is nearly the opposite of the doctrine popularly attributed to him. That we are made righteous by faith – and free and peaceful and full of grace and so forth – does not mean that God decides to accept faith as a *substitute* for actual virtue. We are justified by faith because faith is intent listening to the gospel, because the gospel communicates God's "good things," and because in hearkening we are shaped to what we hear. Justification is "without works" not because we are excused from works, but because the good in good works is being formed in believers antecedently to their working, by God's good address to them. When God looks at a believer and says, "You are righteous for Christ's sake," this is not fiction or even an exercise of clemency, but a statement of fact.

It is "for Christ's sake" that believers are righteous, in that the gospel-word to which faith hearkens is both about him and spoken by him. This enables Luther's other and better known statement of why faith makes righteous – taken straight from the fathers: "Faith...unites the soul with Christ, as a bride with her bridegroom. From this marriage it follows...that Christ and the soul have everything together..."[47] As the soul is united with the gospel it hears, it is united with Christ whose word this is, so that the two become one personal subject, of the believer's sin and of Christ's divine righteousness.

Three points are to be noted about Luther's version of the "happy exchange," of the marriage of Christ with the soul. First, he does not intend a trope. On account of the ontological relation of soul and word, the believer is no longer an individual; Christ who speaks to the believer and the believer make but one moral subject between them, and it is the moral quality of *this* subject which is both effective in the believer's works and will be judged by the Father. Second, it is Christ's righteousness and not the believer's sin that constitutes the moral quality of their joint subject because the believer's sin is "swallowed up" by Christ's righteousness.[48] Third, Christ's righteousness swallows up our sin because – here the communion of attributes! – Christ is righteous with God's own righteousness, before which creatures' sin counts for nothing.[49]

We have but one more step, to be back with this section's opening citation of Luther, and with deification. It was a standard maxim of medieval theology that there is no real distinction between God and his attributes: he not only has, for central instance, being, he *is* being. Luther accepts this, and radicalizes it. His argument can be laid out as an enthymeme: God's "good things" are God himself; God is his own Word; therefore the "good things" in God's Word are God himself; and therefore what we "have" as we hear that Word is God himself.[50]

Western theology has typically insisted that as God sanctifies us, what we become is truly human. That is right. But what if to be human means to be destined to live by God's life?

## PERSPICUITAS

Secular historians of culture sometimes praise Luther for "restoring the Bible to the people" or some such achievement. Such praises have more lately been derided by theologians. But perhaps these observers see something that is really there.

To be sure, legends about "dark ages" have needed debunking. Luther's vernacular version was far from the first. Bibles were scarce until Luther's time not because priestcraft withheld them from the people, but because the economics of production made all books scarce; prosperous families in England handed down their Tyndale Bibles through the generations. The papal magisterium claimed a special right of authoritative interpretation, but so did Lutheran and Calvinist authorities; and none of these made the claim with such complacency as does modernity's guild of variously "critical" exegetes.

But all that acknowledged, Luther somehow made a church- and world-historical difference in the way the Bible functions publicly. It is what Luther thought the Bible is, and what he thought it is for, that this section will commend. This last set of reflections thus has a different scope than its predecessors, but must certainly be included.

Luther thought the Bible was "clear," that is, that taking the book as a whole, and allowing time for reading and rereading, we could be confident of making out its meaning.[51] He had no need to deny that at any time there will be places in Scripture whose literal sense eludes scholarship, only that "the matter"[52] of Scripture is irretrievably obscured by them.[53] It was with this assurance that he sent out his translations and commentaries.

Unless we are antecedently convinced the Bible does *not* make sense, Luther's confidence must at first seem unremarkable. That we should presume a book as a whole will make sense, and that given time we can discover what that is, is affirmed by the practice also of those who write books to deny that books can have a discernible sense.

But then we may remember that modernity's academic exegesis has been based on *not* taking the Bible as a whole; and on methodological inattention to all pre-modern interpretation, that is, on *not* allowing reading to take its appropriate time. Each successive mode of "critique" has disintegrated the text presented to us into units of its newly discovered sort, and has made these isolates the object of interpretation. And each successive mode has seen previous exegetical efforts as valuable only in leading up to it, denying what once seemed obvious, that in an extended interpretive discourse, the best insight may appear at any time.

The elements of Luther's view are linked. It is because the Scripture has in fact a singular "matter" that it makes a coherent whole. "Take Christ out of Scripture, and what will you find left over?"[54] This one matter is not a doctrine, not even the doctrine about Christ; it is simply Christ himself, or insofar as we think of Scripture as text, it is the narrative of Christ, that is, the form of discourse by which text renders persons. We may take Luther's preface to the books of Moses as a statement of how this works.[55]

Luther's initial thesis is that the Pentateuch is a book of law. His introductions to the books in succession, however, do not discuss their legal doctrine; they trace the history by which God created for himself a people of his law. In Luther's characteristic reading, drawn from his exegesis of Paul, the law as such, and just so this history of God's people, have "the office" of bringing humankind to Christ by undoing the alternative and otherwise universally attempted path to salvation, the path of our own efforts. The text of the law brings those who hear or read it to death, and so to the place where resurrection can happen; and history under the law brings the nation to death, and so to the place where Christ can appear.

Thus Luther's exposition of the Pentateuch as "law" – and this is what is regularly not noted – is a *dramatic* exposition. Luther did not intend to introduce a topic unprepared, when toward the end he says: "Finally, I must surely suggest something of the spiritual meaning, which the Mosaic and Levitical Law and priesthood present."[56] For classic spiritual exegesis was exegesis of the Old Testament precisely as dramatic narrative, teasing out the "figures" by which any interesting narrative holds together.[57]

It turns out, moreover, that Luther must treat spiritual meaning so briefly not because it is of secondary importance, but because proper introduction of the Pentateuch's spiritual meaning would burst the limits of a preface. For "Moses is indeed a fountain of all wisdom and understanding . . . ," from which "the New Testament flows and in which it is founded."[58] The proper introduction to the Pentateuch's spiritual meaning is the whole New Testament.

Within his space allotted, Luther can give only a quick maxim and sample. "If you will interpret well and surely, take Christ for your matter. For he is the one, whom everything solely intends. So make the high priest Aaron be no one but Christ alone, as the Epistle to the Hebrews does... Moreover it is certain that Christ is sacrifice and altar also..."[59]

So it was as a great metanarrative of God in Christ with us, that Luther turned the Scriptures over to the public. He did it in confidence that the narrative was clear, indeed a page-turner. That is what made the world-historical difference. If we could relearn from Luther to trust the eminently readable story of God with us, who knows what might again happen?

### Notes

1. A matter which is far from as clear as might be supposed, and is yearly becoming more puzzling.
2. *Timeo Danaos et dona ferentes* has long been a maxim among the Orthodox, who descend more directly from those Greeks.
3. The word itself is equally well translated "word" or "reason."
4. WA 42, 13, 13.
5. WA 42, 13, 15.
6. Here we must acknowledge the revisionary Luther scholarship of Tuomo Maner-maa and his associates at the University of Helsinki, and of David Yeago, whose full-scale study of the catholic Luther will shortly appear. We will instance the Finns' work several times; a sample is available in English in Carl E. Braaten and Robert W. Jenson, eds., *Union with Christ: The New Finnish Interpretation of Luther* (Grand Rapids: Wm. B. Eerdmans Publishing Co., 1998).
7. The single most impressive monument of this effort is doubtless Martin Chem-nitz' *De duabis naturis in Christo* (Jena, 1570), ET *Two Natures in Christ*, trans. Jacob Preus (St. Louis: Concordia Publishing House, 1971).
8. See Walter Sparn, *Wiederkehr der Metaphysik* (Stuttgart: Calwer Verlag, 1976).
9. The council probably *could* not have said anything material, without exacerbating the divisions it was called to heal.
10. The formula of Pope Leo's "Tome," which had been appended to Chalcedon's decrees as authorized interpretation; *Decrees of the Ecumenical Councils*, ed. N. P. Tanner (Washington, DC: Georgetown University Press, 1990), I:79, 3–7. The formula became the maxim of Western Christology.
11. To this, with the necessary citations, see Robert W. Jenson, *Systematic Theology* (New York, Oxford University Press, 1997–99), II:254–55.
12. E.g., Thomas Aquinas, *Summa theologiae*, iii.75.4.
13. Ibid., iii.78.3–5; 82.1–3.
14. Which I will here draw from the mature work of their leader, Johannes Brenz. *De personali unione duarum naturarum in Christo* (Tübingen: 1561); *Von der Majestät unsers lieben Herrn und einigen Heilands Jesu Christi* (Tübingen: 1562).
15. The dogmaticians distinguished various genera of the communication of attributes; our problem falls under the *genus maiestaticum*.

16. Some of his polemics could as well have been directed against his own *Babylonian Captivity of the Church* as now against Ökolampadius or Zwingli.
17. At Marburg, he did not write in the table-top dust that Zwingli was of another exegetical tradition, but that he was of another "spirit."
18. Zwingli's word for his weak but in fact fairly traditional version of the communion of attributes.
19. WA 26, 319: "Hüt dich. Hüt dich – sage ich – für der Alleosi. Sie ist des Teuffels Larven. Denn sie richtet zu letzt ein solchen Christum zu, nach dem ich nicht gern ein Christen sein."
20. WA 26, 332: "Mir aber des Gottes nicht!"
21. WA 26, 333. Note that this does not require the embodiment of the Father or the Spirit; in patristic fashion, Luther assumes that the person of the Son is always the audible or visible presence of the other trinitarian hypostases.
22. Ibid.: "Nein Geselle! Wo du mir Gott himsetztest, da mustu mir die Menscheit mit hinsetzten."
23. WA 26, 332.
24. E.g., WA 26, 330–31.
25. WA 26, 324.
26. WA 26, 322.
27. WA 26, 320. If a genus of the *communicatio idiomatum* were to be posited following this proposition of Luther's, it would be a *genus tapeinoticon*.
28. *Not*, of course, of some principle of incarnation.
29. See David Tracy, "The Hidden and Incomprehensible God," *Reflections* (Autumn 2000), 62–88. We must hope that the large work Tracy is preparing on this theme does in fact soon appear.
30. WA 18, 784.
31. Romans 11:28–36.
32. It may be worth noting that this is a different phenomenon than the necessity of analogy, or the "death of a thousand qualifications."
33. E.g., WA 18, 689.
34. Isaiah 53:2. The chapter as a whole was very near to being the whole atonement-theology of the most primal church.
35. The evil of "re-imaging" and the like, is not so much the always infantile results, as the activity itself, by whomever and for whatever undertaken.
36. WA 1, 28: "In ipsa fide, Christus adest."
37. WA 40/I, 228.
38. WA 17/I, 438.
39. For the overwhelming evidence, see Simo Peura, *Mehr als ein Mensch?: die Vergöttlichung als Thema der Theologie Martin Luthers von 1513 bis 1519* (Mainz: P. von Zabern, 1994).
40. WA 7, 24.
41. Ibid.
42. A mere dispositional property.
43. WA 20, 26–27.
44. If used with skepticism about the notion of Luther's "discovery," Ernst Bizer, *Fides ex auditu: Eine Untersuchung über die Entdeckung der Gerechtigkeit Gottes durch Martin Luther* (Neukirchen Kreis Moers: Verlag der Buchhandlung des Erziehungsvereins, 1958).

45. As has regularly been noted, the objects of hearing are intrinsically extended in time, as the objects of sight are in space. Thus to hear the world is to apprehend it in its temporality. And if the doctrine of creation is true, to apprehend the world in its temporality is to apprehend it teleologically.

46. WA 1, 29.

47. WA 1, 25.

48. WA 1, 32.

49. Ibid.

50. The centrality of this argument in all Luther's theology is a chief burden of the ground-breaking work of Tuomo Mannermaa, *Der im Glauben gegenwärtige Christus: Rechtfertigung und Vergottung zum ökumenischen Dialog* (Hanover: Lutherisches Verlagshaus, 1989).

51. E.g., WA 18, 606–08.

52. *res Scripturae.*

53. WA 18, 606.

54. Ibid. The answer to Luther's question is, of course: the bits of antique religious history chewed over and over by conventions of academic exegetes.

55. WA DB 8, 11–31.

56. WA DB 8, 29.

57. This is established once and for all by Henri de Lubac, *Exègese Médiévale: les quatre sens de l'Écriture* (Paris: Aubier, 1959–64). See the English translation as *Medieval Exegesis*, trans. Mark Sebanc (Grand Rapids: Wm. B. Eerdmans Publishing Co.; Edinburgh: T&T Clark, 1998– ).

58. WA DB 8, 29.

59. Ibid.

# 18 Luther in the worldwide church today

GÜNTHER GASSMANN

## THE LIBERATION OF MARTIN LUTHER FROM HIS CAPTIVITY

It is obvious that for centuries after the Reformation and for the majority of his followers Martin Luther was not a theologian of the worldwide church. Rather, already in the seventeenth century, in Lutheran Orthodoxy, he was considered to be the father, founder, and foremost – if not normative – theologian of the Lutheran church and tradition. Luther became the Lutheran par excellence. He was not only *the* Lutheran, but *the German* Lutheran, and as a central figure and cornerstone of German Lutheran identity his critical and even polemical position over against the Roman Catholic and Reformed traditions became prominent while his vision of the universal church was forgotten or ignored.

Throughout the ensuing nearly four centuries after his appearance as a reformer, Luther was owned and reinterpreted, misrepresented and misused as the chief ideologist and hero of Lutheran Protestantism. During the Enlightenment period of the eighteenth century, Luther was seen as the Christian hero, who had liberated Protestant Germany from the dictates of a foreign power, the papacy in Rome. He had brought freedom from the yoke of tradition and the bondage of conscience. In the nineteenth century Luther was praised as the grandiose representative of the German national spirit, while in the twentieth century at the time of World War II such distorted images were replaced by a sharply contrasting one when some Anglo-Saxon writers considered Luther as initiator of a movement of authoritarian ideology that led, by way of Bismarck, finally to Adolf Hitler's Nazism.

These are just some examples of the ways in which Luther had been the captive of diverse and often nationalistic and confessionalistic interpretations by his Lutheran and general Protestant friends. However, we must not forget that despite this predominantly German captivity of Luther there have always been people outside that country who were seeking to understand Luther more adequately. There were also in his homeland individuals who tried to penetrate through the dominant layers of interpretation in order to come closer to the original again and to receive inspiration from him for their own faith and thinking.

One wonderful example of those who already in their time viewed Luther in a wider horizon and perspective is the interpretation of the great Thomas Carlyle, who saw in Luther the eminent revolutionary hero of history whose thinking was at the root of a process that led to a free and democratic America. But even here as well as in all portrayals of Luther the person, work, and impact of the reformer were shaped by the hermeneutical presuppositions of his interpreters – a problem, however, that can never be fully avoided. All understanding and interpretation is influenced by particular pre-understandings. Yet there are certainly approximations to an accurate grasp of the truth of a person or a reality, and in the case of Luther only constant new interpretation can save him from becoming a lifeless historical monument.

In the twentieth century a significant effort was undertaken to bring the true and real Luther to light as far as possible, freed from his captivity by those who shaped him according to their narrow nationalistic and confessionalistic presuppositions. This liberation of Luther happened during the first half of the century through the interplay of several developments. There was, first of all and most important, the new wave of research on the person and work of Martin Luther, facilitated by the new critical edition of his writings in the process of publication (and still in this process), the "Weimar" edition. This "Luther renaissance" removed the distortions and limitations of earlier presentations of Luther.

A further development, also beginning during the first decades of the twentieth century, that helped to liberate Luther from being jealously embraced as a Lutheran-Protestant property was the new Roman Catholic view of the Reformation and of Luther. This initiated an increasingly active Roman Catholic research on Luther's personal, spiritual, and theological stature and his impact on church history. Luther was de-confessionalized and regarded as being part of a common theological and spiritual tradition.

A third development that helped to bring Luther into the wider horizon of worldwide Christianity was the ecumenical movement. In this movement Martin Luther was discovered as Lutheranism's gift to world Christianity. Thus an international and multifaceted Luther-reception happened in the twentieth century. Why and how did this occur? What made Luther, beyond his German Lutheran tribe, so interesting, even fascinating? In what sense can we speak of Luther as one of the great teachers and inspirers of the Christian church?

## LUTHER'S VISION OF THE UNIVERSAL CHURCH

An extraordinary person in church history will not be in a position to fabricate and predestine his or her own history of impact and influence (*Wirkungsgeschichte*) and history of reception. Rather, this will depend on the free mechanism of a process of reception by which a person and his/her work is recognized and received by those of a later time who consider this person and work as relevant for their period and situation. However, such reception is facilitated if the person in question exhibits characteristics that appeal to or provoke the questions and concerns of those who are the players in a reception process. This explains why in specific historical constellations a particular person of the past is rediscovered while in other phases of history this same person may again disappear from historical consciousness.

This may further explain why sometimes only one specific trait/characteristic of a historical personality is brought back from history into the present, and why another trait reappears in yet another moment and context. Thus, such rediscovery is always conditioned by the two actors/sides in the process, the one who is to be received and those who receive. Without entering further into this hermeneutical consideration, we can conclude that obviously there are in Martin Luther's personality, faith, and thinking such elements and perspectives that were calling for and facilitated his broad reception in the worldwide church today.

Despite his sharp criticism and rejection of the late medieval Roman system and his lively controversies with the Zwinglian reforming movement and his harsh words against the Anabaptists and Spiritualists (*Schwärmer*), Luther thought and taught as a theologian of the universal/catholic church. In many ways he was still pre-confessional, even though one of the later confessions took on his name. The wide, universal ecclesial horizon of his thinking became visible already early in his Reformation career. Three interrelated insights and perspectives emerged in his thinking: (1) The late medieval church of the West cannot claim to be *the* universal, catholic church because it has itself become a particular (confessional) church within Christianity. (2) The whole Christian church on earth is the proper frame of reference for every ecclesiological reflection. (3) The universal, catholic church has its center in Jesus Christ and this allows for a broad sphere of liberty and diversity.

(1) Already in 1518 during his encounter with Cardinal Cajetan at Augsburg, Luther begins to recognize that Catholic positions, which he had regarded so far as theological opinions of certain schools, are now represented

by the cardinal as the official, strictly papalist and anti-conciliarist position of the church (WA 2, 6–26/LW 31, 259–92; BR 1, 213–23, 233–46/LW 48, 83–89). For Luther, such opinions that are now made official positions cannot claim universal truth. Similarly, he considers the different religious orders as "sects" because of their belligerent exchange of diverse and different theological opinions (WA 6, 537/LW 36, 73). There is no true unity in the papal church, which he regards later as a part or piece of the holy Christian church. For Luther, the holy church is not bound to Rome but extends as far as the world does and is assembled in one faith (WA 6, 300, 35 [1520]). He concludes later: "Because there is no Roman nor Nurembergian nor Wittenbergian church there is but one Christian church, into which all belong who believe in Christ" (WA 47, 236, 5 [1537]). His discovery of the Roman Church being only a part of the universal church, an anticipation of the later confessional/denominational structure of Christianity, enables Luther to look beyond the church of his particular time and place to the one, holy, universal/catholic/Christian church.

(2) The discovery of this wide horizon of the whole Christian church on earth is also generally associated with Luther's disputation with Johann Eck in July 1519 at Leipzig. Here, Luther used the term and concept of the *ecclesia universalis*, the universal church, when he rejected the confinement of this universal church to the catholic church of the West. As examples of the wider, comprehensive nature of the Christian church he referred to the Greek Church of the Eastern/Oriental tradition, which for centuries has never been under the pope and yet without doubt belongs to world Christianity. His other example was the Bohemian Church in the tradition of Jan Hus, which has explicitly confessed through Hus at Constance in 1415 that it belongs to the one universal church (WA 2, 279). Luther also mentioned the "Muscovites," White Russians, Greeks, and many other great nations of the world (WA 6, 287/LW 39, 58). He mentioned Christians in India, Persia, and the whole Orient (WA 54, 213/LW 41, 271; cf. also WA 38, 264/LW 38, 224).

This universal dimension of the church beyond Rome and the Latin West is captured marvelously in Luther's explanation of the third article of the Creed in his *Small Catechism*. There he teaches Christian lay people to better understand their faith and give an account of it, saying that, according to this article, "the Holy Spirit has called me through the Gospel, enlightened me with his gifts, and sanctified and kept me in true faith. In the same way he (the Holy Spirit) calls, gathers, enlightens, and sanctifies the whole Christian church on earth (*die ganze Christenheit auf Erden*), and keeps it united with Jesus Christ in the one true faith" (*Small Catechism*, II:3). The individual, irreplaceable Christian and the whole Christian church on earth – these two are for Luther the decisive dimensions of the triune God's action and presence. The focus on one specific person and at the same time on the worldwide company of believers is simultaneous. The universal church, the one side of this spectrum, is the object of belief and confession, but it also becomes visible and tangible in the different churches in all places and of all times, as the above references indicate. This true and universal church is also present in Rome, but not only there (WA 26, 147, 506; 40/I, 69; 43, 597; 51, 479/LW 40, 231; 37, 367; 26, 24; 5, 245; 41, 194f.), and it is present even among the Spiritualists/Enthusiasts (WA 40/I, 71/LW 26, 25f.). Luther did not want, however, that his followers use his name for their community. They should call themselves "Christians" (WA 8, 685/LW 45, 70).

(3) Viewing the church in its universal extension and nature leads Luther to connect this ecclesiological perspective with the characteristics of freedom and diversity. The church catholic is not bound to a particular place and a particular institution. It is present where true Christians are present in the world and where the church has its center clearly in Jesus Christ, where his Word remains alive, his sacraments are celebrated, and the confession of Jesus Christ goes on. To this foundation the church is bound, everything else is free. Where this foundation is maintained, the church can recognize the office of bishop (WA 50, 247f.) and can accept different ceremonies, rites, liturgical modes, forms of piety, etc. Thus, the "holy catholic or Christian church is in all places of the world and at each time, quite apart from the diversity or difference of the outward life and orders, customs and ceremonies" (WA 22, 299f. [1527]).

Martin Luther's framework of theological reflection was both the immediate and very concrete challenges he faced in his ecclesial environment and the wide-open dimension of the universal and catholic church as a reality to be believed and also to be experienced. He presupposed the presence of this whole Christian church on earth and related it to the existing partial and particular expressions of this church. This trans-provincial and pre-confessional ecclesiological horizon of Luther has certainly contributed to the wide reception of his person and work four centuries later in the worldwide church today.

## THE "LUTHER RENAISSANCE" IN THE TWENTIETH CENTURY

Luther did not disappear from the ecclesial scene after the dawn of the confessional age during the second half of the sixteenth century. On the contrary. When the late medieval Catholic church re-established itself as the *Roman* Catholic Church at the Council of Trent (1545–63) and the Lutheran, Reformed, and Anglican reform movements became institutionalized as churches (cf. for Lutheranism chapter 16 above), Luther became the key figure of Lutheranism. Already in the *Summary Formulation* of the introduction to the *Solid Declaration* part of the *Formula of Concord* of 1577, the last document in the corpus of Lutheran confessional texts, Luther's theology is presented, under the Word of God and in relation to the confessional texts, as being of normative significance. Luther was elevated to the honour of the "church father" of Lutheranism.

A new effort to understand the "real" Luther, to free him from the distorting interpretations of the past, set in during the first decades of the twentieth century. The shock of World War I, which had swept away the idealistic and nationalistic illusions and aberrations as well as their legitimating theological liberalism, has certainly contributed to the coming of the "Luther renaissance." "Back to the sources," back to Luther's own writings and those of his contemporaries, was one of the presuppositions of the new interest in Luther. The new, critical Weimar Edition of his works became an essential tool of research and also a basis for translations into other languages. Initiated in 1883, the "Weimarana," *D. Martin Luthers Werke. Kritische Gesamtausgabe*, has only recently been completed in 127 volumes. For Luther research in North America, the so-called "Walch Edition" of Halle from 1740–53 in 24 volumes was printed at St. Louis, Missouri, from 1880–1910 in a revised and expanded edition, while English translations in several volumes appeared at Minneapolis (1803–1910) and Philadelphia (1915–32) during the period of the Luther renaissance.

A rapidly growing number of studies on Luther in the framework of the Luther renaissance were based on an examination of the sources (now becoming more broadly available by means of the "Weimarana") and interpreted his life and thinking in relation both to his own time and to the modern world by way of showing forth Luther's significant impact on European intellectual history. Karl Holl (1866–1926) was the outstanding pioneer of the new wave of Luther studies (his own Luther studies appeared in 1921), and together with his "Holl school" of Luther scholars and other representatives of the Luther renaissance (Heinrich Boehmer, Werner Elert, Hanns Rückert, Carl Stange, Ernst Wolf, and others) brought Luther back to the center of serious theological and historical inquiry.

The new preoccupation with Luther was not limited to Germany. Theologians of the "Lund school" in Sweden such as Anders Nygren, Ragnar Bring, and Gustav Aulén initiated a highly important period of Luther research in their country and beyond during the 1920s and 1930s. They related their interest in scientific methodology and in history to their efforts to better understand Luther's theological thinking with the help of motive research.

In North America, also, a new era of Luther studies began during this time under the inspiration of Preserved Smith (1880–1941). It reached an impressive quantitative and qualitative level after World War II. The movement of dialectical theology, another protest child of the shock of World War I and led by Swiss theologian Karl Barth, contributed to the new interest in Luther studies by its return to fundamental Reformation ideas and perspectives. To this broader context of the Luther renaissance belong, finally, the beginnings of a change in Roman Catholic interpretation of the Reformation and of Luther.

## THE INTERNATIONAL SCOPE OF LUTHER STUDIES

As a result of the Luther renaissance, hundreds of books and articles in Europe and North America on Luther's life, his thinking, his place in history, and his influence on European society and culture were now available and have proved to be of help for those who during the crisis of World War II were looking for a firm spiritual and theological basis of their Christian confession in the face of idolatry and inhumanity. After World War II, Luther studies entered a new and even more intensive phase. There was continuity with the foundations laid by the Luther renaissance, the publishing process of the Weimar Edition was restarted, but there were also new questions directed to Luther's work that were provoked by the experience of Nazism and the war. Most important was, however, a further "internationalization" of Luther studies beyond Germany enabled, in part, by the ecumenical movement as well as by Roman Catholic Luther research. Critical editions of Luther's works were published or are still in the process of being published. The most widely known and, after the "Weimarana," the most comprehensive translation is *Luther's Works* with fifty-five volumes, published in St. Louis and Philadelphia from 1955 to 1986. Smaller and larger editions of Luther's works have come out or are published in all European countries with a Lutheran presence, even where it is a Christian minority as in France, but also in Italian, Spanish, Portugese (Brazil), Japanese, Korean, and other languages. A Chinese edition is in preparation.

In Europe, the center of Luther research continued to be in Germany with hundreds of publications during the last decades on many aspects of Luther's life, work, historical context, his impact and continuing significance. Monumental biographical studies appeared, such as the three-volume biography by Martin Brecht. Paul Althaus, Heinrich Bornkamm,

Walter von Loewenich, the Dutch historian Heiko Oberman during his pro-
fessorial career in Germany, Gerhard Ebeling, and Bernhard Lohse have with
their comprehensive presentations of Luther's theology and other studies
contributed significantly to a wider appreciation of Luther's theology. Secular historians in former socialist East Germany (GDR) presented a Marxist
reinterpretation of Luther (contrary to the old image of a servant of the
princes) and considered him in the line of Friedrich Engels as one of the ini-
tiators of the early bourgeois revolution while recognizing also his primary
role as a theologian.

In Lutheran northern Europe, the study of Luther's theology has continued with important contributions on Luther's understanding of the work of
the Holy Spirit and sanctification, creation and ethics, and soteriology, especially by, among others, Regin Prenter in Denmark and Gustav Wingren
and Gunnar Hillerdal in Sweden, while a new and very active school of
Luther research has emerged in Finland. Tuomo Mannermaa, professor at
the University of Helsinki, and a circle of younger researchers have developed a new approach to several aspects of Luther's theology. The original
impulse for their enterprise came from the bilateral theological dialogue
between the Evangelical Lutheran Church of Finland and the Russian
Orthodox Church since the 1970s. In order to find a comparable concept to
the Orthodox view of the *theosis*, the deification of the human person, the
Helsinki scholars have moved beyond the German Protestant tradition of
negating ontological perspectives in Luther's theology by showing that, and
how, such perspectives are, indeed, present. Such perspectives can help explain the relationship between humans and God also in the sense of human
participation in Christ through his presence in our faith, within us (*Christus
in nobis*), by which we receive the grace and righteousness of God.

In Great Britain, Luther's theology had played a not insignificant role
in the early phase of the English Reformation (Thomas Cranmer, William
Tyndale, Robert Barnes, et al.). However, Luther's theological presence and
influence were soon replaced by Calvin and Reformed theology, and during
the following centuries only marginal references were made to Luther, often
in the sense of a caricature of the not very gentlemanlike German reformer.
After World War II, however, Luther was rediscovered by historians and
theologians eager to do him justice. During the first decade after the war,
Gordon Rupp has claimed, more publications on Luther came out than in the
centuries before. Among these and the many that followed, together with a
new wave of Reformation studies that considered the English Reformation
as part of a comprehensive European Reformation movement, were studies by James Atkinson, James Cargill Thompson, Brian Gerrish, Thomas
Torrance, Philip Watson, and especially Gordon Rupp. These and other

historians and theologians have liberated Luther from distorting clichés and awakened among many students, theologians, historians, and lay people a new interest in a fascinating reformer.

Together with the Anglican, Methodist, and Reformed interpreters in Great Britain, Luther was also re-studied by Lutheran and Reformed scholars in France (esp. Marc Lienhard), the Netherlands (e.g. Willem J. Kooiman), Italy (e.g. Giovanni Miegge), and Switzerland, while such studies were very much limited in Eastern Europe until the political changes of 1989/90 provided freedom of research again. But even under communist oppression there was a continuing interest in Luther and the creative studies on Luther's "two-kingdom" concept by the Slovak theologian Igor Kiss found attention also in the West.

Contrary to Great Britain where there has been only a tiny Lutheran minority of mostly expatriates, North America with its fairly large number of Lutheran immigrants provided a necessary and fertile ground for encounters with Martin Luther, both popular and scholarly. After a lively interest in Luther had already surfaced in the nineteenth century, North American studies on the Reformation and on Luther, both by Lutherans and members of other traditions, reached an impressive level, quantitatively as well as qualitatively, in the second half of the twentieth century.

One of the Luther scholars, Scott Hendrix (cf. his "American Luther Research in the Twentieth Century", *Lutheran Quarterly* 15 [2001], 1–23), has structured the mountain of Luther studies by theologians, church historians, and researchers in other fields into three characteristic interests and emphases: (1) The spirit and impact of the person of Luther. In this predominantly biographical orientation, the "pioneer" Preserved Smith, already mentioned above, is followed by Roland Bainton whose book on Luther, *Here I Stand* (1950), has become the most widely read book on the reformer. At the other end of the spectrum we find Erik Erikson's much discussed psychoanalytical study *Young Man Luther* (1958). Further biographical presentations followed (e.g., by Mark U. Edwards Jr., Eric Gritsch, H. G. Haile, James Kittelson).

(2) Other studies focused on an interpretation of Luther in the historical and theological-intellectual context of the late Middle Ages, Renaissance, and Reformation (e.g. Harold Grimm, Ernst Schwiebert).

(3) Luther's theology. There seems to exist as yet no comprehensive presentation of Luther's theology, and German books on this topic are translated and widely used (the latest one being Bernhard Lohse's *Martin Luther's Theology: Its Historical and Systematic Development*, 1999). However, there are numerous studies on specific aspects of Luther's thinking, for example on his social ethics (F. Edward Cranz, George W. Forell, Carter Lindberg),

relation to mysticism (Bengt Hoffman, Steven Ozment), presentation of the "catholic Luther" (Carl Braaten, Robert Jenson, Carolyn Schneider, David Yeago), and a contrary position that points out the continuing reality of Christians being simultaneously justified and sinners (Gerhard Forde, Timothy Wengert), and accordingly denies any connection between Luther and mysticism and is also very critical of an ontological, internal view of justification such as that emphasized by Finnish Luther research (see above). Furthermore, other studies deal with Luther's interpretation of Holy Scripture (Heinz Bluhm, Kenneth Hagen, Jaroslav Pelikan, David Steinmetz) and with his significance as reformer of education (Marilyn Harran, Lewis W. Spitz).

One remarkable result of North American Luther studies that is of lasting importance is the preparation and publication of the American Edition of *Luther's Works* (see above). It combines historical-critical editorial competence with accessibility for modern readers and has, indeed, made Luther available to thousands of pastors, theological students, and lay people. In Australia, Luther studies were inspired especially by the German/Australian scholar Hermann Sasse.

An important new perspective on the person and work of Martin Luther has been introduced by theologians (e.g. Walter Altmann, Yoshikazu Tokuzen) in Africa, Asia, and, especially, Latin America. Here, the general hermeneutical reality, often not acknowledged by Europeans and North Americans, that the theological, social-political, and cultural context of the interpreter, together with his/her corresponding pre-understanding, becomes part of his/her interpretation, is not only acknowledged but explicitly applied. Accordingly, Luther's person and work are interpreted as a thought-provoking help for theological reflection within a situation of poverty, injustice, dependency, exploitation, and oppression. This is facilitated by the recognition that there exists a certain similarity between Third World countries and the situation prevailing at Luther's time to which he clearly relates: economic misery, low literacy, lack of liberty, oppression by the rich, etc. In these interpretations, Luther's addressees now become the poor and alienated, and many of his social-ethical statements are rediscovered and reinterpreted by drawing them out into contemporary situations while holding fast to their decisive theological-spiritual foundations. Some examples are: Justification by faith and through grace alone leads to participation in God's reign with the aim of transforming evil social structures; God's call comes to us in the needy; in our commitment to the suffering people our gratitude to God is demonstrated; God is served in the oppressed; grounded in her/his justification, the liberty of the Christian in faith before God and in service to others leads to the freedom to use his/her reason, learn from non-Christians, resist oppressive forces, work for more justice; etc. Luther, thus, becomes relevant in new and unexpected ways as a theologian who speaks to the worldwide church.

## THE RADICAL CHANGE OF CATHOLIC PERCEPTIONS OF LUTHER

Parallel to the Protestant-Lutheran captivity of Luther during the centuries after the Reformation has been its negative reflection in Roman Catholic publications. Until the first half of the twentieth century works about and references to Luther continued the tradition established by the extremely negative portrayal of Luther in a first Roman Catholic biography written by Johann Cochlaeus (1479–1552). Here, Luther was condemned as a son of Satan, an antichrist. Accordingly, the way was opened to a flow of serious literature as well as pamphlets in which in a highly polemical style Luther was described as the destroyer of the unity of the Latin church, a heretic who had betrayed the true faith, and a psychologically and morally ill and inferior creature. Even at the beginning of the twentieth century, serious and knowledgeable Roman Catholic historians such as Heinrich Denifle (*Luther und Luthertum in ihrer ersten Entwicklung*, 1904–09) and Hartmut Grisar continued to describe Luther's destructive impact on people or regarded him simply as sick. Thirty years later a historical change in the Roman Catholic portrayal of Luther was signaled and advanced by Joseph Lortz' epochal work *The Reformation in Germany* (1939; ET 1968/69). Lortz rehabilitates Luther as a serious religious personality, who is forced by the lamentable condition of the church of his time and the aberrations of the theological schools to take on a reforming position. Not Luther, but the church of his time is to a large degree responsible for the split within the church.

This change in the Roman Catholic position is not yet shared by all. But Lortz has found an increasing number of followers, and during the last decades also outside Germany. The first generation of the new school of Catholic Luther research followed Lortz in its critique of past Roman Catholic depictions of Luther, in its realistic description of the condition of the late medieval church, and in its new understanding of Luther as a religious personality and as of historical significance, as – in many of his views – a "catholic Luther" who was still part of the catholic faith tradition. The second generation of Roman Catholic Luther researchers (e.g. Albert Brandenburg, Peter Manns, Harry McSorley, Daniel Olivier, Otto Hermann Pesch, Jared Wicks) has taken a further step. These theologians and historians no longer interpret Luther "backwards," comparing him with the ecclesial and theological tradition of his time in order to discern where he has remained "catholic" and where he has left this tradition. Rather, they seek to understand Luther by studying specific aspects of his theology, relate him to other leading theologians such as Thomas Aquinas, advocate a reception of his spiritual and theological insights that are of continuing relevance, and thus see him as part of a common Christian tradition or are even prepared to call him "father in the faith" (Peter Manns).

A certain official Roman Catholic legitimization received the new Roman Catholic view of Luther and his theology in a speech of Cardinal Jan Willebrands at the Fifth Assembly of the Lutheran World Federation in Evian, France, in 1970. There the cardinal affirmed the new directions and results of Roman Catholic Luther studies by emphasizing especially Luther's deep understanding of the concept of faith and justification in which Luther can be "our common teacher" (*Sent Into the World*, The Proceedings of the Fifth Assembly of the Lutheran World Federation [Minneapolis: Augsburg Publishing House, 1971], 62–64).

Ten years later, on the occasion of Martin Luther's 500th birthday in 1983, another important step was taken by the official international Roman Catholic/Lutheran Joint Commission. In its statement *Martin Luther – Witness to Jesus Christ* (printed in Roman Catholic/Lutheran Joint Commission, *Facing Unity* [Geneva: Lutheran World Federation, 1985]), the commission considers the reformer in the framework of the movement "from conflict to reconciliation." It is recognized that "Luther's call for church reform, a call to repentance, is still relevant for us" (p. 73) and that "Luther points beyond his own person in order to confront us all the more inescapably with the promise and the claim of the gospel he confessed" (p. 75). The results of the intensive Catholic reevaluation of Luther as a person and of his Reformation concerns are underlined and Cardinal Willebrand's words (see above) are taken up. The statement shows how Vatican II reflects basic concerns of Luther (pp. 77–78). In a way the question in this statement is no longer "How catholic was Luther?" but "To what degree is there a convergence between Roman Catholic thinking and Luther's theological concerns?" A list of learnings from Luther closes this remarkable text (p. 79).

The radically reversed Roman Catholic understanding of the person, work, and continuing relevance of Luther has led to an attitude and conviction of considering Luther as part of a common heritage. This new perspective has been spread in the churches also by joint Catholic–Lutheran studies and publications, including study guides and other educational materials. Because of its specific and negative historical background, Roman Catholic Luther research and the changed attitude to Luther in general have, more than other denominational studies, "de-confessionalized" Luther. A process has been initiated of revising false clichés and prejudices and introducing in the largest section of world Christianity a more positive picture of the reformer.

## THE RECEPTION OF LUTHER IN THE WORLDWIDE CHURCH

With the international scope of Luther studies and the changed Roman Catholic view of the reformer as well as first Orthodox voices expressing interest in the theology of Luther, the scholarly study and interpretation of Luther and its broader impact have truly become both interconfessional and international. This new reality comes to expression in a lively exchange and discussion between Luther scholars through meetings and publications and especially also at their regular meetings in the International Congresses on Luther Research under the auspices of the Lutheran World Federation. These congresses have met every five or six years since 1956 and Catholic scholars have participated in them since 1966. Another means of communication and tool for research is the international Luther bibliography, published since 1957 in the annual *Lutherjahrbuch*, listing each year several hundred new titles of books and articles dealing with the person and work of the reformer. These studies and exchanges have significantly contributed to the reception of the person and work of Luther in the worldwide church.

But there have been other factors also in this reception process. This process would not have been possible without the emergence of the ecumenical movement and its impact on twentieth-century church history. One of the goals of the ecumenical movement is to move Christians beyond mutual respect and understanding to a sharing, an exchange of the specific gifts of theological insight and spiritual experience that each Christian tradition has to offer. In this process of sharing and exchange these gifts become increasingly available to all who look for them and thus become part of the spiritual treasure of world Christianity. Thus, medieval women prophets and mystics such as Hildegard von Bingen and Julian of Norwich or twentieth-century martyrs such as Lutheran pastor Dietrich Bonhoeffer and Catholic Archbishop Oscar Romero have become part of common Christian heritage and inspiration. Martin Luther was and is discovered to be such a gift of Lutheranism to world Christianity and many willingly receive this gift. To make this gift available, popular brochures and general books on the reformer are brought out in diverse languages, together with documentary films, videos, extensive references to Luther in dictionaries as well as in books on literature, culture, and philosophy, presentations of Luther in the performing arts (e.g. by John Osborne) and, innumerably, in the visual arts.

Another contributing factor to the worldwide reception of Luther has been, quite naturally, the movement of Lutheranism from Europe to all continents through emigration (North and South America, Australia) and mission (Africa and Asia). Emigrants and missionaries brought Luther with them – in whatever package – and made him known in their new homelands. The more than 140 Lutheran churches and several united churches all use Luther's *Small Catechism* for catechetical instruction, they have included Luther's hymns in their hymnbooks, use his prayers, inform about him in articles and books, refer to his thoughts in sermons, and communicate Luther to their sisters and brothers in other denominations. One should also not underestimate the fact that in the past Luther has become a much referred to figure of cultural history far beyond Germany and that this has also contributed to the growing and broadening interest within Christianity in his life and work.

Decisive, however, in the process of receiving Luther as a theologian and teacher of the Christian church is the attraction and fascination that are created by his personality, spirituality, and thinking. To believe like and with Luther has for many become a strong motive of their interest in the reformer. They are impressed and moved by his confident, unshakable faith, imaginative preaching, poetic as well as down-to-earth language, joyful earthiness, deep piety, cruciform realism, sovereign exercise of Christian liberty, courage to resist the powerful, radical commitment to God's calling, and other characteristics of his personality. And there are Luther's theological insights that are rediscovered, reinterpreted, and reaffirmed again and again because they seem to assume fresh light and relevance in everchanging situations and times and now also in other Christian traditions than his own: focus on the primary and exclusive initiative of God for our salvation; God's condescension and presence in Christ and through Word and sacrament, the external means of God's grace; the unconditional and liberating acceptance – justification – of fallible human beings; the gift of the Holy Spirit who creates faith and enlivens the church; the dignity and responsibility of all Christians before God and in service to their neighbors; the glorious liberty of the justified ones; the distinction between God's reign in the church and God's sustaining and providential reign in the world; the law and gospel dialectic; the dynamic interpretation of the authority of the Bible with the gospel as its criterion; the call addressed to the churches to constant renewal; Christian unity based on the fundamentals of faith together with great liberty in outward forms and theological positions – and other theological perspectives that have not lost their contemporary significance as long as they are not simply repeated but interpreted.

There are facets in Luther's work that are time-bound or even wrong and inexcusable, like his statements about the Jews and the rebellious peasants. But there is also such an inexhaustible richness surrounding his personality and embedded in his work, that the worldwide church has rightly taken hold of him as a model of faith and source of inspiration.

# Select bibliography

## Luther's life

Bainton, Roland H. *Here I Stand. A Life of Martin Luther.* Nashville: Abingdon Press, 1978; London: Penguin, 2002.

Beutel, Albrecht. *Martin Luther* (Beck'sche Reihe Autorenbücher 621). Munich: Verlag C. H. Beck, 1991.

Bott, Gerhard, Ebeling, Gerhard, and Moeller, Bernd, eds. *Martin Luther. Sein Leben in Bildern und Texten.* Frankfurt a M.: Insel-Verlag, 1983.

Brecht, Martin. *Martin Luther.* 3 vols. Stuttgart: Calwer Verlag, 1981–87. Eng. trans. James L. Schaaf, Minneapolis: Fortress Press, 1985–93.

Ebeling, Gerhard. *Lutherstudien.* 5 vols. Tübingen: Verlag C. B. Mohr (Paul Siebeck), 1971–89.

Grosshans, Hans-Peter. *Luther.* London: HarperCollins Publishers, 1997.

Haile, Harry Gerald. *Luther: An Experiment in Biography.* Garden City, NY: Doubleday, 1980.

Junghans, Helmar. *Martin Luther: Exploring His Life and Times, 1483–1546.* CD ROM. Minneapolis: Fortress Press, 1998.

Junghans, Helmar, ed. *Leben und Werk Martin Luthers von 1526 bis 1546.* Berlin: Evangelische Verlagsanstalt, 1983.

Kittelson, James M. *Luther the Reformer: The Story of the Man and His Career.* Minneapolis: Augsburg, 1986.

Lohse, Bernhard. *Martin Luther: An Introduction to His Life and Work.* Trans. Robert Schultz. Philadelphia: Fortress Press, 1986.

Oberman, Heiko A. *Luther: Man Between God and the Devil.* Trans. Eileen Walliser-Schwarzbart. New York: Image Books, 1992.

Schwarz, Reinhard. *Luther.* Göttingen: UTB, 1998.

Smith, Preserved, *The Life and Letters of Martin Luther.* London: Hodder & Stoughton, 1993.

Todd, John Murray. *Luther. A Life.* New York: Crossroad, 1982.

von Loewenich, Walther. *Martin Luther: The Man and His Work,* trans. Lawrence W. Denef. Minneapolis: Augsburg, 1986.

## Luther's Wittenberg

Bellmann, Fritz, Harksen, Marie-Luise, and Werner, Roland, eds. *Die Denkmale der Lutherstadt Wittenberg.* Weimar: Böhlau, 1979.

Bünger, Fritz and Wentz, Gottfried, eds. *Das Bistum Brandenburg.* Part 2. Germania Sacra, Abt. 1: Die Bistümer der Kirchenprovinz Magdeburg, Vol. III. Berlin: de Gruyter, 1941.

Hennen, Insa Christiane. *Zu den Quellen!: Katalog zur Dauerausstellung im Melanchthonhaus, Redaktion.* Wittenberg: Reformationsgeschichtliche Museen Wittenberg, 1997.

Junghans, Helmar, ed. *Leben und Werk Martin Luthers von 1526 bis 1546.* Berlin: Evangelische Verlagsanstalt; Göttingen: Vandenhoeck & Ruprecht, 1983.

*Martin Luther und Wittenberg.* Munich/Berlin: Koehler und Amelang, 1996.

*Katalog der Hauptausstellung in der Lutherhalle Wittenberg.* Berlin: Schelzky & Jepp, 1993.

Oehmig, Stefan, ed. *700 Jahre Wittenberg: Stadt, Universität, Reformation.* Weimar: Böhlau, 1995.

Steffens, Martin and Hennen, Insa Christiane, eds. *Von der Kapelle zum Nationaldenkmal: die Wittenberger Schloßkirche.* Wittenberg: Stiftung Luthergedenkstätten in Sachsen-Anhalt, 1998.

### *Luther as Bible translator*

Bluhm, Heinz. *Martin Luther: Creative Translator.* St. Louis: Concordia Publishing House, 1965. An informative survey of Luther's work, with helpful samples of his translations.

Bornkamm, Heinrich. *Luther and the Old Testament.* New edn., trans. Eric W. Gritsch and Ruth C. Gritsch. Ramsey, NJ: Sigler Press, 2000. Rpt. 1969 edn.

Brecht, Martin. *Martin Luther.* Trans. James L. Schaaf. 3 vols. Minneapolis: Fortress Press, 1999. Vol. II, chs. 1, 6. III, ch. 4. The most contemporary, detailed German study of Luther's life and work. The chapters and sections narrate the story of Luther's work as a Bible translator, with a bibliography.

Gritsch, Eric W. *Martin – God's Court Jester. Luther in Retrospect.* 2nd edn. Ramsey, NJ: Sigler Press, 1990. Rpt. 1983 edn. Ch. 5 on "Scripture and tradition." Describes the theological context of Luther's translation of the Bible.

Hobbs, Gerald, R. "Bible Translations," in Hillerbrand, Hans J., ed. *The Oxford Encyclopedia of the Reformation.* 4 vols. New York and Oxford: Oxford University Press, 1996. I:163–66. Survey of most translations of the Bible in the sixteenth century.

Lotz, David, W. "Luther on Biblical Authority," in *Encounters with Luther.* Lectures, discussions and sermons at the "Martin Luther Colloquia 1975–1979." Vol. II, ed. Eric W. Gritsch. Gettysburg, PA: Institute for Luther Studies, 1982, pp. 127–44.

Luther, Martin. "On Translating: an Open Letter," 1530, LW 35, 177–202. "Defense of the Translation of the Psalms," LW 35, 209–23.

Steinmetz, David, C., ed. *The Bible in the Sixteenth Century.* Papers of the Second International Colloquium on Sixteenth Century Biblical Exegesis, Durham, North Carolina, 1982. Durham, NC: Duke University Press, 1990. Helpful background material.

Wood, A. Skevington. *Captive to the Word. Martin Luther: Doctor of Sacred Scripture.* Grand Rapids: Wm. B. Eerdmans Publishing Company, 1969. A theological biography with some attention to Luther's work as a Bible translator.

Readers of German will encounter two thorough studies:

Raeder, Siegfried. *Luther als Ausleger und Übersetzer der Heiligen Schrift [Luther as Interpreter and Translator of Holy Scripture]*, Leben und Werk Martin Luthers von 1526–1546. Festgabe zu seinem 500. Geburtstag. 2 vols. Ed. Helmar Junghans. Göttingen: Vandenhoeck & Ruprecht, 1983, I:253–78.

Stolt, Birgit. *Luthers Übersetzungstheorie und Übersetzungspraxis [Luther's Theory of Translation and His Praxis of Translation]*, Leben und Werk ... I:241–52.

### Luther's theology

Althaus, Paul. *The Theology of Martin Luther.* Trans. Robert C. Schultz. Philadelphia: Fortress Press, 1966.

Ebeling, Gerhard. *Luther: An Introduction to His Thought.* Trans. R. A. Wilson. Philadelphia: Fortress Press, 1970.

Gerrish, Brian A. *Grace and Reason: A Study in the Theology of Martin Luther.* Oxford: Oxford University Press, 1962.

Loeschen. John R. *Wrestling with Luther: An Introduction to the Study of His Thought.* St. Louis: Concordia, 1976.

Mannermaa, Tuomo. Der im Glauben gegenwärtige Christus: Rechtfertigung und Vergottung zum ökumenischen Dialog. Hanover: Lutherisches Verlagshaus, 1989.

McGrath, Alister E. *Luther's Theology of the Cross: Martin Luther's Theological Breakthrough.* Grand Rapids: Baker, 1990.

Ngien, Dennis. *The Suffering of God According to Martin Luther's 'Theologia Crucis'.* American University Studies. New York: Peter Lang, 1995.

Pelikan, Jaroslav. *Reformation of Church and Dogma.* Vol. IV of *The Christian Tradition: A History of the Development of Doctrine.* Chicago: University of Chicago Press, 1984.

Seeberg, Reinhold. *Text-book of the History of Doctrines.* Trans. Charles E. Hay. Grand Rapids: Baker, 1952.

von Loewenich, Walther. *Luther's Theology of the Cross.* Trans. Herbert J. A. Bouman. Minneapolis: Augsburg, 1976.

Watson, Philip S. *Let God Be God: An Interpretation of the Theology of Martin Luther.* Philadelphia: Fortress Press, 1947.

### Luther's moral theology
Primary sources:

*Concerning the Blessed Sacrament of the Holy and True Body of Christ and the Brotherhoods*, 1519 (WA 2, 742–58).

*The Freedom of a Christian*, 1520, in *Luther's Works*, vol. XXXI. Ed. Harold J. Grimm, trans. from the Latin by W. A. Lambert, and rev. by Grimm. Philadelphia: Muhlenberg Press, 1957, 327–77.

*Treatise on Good Works*, 1520, in *Luther's Works*, vol. XLIV. Ed. James Atkinson, trans. from the German by W. A. Lambert and rev. by Atkinson. Philadelphia: Fortress Press, 1966, 15–114.

*Temporal Authority: To What Extent It Should Be Obeyed*, 1523, in *Luther's Works*, vol. XLV. Ed. Walther I. Brandt, trans. from the German by J. J. Schindel and rev. by Brandt. Philadelphia: Muhlenberg Press, 1962, 75–129.

*Lectures on Galatians*, 1535, in *Luther's Works*, vols. XXVI, XXVII. Ed. and trans. from the Latin by Jaroslav Pelikan. St. Louis: Concordia Publishing House, 1963, 1964.

*Luthers Psalmenauslegung.* vol. II, ed. Chr. Eberle. Stuttgart: Evang. Bücherstiftung, 1987.

*The Book of Concord: The Confessions of the Evangelical Lutheran Church.* Ed. Robert Kolb and Timothy J. Wengert, trans. Charles Arand et. al. Minneapolis: Fortress Press, 2000. Cf. the older English edition edited by Theodore G. Tappert in collaboration with Jaroslav Pelikan, Robert H. Fischer, and Arthur C. Piepkorn. Philadelphia: Fortress Press, 1959.

*The Book of Concord on CD-ROM.* Ed. Robert Kolb and Timothy J. Wengert. Minneapolis: Fortress Press, 2000.

Secondary sources:

Althaus, Paul. *The Ethics of Martin Luther.* Trans. from the German and with a Foreword by Robert C. Schultz. Philadelphia: Fortress Press, 1972.

Bayer, Oswald. "Luther's Ethics as Pastoral Care," *Lutheran Quarterly* 4/2 (1990), 125–42.

*Freiheit als Antwort. Zur theologischen Ethik.* Tübingen: Verlag C. B. Mohr, 1995.

"Nature and Institution. Luther's doctrine of the three estates," trans. C. Helmer, *Lutheran Quarterly* 12/2 (1998), 125–59.

Bloomquist, Karen L. and Stumme, John R., eds. *The Promise of Lutheran Ethics.* Minneapolis: Fortress Press, 1998. Includes an extended bibliography.

Forell, George W. *Faith Active in Love: An Investigation of the Principles Underlying Luther's Social Ethics.* Minneapolis: Augsburg Publishing House, 1954.

"Freedom as Love: Luther's Treatise on Good Works," in Bielfeldt, Dennis D. and Schwarzwäller, Klaus, eds., *Freedom as Love in Martin Luther.* New York: Peter Lang, 1995, 79–84.

Holl, Karl. *The Reconstruction of Morality.* Ed. James Luther Adams and Walter F. Bense, trans. from the German by Fred W. Meuser and Walter R. Wietzke. Minneapolis: Augsburg Publishing House, 1979.

Hütter, Reinhard. "The Twofold Center of Lutheran Ethics: Christian Freedom and God's Commandments," in Bloomquist, Karen L. and Stumme, John R., eds., *The Promise of Lutheran Ethics.* Minneapolis: Fortress Press, 1998, 31–54.

Lehman, Paul L. *The Decalogue and a Human Future. The Meaning of the Commandments for Making and Keeping Human Life Human.* Grand Rapids: Eerdmans, 1995.

Peters, Albrecht. *Kommentar zu Luthers Katechismen.* Vol. I, *Die Zehn Gebote.* Göttingen: Vandenhoeck & Ruprecht, 1990.

Raunio, Antti. "Natural Law and Faith: The Forgotten Foundations in Ethics in Luther's Theology," in Braaten, Carl E. and Jenson, Robert W. eds., *Union with Christ: The New Finnish Interpretation of Luther.* Grand Rapids: Eerdmans, 1998, 96–124.

Troeltsch, Ernst. *The Social Teaching of the Christian Churches.* Vol. II, trans. from the German by Olive Wyon. New York: Harper & Row, 1960, 465–576.

Wannenwetsch, Bernd. "The Political Worship of the Church: A Critical and Empowering Practice," *Modern Theology* 12 (1996), 269–99.

"Caritas fide formata. 'Herz und Affekte' als Schlüssel zu 'Glaube und Liebe,'" *Kerygma und Dogma* 46 (2000), 205–24.

*Gottesdienst als Lebensform. Ethik für Christenbürger.* Stuttgart, Berlin, Cologne: Kohlhammer, 1997.

Wingren, Gustaf. *Luther on Vocation.* Trans. from the Swedish by Carl C. Rasmussen. Philadelphia: Muhlenberg Press, 1957.

Yeago, David. "Martin Luther on Grace, Law and Moral Life. Prolegomena to an Ecumenical Discussion of Veritatis Splendor," *The Thomist* 62 (1998), 163–91.

### Luther's spiritual journey

Asendorf, Ulrich. *Eschatologie bei Luther.* Göttingen: Vandenhoeck & Ruprecht, 1967.

Gassmann, Günther and Hendrix, Scott. *Fortress Introduction to the Lutheran Confessions.* Minneapolis: Fortress Press, 1999.

Gerrish, B. A. " 'To the Unknown God': Luther and Calvin on the Hiddenness of God," in *The Old Protestantism and the New: Essays on the Reformation Heritage.* Edinburgh: T&T Clark, 1982.

"The Chief Article – Then and Now," in *Continuing the Reformation: Essays on Modern Religious Thought.* Chicago: University of Chicago Press, 1993.

"Doctor Martin Luther: Subjectivity and Doctrine in the Lutheran Reformation," in *Continuing the Reformation: Essays on Modern Religious Thought.* Chicago: University of Chicago Press, 1993.

Hoffman, Bengt R. *Luther and the Mystics: A Reexamination of Luther's Spiritual Experience and His Relationship to the Mystics.* Minneapolis: Augsburg Publishing House, 1976.

Lienhard, Marc. *Luther's Witness to Jesus Christ: Stages and Themes of the Reformer's Christology.* Trans. Edwin H. Robertson. Minneapolis: Augsburg Publishing House, 1982.

Lohse, Bernhard. *Martin Luther's Theology: Its Historical and Systematic Development.* Ed. and trans. Roy A. Harrisville. Minneapolis: Fortress Press, 1999.

Lull, Timothy F., ed. *Martin Luther's Basic Theological Writings.* Minneapolis: Fortress Press, 1989.

Matheson, Peter. *The Imaginative World of the Reformation.* Edinburgh: T&T Clark, 2000.

Oberman, Heiko A. "Simul genitus et raptus. Luther und die Mystik," in *Die Reformation: Von Wittenberg nach Genf.* Göttingen: Vandenhoeck & Ruprecht, 1986.

Steinmetz, David C. "Luther and the Hidden God," in *Luther in Context.* Bloomington, IN: Indiana University Press, 1986.

Wicks, Jared. *Luther and His Spiritual Legacy.* Wilmington, DE: Michael Glazier, 1983.

Wingren, Gustaf. *Luther on Vocation.* Trans. Carl C. Rasmussen. Philadelphia: Muhlenberg Press, 1957.

### Luther's struggle with social-ethical issues

Lindberg, Carter. *Beyond Charity: Reformation Initiatives for the Poor.* Minneapolis: Fortress Press, 1993.

"Luther on Poverty," *Lutheran Quarterly* 15 (Spring 2001), 85–101.

Pawlas, Andreas. *Die lutherische Berufs- und Wirtschaftsethik: Eine Einführung.* Neukirchen-Vluyn: Neukirchener, 2000.

Prien, Hans-Jürgen. *Luthers Wirtschaftsethik*. Göttingen: Vandenhoeck & Ruprecht, 1992.

Rieth, Ricardo. *"Habsucht" bei Martin Luther. Ökonomisches und theologisches Denken, Tradition und soziale Wirklichkeit im Zeitalter der Reformation*. Weimar: Böhlaus, 1996.

Strohm, Theodor. "Luthers Wirtschafts- und Sozialethik," in Junghans, Helmar, ed., *Leben und Werk Martin Luthers von 1526 bis 1546*. Berlin: Evangelische Verlagsanstalt, 1983, 205–23.

" 'Theologie der Diakonie' in der Perspektive der Reformation: Zur Wirkungs-geschichte des Diakonieverständnisses Martin Luthers," in Philippi, Paul and Strohm, Theodor, eds., *Theologie der Diakonie: Ein Europäischer Forschungsaus-tausch*. Heidelberg: Heidelberger Verlagsanstalt, 1989, 175–208.

Witte, John, Jr. *Law and Protestantism: The Legal Teachings of the Lutheran Refor-mation*. Cambridge: Cambridge University Press, 2002.

*Luther's political encounters*

Allen, J. W. *A History of Political Thought in the Sixteenth Century*. London: Methuen, 1957.

Cargill Thompson, W. D. J. *The Political Thought of Martin Luther*. Ed. Philip Broad-head. Totowa, NJ: Barnes & Noble, 1984.

Carlyle, R. W. and Carlyle, A. J. *A History of Medieval Political Theory in the West*. New York, Barnes & Noble, 1964.

Cranz, F. Edward. *An Essay on the Development of Luther's Thought on Justice, Law, and Society*. Ed. Gerald Christianson and Thomas M. Izbicki with a new Introduction by Scott Hendrix. Mifflintown, PA: Sigler Press, 1997. Originally published in 1959.

Gritsch, Eric W. "The Use and Abuse of Luther's Political Advice," *Lutherjahrbuch* 1990, 207–19.

Höpfl, Harro. "Luther, Martin," in David Miller, ed., *The Blackwell Encyclopedia of Political Thought*. New York: Blackwell, 1987.

Hoffmann, Manfred, ed. *Martin Luther and the Modern Mind: Freedom, Con-science, Toleration, and Rights*. New York and Toronto: Edwin Mellen Press, 1985.

Keen, Ralph. *Divine and Human Authority in Reformation Thought: German Theolo-gians on Political Order, 1520–1555*. Nieuwkoop: B. De Graaf, 1997.

Kingdon, Robert. *Church and Society in Reformation Europe*. London: Variorum, 1985.

Kouri, E. I. and Scott, Tom, eds. *Politics and Society in Reformation Europe: Essays for Sir Geoffrey Elton on his Sixty-Fifth Birthday*. London: Macmillan, 1987.

Lau, Franz. *Luthers Lehre von den beiden Reichen*. Berlin: Evangelische Verlagsanstalt, 1952.

Lindberg, Carter. "Conflicting Models of Ministry: Luther, Karlstadt, and Müntzer," *Concordia Theological Quarterly* 41/4 (1977), 35–50.

Ozment, Steven. *Protestants: The Birth of a Revolution*. New York: Doubleday, 1992.

Skinner, Quentin. *The Foundations of Modern Political Thought*. Vol. II, *The Age of the Reformation*. Cambridge: Cambridge University Press, 1978.

Tonkin, John. *The Church and the Secular Order in Reformation Thought*. New York, Columbia University Press, 1971.

Tracy, James D., ed. *Luther and the Modern State in Germany*. Kirksville, MO: Sixteenth Century Journal Publishers, 1986.

Whitford, David M. *Tyranny and Resistance: The Magdeburg Confession and the Lutheran Tradition*. St. Louis: Concordia, 2001.

Wolgast, Eike. *Die Wittenberger Theologie und die Politik der evangelischen Stände: Studien zu Luthers Gutachten in Politik*. Gütersloh: Gütersloher Verlagshaus Mohn, 1977.

*Luther's polemical controversies*

Bagchi, David V. N. *Luther's Earliest Opponents: Catholic Controversialists, 1518–1525*. Minneapolis: Fortress Press, 1991.

Chrisman, Miriam Usher. *Conflicting Visions of Reform: German Lay Propaganda Pamphlets, 1519–1530*. Studies in German Histories. New Jersey: Humanities Press, 1996.

Edwards, Jr., Mark U. *Luther and the False Brethren*. Stanford, CA: Stanford University Press, 1975.

Edwards, Jr., Mark U. *Luther's Last Battles: Politics and Polemics, 1531–1546*. Ithaca: Cornell University Press, 1983.

*Printing, Propaganda, and Martin Luther*. Berkeley: University of California Press, 1994.

Köhler, Hans-Joachim. "Erste Schritte zu einem Meinungsprofil der frühen Reformationszeit," in Press, Volker and Stievermann, Dieter, eds., *Martin Luther: Probleme seiner Zeit*. Stuttgart: Klett-Cotta, 1986.

"The *Flugschriften* and their Importance in Religious Debate: A Quantitative Approach," in Zambelli, Paola, ed., *'Astrologi hallucinati': Stars and the End of the Word in Luther's Time*. New York: Walter de Gruyter, 1986.

Matheson, Peter. *The Rhetoric of the Reformation*. Edinburgh: T&T Clark, 1998.

Maurer, Wilhelm. *Luther und die Schwärmer*. Berlin: Lutherisches Verlagshaus, 1952.

Oberman, Heiko A. *The Roots of Anti-Semitism in the Age of Renaissance and Reformation*. Trans. James I. Porter. Philadelphia: Fortress Press, 1981.

Scribner, Robert. *For the Sake of Simple Folk: Popular Propaganda for the German Reformation*. Cambridge: Cambridge University Press, 1981.

Zorzin, Alejandro. *Karlstadt als Flugschriftenautor*. Göttingen: Vandenhoeck & Ruprecht, 1990.

*Luther's function in an age of confessionalization*

Dingel, Irene. *Concordia controversa. Die öffentlichen Diskussionen um das lutherische Konkordienwerk am Ende des 16. Jahrhunderts*. Gütersloh: Gütersloher Verlagshaus, 1996.

Kolb, Robert. *Confessing the Faith: Reformers Define the Church, 1530–1580*. Saint Louis: Concordia, 1991.

*Martin Luther as Prophet, Teacher, and Hero: Images of the Reformer, 1520–1620*. Grand Rapids: Baker, 1999.

Lund, Eric, ed. *Documents from the History of Lutheranism 1517–1750*. Minneapolis: Fortress Press, 2002.

Mostert, Walter. "Luther, Martin. III. Wirkungsgeschichte," in Gerhard Krause, Gerhard Müller in Gemeinschaft mit Horst Robert Balz et al., eds., *Theologische Realenzyklopädie* XXI. Berlin: de Gruyter, 1991.

Pelikan, Jaroslav, ed. *Interpreters of Luther: Essays in Honor of Wilhelm Pauck.* Philadelphia: Fortress Press, 1968.

Schilling, Johannes. "Lutherausgaben," in Gerhard Krause, Gerhard Müller in Gemeinschaft mit Horst Robert Balz et al., eds., *Theologische Realenzyklopädie* XXI. Berlin: de Gruyter, 1991.

Schönstädt, Hans-Jürgen. *Antichrist, Weltheilsgeschehen und Gottes Werkzeug. Römische Kirche, Reformation und Luther im Spiegel des Reformationsjubiläums 1617.* Wiesbaden: Steiner, 1978.

Stephan, Horst. *Luther in den Wandlungen seiner Kirche.* Giessen: Töpelmann, 1907.

Volz, Hans. *Die Lutherpredigten des Johannes Mathesius: Kritische Untersuchung zur Geschichtsschreibung im Zeitalter der Reformation.* Halle: Waisenhaus, 1929.

Wolgast, Eike. "Biographie als Autoritätsstiftung: Die ersten evangelischen Luther-biographien," in Berschin, Walter, ed., *Biographie zwischen Renaissance und Barock.* Heidelbert: Matthes, 1993.

Zeeden, Ernst Walter. *Martin Luther und die Reformation im Urteil des deutschen Luthertums: Studien zum Selbstverständnis des lutherischen Protestantismus von Luthers Tode bis zum Beginn der Goethezeit.* 2 vols. Freiburg/B: Herder, 1952.

Supplemental titles:

Bäumer, Remigius. *Johannes Cochläus (1479–1552): Leben und Werk im Dienst der katholischen Reform.* Münster: Aschendorff, 1980.

Herrmann, Wolfgang. "Die Lutherpredigten des Cyriacus Spangenberg," *Mansfelder Blätter* 39 (1934/35), 7–95.

Moeller, Bernd, ed. *Luther in der Neuzeit: Wissenschaftliches Symposion des Vereins für Reformationsgeschichte.* Gütersloh: Mohn, 1983.

Nischan, Bodo. "Reformation or Deformation? Lutheran and Reformed Views of Martin Luther in Brandenburg's 'Second Reformation,'" in Sessions, Kyle C. and Bebb, Phillip N., eds., *Pietas et Societas: New Trends in Reformation Social History: Essays in Memory of Harold J. Grimm.* Kirksville: Sixteenth Century Journal, 1985.

Söderlund, Rune. *Ex praevisa fide. Zum Verständnis der Prädestinationslehre in der lutherischen Orthodoxie.* Hamburg: Lutherisches Verlagshaus, 1983.

*Luther in the worldwide church today*

Edwards, Jr., Mark U. and Tavard, George, eds. *Luther: A Reformer for the Churches: An Ecumenical Study Guide.* Philadelphia and New York: Fortress Press and Paulist Press, 1983.

Manns, P. and Meyer, H., eds. *Luther's Ecumenical Significance: An Interconfessional Consultation.* Philadelphia and New York: Fortress Press and Paulist Press, 1984.

Yule, George, ed. *Luther: Theologian for Catholics and Protestants.* Edinburgh: T&T Clark, 1985.

*Further resources*

Gassmann, Günther, Duane H. Larson and Mark W. Oldenburg, *Historical Dictionary of Lutheranism.* Lanham, MA: The Scarecrow Press, 2001.

Lutherjahrbuch – Annual bibliographies of Luther studies.

*Luthers Werke auf CD-ROM.* Ann Arbor, MI: Bell & Howell Information and Learning and Cambridge, United Kingdom: Chadwyck-Healey Ltd., 2000. (http://luther.chadwyck.com)

Pelikan, Jaroslav and Lehmann, Helmut T., eds. *Luther's Works on CD-ROM*. Minneapolis and St. Louis: Fortress Press and Concordia Publishing House, 2002.

http://chaucer.library.emory.edu/luther/luther_site/luther_frame.html Facsimile and English translation of Johann Bugenhagen Pomeranus' *A Christian sermon over the body and at the funeral of the venerable* Dr. Martin Luther (1546)

http://luther.bc.edu/default.html Index Verborum (Index to Luther's German writings)

http://www.acronet.net/~robokopp/luther.html Luther's Hymns (German/English/Melody)

http://www.concordance.com/luther.htm Concordances to some of Luther's writings (English)

http://www.ctsfw.edu/etext/luther/ Lutheran Electronic Archive from Project Wittenberg

http://www.ctsfw.edu/etext/luther/hymns/homl/ Luther's Hymns (Project Wittenberg)

http://www.cuw.edu/lutherdigest/ *Luther Digest* (An annual abridgement of Luther studies)

http://www.educ.msu.edu/homepages/laurence/reformation/Luther/Luther.htm Includes Luther links

http://www.hti.umich.edu/l/luther/ *Die Bibel*, Martin Luther translation from Humanities Text Initiative, University of Michigan

http://www.iclnet.org/pub/resources/text/wittenberg/wittenberg-home.html Project Wittenberg

http://www.luther.de/e/ Martin Luther

http://www.newadvent.org/cathen/09438b.htm *Catholic Encyclopedia*

http://www.utm.edu/research/iep/l/luther.htm The Internet Encyclopedia of Philosophy

http://www.wittenberg.de Lutherstadt Wittenberg

# Index